West Meets East:
100 Essays from University Students in the U.S.A.

东西交汇：美国大学生优秀作文 100 篇

Edited by **Licheng Gu**
主编　顾利程

北京语言大学出版社
BEIJING LANGUAGE AND CULTURE UNIVERSITY PRESS

PHOENIX TREE PUBLISHING INC.

图书在版编目（CIP）数据

东西交汇：美国大学生优秀作文 100 篇 / 顾利程主编. -- 北京：北京语言大学出版社，2023.6
ISBN 978-7-5619-6342-5

Ⅰ. ①东… Ⅱ. ①顾… Ⅲ. ①汉语 - 阅读教学-对外汉语教学 - 教学参考资料 ②汉语 - 写作 - 对外汉语教学 - 教学参考资料 Ⅳ. ①H195.4

中国国家版本馆 CIP 数据核字 (2023) 第 173377 号

东西交汇：美国大学生优秀作文 100 篇
DONGXI JIAOHUI: MEIGUO DAXUESHENG YOUXIU ZUOWEN 100 PIAN

责任编辑：唐琪佳　　英文编辑：张铁鋆
装帧设计：邱　彬　　插图绘制：黄　莉
排版制作：北京青侣文化创意设计有限公司
部分供图：壹图网、视觉中国、中国新闻图片网
责任印制：周　燚

出版发行：北京语言大学出版社
社　　址：北京市海淀区学院路 15 号，100083
网　　址：www.blcup.com
电子信箱：service@blcup.com
电　　话：编辑部　8610-82303647/3592/3395
国内发行　8610-82303650/3591/3648
海外发行　8610-82303365/3080/3668
北语书店　8610-82303653
网购咨询　8610-82303908
印　　刷：天津嘉恒印务有限公司

版　　次：2023 年 6 月第 1 版　　印　　次：2023 年 6 月第 1 次印刷
开　　本：787 毫米 × 1092 毫米　1/16　　印　　张：39.25
字　　数：658 千字
39900

PRINTED IN CHINA
凡有印装质量问题，本社负责调换。售后QQ号1367565611，电话8610-82303590

谨将此书献给我生命中最重要的三个女人：

在清贫中生我养我的慈祥母亲司桂明

在繁忙中鼎力支持我事业的夫人吕行

在欢乐中给我创作灵感的女儿顾文迪

This book is dedicated to the three most important women in my life:

My mother Si Guiming, who, in hardship, fed and clothed me in my early years in China.

My wife Lucy Xing Lu, who, despite being extremely busy herself, supports me unconditionally in my career.

My daughter, Wendi Lulu Gu, whose positivity and cheerfulness has always been a source of inspiration for my research.

目录

中国故事

CONTENTS

My Chinese Stories

中文之路

深情厚谊

Journeys of Learning Chinese

Deep Friendships

血浓于水

文化交流

Blood Is Thicker than Water

Cultural Exchange

昔为今用

有感而发

The Past Guides the Present

Reflections

时事评论

Current Affairs Commentary

序言

刘利　Liu Li

顾利程教授任职于美国西北大学，从事中文教育30余年，勤勉治教，多所创获。2019年曾出版专著《美国汉语教学动态研究》，开创国别中文教育系统研究之先河。近来又编就《东西交汇：美国大学生优秀作文100篇》（以下简称“文集”）一书，将美国60余所名校学生的中文优秀作文萃于一编，不仅展示了编者本人的育人成就，也展示了国际中文教育事业如今在美国结出的硕果。

文集汇聚的文章，题材广泛，情感真挚，思考深入，令人印象深刻。言为心声。写作，是语言学习的高级阶段，体现的不仅是学习者的文字能力，更是其文化理念和情感认同的呈现。这些能力的养成绝非朝夕之功，而是源自情景的浸润、人性的互通，以及身临其境的体验和认同。1879年，第一位受聘进入美国哈佛大学的中文教师戈鲲化，面对的还是冷冷清清的课堂，尽管他以诗歌之美和人格魅力打动了很多人，但中文——这种陌生而艰深的语言却仍然被当时的美国人视为畏途。100多

Preface

Professor Licheng Gu works at Northwestern University in the United States. In his over 30 years of active engagement in Chinese education, he has made many achievements and worked diligently in teaching and research in this area. In 2019, he published the book *Chinese Teaching in America: An Analysis of Its Past, Present and Future*, creating a precedent for research on Chinese education systems in other countries. Recently, he edited the book *West Meets East: 100 Essays from University Students in the U.S.A.*, which is comprised of outstanding Chinese essays written by students from more than 60 prestigious universities around the United States, showcasing not only the editor's achievements in teaching, but also the widespread success of international Chinese education in the United States.

The essays in this anthology feature a wide range of themes, sincere emotions, and deep reflections, leaving a lasting impact on the readers. Words are the voice of the heart. Writing is an advanced stage of language learning, showcasing not only the learners' writing abilities but also their cultural beliefs and emotional identities. The development of these abilities is by no means achieved overnight, but rather through immersion in specific environments, mutual communication, and special experiences. In 1879, Ge Kunhua, the first Chinese professor hired into Harvard University in the United States, faced an empty and silent classroom. Although he touched many people with the beauty of his poetry and his charisma, Chinese

北京语言
毕业典礼

9届春季
授予仪式

年之后，这么多名校学子热情拥抱中文和中华文化，并且能以中文为载体，表达自己的所见所闻、所思所感，足见中美友谊的深入发展和海外中文教师做出的卓著贡献。

语言与文化在学术研究上固然是两个范畴，但是在语言教学中却常常是互为表里、密不可分的。从学习者来说，学习一门外语的最初动力往往源自对一种文化的好奇与好感，但这样的感觉却能够引导学习者走向“人同此心，心同此理”的认同与理解；反过来，文化的认知与感受又会直接影响语言学习的效率和水平。中国自古就有“诗言志”的传统，这里的“志”，指的就是写作者的认识、思想、情感、抱负等。“在心为志，发言为诗”，融合了主观情感和理性认知的“作文”，发乎真情，形诸笔端，确实是突破文化隔阂、提升语言能力的极佳方式。因此，写作既是训练语言运用能力的有效抓手，也是观察语言教学成效的明亮窗口。

文集内容丰富，编排别具匠心。100 篇精选的文章被编者分为八个板块，其中“中国故事”尤为吸引读者的目光。这些文章大都源自作者在中国的亲身经历，文字虽不免稚嫩，情感却十分真挚。西北大学刘可阳的作品《谁是亲妈》读来让人忍俊不禁，虽然语言轻快活泼，但巧妙地用“两个妈妈”的风格折射中美文化，特别是亲子关系的微妙差异，观察精准，描述传神。同样来自西北大学的黄大伟生动记述了他和后海边的“煎饼哥”由陌生到熟悉，再到理解认同、互相帮助的交往过程：一个善良热情的美国小伙子和一个勤劳朴实的中国家庭，他们之间那种超越语言隔阂的感情，读来令人动容。虽然只是一篇小作文，但是作者的叙事能力表现得非常充分，他对人物的神态、语言、摊煎饼的动作都有精准的描写，寥寥几笔就把读者带入所描绘的情境中去，体现出很好

was still regarded as a strange, difficult, and daunting language in the eyes of Americans at that time. 100 years later, countless students from prestigious American universities embrace Chinese language and culture enthusiastically, using Chinese as a means to express what they see, hear, think, and feel. This shows the in-depth development of the Sino-U.S. friendship and the outstanding contributions made by overseas Chinese teachers.

Although language and culture are two different categories in academic research, they tend to be closely connected and almost inseparable in language teaching. From the perspective of a learner, the initial motivation to learn a foreign language often stems from a sense of curiosity about a culture, allowing students to feel that they "share the same heart and same goals (人同此心，心同此理)". In turn, the cognition and experience of culture directly affect the efficiency and level of language learning. Since ancient times, China has had the tradition of "expressing one's will through poetry (诗言志)", with "will (志)" revealing the author's realizations, thoughts, feelings, and aspirations. As "poetry stems from the heart; speech stems from poetry (在心为志，发言为诗)", these essays allow authors to express their true feelings through writing – indeed, an excellent way to break through cultural barriers while improving language skills. Therefore, writing is not only an effective starting point on the journey of language learning, but also a bright window observing the effectiveness of language teaching.

This anthology is rich in content and ingenious in arrangement. The 100 selected essays were divided into eight sections by the editor, among which the "My Chinese Stories" Section particularly attracts readers' attention. Most of these essays are inspired by the students' personal experiences in China. Although the writing may come off as simplistic, the essays show the authors' most sincere emotions. After reading "Who Is My Biological Mother" by Alec D'Alelio from Northwestern University, people can't help but laugh in amusement. Although the language is brisk and lively, it skillfully incorporates the characteristics of "two mothers" to reflect the subtle differences between American and Chinese cultures. The observations are accurate and the description is evocative, especially when it comes to portraying parent-child relationships in the two cultures. David Jameson Harris, who is also from Northwestern University, vividly describes a conversation he had with a man selling

的文字修养。

文集也不乏对中华文化的深入思考，很多文章都闪烁着思想的洞见和智慧的火花。来自普林斯顿大学的董安琪同学续写了陶渊明的《桃花源记》。“桃花源”虽然出自想象，但已经沉淀为中华文化中的一个重要象征意象，董安琪同学敏锐地把握到了这一点，并在深入理解原作的基础上，将自己充满哲理的思考融入虚构的叙事，构思之精巧、细节之生动、表述之准确，令人惊喜。像这样的精彩之作，书中还有很多，既覆盖源远流长的文化传统，也有日新月异的当今现实，既有对文化差异的敏锐感受，也有对人性相通之处的深刻洞察，表现出新鲜而丰富的视角，描绘出生机勃勃的图景。

当今世界正日益走向开放包容，中文不仅是中外文化交流的通道，也包含着人类心灵共振的密码。不久前，一位意大利航天员借用王羲之《兰亭集序》中的几句话表达了自己面对浩瀚宇宙时的感受：“仰观宇宙之大，俯察品类之盛，所以游目骋怀，足以极视听之娱，信可乐也。”这段1600多年前中国文人笔下的文字，通过这位航天员之手，赢得了全世界的喜爱。我想这不只是中文的魅力，也是人类内在相通的情感所产生的共鸣。相信如此由不同语言发出的点点星光，最终会交织起来，汇成人类相互理解的思想虹桥。

感谢编者的信任，把这部集萃之作交给北京语言大学出版社出版。作为中国唯一一所以国际中文教育为主要使命的大学，北京语言大学在过去60年里，培养了20多万通晓中文和中华文化的优秀人才，其中很多人成为了中文教师；北京语言大学也向世界各国派出了大量优秀的中文教师，其中不少人在美国任教。中外师生携手努力，共同成就了今天

pancakes in Beijing. From starting off as strangers to growing more familiar with each other, they fostered a sense of mutual understanding and recognition and helped each other: a kind and enthusiastic American boy and a hard-working and simple Chinese family, tied together by a special relationship that transcends language barriers. Although it is only a short essay, the author's excellent narrative ability is fully demonstrated, and the writer describes the man's demeanor, language, and movements during the pancake spreading process in great detail. With a few strokes, readers are immediately captivated, reflecting the author's excellent writing skills.

There is also no lack of in-depth reflections on Chinese culture in the anthology, and many essays shine with unique insights and wisdom. Angel Dong from Princeton University wrote a continuation of Tao Yuanming's renowned "Peach Blossom Spring." Although "Peach Blossom Spring" stems from imagination, it has already become an important symbolic image in Chinese culture. Angel Dong grasped this point precisely, and based on a deep understanding of the original work, she integrated her own philosophical perceptions into the fictional narrative. The exquisiteness and vividness of details are astonishing. There are many other wonderful works like this in the anthology, with content spanning from long-standing cultural tradition to the ever-changing occurrences in the society today. The anthology not only features a keen sense of cultural differences, but it also offers deep insights into the underlying similarities of human nature, showing a fresh and diverse perspective that paints a vibrant picture in readers' minds.

Today's world is becoming increasingly open and inclusive. Chinese is not only a channel for effective cultural exchanges between China and foreign countries, but also contains the code of human spiritual resonance. Not long ago, an Italian astronaut quoted a few words from Wang Xizhi's "Preface to the Poems Collected from the Orchid Pavilion" to express his feelings when facing the vast universe: "Looking up at the vastness of the universe and looking down at the abundance of living things, as our eyes wander, so do our minds too. Indeed, it is a pure delight for our all senses." This text appeared in the works of Chinese literati over 1,600 years ago, and it became popular around the world through the astronaut. I think this shows not only the charm of Chinese language, but also the resonance generated by the inner emotions of human beings. I believe that the shining stars emitted by different

国际中文教育事业的繁荣局面。这部中英双语对照的作文集，是以顾利程教授为代表的海外中文教师们长久耕耘的结晶，也是国际中文教育宏大叙事中的精彩篇章，它为各国中文学习者和教育工作者提供了难得的借鉴，相信读者们含英咀华，一定能够从中获得更多的启示，从而使更多的人加入学习中文和推动中外文化交流的事业中来。

刘利
北京语言大学校长、教授
2022 年 11 月 28 日

languages will eventually intertwine, converging into a bright bridge of thought to foster mutual understanding across all human beings.

Thanks go to Professor Gu for entrusting this anthology to Beijing Language and Culture University Press for publication. As the only university in China whose main mission is to teach foreign students Chinese, in the past 60 years, BLCU has trained over 200,000 outstanding individuals who are proficient in Chinese language and culture, many of whom have become Chinese teachers; BLCU has also sent a large number of excellent Chinese teachers to countries all around the world, many of whom teach in the United States. Chinese and foreign teachers have worked together with their students for decades to achieve the prosperity of today's international Chinese education. This collection of bilingual essays is the crystallization of the persisting hard work of overseas Chinese teachers represented by Professor Licheng Gu, and it is also a wonderful chapter in the grand narrative of international Chinese education. Not only does it provide a unique reference for Chinese language learners and educators from all over the world, but I believe that readers will also be able to gain a lot of inspiration from the collection. As a result, more people will join in on the cause of learning Chinese while promoting cultural exchanges between China and foreign countries.

Liu Li

Professor and President

Beijing Language and Culture University

November 28th, 2022

致读者的信

夏彼洛 Morton Schapiro

《东西交汇：美国大学生优秀作文100篇》是由我的朋友兼同事顾利程教授主编的。我们的重要使命之一就是将世界引入西北大学，将西北大学推向世界。我们在这一点上成功了，而这一本由美国大学生撰写的故事集就是一个证明。今天的社会一切都变得越来越紧密，越来越息息相关，所以我们更需要加强跨国界、跨语言和跨文化的合作。出于这些原因，我们必须让学生意识到，只有获得强大的跨文化交流的能力，他们才能解决当今世界面临的问题，才能成为富有远见卓识的全球领导者。这部故事集充分证明我们的教师履行了对学生的承诺，而我们的学生也成功地融入了全球社会。

这些故事包括学生们对中国诗歌和小说的理解和反思，以及观看中国电影和戏剧获得的感受。在中国留过学的学生分享了他们在中国旅行的独特经历，描述了他们遇到的人和事，特别是这些人和事是如何帮助他们深入培养自我意识并从中获得成长的。学生们在沉浸于中国文化的同时，也通过旅行和语言交流与当地人建立了深厚的友谊，并深刻地体

A Letter to Readers

The collection of student essays in this book, *West Meets East: 100 Essays from University Students in the U.S.A.*, edited by my friend and colleague Professor Licheng Gu, illustrates the successes of a key initiative to bring the world to Northwestern University and Northwestern University to the world. As our societies become more and more connected, we will require greater cooperation across borders, languages, and cultures. For these reasons, we must prepare students to be thoughtful global leaders, to appreciate that solving critical problems requires broad, cross-cultural understanding. This collection of essays serves as a wonderful testament to our faculty fulfilling their commitment to students, and to our students' success in embracing global citizenship.

These short essays include students' understanding and reflections on Chinese poems and novels, and lessons learned from watching Chinese movies and operas. Students who studied abroad in China share their experiences of traveling within the country, and of how the people they met and the activities in which they engaged helped them develop self-awareness and maturity. The students' immersion in Chinese culture through travel and participation in language exchange allowed them to build deep friendship with local Chinese people and to clearly see the importance of being adaptive to different environment, respecting different cultures and recognizing different values.

会到了适应不同环境、尊重不同文化和承认不同价值观的重要性。

西北大学每年大约会有三百名学生注册汉语课程。除了在课堂上教授中国语言和文化以外，顾教授和他的同事们还鼓励学生把中文带到课外，其中包括同学之间的语言交流和教师组织的各种活动，如下午茶、在中国餐馆用餐、包饺子等等。此外，他们还举办中文演讲比赛、中国新年庆祝活动，以及帮学生争取去海外学习不同科目的机会。

About three hundred students enroll in Chinese language courses at Northwestern University each year. In addition to teaching Chinese language and culture in the classroom, Professor Gu and his colleagues encourage students to put Chinese to use outside of the classroom through language tables and a variety of faculty-planned activities such as tea hours, dining at Chinese restaurants, and lessons on how to make dumplings. They also host Chinese language speech competitions and Chinese New Year celebrations and performances, as well as overseas study opportunities in various academic disciplines.

顾利程教授是一位非常敬业的教师，在西北大学已任教30年。他不仅仅是一位杰出的教师，还是西北大学国际关系办公室的东亚事务联络官和西北大学中国留学项目主任。

在担任校长职务期间，我有幸多次访问中国，并见到了在西北大学北京暑期项目学习政治经济和公共卫生的学生。顾教授自1999年开始主管这些项目，先是在清华大学（1999年至2009年），然后在北京大学（2010年至今）。对我来说，在中国最难忘的经历是和我们的学生一起爬长城、游故宫，以及参观秦始皇陵兵马俑。

学生们用中文记录了他们在中国的难忘经历，作为作业交给了顾教授。时光流逝，经过这么多年，有些人可能已经淡忘了他们曾经分享过的经验和感想，但顾教授没有忘记。他一直珍藏着这些美丽的故事，在征得学生同意后，精选了一部分，结集成册。

我们的未来取决于如何将当今的年轻人培养成真正具有全球意识的领导者。我在西北大学校长的岗位上已经工作了13年，我想特别褒扬顾利程教授这些年所做的一切，这些工作帮助我们的学生和大学成为跨国界、跨文化的典范。感谢顾利程教授的辛苦付出，也感谢我们的学生愿意在这里分享他们的故事。

夏彼洛

西北大学校长、教授

2022年6月29日

Professor Licheng Gu is a dedicated teacher, celebrating thirty years at Northwestern University in 2022. He has been invaluable not only as a teacher, but also as our East Asia liaison in our International Relations Office and as director of our study abroad programs in China.

I am honored and grateful to have been able to travel to China many times during my presidency and, while there, to have met with our students studying on Northwestern University's Summer in Beijing Political Economy and Public Health programs. Professor Gu has guided these programs since their inception in 1999, first at Tsinghua University (1999-2009) and then at Peking University (2010-present). Highlights for me included climbing the Great Wall with our students, touring the Imperial Palace together, and visiting the magnificent Terracotta Warriors and Horses in Xi'an.

Students documented their experiences in essays handed in as homework. Over the years, some may have forgotten about the reflections shared when they were younger, but Professor Gu did not. He kept and treasured these essays, and, with the students' permission, shares some of them in this book.

Our collective future depends on the successful nurturing of today's young people into truly globally minded leaders. As I leave Northwestern University after thirteen rewarding years, I applaud Professor Licheng Gu for helping our students and our university become exemplars of international and cross-cultural exchange and understanding, and I thank our students for sharing their stories.

Morton Schapiro

Professor and President

Northwestern University

June 29th, 2022

编者的话

顾利程　Licheng Gu

编者在美国大学从事中文教学30余年，并且成功组织了21届汉语桥演讲比赛，有幸在全美范围内收集到了众多题材广泛、风格迥异的优秀学生作文。经过精心筛选，编辑成这本《东西交汇：美国大学生优秀作文100篇》，献给中美两国读者。

这100篇作文中英对照，风格不同，主题各异。有的讲述中国故事、留学经历，有的介绍学习中文过程中的感受和体验。

这100篇作文的语言或许显得有几分质朴，甚至略微带有英文写作的风格，但是都能够表达美国学生对中文的热爱及对中国文化的向往。这些作文略加编辑之后，成为一篇篇范文，给其他学习中文的学生树立了榜样。中国读者也可以通过阅读这些中文作文，领略这些美国学生独特的视角、幽默的方式、深刻的思辨，以及积极的人生态度。每篇作文配备的英文译文，可以帮助学生的亲友及其他美国读者了解中国及中国文化，也能帮助中国学生提高英文阅读及写作水平。这部作文集的中英两种文字，既能帮助美国人学习中文、了解中国，又能帮助中国人学习英文、了解美国。各取所需，各得其所。

Chief Editor's Preface

I have been teaching Chinese in American universities for over 30 years and organized Chinese Bridge Speech Contests for 21 years. I am fortunate to have collected many outstanding essays with a wide range of topics and diverse writing styles from students across the United States. These essays combine to become this book, *West Meets East: 100 Essays from University Students in the U.S.A.*, dedicated to readers in China and America.

These 100 essays are presented in Chinese and English, with different styles and themes. Some feature Chinese stories and students' experiences while studying abroad, and others introduce students' feelings and discoveries on their journey of learning Chinese.

While the language used in these 100 essays may come off as simple or even closely resemble the English writing style, they all express American students' love for Chinese language and their desire to learn more about Chinese culture. After slight editing, these essays became sample essays that serve as examples for other students studying Chinese. By reading these essays, Chinese readers can also appreciate the unique perspectives, humorous methods, profound thinking, and positive life attitudes of these American students. Each essay is also supplemented with an English translation, which can help students' relatives, friends, and other American readers understand China and Chinese culture. It can also help Chinese students improve their English reading and writing skills. Not only can this collection of essays, presented in both Chinese and English, help Americans learn Chinese and understand China, but it can also help Chinese people learn English and better understand the United States. As a result, it is our hope that everyone can gain valuable insights as they read.

这100篇作文是从美国60余所不同类型大学的300多篇学生作文中精选出来的。这60余所大学中有常春藤顶尖私立大学，如普林斯顿大学、哈佛大学、哥伦比亚大学；有“巨无霸”公立大学，如密歇根大学、印第安纳大学、明尼苏达大学；有综合科研型大学，如芝加哥大学、斯坦福大学、杜克大学；也有闻名遐迩的文理学院，如欧柏林学院、明德学院、史密斯学院；甚至还有军事学院。从地域上看，100篇作文来自全美各地，其中包括高校林立的东西两岸、各具特色的南方北方、崇文重教的中部地区，最远的来自孤悬太平洋的夏威夷大学。撰稿学生有本科生，有研究生，也有刚刚离开学校走上工作岗位的毕业生。学生作者均为美国文化背景，其中包括一些亚裔学生。

从中文水平上来看，这100篇作文的语言水平有高有低。有的是初级学习者，有的是高水平的学生。虽然学生的中文水平参差不齐，但这

The 100 essays were carefully selected from more than 300 student essays across more than 60 universities in the United States. Among these universities are top Ivy League private universities, including Princeton, Harvard, and Columbia; there are public universities, such as the University of Michigan, Indiana University, and the University of Minnesota; there are comprehensive research universities like the University of Chicago, Stanford, and Duke; there are also well-known liberal arts colleges including Oberlin College, Middlebury College, and Smith College; there is even a military college. From a geographical standpoint, the 100 essays come from all around the United States, including the east and west coasts with renowned universities, the south and north with unique characteristics, the central region with its strong educational focus, and even the University of Hawai'i, which is isolated in the Pacific Ocean and is the furthest away. The authors of these essays include undergraduate and graduate students, along with graduates who have just left school and recently entered the workforce. The students all come from American cultural backgrounds, including some Asian-American students.

In terms of Chinese skills, the language level in the 100 essays vary from high to low. Some students are beginners, while some are more advanced. Although the students'

并不影响他们作文的内涵。譬如《翠湖公园里的故事》一文，就出自一个本科二年级水平的学生之手。该文讲述了作者在昆明暑期班留学期间，与当地人结下的友谊。该文使用的语言非常简单，但是却把昆明翠湖公园里休闲老人的表现描写得惟妙惟肖，让人忍俊不禁，是一个绝好的中国故事。另一篇高年级的作文，《三位诗人笔下的杨贵妃》则凸显了作者对李白、杜甫、白居易三位诗人写作特点的精准掌握。文中所使用的文字典雅高端，带有几分诗情画意。这两篇作文的语言水平相差甚远，但是在立意上却不分伯仲，各有千秋。

这100篇作文根据主题分成如下八个板块：中国故事、中文之路、深情厚谊、血浓于水、文化交流、昔为今用、有感而发、时事评论。为了帮助读者阅读理解，每个板块前面都配有一篇导读。

这些作文有很多不同之处，但是它们之间有一个共同点，那就是它们都表现了同学们对中文的挚爱，对中国的向往。文风上的捐华务实、朴实自然亦可借鉴。

相信100篇优秀作文的创作者能够成为100名维系中美友谊的民间大使，为增进中美人民之间的相互了解，为增强中美两国人民之间的友谊，为维护世界和平，添砖加瓦，铺路搭桥。这正是编者编辑这本《东西交汇：美国大学生优秀作文100篇》的初心。

顾利程

西北大学教授、东亚事务联络官

北京语言大学客座教授

2022年9月15日

Chinese proficiency varies, this does not affect the connotation and meaning behind their compositions. For example, "Stories in Green Lake Park" was written by a second-year undergraduate student. The essay describes the friendship the author developed with the local people during her summer school in Kunming, China. Although the language incorporated in this essay is simple, it effectively depicts the behavior of the people in the park so vividly that readers can't help but laugh after reading the excellent and humorous story. Another essay, "Imperial Consort Yang as Described by Three Poets," was written by an upperclassman. This essay highlights the author's precise grasp of the unique writing characteristics of three famous poets, i.e., Li Bai, Du Fu, and Bai Juyi. The language and vocabulary used in this essay are elegant and advanced, including poetic techniques as well. The language level of these two compositions is extremely different, but in terms of conception, there is no difference as each essay has its own merits.

The 100 essays are divided into the following eight sections, categorized based on theme, i.e., My Chinese Stories, Journeys of Learning Chinese, Deep Friendships, Blood Is Thicker than Water, Cultural Exchange, The Past Guides the Present, Reflections, and Current Affairs Commentary. To help readers better comprehend the content of the essays, each section is preceded by an introduction.

There are many differences among these essays, but they have one commonality; that is, they all show the students' passion for Chinese language and interest in China. Readers can also benefit from reading essays in their pragmatic and simple writing style.

I believe that the creators of the 100 excellent essays can become 100 non-governmental ambassadors to maintain the friendship between China and the United States, to enhance the mutual understanding between the Chinese and American people, and to preserve world peace by bridging cultural divides. This precisely describes the original intention of the editor in compiling and putting together this book, *West Meets East: 100 Essays from University Students in the U.S.A.*

Licheng Gu

Professor and East Asia Liaison at Northwestern University

Visiting Professor at Beijing Language and Culture University

September 15th, 2022

中国故事

My Chinese Stories

导　读

本板块收集了十三名美国大学生讲述的“我的中国故事”。从内容上讲，一个故事一定要有人物、时间、地点以及情节的发展。从框架来讲，首先要设计好一个醒目的标题，简洁的开始，合理的发展，流畅的转折，跌宕起伏的高潮以及最后令人深思的结尾。纵观整个板块，这十三篇文章的人物都是第一人称“我”，讲的都是“我”在中国遇到的人和事。有的故事发生在偏僻的乡下小镇，有的故事发生在游人如织的旅游胜地，有的故事发生在传统的北京胡同里，有的故事发生在上海古老的弄堂里，有的故事发生在宽敞的公园里，有的还发生在窄小的出租车里。每一篇故事都是那样感人，那样令人回味无穷。

在《煎饼哥与煎饼弟》这个故事里，西北大学的黄大伟同学讲述了他与外来务工人员周大力结下的深厚友情。为了给大力的女儿兰兰挣医药费，这一中一洋两个朋友在炎热的夏天一天就摊出了八百多个煎饼。为了走上星光大道的舞台，大力教大伟唱中国歌，大伟教大力弹吉他。通过与一个外来务工者的交往，美国青年大伟不仅提高了中文水平，而且学会了怎样克服困难，怎样在逆境中保持积极向上的心态。

读者在享受这个美丽故事的同时，还可以学习作者对摊煎饼这个过程的描述。“只见他潇洒地把面糊舀到饼铛上，灵巧地一划，推出了一个圆圆的煎饼。稍后用铲子一挑，煎饼在空中翻了一个个儿，平稳地落在饼铛上。”首先看几个单音节动词的选用，如“舀”“划”“推”“挑”“翻”和“落”，再来看选用的描述动作的副词，如“潇洒地”“灵巧地”“平稳地”等等，短短几句话，一个精明能干的人物就已经跃然纸上了。

Introduction

This section consists of the Chinese stories written by thirteen American college students. In terms of content, a story must have characters, time, place, and plot development. From the perspective of the overall framework, we begin by designing a striking title, a concise start, a reasonable development, smooth transitions, ups and downs of the climax, and finally a thought-provoking conclusion. Looking at the entire section, these thirteen stories are all written in the first person, and they talk about the people and things that "I" (the author) personally encountered in China. The stories happened in remote rural towns, tourist attractions full of visitors, traditional Beijing alleys, old alleys in Shanghai, spacious parks, small taxis... Every story is so touching and memorable.

In the story "Pancake Brothers," David Harris, a student who studies at Northwestern University, shared a story about the profound friendship he formed with Zhou Dali, a migrant worker. To cover medical expenses for Dali's daughter Lanlan, the two friends, one Chinese and one foreign, made over 800 pancakes on a hot summer day. Furthermore, to get on the stage of Starlet Road, Dali taught David to sing Chinese songs while David taught Dali to play the guitar. As a young American, David not only significantly improved his Chinese as he spent time with Dali but also learned how to overcome difficulties and remain positive in the face of adversity.

While enjoying this beautiful story, readers can also learn from the author's description of the process of pancake spreading. "He elegantly poured some soft flour paste onto the hot pan. With a gentle scrape, he made a perfect circle and made an extremely thin pancake. Later, he raised the pancake with a spatula and tossed the whole pancake into the air. The pancake flipped in the air and landed steadily on the hot pan." First, we should look at the diverse selection of several monosyllabic verbs, such as pour, scrape, toss, flip, and land. We can then observe the adverbs used to describe the actions, such as elegantly, extremely, and steadily. In

讲一个故事不仅要有细致入微的描述，还应该有突出人物性格的对话。在《出租车里的故事》一文中，北弗吉尼亚社区学院的文理爱同学就引用了大量司机师傅的问话："你来自哪个国家？""你是北京人吗？""你有没有孩子？""你喜欢什么样的音乐？"

这些互相了解认识的初步问答说完以后，他们的对话慢慢也会进入实质性的阶段："你觉得什么是'现代中国的特色'？""消除贫困、共同富裕是现代中国的特色。"

下面来自司机师傅的问候更显出了国人对美国留学生的关爱："美国的学费真的像别人说的那么贵吗？""你在美国的家人还好吗？他们会不会考虑跟你一样搬到中国来？"

通过以上的对话，和蔼可亲、关心他人的中国出租车司机的形象就准确地刻画出来了。所以在这一板块中，希望读者在欣赏这十三篇故事的同时，也学习作者对行为动作的描写、对人物之间对话的掌控。

just a few sentences, it seems as if a shrewd and capable character has already leapt his way into life on the paper.

Telling a story requires not only nuanced descriptions, but also dialogue that highlights the distinct personality traits of the characters. In "Stories in Cabs," Raven Witherspoon, a student from Northern Virginia Community College, quotes a lot of her conversations with the taxi driver: "Which country are you from?" "Are you from Beijing?" "Do you have children?" "What kind of music do you like?"

Following their initial "get to know you" dialogue, their conversation gradually enters a more substantive stage: "What do you think are modern China's 'special characteristics'?" "Eradicating poverty, and seeking common prosperity, those are the special characteristics of modern China."

The following questions from the driver further show the concern and care that Chinese people have toward American students who are studying abroad: "Is American college tuition really as expensive as people say it is?" "Are your family members in the U.S. doing alright? Will they consider moving to China like you?"

Through the above dialogue, the image of an amiable and caring Chinese taxi driver is accurately portrayed. Therefore, in this section, I hope that while readers appreciate these thirteen stories, they will also learn from the authors' description of actions and control of dialogues between the characters.

煎饼哥与煎饼弟

作者：黄大伟　指导教师：顾利程　西北大学

大力积极的生活态度激励我勇敢地面对困境，勇于承担，永不言退。

我是 David Harris，中文名字叫黄大伟，是一名美国西北大学在北京的留学生。有一天，我去后海玩儿，逛到中午有些饿了。我正想买些东西吃，突然从旁边小胡同里飘来了一阵轻快的歌声和一股特别的香味。我走近一看，原来是一个煎饼摊儿。只见那个摊煎饼的老板浑身是汗地忙活着，煎饼摊儿前还有五六个人排队等着。虽然老板在高温里烘烤着，可是兴致却很高，一边摊煎饼，一边唱歌。好像是在娱乐他的顾客，更像是在娱乐他自己。排队买煎饼的人似乎也没有了往日的焦躁，而是悠闲地站在那里闻着摊煎饼的香味，享受着老板那有一句没一句的歌声，等着自己的煎饼出锅。我被这情景吸引住了，也身不由己地排在队后，准备买一个煎饼尝尝。

排到我了，老板问：“小伙子，你要几个？”

“我要一个。”

“几个鸡蛋？”

“两个。”

“要不要辣酱？”

“当然要。”

老板一边问着，一边熟练地摊着煎饼。只见他潇洒地把面糊舀到饼铛上，灵巧地一划，推出了一个圆圆的煎饼。稍后用铲子一挑，煎饼在空中翻了一个个儿，

Pancake Brothers

Author: David Jameson Harris   Instructor: Licheng Gu   Northwestern University

Dali's positive attitude toward life inspires me to bravely face misfortunes, take up responsibilities, and remain strong and hopeful in life.

My name is David Harris, and my Chinse name is Huang Dawei. I am a Northwestern student studying abroad in Beijing. One day, I was hanging out in Houhai, a popular tourist spot in Beijing. It was almost noon and I was a little hungry. I wanted to buy some snacks for lunch when I heard someone singing and smelled something good in a small alley nearby. Following the song and smell of food, I walked ahead and found a pancake stand. The vendor was busy cooking pancakes there, streaming with sweat, and five or six customers were waiting for their pancakes. It was a hot day. Cooking in front of a burning stove was even hotter. But that did not seem to bother the man. He was working swiftly and happily. He was cooking and singing, as if to entertain his customers as well as himself. The customers lost their usual impatience. They waited for their pancakes while enjoying the good smell and the intermittent singing. Out of curiosity, I joined the line and planned to buy a pancake.

When it was my turn, the man asked, "How many would you like to have, guy?"

"Just one."

"How many eggs would you like to have?"

"Two, please."

"Spicy or plain?"

"Spicy, of course."

While talking, the man never stopped working on my pancake. He elegantly poured

平稳地落在饼铛上。接着，老板一丝不苟地加上鸡蛋、辣酱、香菜、葱花、薄脆。不到两分钟，一套香喷喷、热腾腾的煎饼果子已经送到了我的手上。我迫不及待地咬了一口，嘿，内焦外嫩，香辣可口，好吃极了！因为后边暂时没有别的顾客，我就边吃边和摊煎饼的老板攀谈了起来。

他叫周大力，从内蒙古来。他和太太生了一个女儿叫兰兰，兰兰不幸患了癌症。为了给兰兰治病，他们来到了北京。兰兰不到五岁，就已经做了四次手术、十二次化疗。为了给兰兰治病，大力拼命地工作。他一个人每天打两份工：白天在胡同里摊煎饼，晚上给一所学校做保安。他们每天吃得简简单单，住得窄小、

some soft flour paste onto the hot pan. With a gentle scrape, he made a perfect circle and made an extremely thin pancake. Later, he raised the pancake with a spatula and tossed the whole pancake into the air. The pancake flipped in the air and landed steadily on the hot pan. Then the vendor added eggs, thick pepper, coriander, chopped spring and snap with unfailing precision. In less than two minutes, I received a freshly cooked pancake in my hand. I couldn't wait to take a hearty bite. Wow, it tasted so good! The inside was crispy and crunchy while the outside was tender and soft. It just happened that no other customers were waiting behind, I chatted with the man and found out about his life.

The man is called Zhou Dali. He was from Inner Mongolia in China. He and his wife had a young daughter, Lanlan. Unfortunately, Lanlan had cancer. To give her proper medical treatment, Dali and his family came to Beijing. Lanlan was only five years old, but she had four major operations and a dozen of chemotherapies already. Dali had to work like crazy to pay the medical bills. Dali worked on two jobs. In the day time, Dali sold pancakes on streets in Beijing, and at night he worked as a security guard for a school. The family ate the simplest food and lived in a shabby place. Although experiencing hardships, Dali had great passion in life. He never complained or gave up hope, nor did he beg for sympathy or charity. He worked hard and lived a happy life every day. Whenever he had a minute from work, he would sing songs for Lanlan. His songs kept Lanlan happy and hopeful. His songs also kept him going ahead with faith.

I was touched by Dali's misfortune and his positive attitude toward life. We became friends from then on. I came to visit Dali and Lanlan every two days. I played with Lanlan and taught her English. Dali taught me to speak Chinese and cook pancakes, and I taught Dali to sing songs and play the guitar.

Dali was a good teacher on cooking pancakes. I learned the skills of cooking pancakes very fast. Whenever we two cooked and sold pancakes on streets in Beijing, we could always attract a lot of customers. Customers warmly called Dali "Big Brother Pancake from China," and called me "Younger Brother Pancake from the U.S." Many people came to take videos or pictures of us. In the busiest day, we two cooked and sold over 800 pancakes. We were so exhausted by the end of the day, but we were very happy. We knew that we had made some

局促。虽然日子很辛苦，但是大力仍然对生活充满了热情。他没有恨天怨地，没有自暴自弃，更没有去向别人乞求同情或者施舍。他每天勤奋地工作，愉快地生活。一有时间，他就给兰兰唱歌，带给她欢乐和希望，同时也以此来鼓励自己。

我被大力的不幸震撼，也被他积极的生活态度感动，主动跟他交上了朋友。我每隔一天就来大力家看望他们，并且跟兰兰玩儿，教她英语。大力教我说中文，摊煎饼；我教大力唱歌，弹吉他。

大力是个好师傅，所以我摊煎饼的手艺越来越好。我们每次在胡同里摊煎饼时，总能吸引很多顾客。大家亲切地称大力为“中国煎饼哥”，称我为“美国煎饼弟”，并且用手机给我们拍视频、拍照片。最忙的时候，我们哥儿俩一天就摊了八百多个煎饼。虽然很辛苦，但是我们很愉快，因为我们又给兰兰挣到了一些医药费。

大力也是个好学生。他很有音乐天赋。歌越唱越好，吉他也越弹越棒。我们在街头巷尾演唱时总能吸引很多人观看。最后，我和大力一起唱到了北京电视台，做了《北京客》节目的嘉宾。不久，我们又一起唱到了中央电视台，走上了《星光大道》。我们的歌声给人们带来音乐的享受，我们的故事打动了众多的中美百姓。

跟大力在一起，我不仅提高了中文水平，学会了很多中国歌，同时也学会了怎样克服困难，面对人生。大力积极的生活态度激励我勇敢地面对困境，勇于承担，永不言退。

money for Lanlan to see her doctor again.

Dali was a good student on learning the guitar. He seemed to have some talent in music. He sang songs and played the guitar better and better. Dali and I often performed together on street corners and attracted a lot of people. We two became so popular that the Beijing TV Station invited us to make a show in "Beijinger." A couple of months later, Dali and I sang songs and played the guitar at the famous "Starlet Road" Program at the China Central TV Station. Our music entertained people. Our story moved numerous people in both China and the U.S.

From my Chinese friend Dali, I not only improved my Chinese, learned many Chinese songs, but also learned how to overcome difficulties and face my life. Dali's positive attitude toward life inspires me to bravely face misfortunes, take up responsibilities, and remain strong and hopeful in life.

美国面孔，中国心

作者：西西　指导教师：陈红　洛尤拉大学

感谢我的父母把我们带到了中国，给了我们终生难忘的生活经历和体验。

我叫西西，是芝加哥洛尤拉大学大一的学生。我虽然看起来和一个普通的美国女孩儿没什么两样，但是我心里觉得我是一个在美国的中国人。

我为什么有这样的感受呢？这要从我十岁那年说起。由于工作的需要，爸爸决定去中国四川成都做生意。为了不和家人分离，爸爸妈妈决定带我和弟弟一起去。我们知道这个消息后，又兴奋激动，又有几分担心害怕，想象不出我们将来的生活会是什么样子。听说四川是大熊猫的故乡，我们是不是很快就可以见到憨态可掬的大熊猫了？我们越想越觉得兴奋和好奇！

离开了熟悉的环境以及多年一起玩耍的小伙伴，经过 14 个小时的长途飞行，飞机穿过蓝色的天空，我们降落在成都的双流国际机场。

新的生活就这样开始了。记得爸爸妈妈当时用了很多手势和司机师傅沟通，几经周折之后，司机师傅才把我们送到了酒店。

时间过得很快，我们都慢慢地融入了成都的生活。我和弟弟都非常喜欢我们的国际学校。除了用我们的母语英语学习各种知识以外，学习汉语也成了我们生活的一部分。不知不觉中，我已经感觉成都是我的第二故乡，而汉语也成了我们的第二语言。我们的同学和老师帮助我们学习，我们的朋友和邻居帮助我们融入当地人的生活。杜甫草堂、武侯祠等名胜古迹让我们感受到了中国历史的深厚，川剧变脸

American Face, Chinese Heart

Author: Cecelia Dolaz Instructor: Hong Chen Loyola University Chicago

> I thank my parents for bringing us to China, providing us with unforgettable life experiences and memories.

My name is Cecelia, and I'm a freshman at Loyola University Chicago. Although I look no different from any ordinary American girl, at heart, I feel like I'm a Chinese person in America.

Why do I feel this way? It all started when I was ten years old. Due to work, my father decided to go to Chengdu, Sichuan in China to do business. In order not to get separated from us, my parents decided to bring my brother and me there as well. After we heard the news, we were excited and a little worried, and we couldn't imagine what our future life would be like. We heard that Sichuan is the hometown of giant pandas, so would we be able to see the chubby and adorable giant pandas soon? The more we thought about it, the more excited and curious we became!

We left the familiar environment and the friends we've played together with for many years, and after a long-distance flight of 14 hours, the plane passed through the blue sky, and we landed at Shuangliu International Airport in Chengdu.

This was how my new life began. I remember that my parents used a lot of hand gestures to communicate with the driver at that time. After many setbacks, the driver finally dropped us off at the hotel.

Time flew by, and we gradually integrated ourselves into life in Chengdu. My brother and I both liked our international school a lot. In addition to learning all kinds of knowledge in our native language English, learning Chinese also became a part of our daily life. Before I knew it, I already felt that Chengdu was my second hometown, and Chinese became our second language. Our classmates and teachers helped us learn, and our friends and neighbors

让我们感受到民间艺术的博大精深。我们都深深地爱上了这里的一切，街边的麻辣小吃，节日的喜庆喧闹，传统的采摘茶叶，神奇的传说故事……这个古老又现代的城市深深地吸引着我们。我每次离开中国，都盼望着早日再回中国的家。

感谢我的父母把我们带到了中国，给了我们终生难忘的生活经历和体验，给了我们一颗中国心，使我们的成长道路更加丰富多彩。我希望将来我有了孩子，也为他们创造这种机会、让他们的生活也和我的一样精彩。

helped us integrate into local life. Visiting historical sites such as Du Fu Thatched Cottage and Wuhou Temple allowed us to feel the profoundness of Chinese history, and the face-changing of Sichuan opera made us feel the breadth and depth of folk art. We all fell in love with everything here, such as the spicy snacks on the street, the jolly and noisy festivals, the traditional tea picking, the magical legends... This ancient yet modern city fascinated us deeply. Every time I leave China, I always look forward to returning to our home in China as soon as possible.

I thank my parents for bringing us to China, providing us with unforgettable life experiences and memories, giving us a Chinese heart, and making our growth journey richer and more colorful. I hope that when I have kids in the future, I will be able to create this opportunity for them as well, making their life as wonderful as mine.

我与中国

作者：谢华　指导教师：郭依鹭　芝加哥大学

如果我们学会不同的语言，了解不同的文化，就可以开阔我们的视野。

我是 Hugh Shepard，中文名字叫谢华，是芝加哥大学一年级的学生。2014年，我 11 岁时，我们家决定要搬去北京，因为爸爸、妈妈都在北京找到了工作。刚到北京时，那里的一切对我们来说都是陌生的，我注意到那里的马路很宽，路上的汽车很多，道路两边耸立着高楼大厦。当时的我知道的中文词很少，害怕用中文跟别人沟通。

我上的学校是耀中国际学校的中学部，英语是主要的教学语言，除了中文课以外，所有的课程都用英语。学校也按照我们的中文水平分班。当时我被分到二年级中文班。这个班的功课很难，有很多我不理解的内容，第一次考试我只拿了 30 分。这让我感到失望和担心，因为我从来没得过那么低的分数。妈妈安慰我说："没关系，这是你第一次在中国考试，只要努力学习，下次就会考好。"妈妈说的话鼓励了我，之后我每天学习中文，后来考试得了 87 分，这让我兴奋不已。在北京生活了一年后，我学会了用中文买票、点菜等，我对北京、对我的学校也更熟悉了。

回美国上大学以后，我继续学中文，并发现美国和中国虽然有很大的文化差异，但是有的方面却很相似。我们在中国的时候，一月份去哈尔滨参加了那里的冰雪节。一月份的哈尔滨非常冷，最高温度是零下 12 摄氏度。载我们去酒店的出租车司机是土生土长的哈尔滨人，听得出来他为自己的城市感到非常自豪。他

China and I

Author: Hugh Shepard   Instructor: Yi-lu Kuo   University of Chicago

> If we study foreign languages, and learn more about different cultures, we can broaden our perspectives.

I'm Hugh Shepard. My Chinese name is Xie Hua, and I'm a freshman at the University of Chicago. In 2014, when I was eleven, my family decided to move to Beijing, because my Mom and Dad were both offered jobs there. When I first arrived in Beijing, everything was unfamiliar to me. I was struck by the wide roads, the numerous cars, and the high-rise buildings on both sides of the roads. At that time, I didn't know many Chinese words, and I was afraid of communicating with people in Chinese.

I attended Yew Chung International School's secondary section. English was the main language of instruction, and with the exception of Chinese class, all classes were taught in English. The school divided us into different classes according to our fluency in Chinese, and at the time I was placed in the Level 2 Chinese class. The content of that class was challenging for me. There was a lot that I didn't understand, and on my first test, I received a score of 30%. I was quite disappointed and worried, because I had never received such a low score on a test before. However, my mother comforted me by saying "Don't worry! This is the first time you are taking a test in China. As long as you study hard, you will do well next time." My mother's words encouraged me, and I studied Chinese every day. On the next test I received a score of 87%, and I was thrilled. After living in Beijing for a year, I became comfortable using Chinese to buy tickets, order food, and I became more familiar with both the city of Beijing and my school.

I continued to study Chinese in college after moving back to America, and also realized that despite the many cultural differences between America and China, there were also many similarities between the two countries. When we lived in China, we traveled to the city of

说外地人来到哈尔滨只有两个目的：第一个就是参观哈尔滨有名的大学，第二个就是参加冰雪节。冰雪节主要是在松花江上的太阳岛举行的。我们在河边看到很多人在结冰的河面上进行滑冰等娱乐活动。河面上的冰非常厚，不需要从桥上过河，可以直接从结冰的河面上走过河。河面上不仅有人走路，还有载着游客的马车。哈尔滨的市中心的建筑也具有俄罗斯建筑的风格。

我现在上芝加哥大学，这里冬天的风雪让我想到在哈尔滨的生活经历。芝加哥大学有一个传统，每年二月份的某一天，同学们早上六点会走到密歇根湖畔看日出。我今年参加了这个活动。记得那天早上也特别冷，我们走路走了快30分钟才到了湖边。可惜的是，因为那天多云，云朵遮住了太阳，我们没有看到日出。虽然没有看到日出，但这仍然是一次有趣的经历。那一天湖面结冰了，地上和湖上也有雪，连成了白茫茫的一片，景色特别优美。我们也看到有人在湖面上走，但是警察让那个人离开湖面，因为密歇根湖的冰很薄，在冰上走很危险。

哈尔滨和芝加哥有很多共同点，比如这两个城市都有很好的大学，冬天也都很冷。很多芝加哥人也跟我们在哈尔滨遇到的司机一样，都为自己的家乡感到自豪。这些经历让我意识到，虽然美国和中国有很多文化、经济、政治方面的差异，但是这两国之间也有很多相似点。如果我们学会不同的语言，了解不同的文化，就可以开阔我们的视野，发现不同地方的特色，进而改善国际关系。

Harbin's famous ice festival in January, at a time when the temperature in Harbin had a high of around negative 12 degrees Celsius. The taxi driver who took us to our hotel was a born-and-raised Harbiner, which became obvious when you heard him speak with pride about his hometown. He told us that there were two main reasons that people visited Harbin: Harbin's famous universities, and the annual ice festival. The main part of the ice festival was held on Sun Island, which is in the middle of the Songhua River. When we walked by the river, we saw a lot of people enjoying themselves on the frozen river, ice skating and having fun. The ice was so thick that to cross the river, you didn't need to walk across a bridge, and you could simply walk across the river on the ice. In fact, not only could you walk across the ice, you could also take an old-fashioned horse-pulled carriage across the ice that catered to tourists. Harbin was also known for its Russian-style architecture in the old downtown area of the city.

I am now a student at the University of Chicago, and the winter weather and snow here remind me of my experience in Harbin. The University of Chicago has a tradition when on one day in February, students wake up at 6 in the morning to walk to Lake Michigan to see the sunrise. This year I participated in the activity, and I remember that it was especially cold that morning. After walking for nearly 30 minutes, we arrived at the lake. But we weren't able to see the sunrise, because it was too cloudy. Although we did not see sunrise that day, still the experience was interesting. The lake was frozen, a layer of snow covered both the ground and the lake, and the scene was beautiful. We also saw a person walking on the lake, but the police told him to get off the lake, because the ice on Lake Michigan was very thin, and walking on the ice was dangerous.

Harbin and Chicago have much in common. Both cities have good universities, and both have freezing winters. Like the taxi driver we met in Harbin, many Chicagoans are very proud of their hometown. These experiences made me realize that, despite the many cultural, economic, and political differences between America and China, the two countries have much in common. If we study foreign languages, and learn more about different cultures, we can broaden our perspectives, and discover interesting characteristics of different places. And this knowledge and experience will contribute to improving international relations.

我的上海故事

作者：钱采琳　指导教师：闫玲　哥伦比亚大学

在中国的经历教会了我以一颗坚韧的心去战胜一切。

我从小便是个乖乖女，一直盲目地听从父母的安排。直到23岁的一天，我突然感到前所未有的迷茫，迫切地想改变自己，于是我决定离开舒适的家，去上海留学。到达上海的第一天，我住进了项目给我们安排的寝室里。那儿又阴又湿，令我感到十分绝望，不禁怀疑起自己——来上海是不是个正确的决定？

第二天早上，我在宿舍附近散步，探索这个对我来讲还是完全陌生的城市。刚刚出门不久，我就发现离我寝室不远的地方有一家星巴克。闻到从店里飘出来的熟悉的香味儿，我突然感觉很温暖，这个城市似乎也没有那么陌生了。我继续向前走着，看到了很窄的弄堂。弄堂里的孩子们在嬉笑奔跑，每户人家都开着门做饭，邻里们在相互问候。整个弄堂充满着孩子的哭笑声、小贩的叫卖声、自行车的铃声、人们的寒暄声。上海百姓简朴而又和谐的生活给我留下了深深的印象。我继续在不同的弄堂里走着……一转弯，眼前的一切让我大吃一惊。刚看到的老上海烟消云散了，出现在我眼前的是宽阔的马路、车水马龙的街道、高耸入云的大楼，完全是一幅现代化国际大都市的景象。这样强烈的对比使我对上海产生了强烈的好奇心。我开始期待在中国生活，期待学习汉语。

来中国之前，我以为在中国学习汉语进步会很快，但实际上学习汉语的前两个月，我基本上没什么进步。这可能是我自己的原因。即使在课上学过了数字，我仍然分不清上海人说的是“十四”还是“四十”。像这样的障碍多的是，但不知

My Experience of Living in Shanghai

Author: Jocelyn Chambers Instructor: Ling Yan Columbia University

My experience in China taught me how to remain resilient when faced with relentless challenges.

Growing up, I was renowned in my neighbourhood for being an obedient little girl who always listened to her parents. One day when I was 23 years old, however, an existential dread that had been following me since high school finally became too overwhelming to ignore. Desperate to change myself, I decided to leave my cosy home and study abroad in Shanghai, China. The first day I arrived in Shanghai, I moved straight into the tiny dormitory the program had arranged. It was bone-chillingly cold and damp there and I was in deep despair. I couldn't help but question my decision to move across the world to come to Shanghai.

The following morning, I set about exploring my new neighbourhood on foot. An alluring smell drew me forward until I unexpectedly stumbled upon something from home: Starbucks Coffee. As the warm aroma of freshly brewed coffee floated out of the store, a sudden sense of familiarity struck me. Perhaps this foreign city wasn't so alien after all. Upon turning the corner, a traditional Shanghai *longtang* neighbourhood appeared out of nowhere. In the narrow alleyway, children were playing and running, neighbours were cooking and greeting each other with their doors open. The alleyway was bustling with the sounds of children laughing and crying, street vendors hawking their wares, rings of bicycles, and neighbours exchanging pleasantries. The simple and harmonious life of Shanghai locals impressed me a lot. I went on in different alleyways. One block later, however, the neighbourhood vanished. To my astonishment, appearing before me now were broad

怎么搞的，我从来没想过放弃学习汉语。令我不可思议的是，我越学习汉语，就越觉得中国神秘。更不可思议的是，我深深地被这个神秘的国家吸引了。我原来计划在中国只待半年，可是一年过去了，两年，三年，四年，我渐渐地适应了这儿的生活。从连“你好”都不会说，到可以和中国朋友流利地聊天儿；从担心找不到工作，到可以管理一个刚开的幼儿园；从一个朋友都没有，到现在有了很多知心朋友。

在中国的经历不但让我找到了真正的自我，而且给了我很大的启发。它不仅点燃了我对汉语和中国历史的热情，也教会了我以一颗坚韧的心去战胜一切。将来，无论我遇到什么障碍，我都会勇敢地跨越它们。我在中国生活的经历给予了我一生都用之不尽的精神财富。

roads, busy streets, and a maze of luminous glass skyscrapers – the scene of an modern international metropolis. Such a remarkable contrast between old and new, traditional and modern intrigued me immensely. I began to look forward to living in China and studying Chinese.

Before moving to China, I had believed that living in Shanghai meant my language skills would rapidly improve. However, the fact is that after two months of studying Chinese, I had essentially made zero progress. It might be my own reason. Even after gaining a solid grasp of numbers, I still couldn't differentiate between *fourteen* and *forty* when pronounced in a Shanghainese accent. There are many obstacles like this. The idea of giving up, however, never crossed my mind. What amazes me is that the more I learn Chinese, the more mysterious I feel about China. What's even more incredible is that I am deeply attracted to this mysterious country.

My original plan was to stay in China for six months. But six months quickly became one year, one year became two years, two years became three years, three years became four years, and four years ultimately made me gradually adapt myself to the life here. From not knowing how to say "hello" to comfortably conversing with Chinese friends, from worrying about finding a job to managing a newly-opened kindergarten, from not having a single acquaintance to making many bosom friends from around the world.

My experience in China not only gave me the courage to trust my inner voice, but also inspired me a lot. It not only ignited my passion in Chinese language and history, but also taught me how to remain resilient when faced with relentless challenges. In future, no matter what obstacles I meet, I will overcome them bravely. My experience in China has given me eternal intellectual wealth.

难忘的中国之行

作者：晏颖　指导教师：温晓虹　休斯敦大学

我喜欢这个文化多元的世界，不同的文化有不同的视角。

我是休斯敦大学大四的学生。我母亲是中国人，父亲是危地马拉人。我虽然在美国出生、长大，但从小就喜欢跟姥姥一起听中文歌，看中文书和中文电视剧。姥姥、姥爷给我讲故事的时候，我总是坚持请他们说中文。我梦想着有一天能去中国。2005年夏天，我第一次去中国的机会来了！

踏上中国的土地，我的第一个印象就是中国人好多啊！那时候我个子很矮，所以在熙熙攘攘的人群中看不见人的脸，一眼望去都是腿。我很快发现，无论是在街上还是在公共汽车上，到哪儿都很拥挤。公共汽车上没有空座位，只能听到售票员报站名，可是看不见她在哪里。既然看不到售票员，我就模仿她报站名，惹得全车人哈哈大笑。我长大后懂得了中国地大物博，世界上六分之一的人都说中文呢。我是半个中国人，也算中国的一分子，我更要把中文学好。到现在，我还记得那时在公共汽车上学的北京的车站名。

中国给我的第二个印象就是会有很多陌生人主动跟我说话。可能是因为我虽然长着一张外国孩子的脸，可是又说着流利的普通话，所以人们会很热情地跟我或者跟我姥姥说："这是个外国小孩儿吧？长得真胖乎！"虽然那时我不太愿意别人说我胖，但是现在我明白了每个国家的文化是不同的。"胖乎乎"在中文里是说这个人很可爱。我还了解到唐朝人就是以胖为美呢。这是我在博物馆看中国

An Unforgettable Trip to China

Author: Wilma Yan-Gutierrez Instructor: Xiaohong Wen University of Houston

I like this world of multicultural diversity. Different cultures often have different perspectives.

I am a senior at the University of Houston. My mother is Chinese, and my father is Guatemalan. Although I was born and raised in the United States, I enjoy listening to Chinese songs, reading Chinese books, and watching Chinese TV dramas with my grandmother since I was a child. When my grandparents told me stories, I insist that they speak Chinese. I dreamed of going to China one day. In the summer of 2005, my first chance to go to China came!

When I set foot on Chinese soil, my first impression was that there were so many people! At that time, I was very short, so I couldn't see people's faces in the crowd; all I could see was a sea of legs. I quickly found that it was crowded everywhere, whether in the street or on the bus. There were not empty seats on the bus, and I could only hear the conductor calling the stops, but I couldn't see where she was. Since I couldn't see her, I imitated her to announce the stops' names, which made everyone on the bus laugh. As I grew older, I learned that China is a place of vast land and rich resources. One-sixth of the people in the world speak Chinese! I am a member of China, half Chinese, so I should learn Chinese well. To this day, I still remember the names of the different bus stops in Beijing.

The second impression was that many strangers would take the initiative to talk to me, maybe because I had the face of a foreigner but spoke fluent Mandarin. People would be very enthusiastic about me or say to my grandmother, "Is this a little foreign kid? She's really chubby!" Although I was reluctant to be called "chubby" at the time, now I understand that each country's culture is different. "Chubby" is a praise in Chinese, which means that the

的艺术展览和学习唐代文化时认识到的。我喜欢这个文化多元的世界，不同的文化有不同的视角，而不同的视角都有自己的独到之处。

在中国时，我发现了很多在美国没有的东西，比如三轮车、胡同，还有蹲式厕所。记得第一次去厕所，我不会蹲，就目不转睛地看着旁边的一位老奶奶。老奶奶觉得莫名其妙，问我："你怎么不上厕所？干吗老看着我？"我也不好意思了，学着她的样子蹲下。我觉得是这位老奶奶教会了我怎么上蹲式厕所的。今天想起来，我觉得蹲式和坐式厕所各有长处。虽然坐式厕所用起来舒服也方便，但蹲式厕所更卫生，因为不会有皮肤接触，还有锻炼身体的作用。

给我印象最深的是火炕，那是我跟姥姥和舅舅参观长城的时候见到的。因为那时候长城还没有缆车，所以我们是徒步爬上山的。快天黑的时候，我们找到了一个可以过夜的农家小院。在这儿，我第一次感受到文化震撼！让我最惊讶的就是睡觉的炕，它是一块大石板，石板下左右两边是砖堆起来的，支撑着那块大石板，中间留有空间放木柴烧火，另一面顶着墙。在我看来它就像一个烧烤炉！要

person is cute. I also learned that people in the Tang Dynasty regarded being "chubby" as beautiful. I learned these facts when visiting Chinese art exhibitions in museums and studying Tang the Dynasty culture. I like this world of multicultural diversity. Different cultures often have different perspectives, which are unique and valuable on their own.

While in China, I found a lot of things that America doesn't have, such as tricycles (a bike with three wheels and a mini truck bed attached to the back), *hutongs* (alleyways), and squat toilets. I remember the first time I went to the toilet. Since I didn't know how to squat, I stared at a grandma next to me. The grandma felt inexplicable and said to me, "Why don't you go to the toilet? Why do you keep looking at me?" I tried to imitate her poses. I think it is her who taught me how to properly use the squat toilets. Thinking about it today, I feel that squatting and sitting toilets have their own advantages. Although the sitting position is comfortable and convenient, the squatting position is more hygienic and eliminates skin contact, and it also has the effect of exercising the body.

The most unforgettable experience was sleeping on a heated *kang* (a bed usually made of stone that was heated by fire, either directly under it or through a source feeding the heat to it). I saw it when I visited the Great Wall with my grandmother and uncle. There was no cable car leading to the Great Wall at that time, so we climbed the mountain on foot. When it was getting dark, we found a small farmyard where we could spend the night. I felt culture shock for the first time here! What surprised me the most was the *kang*. It was a large, flat slate rock with bricks stacked on the left and right sides under the slate to support it. There was space in the middle for firewood to burn, and the backside was against the wall. It looked like a barbeque grill to me! When it was time for bed, I kept crying and refused to get on the *kang*. My grandmother asked me strangely, "What are you waiting for? It's already late and you're not going to bed?!" I cried and pointed to the raging fire under the *kang* and kept saying, "Big fire! Big fire!" Then I ran outside the house and stood under a tree on the side of the mountain looking into the distance, refusing to go back into the house. My grandmother chased after me convincing me that it was safe and finally pulled me back into the house. It was late and I was

睡觉的时候，我不停地哭，不肯上炕。姥姥奇怪地问我：“你还等什么呢？这么晚了还不上床睡觉！”我边哭边指着炕底下的熊熊烈火说：“火！ 火！”然后我跑到屋外站在山边的一棵树下向外望去，不肯再回屋里。姥姥着急地追出屋外，好说歹说才把我拉进屋里。这时候已经非常晚了，我也很困了，终于踮起脚爬上炕，发现它没有我想象的那么烫。那天晚上我睡得很舒服。后来，我接触到环保、节能等理念，我突然想起，那天睡的火炕不就很环保、很节能吗？我又一次敬佩中国人的聪明才智和他们解决问题的机智办法。

我后来又有三次机会去中国旅行、学习和做义工，每次都收获不小。我准备把后来那几次中国之行也都记录下来，和姥姥一起重温那难忘的日子，总结我的收获，加深我对中国文化的理解和热爱。

sleepy. Finally, I climbed tiptoe onto the *kang* and found that it was not as hot as I thought. I slept very well that night. Later, I was educated on environmental protection and energy conservation. And one day I suddenly remembered: Isn't the *kang* that I slept on that day environmentally friendly and energy efficient? Once again, I admire the ingenuity of Chinese people and their witty solutions to problems.

Later, I had three more opportunities to travel, study and volunteer in China. I gained a lot of experience and memories each time. I plan to write all my subsequent trips to China, reliving those unforgettable days to share with my grandmother. This process will deepen my understanding and love of Chinese culture.

翠湖公园里的故事

作者：罗安丽　指导教师：刘芳　欧柏林学院

> 不同文化、不同经历、不同种族、不同年龄的人，只要有善良、诚恳的态度，都能顺利交流，友好相处。

我从高中二年级开始学习中文。那时，学习西班牙文的学生比较多，而我选择了一种神秘而未知的语言——中文。我很快就发现这种语言充满了魅力和活力。在我看来，中文最有吸引力的就是说话就像唱歌一样，写字就像画画儿一样。虽然我很早就对中文产生了兴趣，但是直到上了大学，上了中文课、中国历史课、中国电影课、中国书法课以后，有关中国的一切才真正成为我的最爱。

大学二年级的夏天，我去了一个中文暑期学校。在那里，我遇到了很棒的老师，认识了跟我一样喜欢学习中文的朋友，也提高了我的中文水平，而且萌生了去中国留学的愿望。所以 2019 年的夏天，我去昆明参加了一个暑期班。在这两个月里，我真正体验到了中国的生活和文化。

暑期班的功课很忙。我每天要上五个小时的课，还要用三个小时准备第二天的课。这些我还能对付，但让我有点儿难过的是我几乎没有时间出去看看昆明，交交朋友。除了老师以外，我唯一接触的人就是我的中国同屋。糟糕的是我们不大谈得来。语言沟通不是问题，就是总是想不到一块儿，说不到一块儿。话不投机半句多！索性也就不说什么了。我略感懊丧，不同文化背景的人，交流起来真的是挺难。

带着一些失落的心情，我一个人去了昆明市内有名的公园——翠

Stories in Green Lake Park

Author: Ariana Robin Instructor: Fang Liu Oberlin College

> As long as everyone treats each other with a kind and sincere attitude, people of different cultures, experiences, races, and ages can fully communicate and get along well with each other.

I've been learning Chinese since my sophomore year of high school. At the time, there were more students studying Spanish, but I chose a mysterious and unknown language – Chinese. I quickly discovered that the language is full of charm and energy. In my opinion, the most attractive part about Chinese is that speaking is like singing, and writing is like drawing. Although I became interested in Chinese very early on, it wasn't until I went to college and took Chinese language classes, Chinese history classes, Chinese film classes, and calligraphy classes that everything correlated with China truly became my favorite.

During the summer of my sophomore year in college, I went to a Chinese summer school. There, I met great teachers, met friends who enjoyed learning Chinese just as much as me, and improved my Chinese skills, which led to my desire to study abroad in China. So, in the summer of 2019, I went to Kunming to attend a summer school. Through the course of those two months, I really got to experience the Chinese life and culture.

I was very busy during the summer school. I had five hours of class every day and had to use three hours to prepare for the next day's classes. I could handle that, but what made me a little sad was the fact that I hardly had time to go out to explore Kunming and make some friends. Apart from the teacher, the only person I had contact with was my Chinese roommate, but it was unfortunate because we didn't have much to talk about. Language communication was not a problem, but it was almost impossible for us to think and speak on the same wavelength.

湖。在那里，我很放松，很随意，还可以享受自然，享受优美的环境和悦耳的音乐。我一个人走着走着，误入了公园的“相亲角”，那里是父母为自己的孩子选择对象的地方。一个美国女孩儿的闯入，吸引了所有人的目光。他们一定诧异怎么有个洋“剩女”自己送上门来了。还好我没等他们回过神来就逃跑了。

后来，我一有机会就去翠湖散步，只是要远离那个“相亲角”。虽然我经常会引起陌生人的注意，但是我还是在这里找到了归属感，感到自在。因为每张陌生的面孔都带着善意。

我特别喜欢看人们遛狗，看孩子们嬉戏，看大妈们跳广场舞。我最喜欢的是看三点左右开始的老人们的音乐舞会。这些至少六十岁的老年人，欢快地唱啊、跳啊，愉快而自得其乐。

In a disagreeable conversation, one word more is too many! Therefore, I resorted to not really saying anything at all. I was a little disappointed as it proved to be pretty difficult for people from different cultural backgrounds to communicate effectively.

Feeling a bit disheartened, I went to a famous park in Kunming alone – the Green Lake. There, I felt very relaxed and carefree, and I could enjoy nature, the beautiful environment, and harmonious music. As I walked alone, I stumbled into the park's "Blind Dating Corner," where parents would seek a boyfriend or girlfriend for their children. The sudden intrusion of an American girl caught the attention of almost everyone there. They must've been surprised by how a foreign "leftover girl" delivered herself to the door. Luckily, I ran away before they came back to their senses and could scrutinize me even more.

Later, I would go to the Green Lake for a walk whenever I had the chance, remembering to avoid the "Blind Dating Corner." Even though I often attracted the attention of strangers, I still felt at home and free there – because every unfamiliar face was full of kindness.

I especially enjoyed watching people walk their dogs, watching the kids play, and watching the elderly ladies do square dancing. My favorite part was watching the old people's musical dances that started around three o'clock. These elderly people, who were at least 60 years old, would happily sing, dance, and enjoy themselves.

One day, I courageously walked into the circle of the old people. I was the only young lady and the only foreigner, and it seemed as if I was out of place. I saw several old people whispering to each other, showing their curiosity without being unfriendly. I returned their whispers with a smile. After a while, an old lady handed me a newspaper; I was very surprised – was I about to take an exam? I took the newspaper and read it carefully. They were even more shocked, and with that, they all started laughing. It turned out they just wanted me to put the newspaper on the chair and sit.

When the ladies saw me reading the newspaper, they were extremely surprised and asked me, "Can you read Chinese?" "Yes." I heard many exclamations of "she can speak Chinese," and many elderly people were attracted. They asked me what country I was from. I said that I'm American. There were more expressions of astonishment. I was a little nervous since I didn't know what the Chinese elders' attitudes were toward America.

有一天，我壮着胆子，走进了老人们的圈子。我是唯一的年轻人，也是唯一的外国人，好像与她们格格不入。我见到几位老人相互耳语，显得好奇而并非不友好。我也报以微笑。一会儿，一位老大妈递给我一张报纸，我很诧异，要考试吗？我接过来认真读。她们更诧异，接着都笑了起来。原来她们是要我垫在椅子上坐。

大妈们看见我看报纸，很是惊讶，问我："你能看懂中文？""能。"我听到很多声"她会中文"的惊叹，不少老人被吸引了过来。她们问我是哪国人。我说我是美国人。又是一片惊叹。我稍许有点儿紧张，因为我不知道中国老人们对美国是什么态度。

没想到她们对我非常热情，我一下子放心了，我们开始聊起来。好几位大妈围拢过来，其中一位还递给我一块紫色的糖果。挺难吃，但我还是吃了。她们热心地向我介绍她们的乐器和音响，我大部分听不懂，只是一个劲儿地点头说："好，好！"

一个不速之客一下子成了她们的贵客，我好像已经是她们之中的一员了。我是个很年轻的陌生的外国人，而翠湖的一个老人圈却接受了我，真是让我感到很开心，很激动。我非常后悔没有早些去那里。后来，因为功课太忙，我没能应她们的邀请，去参加大妈们的广场舞。如果有机会，我一定会跟她们一起跳，一起笑。

这是我在昆明最有价值的经历。这个经历教育、鼓励了我。我跟同屋的关系让我怀疑我能不能跟外国人交流，这是完全没有道理的。不同文化、不同经历、不同种族、不同年龄的人，只要有善良、诚恳的态度，都能顺利交流，友好相处。我至今想念翠湖的那些老年人，非常感谢那群热情友好的大妈们。期待着和她们再见面！

I hadn't expected that they treated me very warmly. I immediately felt relieved, and we started chatting with each other. Several ladies gathered around me, and one of them even handed me a piece of purple candy. It tasted pretty bad, but I still ate it. They enthusiastically introduced me to their musical instruments and stereos. I couldn't understand most of what they were saying, but I just kept nodding and saying, "Good, nice!"

An uninvited guest suddenly became their distinguished guest, and in that moment, it seemed as if I was one of them – a part of their community. I was a very young foreigner who was unfamiliar with everything, but I was accepted by the elderly at the Green Lake, which made me feel happy and excited. I really regret not going there sooner. Later, because I was too busy with my schoolwork, I couldn't attend the square dancing with the ladies at their invitation. If I ever get the chance, I will definitely dance with them and laugh with them.

This turned out to be my most valuable experience in Kunming, which educated and encouraged me. My relationship with my roommate made me wonder if I could even communicate with foreigners. This doubt makes absolutely no sense. As long as everyone treats each other with a kind and sincere attitude, people of different cultures, experiences, races, and ages can fully communicate and get along well with each other. I miss the elders at the Green Lake to this day, and I am very grateful that I met those warm and friendly ladies. I look forward to seeing them again!

中国和塞尔维亚

作者：王朋　指导教师：陈红　洛尤拉大学

> 我们彼此有了更深的了解，才能让世界变得更加包容、和谐、平等和自由。

我叫王朋，是芝加哥洛尤拉大学三年级的学生。两年前，我有机会在北京学习生活了半年。那半年的所见所闻给我留下了深刻的印象。

记得我刚刚到北京不久，就利用课余时间，走遍了北京的大街小巷。虽然我去过世界上的许多国家，但是这将是我第一次离开家好几个月。当我走进朝阳区，漫步于各国大使馆之间的时候，我第一次注意到那些建筑与塞尔维亚的建筑惊人地相似。在美丽的蓝天白云下，一座座

China and Serbia

Author: Filip Zigic Instructor: Hong Chen Loyola University

> Better understanding of each other makes the world more tolerant, harmonious, equal and free.

I am Filip Zigic, a junior at Loyola University in Chicago. Two years ago, I studied in Beijing for half a year. I was deeply impressed by what I experienced in Beijing.

I remember soon after I arrived in Beijing, I roamed through many neighborhoods in Beijing when I did not have classes at school. Although I visited many countries all around the world, this was the first time I was away from home for a few months. One day, I was walking by the area in Chaoyang District in Beijing where all the embassies are when I first noticed some similarities with Serbia. I noticed how similar the elegant buildings and the beautiful blue sky above. I'd first arrived in Beijing two weeks before, and I fell in love with everything here.

When you live in another country for a long time, you start to notice little things that you had not noticed before. For example, during my whole life in the United States I did not know that I would miss chocolate so much if I were to leave. I also never thought I would know what it was like to live in a country where everyone was so interested in Serbia. Although I was born and raised in the United States, my entire family is Serbian, and we are all very proud of that. The first time I mentioned to a Chinese person that I was Serbian as well as American, they said, "Wow, I've heard of Serbia! I have also watched the movie *Walter Defends Sarajevo*." I looked at him in confusion and awe, then I responded, "How in the world do you know about that film?" He said it was huge in China 40 years ago. He also said that almost everyone in China had seen it at some point as it was still on television sometimes and was one of the few foreign films in China at the time. I was in shock, and I couldn't believe that this classic Yugoslav film had made such a huge impact in China!

整齐别致的楼房好像把我带到了塞尔维亚。我刚刚到北京两个星期，就已经爱上了这里的一切。

如果在一个国家待上比较长的时间，你就能够注意到这个国家与你的祖国细微的区别。这些差别在很短的时间里你是不会注意到的。如果我一直住在美国没有出国，我就不会意识到我是如此钟爱巧克力。如果我没有在中国待上一段时间，我永远不会知道中国人对塞尔维亚这么感兴趣。虽然我是在美国出生和长大的，但是我的爸爸、妈妈都来自塞尔维亚。我们是美国人，也是塞尔维亚人，我们都为此感到十分骄傲。记得我第一次对一个中国人说："我是美国塞尔维亚人。"他惊奇地说："哇！真的吗？我听说过塞尔维亚！也看过电影《瓦尔特保卫萨拉热窝》。"我疑惑又敬畏地看着他，问道："你是怎么知道那部电影的？"他说大约40年前那部电影是家喻户晓的热播片，是当时中国为数不多的外国电影之一，差不多人人都看过。现在电视上有时候还会播放。我很震惊，我不敢相信这部经典的南斯拉夫电影在中国产生了这么大的影响！

而在美国，这种事情绝对不会发生。谈到塞尔维亚，很多美国人的模糊记忆仅仅是20多年前北约军队对南联盟的大规模轰炸。

我很欣赏中国人愿意和外国人交谈，也从不因为我当时的汉语水平太差而嘲笑我。在北京生活的六个月里，我的汉语水平迅速提高。我喜欢任何时候可以和任何中国人交谈，并留下联系方式，最终变成好朋友。可以说，语言真是人类沟通的桥梁，把我们紧紧地联系在一起。我看到了中文的魅力，越学越喜欢学。

在中国短短的几个月里，我结交了许多新朋友，开阔了眼界，也看到了中国人眼里的塞尔维亚，亲身体验了世界上最迷人的国家之一。我相信通过语言，我们可以更好地互相交流、学习。我们彼此有了更深的了解，才能让世界变得更加包容、和谐、平等和自由。我们都开始明白，其实国与国、人与人之间没有很大的不同。我希望尽我的努力，为中国、美国、塞尔维亚人民的交流沟通发挥我的作用，贡献我的力量！

This sort of scenario never happens in the United States. When it comes to Serbia, many American persons only have vague memories of the massive bombings of the Federal Republic of Yugoslavia by NATO 20 years ago.

I appreciated Chinese people's willingness to talk with a foreigner, and they never derided me too much for my, at the time, poor Chinese skills. In the six months I lived in Beijing, my Chinese level increased rapidly. I loved that any time I wanted to I could talk with nearly any Chinese person, have a relatable conversation, and finally become a friend of them. One could say that language is the bridge of communication that bind together humanity. I have seen the charm of Chinese. The more I learn it, the more I'd like to learn.

I had a wonderful experience during my short few months in China. In that short time, I made many new friends, broadened my outlook, learned about Serbia in Chinese people's eyes, and experienced first-hand one of the most fascinating countries in the world. I believe that language helps us better communicate and learn from each other. Better understanding of each other makes the world more tolerant, harmonious, equal and free. By doing so, we can all begin to understand that none of us are very different from anybody else. I hope I've done my part in my own small way for the communication among Chinese, American and Serbian people!

出租车里的故事

作者：文理爱　指导教师：谭大立　北弗吉尼亚社区学院

我坐在这位司机的车上，感到很温暖，好像又回到了妈妈的怀抱。

我在美国一向自己开车，但是到了北京以后，我发现打车会有一种意想不到的收获。这个收获就是可以跟司机交谈，从他们那里学到很多课堂里学不到的东西。打车让我有机会进一步了解中国人的思想和日常生活。今天我想分享几个出租车里的小故事。

我上出租车以后，司机总是会问："你来自哪个国家？"答完以后，我常常会问像"你是北京人吗？""你有没有孩子？""你喜欢什么样的音乐？"这类的问题。

有一位来自内蒙古的司机，给我留下了深刻的印象。他看起来很不幸福，很无奈。我问了他很多问题，发现他是一个非常不幸的人。他曾经跟他最爱的人结婚，但是后来，他们的爱渐渐变淡了，最终他们离婚了。自从离婚以来，他没有很多机会去看他的孩子。他心情很糟糕，所以感觉好像全世界都是他的敌人。他的世界观和爱情观显然受到了重大挫折。他很现实地跟我说："你们毕业以后不必找好工作，而应该找一位有钱的老公。清华大学有很多富二代。"我当然不同意他的看法，劝他向前看，再次开始新的生活。

谈到富二代，我不由得想起另一个打车经历。我在车上有时会做作业。有一次，我问了司机一个我的功课上的问题："你觉得什么是'现代中国的特色'？"

Stories in Cabs

Author: Raven Witherspoon

Instructor: Dali Tan Northern Virginia Community College

> The warmth I felt while sitting in the cab was like returning home to my mother's hugs.

I always drove on my own when I was in the U.S., but after coming to Beijing, I realized that cab hailing could give me unexpected gains – I could chat with cab drivers and get to know many things that cannot be learned in class.

Cab hailing gave me the opportunity to further understand the perspectives and daily lives of Chinese people. Today, I'd like to share several short stories of my experiences in Beijing cabs.

Whenever I enter a cab, the driver will always ask me: "Which country are you from?" After answering this question, I often ask questions like "Are you from Beijing?" "Do you have children?" "What kind of music do you like?"

One driver from Inner Mongolia left a deep impression on me. He seemed deeply unhappy, resigned to his lack of control over life's circumstances. I asked him many questions and found how unfortunate his life had been. He had married the love of his life, but their love gradually dissipated. In the end, they divorced. Ever since the divorce, he had few opportunities to see his child. His disposition was miserable, as if the whole world were his enemy. His outlook on life and love had clearly suffered deep blows. He advised me: "After you graduate, there's no need to find a good job. You should find a rich husband; there are plenty of '富二代,' the second generation of the rich, at Tsinghua University." Of course, I disagreed with his

他刚一开始还不太明白我的意思，所以我跟他讲了讲我的中文课文的内容。他想了一会儿，然后说道："消除贫困、共同富裕是现代中国的特色。"就此我又引出了一些话题，比方说最近房子价格提高了，我想知道他是怎么看这类问题的。他说："房价上涨是难免的，政府也在努力解决问题，增盖更多的经济适用房。我们还得往前走，向前看。"我很欣赏这位司机师傅的积极态度，笑着跟他开玩笑说："对，我们继续开车，往前走，向前看。"

perspective, and I encouraged him to keep looking forward and begin a new life.

Speaking of the Chinese term for "the second generation of the rich," I can't help but be reminded of another cab hailing experience. I sometimes do assignments during cab rides. I once asked a driver a question from my homework assignment – "What do you think are modern China's 'special characteristics?'" At first he didn't quite understand what I meant, so I further explained the content of my Chinese lesson. He thought for a while, and then said: "Eradicating poverty, and seeking common prosperity, those are the special characteristics of modern China." I then raised a number of other topics such as the recent increase in housing prices. I wanted to know how he viewed these questions. He said, "The increase in housing prices is unavoidable, and the government is working hard to remedy problems by building more economically affordable houses. We must continue looking and moving forward." I admired this driver's positive attitude. I smiled and jokingly said, "You're right, we should keep driving forward and looking ahead."

The warmth I felt while sitting in the cab was like returning home to my mother's hugs. Somehow, he remained incredibly patient despite spending his working hours in a traffic jam in Beijing. He wasn't rushed or flustered; with good humor and an even temper, he chatted with me as he drove. Although our age, gender, and nationality are all different, our worldview is identical. He said, "When you enter my cab, I have a responsibility to make you happy, to make you feel that today is lovely. Whether or not we'll meet again in the future is uncertain, but meeting today is a kind of fate." I completely agreed with his perspective; being able to meet in a cab is like a form of destiny. He and I talked about the economic conditions of his hometown, his children's experiences in college, the Sino-U.S. relationship, environmental protection, and so on.

Many cab drivers have asked me: "Do you like China?" "Is American college tuition really as expensive as people say it is?" "Are your family members in the U.S. doing alright? Will they consider moving to China like you?" The compassion of these cab drivers has moved me. I

我坐在这位司机的车上，感到很温暖，好像又回到了妈妈的怀抱。他在上下班交通堵塞中还耐心得很。他不着急，不着慌，心平气和地开车，和我聊天儿。虽然我们的年龄不同，性别不同，国籍不同，但是我们的观念一模一样。他说："您上了我的车，我就有责任让您高兴，让您觉得今天很美好。咱们将来能不能见面不一定，但是今天见面了就是我们有缘分。"我特别同意他的观点，我们能够在出租车里认识确实是缘分。我们讨论的话题还包括他老家的经济条件、他孩子的大学经历、中美关系、环境保护等问题。

许多司机师傅还会问我："你喜欢中国吗？""美国的学费真的像别人说的那么贵吗？""你在美国的家人还好吗？他们会不会考虑跟你一样搬到中国来？"他们的关爱让我很感动。我认为，在中国期间，除了课堂里面的老师以外，在出租车里，我还有很多老师。三人行，必有我师。坐出租车出行，司机师傅就是我的老师。

believe that during my time in China, in addition to my classroom professors, I also found many teachers in cabs. Where there are three men walking together, one of them must be qualified to be my teacher. When traveling in a cab, the driver is my teacher.

童年的故事

作者：吴波　指导教师：顾利程　西北大学

> 在中国各地游览的经历，大大地开拓了我的眼界，真是应了"行千里路胜读万卷书"的古语。

我2002年出生在俄勒冈州的波特兰市。我有一个快乐的童年。父母放假的时候总会带着我到处旅游，希望我能多接触外面的世界。

四岁时，我第一次去中国，住在广州祈福新村的外公外婆家。那儿气候温暖，到处鲜花盛开，绿草如茵，果树飘香。新村内还有一个很大的人工湖，人工湖中心还有一个小岛，上面有几只白天鹅。外公外婆经常带我到湖中划船，白天鹅也常常跟在我们的小船边游来游去，我向它们泼水，它们也不跑，一点儿都不怕人，好可爱。

在广州期间，我还进了新村的双语国际幼儿园。每天从幼儿园放学回家，有一大乐趣，那就是和蝌蚪一起玩儿。外婆家门口，有一条长长的小溪。春天，小溪里游着很多拖着长长扁尾巴的小蝌蚪。它们抖动着小尾巴，在水中欢快地来回游动，非常可爱。我会脱了鞋走到小溪中，用小棍子轻轻地拨弄小蝌蚪的尾巴，逗它们玩儿。我对蝌蚪变成青蛙的过程有很大的兴趣。我注意到，小蝌蚪先长出两条后腿，十几天后又长出两条前腿，可以出水爬行，再过些日子，长长的尾巴就没有了，变成活蹦乱跳的小青蛙了。

九岁那年，父母正好有了长假，他们又一次带我去了中国。我们先从杭州出发，一路向北，游览了许多南方城市——上海、苏州、无锡、南京，还去了中国的首都——北京。美丽的风景，不一样的风土人情，各种各样的美味佳肴都让

My Childhood Stories

Author: Ethan Wu Instructor: Licheng Gu Northwestern University

These experiences of traveling around China have broadened my horizons even more, fitting the old saying "Walking ten thousand *li* is better than reading ten thousand books."

I was born in Portland, Oregon in 2002. I had a happy childhood. When my parents were on vacation, they would always take the time to bring me on trips around the world, hoping me to get more contact with the outside world.

When I was four, I went to China for the first time, staying at my maternal grandparents' home in Clifford Estates, Guangzhou. There, the climate was warm, flowers were in bloom everywhere, the grass was green, and the sweet scent of the fruit trees permeated everywhere. There was a large man-made lake in the village, and in the middle of the lake was a small island where several white swans nested. My grandparents would frequently take me to play on the lake in a rowboat, and the swans would often follow our little boat, swimming alongside us. Even when I splashed them with water, they wouldn't run away, as they were completely unafraid of people – so cute.

During my stay in Guangzhou, I also attended the village's bilingual international kindergarten. Every day on the way home from school, I had a very fun hobby, that is, playing with tadpoles. In front of my grandmother's house, there was a long stream. In spring, there would be many tadpoles swimming in the stream, dragging their long, flat tails. They would wiggle their little tails, happily swimming back and forth which I found adorable. I would take off my shoes and walk into the stream, using a small stick to gently poke the tadpoles' tails to play. I was really interested in the process of how tadpoles would become frogs. I noticed that

我久久难以忘怀。我喜欢上了上海小笼包、老北京炸酱面、醒脑开胃的酸辣汤，还有看着吓人但特别好吃的皮蛋。行程中最让我震撼的是那历史悠久的古代建筑——长城。远看长城就像一条巨龙，在崇山峻岭之间穿行，连绵起伏，曲折蜿蜒。一座座坚固的烽火台，耸立在山头，就像一个个城堡。秦始皇建立秦朝以后修建的长城，从东到西超过一万里（五千千米），所以称为“万里长城”，这个名字一直沿用到今天。实际上，后代陆续修建的长城总长度有两万多千米，而我们今天看到的长城主要是明长城。长城在世界历史上真是一个伟大的奇迹！我试着攀登长城，可是上面风很大，台阶又高又多，我实在爬不上去。人们常说，不到长城非好汉，我只能把这个挑战留给下一次了。

时间过得真快，童年的生活像一道闪电，在我眼前一闪而过，但童年的种种欢声笑语并没有因此消失，至今回味无穷。在中国各地游览的经历，大大地开拓了我的眼界，真是应了“行千里路胜读万卷书”的古语。希望我有机会再去中国看望我的外公外婆，再去看看我儿时的朋友——小蝌蚪，再去尝尝上海小笼包。当然，我长大了，这次一定要爬上长城，当一名好汉！

the small tadpoles would first grow their two back legs, and a dozen days later, their front legs would develop, allowing them to climb out of the water. A few days after, their long tails would disappear, and they would become lively little frogs.

When I was nine, my parents had another long vacation, and brought me to China once again. We started in Hangzhou; heading north, we visited many southern cities – Shanghai, Suzhou, Wuxi, and Nanjing. We also visited the capital of China – Beijing. The beautiful scenery, varied customs, and all kinds of delicious delicacies created an unforgettable memory. I really liked Shanghai's *xiaolongbao*, Old Beijing's noodles served with fried bean sauce, the refreshing and appetizing sour and spicy soup, and the seemingly scary but very delicious preserved eggs. What awed me the most on this journey was the ancient and storied piece of architecture – the Great Wall. From a distance, the Great Wall seemed like an enormous dragon winding and snaking through the mountains. Many sturdy watch towers stand on the top of the mountain, like castles. The Great Wall built after Qinshihuang established the Qin Dynasty, was over 10,000 *li* (5,000 kilometers) long from east to west, so it is called "the 10,000-*li* Long Wall." This name has been used ever since. In fact, the Great Wall has been extended by future generations, and now extends more than 20,000 kilometers long. What we see today of the Great Wall is mainly that of the Ming Dynasty. The Great Wall is really one of the miracles in the history of the world! I tried to climb the Great Wall, but it was very windy up there and the steps were so high and many that I couldn't climb up. People often say that if you don't go to the Great Wall, you cannot be called a true man, so I could only leave this challenge for next time.

Time flies so fast. Childhood is like a flash of lightning, flashing before my eyes, but all the laughter and happiness of childhood have not disappeared with the passage of time, and I hold these memories dearly even today. These experiences of traveling around China have broadened my horizons even more, fitting the old saying "Walking ten thousand *li* is better than reading ten thousand books." I hope that I will have the opportunity to go to China again to see my grandparents again, go to see my childhood friend – the little tadpoles, and then try Shanghai's *xiaolongbao*. Of course, I'm now grown up: I must climb the Great Wall this time and be a true man!

故乡行

作者：吕若曦　指导教师：顾利程　西北大学

> 那雄伟秀丽的高山，昂首挺拔的青松，冉冉升起的红日，飞流直下的瀑布，都让我流连忘返。

十五岁初中毕业的那个暑假，我跟爸爸回中国玩儿了一个月。这次旅行让我更多地了解了中国文化，领略了中国风光，还见到了国内的很多亲人。我们从芝加哥直飞上海，再坐火车去爸爸的家乡——江苏省高邮市三垛镇。在那里住了两天以后，我们开车去了武汉，看望那里的家人。在武汉玩儿了几天以后，我们又去了黄山。我们在黄山住了一个晚上，然后又坐动车去北京看望我的表姐。我跟表姐在北京玩儿了一个

A Trip to My Homeland

Author: Chelsea Lu Instructor: Licheng Gu Northwestern University

When I was 15, during the summer after graduating from middle school, my dad and I went on vacation back to China for a month. This trip allowed me to learn more about Chinese culture, appreciate the scenery of China, and meet many relatives at home. We flew directly from Chicago to Shanghai, and then took the train to my dad's hometown – a small town called Sanduo, which is a part of Gaoyou City, Jiangsu Province. After staying there for two days, we drove to Wuhan to visit our family members. After a few days in Wuhan, we went to Mount Huangshan. We stayed in Mount Huangshan for one night, and then took the bullet train to Beijing to visit my cousin. After spending a week in Beijing with my cousin, we took the high-speed train to Xi'an. Using many different modes of transportation, we traveled across more than half of China within a month, and what I saw and heard will never be forgotten.

The majestic and beautiful mountains, the tall green pines, the rising red sun, and the rushing waterfalls all made me linger.

I really enjoy climbing Mount Huangshan; although mountain climbing is very exhausting, the scenery there is so beautiful. The majestic and beautiful mountains, the tall green pines, the rising red sun, and the rushing waterfalls all made me linger, just like the famous Chinese saying, "After returning from Mount Huangshan, you have no desire to visit any other mountains." As I traversed across the beautiful mountains and rivers of China, not only did I witness stunning scenery, but I also tasted delicious food. Within the month I spent in China, I had a lot of Chinese meals and special snacks. For example, I tried Shanghai's local dishes, Nanjing's dried salted duck, Hunan's stinky tofu, and Xi'an's pita bread in mutton soup. To help me communicate with local students, my dad even signed me up for a summer camp in Xi'an.

星期，接着坐高铁去西安。我们乘坐很多不同的交通工具，在一个月内游历了大半个中国，所见所闻让我久久不能忘记。

我很喜欢爬黄山，虽然爬山非常累，但那里的风景太美了。那雄伟秀丽的高山，昂首挺拔的青松，冉冉升起的红日，飞流直下的瀑布，都让我流连忘返，真是应了那句俗话，“黄山归来不看山”。在中国的美丽山川中，我不仅大饱了眼福，而且大饱了口福。在中国一个月的时间里，我吃到了很多中国大餐和特色小吃。譬如，我吃到了上海的本帮菜、南京的板鸭、湖南的臭豆腐，还有西安的羊肉泡馍。为了让我多跟当地学生交流，我爸爸还在西安给我报名参加了一个夏令营。在一个星期的夏令营里，老师给我们讲中国的历史故事，带我们去参观兵马俑以及各类寺庙和博物馆，使我对中国的历史有了更深刻的了解。

这次旅行我们去了很多地方，但是访问爸爸长大的小镇给我留下的印象最深。我爸爸是在三垛镇长大的，那里还有爷爷、奶奶亲手盖的房子。在我的眼里，那个老屋真的是又老又小，破烂不堪，但是院子里的一草一木都让爸爸沉浸在对儿时的回忆当中，看得出爸爸对老屋的一砖一瓦都充满了深情厚意。爸爸离开三垛很长时间了，三垛发生了很大的变化。他以前熟悉的街道不见了，儿时的朋友找不到了，以前的工厂不见了，就连他读过的小学也没有了。我们眼前看到的是一座座崭新的现代化建筑。面对家乡这些翻天覆地的变化，我从爸爸的脸上看到了惊喜，同时也看到了伤感、失落，以及一丝淡淡的哀愁。我想告诉爸爸，中国不能永远停留在过去，中国在和世界一起变化，这不是以个人意愿为转移的。然而我自始至终什么也没有说，相信爸爸是明白的。

During the one-week summer camp, the teacher told us about historical stories of China and took us to visit the Terracotta Warriors and Horses as well as various temples and museums, which gave me a deeper understanding of ancient Chinese history.

Although I have gone to many places during this trip, the visit to the small town where my dad grew up left the greatest impression on me. My dad grew up in Sanduo. At Sanduo, there is also a house built by my grandparents. From my perspective, the house looked very old, small, and dilapidated, but the grass and trees in the yard all made my dad immersed in his childhood memories. I could tell that my dad felt deeply attached and affectionate toward every brick and every tile of the house. My dad had been away from Sanduo for a long time, and a lot had changed since then. The streets he used to know are gone, his childhood friends are gone, the old factories are gone, and even the elementary school he attended as a child is gone. What we now see in front of us are brand new modern buildings. Along with these dramatic changes and innovations in his hometown, I saw my dad's expression of surprise, but I also saw sadness, loss, and a tinge of sorrow. I would like to tell my dad that China cannot be stuck in the past forever; China is changing with the world, and this is not a change that can be controlled by personal will. However, I didn't actually say anything as I believe that my dad understands this concept.

杭州大使环球行

作者：康宝莉　指导教师：闫玲　哥伦比亚大学

> 在中国和其他国家不同的城市唱中文歌曲时，我将音乐视若治愈心灵、凝聚一切的法宝。

像其他青少年一样，业余时间我很喜欢在油管上观看各种各样的视频。2015 年暑假，我看到了一个美国小女孩儿说中文的小视频，她谈到一个令人兴奋的旅游真人秀选拔赛，名字叫“2015 年杭州大使环球行”。这次比赛是由杭州市政府和杭州旅游局联合赞助举办的。他们打算通过该选拔赛在全球选出一个中国家庭和一个美国家庭，胜出的家庭将赢得 30 天的免费环球旅行。我知道杭州在哪儿，以前在中文课上学过，它是中国浙江省的省会，据说也是中国最快乐的城市之一，所以我对这个选拔赛非常感兴趣。乍看起来，这个机会着实好得令人难以置信，所以我跟我当时的中文老师对这个比赛进行了深入细致的研究，希望能够顺利获选。当时我还没去过中国，因此觉得这也是一个相当完美的了解中国的机会，如果让这个机会白白溜走，我一定会遗憾的。

一切准备就绪后，我迅速在网上报了名，还跟爸爸妈妈一起录了一段小视频介绍我们的家庭。我妈妈是演员，爸爸是歌手，表演和唱歌也是我最大的爱好，因此录一段音乐视频对我们一家来说是轻而易举的事情。我们在视频里讲了为什么要参加此次旅行，为了体现自己的诚意，我说了中文，还唱了一首叫《宝贝》的中文歌曲。在网上提交视频以后，漫长而又焦灼的等待过程令我们紧张不安。我们等了三个星期才收到杭州旅游局发来的电子邮件，他们通知我们，我们的家

My Global Tour as a Hangzhou Ambassador

Author: Cayleigh Capaldi Instructor: Ling Yan Columbia University

> When we sang Chinese songs in the various cities of our trip, I saw how music can be a universal language of healing and solidarity.

Like any other teenager, I love watching YouTube videos in my free time. In the summer of 2015, I came across a video of a little American girl speaking Chinese, talking about an exciting tourism reality show called "The Hangzhou Global Tour 2015." This competition was jointly sponsored by the Hangzhou Government and the Hangzhou Tourism Commission. They planned to host a global competition in search of one Chinese family and one American family, who would win a free 30-day trip around the world. I knew where Hangzhou was, as I had studied the city in my Chinese class; Hangzhou is the capital city of Zhejiang Province, also known as one of the happiest cities in the country, so I was very interested in this opportunity. At first glance, it all seemed incredibly good, so I did some in-depth research with my Chinese teacher at the time hoping to win. At that point I had never been to China before, so it seemed like this was the perfect opportunity to get to know the country. It would be a shame if I let this chance slip away.

After some preparation, I signed up online and recorded a short video with my mom and dad to introduce our family. My mom is an actress, my dad is a singer, and acting and singing are my biggest hobbies so it seemed that a music video would be the perfect way to showcase our family. In the video, we shared why we wanted to go on this adventure, and to show my sincerity, I spoke Chinese and sang the Chinese song "*Baobei*." After submitting the video online, we waited three weeks before receiving an email from the Hangzhou Tourism

庭被选中了!

2015 年 7 月底，我们一家乘坐飞机从旧金山飞到了杭州。我记得初到杭州时心中忐忑不安，虽然我已经学了五年的中文，但我仍然担心自己的中文水平不够高，影响此次的杭州之行。但是，在杭州住了一个星期以后，我的恐惧很快就消失了。我们先在杭州了解了当地的历史和文化，每天去看杭州丰富又多元的自然景观，比如中国最有名的湖泊之一——西湖。绿树环抱的西湖给我留下了特别深刻的印象：广阔辽远的湖面给人一种苍茫之感，漫步苏堤之上，品味此番妙处让人顿生安定之心。若停留驻足观看，只见翠绿的荷叶衬托着一株株淡粉的荷花，它们亭亭玉立，有的含苞待放，有的招蜂引蝶，吸引了无数游客拍照留念。西湖为杭州树立宁静和谐的城市形象起到了举足轻重的作用，扮演了整个城市名片的中心角色。而今回想起来，我仍记得我们在杭州度过的美好时光：晨起，驱车前往杭州附近的茶场，学习中国传统的茶道以及风俗，像古代的姑娘一样，用自己的嘴唇采茶；日落，伴着微风在西湖上划船，穿梭其间，听取附近蛙声、蝉声一片；当然，拐进街边小店欣赏二胡和古琴演奏的美妙乐曲，也是我们一家人最喜爱的休闲活动。离开杭州以后，我们便踏上了丝绸之路的旅途，一路向西，最后到达美国纽约。30 天的时间里，我们跨越了三大洲、七个国家、十一座城市和岛屿：有中国的杭州和敦煌，希腊的雅典、米克诺斯岛、圣托里尼岛，克罗地亚的杜布罗夫尼克，意大利的威尼斯，瑞士的日内瓦，法国的巴黎，还有美国的波士

Commission. The long and anxious waiting process made us incredibly nervous – but luckily, the email we received said that our family had won!

At the end of July in 2015, my family and I flew from San Francisco to Hangzhou. I remember feeling uneasy when I first arrived; even though I had been studying Chinese for five years, I was terrified that my language level was not high enough for me to do my job as Hangzhou's Official Tourism Ambassador. However, after spending a week in Hangzhou, my fears quickly disappeared. We first learned about the history and culture of the city, and every day we experienced Hangzhou's colorful and diverse scenic landscapes. One such natural beauty was the West Lake, one of the most famous lakes in China. Surrounded by lush green trees, the West Lake left a lasting impression on me: the vast and far-reaching water gives you a feeling of boundlessness, and walking along the Su Causeway allowed me to savor the idyllic elegance and feel a deep sense of peace. If you pause and look, you can see pale pink lotus flowers in bloom framed by emerald green lotus leaves, attracting bees and butterflies and drawing the attention of countless tourists eagerly snapping pictures. The West Lake has played a central role in establishing the city's peaceful and harmonious reputation, and has become Hangzhou's most well-known image. Looking back now, I still remember the incredible times we had in Hangzhou: waking up early, driving to a nearby tea farm, learning about the traditional tea ceremony and Chinese tea customs, and picking green tea leaves with our lips like the women of ancient times; rowing a boat across the West Lake, feeling the light breeze

顿和纽约。作为来自美国的杭州大使，每到一地，我们都会给人们宣传介绍杭州，负责把杭州的快乐带给全世界。与我们同行的还有一个杭州三口之家；一个美国亚利桑那州威肯堡的社交媒体专家和一个中国杭州的社交媒体专家，他们每天在网上写博客记录我们的出行日常；另外还有一个从中国香港来的电影摄制组，每天拍摄专业的视频和音频，发给中国和世界其他国家的一百多个新闻频道、电视台以及广播电台。我们的拍摄时间表非常严格，行程紧张却也充实。

这次旅行让我收获颇丰，特别是在中国的时候，那些丰富多彩的经历开阔了我的视野，让我成为了更好的自己。我和家人也充分享受了音乐的独特魅力，在中国和其他国家不同的城市唱中文歌曲时，我将音乐视若治愈心灵、凝聚一切的法宝。我也看到了音乐在帮助各国人民构筑新联系、建立新友谊方面所发挥的作用。不过，最为重要的是，我意识到跟其他参赛者一样能说中文是一件多么幸运的事情！纵观当今世界，会说中文是一项多么特殊的技能啊！所以我觉得自己异常幸运，可以参加这样特殊的旅行，领略中国精彩的历史、文化，感受中文的力量。

and listening to the croaks and chirps of nearby frogs and cicadas; and of course, exploring the small shops where we enjoying the beautiful music of the *erhu* and the *guqin* was one of my family's favorite pastimes. After leaving Hangzhou, we embarked on a journey across the Silk Road, traveling west until we reached New York, U.S.A. In thirty days, we traveled to three continents, seven countries, and eleven cities and islands: Hangzhou and Dunhuang in China; Athens, Mykonos, and Santorini in Greek; Dubrovnik in Croatia; Venice in Italy; Geneva in Switzerland; Paris in France; Boston and New York City in the U.S. As the U.S. Tourism Ambassadors for Hangzhou, my family and I introduced Hangzhou to the people we met along the way, spreading the happiness of the city across the world. We were also accompanied by a family of three from Hangzhou; asocial media expert from Wickenburg of Arizona, the U.S, and one from Hangzhou, China, who both wrote daily blogs to record our travels; and a film crew from Hong Kong, China who shot professional footage that was sent to over 100 media outlets from China and other countries in the world. Our shooting schedule was strict, and our itinerary was packed.

I learned so much during my travels, especially when I was in China. These rich and colorful experiences broadened my horizons and made me a better version of myself. My family and I also felt the unique power of music, because when we sang Chinese songs in the various cities of our trip, I saw how music can be a universal language of healing and solidarity. I witnessed first-hand the role of music in helping people establish new friendships and connections. But most importantly, I realized how lucky I was to speak Chinese with people I had never met before! Looking at the world today, it is truly a special skill to be able to speak Chinese! I feel blessed to have been a part of this adventure, to learn about China's history and culture, and to appreciate the power of the Chinese language.

我的中国亲戚

作者：施嘉铭　指导教师：顾利程　西北大学

真是礼重情义更重，血浓于水呀。

今年暑假，我跟着父母回中国看望爷爷、奶奶、姥爷、姥姥。同时也见到了许多亲戚。我被他们的热情感动了，也被他们的称谓搞糊涂了。

爷爷、奶奶住在北京。见到我们，他们高兴极了。两位老人拉着我的手，问这问那，还往我手里塞钱，让我自己去买喜欢的东西。

这时爸爸的兄弟姐妹及他们的家人来看我们了。爸爸要我叫这对夫妇“伯父”“伯母”，叫那对夫妇“叔叔”“婶婶”，叫那对夫妇“姑姑”“姑父”。我都一一叫了，虽然我记不清谁是谁。在美国，我只要叫他们“uncle”“aunt”就行了。在中国，称谓怎么这么麻烦呢？当我的头脑还没有清醒过来，爸爸又开始给我介绍孩子们了。这个是你“堂哥”，那个是你“堂妹”，那个是你“表哥”，这个是你“表姐”……一圈叫下来，我早已经糊涂了。他们不都是我的“cousin”吗？

接下来是一家祖孙三代二十多人在一起聚餐。我悄悄问旁边的一个“cousin”：“为什么他们有的是我的堂哥，有的是我的表哥？”他这样解释道：堂哥、堂弟、堂姐、堂妹都是我伯父或者叔叔的孩子，跟我同姓，血缘更近些。而姑姑嫁给了别人，姑姑家孩子就是我的表哥、表弟、表姐、表妹，他们跟父亲姓，跟我不同姓。听了这些，我也只好似懂非懂地低头吃饭了。虽然我分不清他们谁是我的什么亲戚，但是他们都非常照顾我，往我的碗里夹菜，给我的杯里倒水，还跟我约

My Chinese Relatives

Author: Sydney Shi Instructor: Licheng Gu Northwestern University

Over this summer break, I went back to China with my parents to visit my grandparents. At the same time, I also met many other relatives. While I was moved by everyone's warmth and enthusiasm, I was also confused by their titles.

> Indeed, I received precious gifts full of profound kinship – blood is thicker than water.

My grandparents on my dad's side live in Beijing. They were very happy to see us. The two elders took my hand and asked me a plethora of questions, and they even stuffed money into my hand, urging me to go buy things I like.

Then my dad's siblings and their families came over to see us. Dad asked me to call the couple "*bofu*" and "*bomu*," the other couple "*shushu*" and "*shenshen*," and the last couple "*gugu*" and " *gufu*." I greeted them all one by one, although I couldn't remember who was who. In America, I would just call them "uncle" or "aunt." Why are Chinese family titles so troublesome? Before I could clear up my mind, my dad started introducing me to all the kids. "This is your '*tangge*,' and that is your '*tangmei*.' That is your '*biaoge*,' and this is your '*biaojie*.'" As I went around to greet them, I was already confused. Aren't they all just my "cousins?"

Next came the family dinner with more than 20 people from three different generations. I quietly asked a "cousin" next to me why some of them were called my "*tangge*" while others were called my "*biaoge*." He explained that *tangge*, *tangdi*, *tangjie*, and *tangmei* are all the children of my uncles, meaning they have the same surname as me and our bloodlines are more closely related. However, my aunt got married to someone else, so their children are called my *biaoge*, *biaodi*, *biaojie*, and *biaomei*, meaning they don't have the same surname as me. After hearing all of this but barely comprehending anything, I had no choice but to bow my head

定第二天带我去爬长城。临走时他们又送了我很多贵重的礼物，拉着我的手，恋恋不舍。真是礼重情义更重，血浓于水呀。

晚上我问妈妈，到了姥姥、姥爷家，是不是也这样叫他们啊？妈妈赶紧解释道："姥姥、姥爷是中国北方的叫法。到了位于南方的成都，要叫'外婆''外公'。而且妈妈的兄弟要叫舅舅，舅舅的妻子要叫舅妈。妈妈的姐妹要叫姨，她们的丈夫要叫姨父。舅舅家和姨家孩子的称谓比较简单，都是表兄妹。"

天啊，这怎么是"简单"呢？！我赶紧准备一张家庭关系表吧。

down and eat. Although I couldn't distinguish between the titles of my relatives, they all took really good care of me; they put food into my bowl, poured water into my cup, and decided to take me to climb the Great Wall the next day. Before departing, they all gave me precious gifts and held into my hand, showing expressions of reluctance as they prepared to leave. Indeed, I received precious gifts full of profound kinship – blood is thicker than water.

At night, I asked my mom if I would call her parents the same thing when I went to *laolao* and *laoye*'s house. My mom quickly explained: "*Laolao* and *laoye* are what you would call them in northern China. When we arrive in Chengdu, you should call them '*waipo*' and '*waigong*.' Also, you should call my brother '*jiujiu*' and his wife '*jiuma*.' My sisters are called '*yi*,' and their husbands are called '*yifu*.' Their children are relatively simple, all just cousins."

My goodness, how is this "simple?!" Let me hurry and prepare a family relationship chart.

我的中国故事

作者：米瑞　指导教师：洪玮　普渡大学

> 你只有亲自去看过，才知道中国有多么美好，否则你永远不会知道真正的中国是什么样子。

我叫 Miriam Frank，是在美国出生和长大的。我曾经是北京语言大学的一名留学生。我在中国生活了五年，精彩的过程像个五彩斑斓的梦，让我沉醉其中。每当我意识到这不是一个梦，而是一个生动的故事时，我就会忍不住一遍又一遍地向他人讲述。

可以肯定的是，我对中国的了解和兴趣始于我的家乡，也就是普渡大学所在地印第安纳州的西拉斐特市。这个典型的大学城住着很多国际学生和员工，其中一部分就是中国人。生活在这样的环境中，让我对中国的真实面貌非常感兴趣，也非常好奇。我记得第一次去亚洲市场闲逛，看到了大白兔奶糖。糖纸上的大白兔让我想起了《爱丽丝漫游奇境记》里神奇的兔子，那三个汉字更是让我浮想联翩。剥了一块放到嘴里，真是又香又甜。我眯起眼睛，晃起了脑袋，像是一只幸福的兔子。是怎样的文明创造了这种神奇的文字和语言？从那时起，我在心中悄悄种下了对中国好奇的种子，开启了我对中国的向往之旅。

之后，我常常跑到图书馆，疯狂地搜索我能找到的所有中国电视剧和电影，然后借回去在家彻夜观看。上高中时，我在普渡大学孔子学院学了一门中文课程，并取得了优异的成绩，这让我坚定了去中国学习中文的信心。

高中毕业后，我有幸获得了中国政府全额奖学金，就读于北京语言大学，主修中文。在四年的时间里，我完全沉浸在中文学习中，并且在预科的第一年就通

My Chinese Story

Author: Miriam Frank   Instructor: Wei Hong   Purdue University

> You can only understand how beautiful China is when you see it for yourself; otherwise, you'll never know what the real China is like.

My name is Miriam Frank, and I was born and raised in the United States. I used to be an international student at Beijing Language and Culture University. I've lived in China for 5 years, and the whole process has been as wonderful as a colorful dream, always captivating me. Whenever I realize this isn't a dream but a vivid life story, I can't help but share it with others over and over again.

I'm certain that my knowledge and interest in China stemmed from my hometown, West Lafayette, Indiana, where Purdue University is located. This typical university town is home to many international students and employees, some of whom are Chinese. Living in such an environment made me very interested in and curious about what China is actually like. I remember wandering around an Asian market for the first time and seeing the White Rabbit Creamy Candy. The big white rabbit on the candy wrapper reminded me of the magical rabbit in *Alice in Wonderland*, and the three Chinese characters made me lost in thought even more. As I peeled a piece and put it in my mouth, it was really fragrant and sweet. I narrowed my eyes and shook my head like a happy rabbit. What kind of civilization created this magical writing and language? Since then, I've quietly planted the seeds of curiosity about China in my heart, setting off my desire to visit China one day.

Afterwards, I'd often run to the library, frantically searching for all the Chinese TV dramas and movies I could find and borrowing them to watch at home overnight. When I was in high school, I took a Chinese course at the Confucius Institute at Purdue University and received excellent grades, validating my determination to study Chinese in China.

过了 HSK 五级考试。所以我从大二就开始直接学习专业内容了。在北语的四年里，我利用课余时间几乎走遍了中国的每个省份，见证了北京、上海和深圳等城市日新月异的变化。2015 年，我还花了整整一个月的时间在四川省攀枝花的一个小镇过春节，体验了中国农村的宁静和朴素。

更加值得庆贺的是，我在中国第一次坠入爱河，遇到了我的人生伴侣。正是在中国，我觉得自己真正体验了生活的美好，迎接了挑战，学会了爱和被爱，精神上一天天变得更加坚强。时至今日，人们还会问我：你在中国受到的文化冲击大吗？能不能适应？每当听到这样的问题，我都会跟他们说，你只有亲自去看过，才知道中国有多么美好，否则你永远不会知道真正的中国是什么样子。真正的中国幅员辽阔，历史源远流长，人民淳厚朴实，与人为善。所谓东西方文化巨大差异的表象下，真实的中国充满了惊喜。只有走近体验，到那里旅游，到那里

After graduating from high school, I was fortunate enough to receive a full scholarship from the Chinese government to study at Beijing Language and Culture University (BLCU), majoring in Chinese. In these four years, I was completely immersed in Chinese learning and passed the HSK Level 5 within the first year of preparatory courses. So, I started to study major-related content directly in my sophomore year. During my four years at BLCU, I used my spare time to travel to almost every province in China, witnessing the rapid changes in cities such as Beijing, Shanghai, and Shenzhen. In 2015, I also spent an entire month celebrating the Spring Festival in a small town in Panzhihua, Sichuan Province, experiencing the tranquility and simplicity of rural China.

What I feel even luckier about is that I fell in love for the first time in China, where I met my life partner. It was in China that I felt like I truly experienced the beauty of life, faced challenges, learned to love and be loved, and developed a stronger mentality with each passing day. To this day, people still ask me: Did you have a big culture shock in China? Were you able to adapt? Whenever I hear questions like these, I always tell them that you can only understand how beautiful China is when you see it for yourself; otherwise, you'll never know what the real China is like. The real China has a vast territory and a long history. Its people are honest and simple, and they are kind to others. Beneath the thick surface of the so-called cultural differences between the East and the West, the real China is full of surprises. We can only truly appreciate its greatness and depth if we travel there, live there, and experience things firsthand. Ever since I set foot on Chinese soil, I've had a strong desire in my heart to share the knowledge and experience I've gained, as well as my understanding of Chinese culture, with my relatives, friends, and students.

After graduating from Beijing Language and Culture University, I started to pursue a Master's degree in Chinese language education at Indiana University, and I'm the only Chinese teaching assistant in our department whose native language is not Chinese. Because I've gone through the entire process of learning Chinese as a non-native speaker, it's easier for me to explain the difficulties of Chinese learning to American college students while teaching them my unique methods and techniques for learning Chinese. During my days spent teaching Chinese at Indiana University, I felt like I was a bridge between China and America, passing on

居住，才能真正领略到它的伟大和深度。自从我踏上中国的土地，我的内心就有一种强烈的愿望，想把我所拥有的知识和经验，以及我对中国文化的理解，分享给我的亲人、朋友和学生。

从北京语言大学毕业后，我开始在印第安纳大学攻读汉语教育学硕士学位，我是我们系唯一一名母语不是中文的中文助教。因为我经历过一个非母语者学习中文的所有过程，我更容易向美国大学生解释中文学习的难点，并教给他们我学习中文的独特方法和技巧。在印第安纳大学教中文的日子里，我觉得我像是中美之间的桥梁，向那些喜欢中文的人传递中国语言和文化。学生来自不同的专业，对中国的未来发展充满期待，并希望学好中文成为国际人才，更好地与中国公司交流。我找到了各种可能的方法来启发我的学生，让他们意识到一个外国人也可以学好中文，并以中文为媒介了解中国文化。我愿意通过自己的亲身经历，向美国人传播中国语言和文化，做中国文化的代言人。

the Chinese language and culture to those who love Chinese. Students from different majors all have high expectations for the future development of China and hope to learn Chinese well to make an international impact and better communicate with Chinese companies. I've found every possible way to inspire my students to realize that a foreigner can also learn Chinese well and use it as a medium to understand Chinese culture. I'm willing to spread the Chinese language and culture to Americans through my own personal experience and be a spokesperson for Chinese culture.

中文之路

Journeys of Learning Chinese

导 读

在这一板块里，十二名作者分别介绍了自己学习中文的过程。有的作者讲述他们是怎么开始学习中文的，有的作者介绍自己学习中文过程中遇到的困难和得到的经验教训，有的作者分享他们学习中文的体会和收获。作者们最后纷纷强调学习中文的重要性，并且表达了将继续学好中文的意愿。

在这一板块里，作者们为学好中文提出了各种各样的建议。明德学院的王淑蔓同学强调要想学好中文，就必须敢于开口，敢于实践。要利用一切机会开口讲话。她特别强调发音清晰、四声正确的重要性，特别是在学习中文的初级阶段。西北大学的李洪锴同学建议大家学写汉字的时候要从偏旁部首着眼，找出汉字组成的规律，从此不必死记硬背。华盛顿大学（西雅图）的孔禄同学建议大家"看中国电视剧，学习中国历史，看中文书，学成语，学典故，了解传说等等"。他说他自己就是通过这些活动提高了中文水平。杜克大学的孙逊同学建议读古典小说《三国演义》里面的故事，背诵李白、杜甫、白居易等人的诗，甚至了解中医的治疗方法。这些都帮助他提高了中文水平，丰富了他的中国文化知识。加州大学戴维斯分校的阮芳同学建议多观看中国电视剧。她看过《还珠格格》《西游记》《封神榜》《神雕侠侣》等等。除了电视剧之外，阮芳同学还通过学唱中国歌曲、唱卡拉 OK 提高了自己的中文听说水平，丰富了中国文化知识。

通过学习中文，同学们开阔了视野，丰富了知识，对周围的世界有了新的认识。达特茅斯学院的娜塔莎同学感叹道："中文确实让我的世界变得不同。我深深感到我学习的是一种不同的、充满活力的文化。"华盛顿大学（西雅图）的柯丽同学也有同感，认为学了中文以后，她"对自己的身份有了新的认识"。最让人

Introduction

In this section, twelve authors shared their own process of learning Chinese. Some authors talked about how they started their journey, some discussed the difficulties they encountered and lessons they learned along the way, and some shared their experiences and what they gained in the process. In the end, the authors all emphasized the importance of learning Chinese and expressed their desire to continue their journey.

In this section, the authors present various suggestions for how to learn Chinese well. Samantha Ward from Middlebury College emphasized that if you want to learn Chinese well, you must have the courage to continuously speak and practice. You should also leverage every opportunity to communicate in Chinese. She especially emphasizes the importance of clear pronunciation and getting the four tones correct, particularly during the initial stage of learning Chinese. Thomas Li from Northwestern University suggested that when learning to write Chinese characters, you should focus on the radicals and learn the patterns and rules to prevent rote memorization. Luke Khoury from the University of Washington (Seattle) suggested "watching Chinese TV series, studying Chinese history, reading Chinese books, and studying idioms, allusions, legends, to name a few." He supports this by claiming that he himself has improved his Chinese through these activities. Henry Sun, a student at Duke University, suggested reading the stories in the classical novel *Romance of the Three Kingdoms*, reciting poems by Li Bai, Du Fu, and Bai Juyi, and even understanding the methods of traditional Chinese medical treatment. These tactics have helped him improve his Chinese proficiency and enriched his knowledge of Chinese culture. Phuong Nguyen, a student at the University of California, Davis, proposed watching more Chinese dramas. She has watched classics including *My Fair Princess, Journey to the West, Gods of Honor, The Return of the Condor Heroes*, etc. In addition to dramas, Phuong has also improved her Chinese listening and speaking skills by learning to sing Chinese songs through karaoke, enhancing her knowledge of Chinese culture.

感觉耳目一新的是达特茅斯学院施米丽同学的文章《学习中文的五种感觉》。她在文章中指出："学习中文的过程对我来说是一个多么奇妙的过程，使我的听觉、视觉、嗅觉、味觉和触觉都发生了变化，都变得更丰富、敏锐。"在讲听觉时，米丽写道："学习中文让我听到了以前从来没有听到过的声音。……有的音节发一声，有的发二声，有的发三声，有的发四声，有的发半三声，有的发轻声。有时我能听到一串四个不同音节的成语，有时又听到重重叠叠的音节，像一部交响曲。"在讲视觉时，米丽写道："当你懂得笔画组合的意义时，就会感觉奇妙无比。我现在看每一个汉字，几乎就是在欣赏一幅画儿。"在讲到嗅觉和味觉时，米丽写道："我们做葱油饼和麻婆豆腐，它们的香味从新鲜到熟悉；从开始吃一口就兴奋地叫一声，到现在吃一口就能知道油、盐多不多，花椒麻不麻，我的味觉和嗅觉因为吃各种各样美味的中国食物，得到了享受，也得到了锻炼。"在讲到触觉时，米丽写道："我握着毛笔，手和笔杆的接触，用手触摸练字用的宣纸，毛笔在写字的时候，软软的笔尖慢慢散开，和宣纸完美地接触。这些都让我有一种触摸中国历史的感觉。"

同学们在练习写作的过程中，可以考虑如何像这十二名作者一样，通过独特的视角，细微的观察，生动的描写及概括性的总结，写出自己的好文章。

By learning Chinese, students broaden their horizons, enrich their knowledge, and gain a new understanding of the world around them. Natasha Raman, a student from Dartmouth College, exclaimed: "Chinese language has made a difference in my world. I truly feel that I am studying a different and dynamic culture." Lydia Crook from the University of Washington (Seattle) also felt the same way, reflecting that after learning Chinese, she has a new understanding of her identity. The most eye-opening piece is "The Five Senses of Learning Chinese" written by Millie Sach from Dartmouth College. She pointed out in her story: "Through learning Chinese, my senses of hearing, sight, smell, taste, and touch all have changed to be richer and sharper." When it comes to hearing, Millie wrote: "Learning Chinese has exposed me to sounds I have never heard before... syllables can take on the first tone, the second tone, the third tone, the fourth tone, half of the third tone, or even a neutral tone. In some cases, I can hear a string of idioms with the same syllables but four different tones. Sometimes I hear overlapping syllables and tones, like a symphony." When talking about sense of sight, Millie explained: "When you understand what these combinations mean, you will feel amazing. Now, whenever I look at a Chinese character, it is almost as if I am appreciating a painting." When talking about senses of smell and taste, Millie expressed: "We make scallion pancakes and Mapo tofu at home. The dishes' aromas range from fresh and new to familiar. The first moment I took a bite, I screamed excitedly, because it was so unfamiliar. Now, however, I can tell whether there is too much oil, salt, or peppercorns in the food. Through eating a variety of delicious Chinese food, my senses of taste and smell have been engaged and enhanced." When discussing sense of touch, Millie wrote: "I held the brush in my hand and made contact with the rice paper used for calligraphy practice. When the brush drags along the page, the soft tip slowly spreads out, making perfect contact with the rice paper. This experience gave me the sensation of touching Chinese history."

In the process of practicing writing in Chinese, students can learn from these twelve authors and consider how to write their own well-developed stories that highlight their unique perspectives, subtle observations, vivid descriptions, and dynamic summaries.

学习中文的五种感觉

作者：施米丽　指导教师：张淑成　达特茅斯学院

> 学习中文产生的自豪感和享受，是别的东西都比不了的，学习中文真的能让你更有力量！

我叫施米丽，今年十八岁，是达特茅斯学院一年级的学生。我从七年级开始学中文，今年是第七个年头了。

今天我不说中文有多么重要，也不说中国文化多么有意思，只想说说学中文的过程对我来说是一个多么奇妙的过程，使我的听觉、视觉、嗅觉、味觉和触觉都发生了变化，都变得更丰富、敏锐。

先说听觉。学习中文让我听到了以前从来没有听到过的声音。上课时很多同学用中文说话，下课后我和朋友、姐姐用中文聊天儿，听中文歌，我感受到中文声调的特色和魅力。中文里，相同的音节，如果声调不同，就代表不同的意思，这让我觉得很震惊。有的音节发一声，有的发二声，有的发三声，有的发四声，有的发半三声，还有的发轻声。有时我能听到一串四个不同音节的成语，有时又听到重重叠叠的音节，像一部交响曲。我现在去中国城能听懂一些华人在说什么了，这让我非常得意。

让我们转向视觉。每个汉字都有自己的故事，你得非常注意细节才能读懂汉字。我很享受花几个小时来仔细观察、认真思考每个字、每个笔画的意义。对一个没学过中文的人来说，这些笔画的组合没有什么意义。但是，当你懂得笔画组合的意义时，就会感觉奇妙无比。我现在看每一个汉字，几乎就是在欣赏一幅画儿。现在看中国城街上的中文标牌，看电视上的中文字幕，都让我的视觉变得更

The Five Senses of Learning Chinese

Author: Millie Sach Instructor: Shucheng Zhang Dartmouth College

> The sense of pride and enjoyment gained from learning Chinese is incomparable to any other feeling. Learning Chinese can really make you more powerful!

My name is Millie Sach. I am 18 years old. I am a first-year student at Dartmouth College. I have been studying Chinese since the seventh grade, and this year is my seventh year studying it.

Today, I will not talk about how important Chinese language is, or how interesting Chinese culture is. Rather, I want to express how wonderful the process of learning Chinese is. Through learning Chinese, my senses of hearing, sight, smell, taste, and touch all have changed to be richer and sharper.

丰富、更敏锐。

现在说嗅觉和味觉。我和我姐姐喜欢制作和品尝地道的中国菜。在家里，我们做葱油饼和麻婆豆腐，它们的香味从新鲜到熟悉；从开始吃一口就兴奋地叫一声，到现在吃一口就能知道油、盐多不多，花椒麻不麻，我的味觉和嗅觉因为吃各种各样美味的中国食物，得到了享受，也得到了锻炼。

最后是触觉。我曾经学过书法，我握着毛笔，手和笔杆的接触，用手触摸练字用的宣纸，写字的时候，软软的笔尖慢慢散开，和宣纸完美地接触。这些都让我有一种触摸中国历史的感觉。

学习中文，让我对自己有了更多的发现。学习中文产生的自豪感和享受，是别的东西都比不了的，学习中文真的能让你更有力量！

First, sense of hearing. Learning Chinese has exposed me to sounds I have never heard before. In class, my peers speak in Chinese while after class, I continue to chat with my friends and older sister in Chinese, and listen to Chinese songs. I feel the characteristics and charm of Chinese tones. I am astonished by how in Chinese, the same syllable can have different meanings if the tone is different: syllables can take on the first tone, the second tone, the third tone, the fourth tone, half of the third tone, or even a neutral tone. In some cases, I can hear a string of idioms with the same syllables but four different tones. Sometimes I hear overlapping syllables and tones, like a symphony. Now when I go to Chinatown, I can understand some of what Chinese people are saying, which makes me very proud.

Let's now turn to sense of sight. Each Chinese character tells its own story. To understand Chinese characters, you have to pay extreme attention to the details of each character. I enjoy spending hours examining and pondering about the meaning of each character and each stroke. To a person who has never studied Chinese, the combinations of strokes may not make sense. However, when you understand what these combinations mean, you will feel amazing. Now, whenever I look at a Chinese character, it is almost as if I am appreciating a painting. Even just looking at the Chinese signs on the streets of Chinatown and watching the Chinese subtitles on TV programs have enhanced my vision to be richer and sharper.

Now, let's consider senses of smell and taste. My older sister and I love cooking and tasting authentic Chinese food. We make scallion pancakes and Mapo tofu at home. The dishes' aromas range from fresh and new to familiar. The first moment I took a bite, I screamed excitedly, because it was so unfamiliar. Now, however, I can tell whether there is too much oil, salt, or peppercorns in the food. Through eating a variety of delicious Chinese food, my senses of taste and smell have been engaged and enhanced.

Finally is sense of touch. In the past, I have learned the art of calligraphy: I held the brush in my hand and made contact with the rice paper used for calligraphy practice. When the brush drags along the page, the soft tip slowly spreads out, making perfect contact with the rice paper. This experience gave me the sensation of touching Chinese history.

Learning Chinese has allowed me to discover more about myself. The sense of pride and enjoyment gained from learning Chinese is incomparable to any other feeling. Learning Chinese can really make you more powerful!

我从中文学到的

作者：王淑蔓　指导教师：叶信鸿　明德学院

学习外语是一个犯错和改错的过程。我们应该拥抱这些错误，而不是惧怕这些错误！

我第一天学习中文，老师就教我说三个很重要的句子："你好！我叫王淑蔓。我不会说中文。"

我三年前开始学中文。那时候，我常常把这三个句子挂在嘴边。因为当时我特别怕说错，所以我一直跟中国人或老师只说这三个句子。不过，在学习中文的过程中，我发现我需要勇敢地离开舒适圈。为了尽快提高我的中文水平，我需要大胆地尝试说中文，在实践中学习。那时我意识到，要想学好一门外语，就别怕犯错误。所以今天我想跟大家分享我犯的一些错误，特别是这些错误怎么帮助我深刻理解中文和中国文化的。

学习中文一个月以后，我决定找一个语伴。通过我们学校中文系的语言互助项目，我找到了一个语伴。她是一个中国人，叫玛丽。玛丽是一位美丽善良的女同学。我们决定首次见面就去波士顿的唐人街。我们将在那里一边吃饭，一边练习语言。当时玛丽还不知道了我的中文很差，除了"你好"以外，其他的话我一句都不会说。我们来到一家饭馆，坐下来先点菜。玛丽问我要不要点这个菜，我不知道她在说什么，只好摇摇头。玛丽以为我不喜欢吃这个菜，就问我要不要点另外一个菜，我还是摇头。这时候玛丽才知道我根本就没有听懂她的问题。她就问我要不要吃粽子，然后给我讲了粽子的来源。我点头同意了。等菜上来的时候，玛丽给我讲了一些怎么吃粽子和关于端午节的故事，我当然是没有听懂多少。终

What I've Learned from Chinese

Author: Samantha Ward Instructor: Hsin-hung Yeh
Middlebury College

> Studying a foreign language is a process of making mistakes and then fixing them. We should embrace these mistakes, and we shouldn't fear them!

On my first day of studying Chinese, my teacher taught me three important sentences: "Hello! My name is Wang Shuman. I can't speak Chinese."

I started studying Chinese three years ago. At the time, I often repeatedly said these three sentences. Because back then I was afraid to make mistakes, I only used these three sentences when talking with Chinese people or my teachers. But throughout the process of studying Chinese, I realized I had to bravely leave my comfort zone. In order to improve my Chinese level, I had to bravely try to speak Chinese. I had to learn by actually doing. That is when I realized in order to study a foreign language well, you can't be afraid to make mistakes. So today I would like to share a few of the mistakes that I have made, especially how these mistakes helped me form a deeper understanding of Chinese language and Chinese culture.

After studying Chinese for one month, I decided to find a language partner. Through my university's Chinese Language Department's language support program, I ended up finding a language partner. She is a beautiful and nice Chinese classmate with the English name Mary. We decided to meet for the first time in Boston's Chinatown. We would go there to eat and practice our foreign languages. At that time, she didn't know my Chinese wasn't good. Apart from "hello," I couldn't really say anything else. After we arrived at the restaurant, we sat down to order some food. She asked me if I wanted to order a certain dish, but I didn't know what she was saying, so I shook my head. She misunderstood and thought I didn't want to order it, so she asked me if I would like to order another dish. I still just shook my head. This time she knew that I originally didn't understand her question. She asked me if I wanted to eat

于我们的粽子来了，这时我已经很饿了。这是我第一次吃粽子。虽然玛丽已经给我讲了怎么吃粽子，但是我完全没有听懂。我以为跟吃菜包饭团一样，拿起粽子就咬了一口。玛丽大吃一惊，赶快说道："啊！别吃叶子！要把包粽子的叶子剥开，吃里面的东西。"玛丽边说边给我做示范。当众出丑的我觉得非常不好意思。我学着玛丽的样子，剥开了粽子，吃了起来。真是太好吃了！这次经历让我意识到，如果你没有听懂别人问你的话，你就应该告诉他！不能不懂装懂。当然我也学到了吃粽子不能吃叶子！

学习中文三个月以后，我意识到发音很重要。我们学校为所有学中文的学生提供免费的辅导员服务。当时，我的中文水平很低，不过我的辅导员很耐心。她问我："你最喜欢什么动物？"听懂她的问题以后，我感到特别激动。我听懂了！我听懂了！我得意地回答："大虾！"那时候，我还分辨不出"虾"和"象"的区别。

zongzi, then she explained to me the origin of *zongzi*. I agreed! While we waited for our food, she told me about how to eat *zongzi* and about the Dragon Boat Festival. Of course, I didn't understand much. When the *zongzi* finally came, I was already so hungry. This was my first time eating *zongzi*. She had already explained to me how to eat them, but I totally didn't understand. I thought it was like the rice ball wrapped with vegetables, so I picked up the *zongzi* and took a big bite. She was shocked and quickly said, "Oh! Don't eat the leaf! Peel the leaf off the *zongzi* and eat the insides." She said this as she gave me a demonstration. I felt so embarrassed in front of everyone else. I studied her method, peeled open the *zongzi*, and ate it. It was delicious! Through this experience, I realized if you don't understand what someone told you, you should tell them. Don't pretend to understand when you don't. Of course, I also learned when you are eating *zongzi*, don't eat the leaf!

After studying Chinese for three months, I realized that pronunciation is very important. My school provides free Chinese tutoring for all the students that study Chinese. At that time, my Chinese level was very low, but my tutor was very patient. She asked me, "What is your favorite animal? " After I understood her question, I felt so excited. I understood! I understood! I proudly responded, "*Daxia* (big shrimp)!" At that time, I still couldn't differentiate the difference in pronunciation for "*xia* (shrimp)" and "*xiang* (elephant)." I wanted to say "*daxiang*," but instead I said "*daxia*." I told the tutor "I want to ride a *daxia*; a *daxia* is so cute; I want to pet a *daxia*;" etc. After I talked for quite a while, my tutor finally guessed I pronounced it wrongly. She smiled and confirmed with me if it was "big shrimp" or "elephant." We both laughed! Through this mistake, I realized that Chinese pronunciation is very important!

After studying Chinese for a year, I gradually realized the importance of tones. Since the start of learning Chinese, tones were always a big challenge for me. When I just started, I thought as long as Chinese people could understand what I was saying, then that was good enough. It didn't matter if the tone was right or not. Now I know, students studying Chinese absolutely shouldn't think this way. One day I had a Chinese speaking test. The topic I got was "My hobbies." I was happy because I clearly knew that my favorite hobby was reading books. As a result, when I took the speaking test, I very confidently said, "I love 'kǎnshù (cutting down trees).' Every day I 'kǎn (cut down)' different kinds of 'shù (trees),' and study different kinds of

我想说的是“大象”，可是却说成了“大虾”。我告诉辅导员，“我想骑大虾”“大虾很可爱”“我想摸大虾”等。我说了半天以后，辅导员才猜到我发音错了。她笑着跟我确认是“大虾”还是“大象”。弄清楚是“大象”不是“大虾”以后，我们两个都笑了！通过这个错误，我意识到中文的发音特别重要。

学习中文一年以后，我逐渐认识到声调的重要性。自从学习中文以来，声调对我来说一直是一个挑战。刚开始的时候，我以为只要中国人知道我想说什么，那就行了，声调对不对没有太大的关系。现在我认识到，学习中文的学生绝对不应该有这个想法。有一天，中文口语考试，我抽到的话题是“我的爱好”。我很高兴，因为我非常清楚我最大的爱好是看书。于是考试的时候我胸有成竹地说道：“我特别喜欢砍树。我每天都会砍不一样的树，学习不一样的知识。我觉得砍树对我的心理健康非常有好处。每个夏天我至少砍四十本树。”老师看着我，笑着问：“淑蔓，你的意思是‘砍树’还是‘看书’？”然后，她给我解释这两个不同的声调所代表的不同意思。听了老师的解释以后，我脸红了起来。这个错误让我意识到正确的声调是多么重要！我必须说清楚是“看书”，而不是“砍树”，要不然人们可能以为我喜欢毁坏森林！

到了今天，虽然我的中文取得了很大的进步，但是我仍在犯各种各样的错误。比方说，我上个星期告诉我的老师，我喜欢把蜜蜂倒入我的茶里，而其实我想说的是“蜂蜜”！三个月以前，我想告诉我的中国朋友“我的男朋友喜欢吃素”但是我说成了“我的男朋友喜欢吃醋”。这些小错误无所不在，它们已经变成我最喜欢给朋友讲的故事。学习外语是一个犯错和改错的过程。我们应该拥抱这些错误，而不是惧怕这些错误！犯了错误没有关系，只要改正就好。我现在不怕犯错误，我现在能自信地说：“你好！我叫王淑蔓。我会说一点儿中文。”

knowledge. I think 'kǎnshù' is great for my mental health. Every summer I 'kǎn' at least forty 'shù.'" My teacher looked at me, laughed, and asked, "Shuman, are you meaning 'kǎnshù' or 'kànshū (reading books)?'" Then she explained to me how the two different tones represent different meanings. After I listened to her explanation, my face turned red. This mistake made me realize that the correct tones are very important! I must clearly say "kànshū," rather than "kǎnshù," otherwise people will think I love to destroy forests!

Today, although my Chinese has had a lot of improvement, I'm still making all kinds of mistakes. For example, last week I told my teacher I like to put "*mifeng* (bees)" in my tea when I really wanted to say "*fengmi* (honey)." Three months ago, I wanted to tell my Chinese friend "My boyfriend is '*chisu* (vegetarian),'" but instead I said, "My boyfriend is '*chicu* (jealous).'" These little mistakes are omnipresent. They have already become my favorite stories to tell my friends. Studying a foreign language is a process of making mistakes and then fixing them. We should embrace these mistakes, and we shouldn't fear them! Making mistakes isn't a big deal. As long as we fix them, it is fine. Now I am not afraid to make mistakes. Now I can confidently say, "Hello! My name is Wang Shuman. I can speak a little bit of Chinese."

学习外语的重要性

作者：艾娜佳　指导教师：王寄瀛　普渡大学

在我的成长过程中，我对很多事物都感兴趣，但是最吸引我的是外语。今天我想和大家讨论一下学习外语的重要性。

> 拥有跨文化的能力和技巧，就自然而然地比一般人更容易接受其他人的不同思想、价值观和世界观。

首先，我要指出一个问题，那就是，英语国家大多数的人都只会说英语一门语言。

对我来说这是一个非常严重的问题。我认为，多学习一门语言不仅对我们的认知有益处，而且还可以让我们自然地了解另外一个国家的社会、文化和历史。多学习一门外语有助于提高人们的想象力和创造力，还可以培养对他人的认同感和开放的心态。这些都是帮助我们跨越文化的关键技巧。

只会说一种语言的人往往缺乏这些基本而重要的能力，他们很容易心胸狭窄，不愿意倾听和自己的世界观、价值观不同的想法。

在全球化的过程中，能否成为"国际公民"是跨国公司招聘员工的重要标准。在很多情况下，多样性是推动社会进步和发展的基础。无论是在生活中还是在工作上，无论是在私企、学术机构，或者是政府部门，学外语都可以帮助我们从不同的角度认识世界和理解世界。学习外语可以帮助我们向传统的观念发出挑战。现代的知识应该是多元化的、多样化的。拥有跨文化的能力和技巧，就自然而然地比一般人更容易接受其他人的不同思想、价值观和世界观。大体上说，这正是

The Importance of Learning Foreign Languages

Author: Nadya Al-Shawi　Instructor: Chi-ying Alice Wang　Purdue University

> With intercultural competence, one naturally is more inclined to tolerate other people's different ways of thinking, values, and worldviews compared to the average person.

Growing up, I was always passionate about many different things. Among those many things, however, foreign languages were what attracted me the most. Today, I will be discussing the importance of learning foreign languages.

Firstly, I would like to point out a problem: most people from English-speaking countries only speak one language. I think it is a very serious issue. I believe that studying even one extra language will not only yield cognitive benefits, but will also allow one to naturally understand another country's society, culture, and history. Moreover, learning a foreign language aids in the improvement of our imagination and creativity, just as it can also aid in the cultivation of empathy and open-heartedness toward others. These are all key skills fundamental to interculturality.

Unfortunately, those who find themselves to be monolingual often lack these basic yet important skills and abilities, thus causing them to remain narrow-minded and unwilling to respectfully listen to ideas and opinions that differ from their own worldviews and values.

In our world that continues to become more and more globalized, whether or not one is an "international citizen" has turned into an important standard that multinational corporations go by in their search for employees. Under many circumstances, diversity is the foundation for the progression and development of a society. Whether in life or at work, whether it be related to one's personal life, career, academics, or even something beyond the scope of our own lives,

人与人之间引起严重分歧的原因。所以，为了解决这些问题，我们要学习外语。

就我而言，在父母的影响下，我大概中学三年级的时候就发现学外语有多么重要，并且开始专心学习外语。我是在一个比较特殊的家庭中长大的。妈妈来自乌克兰，爸爸来自伊拉克，所以从我从小就沉浸在多元的语言和文化当中，出生在这样的多元家庭让我感到非常幸运。当然，不是每个人都有机会体验我这样的生活。所以，大家更要挑战自己，勇敢地去学习一门外语，这样你才能得到这个世界最有价值的馈赠。

在这个多元家庭中，妈妈教会了我俄语，爸爸教会了我阿拉伯语。我生长在美国，当然也学会了英语。现在，我又在学习中文。中文又给我打开了一扇新

whether in a private company, an academic institution or a government department, learning a foreign language can allow us to understand and learn about the world from various angles. It can help us challenge conventional wisdom and what has been known to be the "norm" for ages. Modern knowledge should be diverse. With intercultural competence, one naturally is more inclined to tolerate other people's different ways of thinking, values, and worldviews compared to the average person. Generally speaking, being incapable of tolerating differences between oneself and others is exactly what causes the serious divisions that we see among people today. Therefore, in order to solve these problems, we need to learn foreign languages.

In terms of my own experience, I realized the significance of studying foreign languages sometime during my final year in middle school and only then began wholeheartedly focusing on it, thanks to my parents. I grew up in a rather unique family. With a Ukrainian mother and an Iraqi father, I have been immersed in diverse languages and cultures since my youth and continue to be ever grateful for having been born into such a family. Of course, not everyone has the opportunity to experience life as I do, which is why people should challenge themselves and be courageous enough to learn a foreign language. Only then will one be able to obtain the most valuable gift offered by our world.

In my diverse household, my mother taught me Russian and my father taught me Arabic. Having been born and raised in the United States, it is a given that I eventually picked up English as well. Now, as I study Chinese, I have been able to open up yet another new window. Through learning Chinese characters, I strengthened my visual thinking ability; through learning the four tones, I improved my listening comprehension; through memorizing and reciting Chinese poetry, I got a glimpse into the profoundness of traditional Chinese culture; through watching films and TV programs, I saw the rapid development of modern Chinese society; and finally, through interacting with Chinese folks, I have met the sincerest of teachers, classmates, and new friends.

Even more amazingly, as someone who has also been studying Japanese and Korean, my experience with studying Chinese has made learning these two languages much easier and more enjoyable in many regards. More notably, I am able to make connections between the three languages, cultures, and societies to further solidify the knowledge I gain through the learning

的窗户。通过学习汉字，我加强了形象思维能力；通过学习四声，我提高了听力水平；通过背诵中国诗词，我窥见了中国传统文化的博大精深；通过观看影视节目，我看到了中国现代社会日新月异的发展；通过跟中国人交流，我认识了彬彬有礼、诚恳待人的师长、同学和朋友。

除了学习中文以外，我还在学习日语和韩语。值得庆幸的是，我的中文习得经验让我觉得日语和韩语容易多了，也有趣多了。主要是，我能把三个国家的语言、文化、历史和社会联系起来，这就巩固了我学过的知识，并且进一步开阔了我的视野。

将来我可能还会学习其他外语，相信一门新的外语会把我带入另一个世界，认识另一些族群。我有说俄语的朋友、说阿拉伯语的朋友、说英语的朋友，还有说汉语的朋友。我相信，将来还会有更多的说不同外语的新朋友。我要成为一个真正的国际公民。

process and broaden my knowledge of an area in the world that I was not previously familiar with prior to my encounter with Chinese.

In the future, I may find myself studying other foreign languages, too. I believe that with each new language, I will be taken into another world, in which I will get to meet new groups of people and communities. I have Russian-speaking friends, Arabic-speaking friends, English-speaking friends, and Chinese-speaking friends, and I know that I may even acquaint myself with people in the future who speak languages I have yet to tackle. I will become a true international citizen.

我与中文的缘分

作者：俐伶　指导教师：李恺　欧柏林学院

> 我要努力致力于中美两国人民之间的相互沟通与了解，这样我们才能永远做朋友。

20世纪90年代，准确地说是1997年。一对美国夫妇的小宝贝到了可以“离开家、到外面闯荡”的年龄了。是啊，宝贝长大了，该让她走出家门了。

这对年轻的父母费尽心思，开始考察旧金山的学校。他们打算让他们的小宝贝上一所双语学校。除了英语之外，让她很熟练地掌握另一种语言。以便让他们的宝贝有更广阔的眼界，有国际视野，心里能装下更大的世界。

旧金山是个非常国际化的城市，找个双语学校不是一件很难的事。夫妻两个开车到一所英法双语学校去考察了一番。嗯，挺不错的一所学校。当他们走出校门时，发现隔壁有一所中美国际学校！

妻子笑着说：“学法语可真没有什么新鲜，看看这所教中文的学校吧！”这对夫妇真是开明而有远见。他们幸运的、大大受益的小宝贝就是我。就这样，因为爸爸妈妈的智慧，我三岁就开始上中美国际学校，读双语课程。开始了我学习中文的历程。

这所国际学校，半天用英文授课，半天用中文授课。我还记得我学会第一个中文词儿的过程。那天，我们三十几个孩子排着队跟老师走进教室，站在教室中间的地毯上。老师说：“大家坐下。”什么是“大家”？什么是“坐下”？孩子们困惑得面面相觑。随后，几个学生坐在地毯上，我们也都跟着坐下。我们很快就懂

My Fated Encounter with Chinese

Author: Lillian Van Cleve Instructor: Kai Li Oberlin College

> I will work hard to facilitate communication and understanding between the people of China and the United States so that we can all be friends forever.

During the 1990's, or to be precise, in 1997, an American couple's baby was old enough to leave home and venture outside. Indeed, the baby is all grown up, so it's about time to let her out of the house.

After much contemplation, the young parents decided to start visiting schools in San Francisco. They planned to send their little one to a bilingual school to make her proficient in another language besides English. This would help their child broaden her worldview and gain an international perspective so that she can hold the larger world close to her heart.

San Francisco is a very international city, so finding a bilingual school was not difficult. The couple drove to an English-French bilingual school and checked out the surroundings. Well, it seemed like a pretty good school. When they walked out of the school gate, they found a Sino-American international school right next door!

The wife smiled and said, "Learning French is really nothing new. Check out this school that teaches Chinese!" This couple was really enlightened and clairvoyant, and the lucky beneficiary of their decision was me. Just like that, because of my parents' wisdom, I started attending the Sino-American international school at the age of three, taking bilingual courses. This started my journey of learning Chinese.

At this international school, half of the day was taught in English, and the other half was taught in Chinese. I still remember the process of learning my first Chinese word. That day, over 30 students lined up to enter the classroom with the teacher, and we stood on the carpet in the middle of the classroom. The teacher said, "Dàjiā zuò xià." What is "dàjiā?" What is "zuò

了，坐下是 sit down。我的大学中文课的同学，都说他们学会的第一句中文是“你好”，可对我来说，最亲切的中国话就是“坐下”。聊天儿要坐下，上课要坐下，喝酒吃饭更要坐下。你们要好好儿听我演讲，都得坐下！

我们的同学家里都至少有一位家长是华人，只有三个学生的家长完全是白人，但是我从来没有注意过这些。我们生活里到处是中国文化，语言、教育、课程、饭菜……同学是华人，老师是华人。对我来说，在这样的环境中长大是很正常的事情。

到小学二年级，我已经八岁了。在这所学校里，每个人都是我的朋友，我生活得很快乐。

有一年快过春节了，学校里已经有浓浓的节日气氛。可是我的家里一点儿动

xià?" The children blankly stared at each other in utter confusion. Afterwards, a few students sat on the carpet, so we all followed suit. We quickly understood that "zuò xià" means sit down. At my university, most of my classmates in Chinese class all say that the first Chinese phrase they learned was "hello," but for me, the most amiable Chinese phrase is "sit down." You have to sit down for chatting, sit down in class, and even sit down for drinking and eating. If you want to respectfully listen to my speech, you all have to sit down!

All of my classmates have at least one Chinese parent, and only three students have completely white parents, but I've never noticed this situation before. My life has been full of Chinese culture, language, education, courses, meals… My classmates and teachers have always been Chinese. To me, it seemed completely normal to grow up in such an environment.

By the time I entered the second grade in elementary school, I was already eight years old. In this school, everyone was my good friend, and my life was full of contentment.

One year, as the Spring Festival was approaching, there was already a strong festive atmosphere around my school, but no such jolly spirits were to be found in my home. I asked my mother, "How do we celebrate the Spring Festival?" My mother responded, "We don't celebrate the Spring Festival!" Pointing to my blue eyes, blonde hair, and white skin, my mother told me a shocking truth: "You are not Chinese, and neither are we."

As reality hit, I couldn't help but wonder: Most of the people in my life are Chinese, why am I not?

At the time, I was just a little girl who didn't care much about beauty, so I didn't look into the mirror all too often; unlike now, I look at myself in the mirror at least eight times a day. Back then, it was natural for me to think that I was no different from all the Chinese children surrounding me.

What my mother said was nothing else than the truth, but for me, it was a bolt from the blue. Based on the environment I grew up in, it only made sense for me, an eight-year-old child, to believe that I was one of the Chinese children; why was this suddenly not the case anymore? I felt so anxious that I immediately started sobbing.

Perhaps I was Chinese in my previous life but was reincarnated into a foreign family in my present life. Fortunately, my foreign parents are so intelligent and far-sighted, allowing me to form such a special bond with China for my whole life.

Appearance is something that cannot be changed, but this did not hinder my interest and

静都没有。我问妈妈：“我们怎么过春节呀？”妈妈说：“我们不过春节。”我说：“我们中国人都过春节！”妈妈指着我蓝色的眼睛、咖啡色的头发和白白的皮肤，告诉我一个令我震惊的真相：“你不是中国人，我们都不是。”

这真是不可思议的事情，我生活中的大多数人都是中国人，我为什么不是？

那时候我还只是个小姑娘，不大懂得臭美，根本不怎么照镜子，不像现在，每天照八回。就理所当然地觉得我和那些中国小朋友没什么两样。

妈妈说的是真相，但对我却是晴天霹雳。从我长大的环境来说，一个八岁的孩子理所当然觉得自己是中国孩子中的一个，怎么突然不是了？我顿时急得大哭。

也许我上辈子是中国人，这一世投胎投到了洋人之家。幸好我的洋人爸妈那么聪明，那么有远见，让我一辈子和中国结了缘。

相貌是没有办法改变的事，但是这丝毫没有妨碍我对中国的语言、历史、文化的兴趣与喜爱。

上小学，上中学，直到上大学，我一直坚持学习中文。到了大学，我发现有不少和我一样长相的，同样是“黄发碧眼”的洋妞、洋小伙儿也在学习中文。我们可以很顺畅地用中文交流，唱中文歌，用中文说绕口令。

中国和美国都是世界上的大国，她们的关系是不是和谐，关系到世界是不是安宁。我要努力致力于中美两国人民之间的相互沟通与了解，这样我们才能永远做朋友。

我也意识到，人与人的关系，和宗教、种族、肤色，没有必然的关系。不同的肤色不应成为不同文化的界限。

孔子说过：四海之内皆兄弟也。他老人家说的四海之内，是把中国和美国都包括在内的！

love for the Chinese language, history, and culture.

Throughout elementary school, middle school, and college, I continued to be persistent in learning Chinese. When I entered college, I discovered that there were quite a few foreign girls and young men with a similar appearance as me, with "blonde hair and blue eyes," who were also learning Chinese. We can communicate fluently in Chinese, sing Chinese songs, and say Chinese tongue twisters.

China and the United States are both major countries in the world, and whether or not their relationship is harmonious directly ties into whether or not the world is peaceful. I will work hard to facilitate communication and understanding between the people of China and the United States so that we can all be friends forever.

I also realized that the relationships between individuals, along with religion, race, and skin color, have no definitive connection to each other. Different skin colors should not be the boundaries of fostering cross-cultural understanding.

As Confucius once said, "All are brothers within the four seas." The reference to the four seas includes both China and the United States!

中文扩展了我的世界

作者：娜塔莎　指导教师：张淑成　达特茅斯学院

我叫娜塔莎，是达特茅斯学院四年级学生。我的专业是历史，中文是我的辅修专业。

> 学习中文，让我接触到了不同的文化和历史，扩展了我的世界。

著名的哲学家维特根斯坦曾说过："我的语言的界限就是我的世界的界限。"这句话让我产生了强烈的共鸣。学习中文，让我接触到了不同的文化和历史，扩展了我的世界。

中国的文化源远流长，博大精深，极富魅力。懂中文让我更多地接触到了中国的诗歌、电影、歌曲等。例如，我最喜欢的中国诗人是李白。他的《静夜思》是一首短小而优美的诗，是我最喜欢的诗歌之一。虽然这首诗已被翻译成英文，但比不上用中文阅读这首诗的感觉。除了读中国诗歌，我还喜欢听中国音乐。从和慧这样的女高音歌唱家到邓丽君这样的流行歌曲偶像，我喜欢各种类型的中国歌曲。能够听懂这些歌的歌词，让我对中国的音乐和文化有了更深的理解。

除了诗歌和音乐，我还喜欢中国舞蹈。我对舞蹈所表现出来的中国特有的文化意义很是着迷，例如在农历新年期间表演的舞龙。这些优美舞蹈的强烈吸引力，促使我开始学习中国舞。在老师的帮助下，我学会了扇子舞和伞舞。通过学习不同类型的舞蹈，我逐渐能体会到中国舞蹈更深层次的优美和意韵。

学习中文也大大增进了我对中国历史的了解。作为一名历史专业的学生，我目前正在撰写一篇关于 20 世纪中国货币政策的论文。为了研究这一主题，我一

Chinese Expands My World

Author: Natasha Raman   Instructor: Shucheng Zhang   Dartmouth College

My name is Natasha, and I am a senior at Dartmouth College. I take History as my major and Chinese as my minor.

The famous philosopher Wittgenstein once said, "The boundaries of my language are the boundaries of my world." This quote particularly resonates with me. Learning Chinese has expanded my world by exposing me to a different culture and history.

> Learning Chinese has expanded my world by exposing me to a different culture and history.

Chinese culture is long-standing, well-establishing, extensive, profound, and charming. Understanding Chinese has given me more exposure to Chinese poetry, movies, songs, etc. For example, my favorite Chinese poet is Li Bai. His poem "Thoughts in a Quiet Night" is short yet beautiful and is one of my favorite poems. Although this poem has been translated into English, the experience of reading it in Chinese is better. Apart from reading Chinese poetry, I also like listening to Chinese music. From the soprano like He Hui to pop idols like Teresa Teng, I love all types of Chinese songs. Being able to understand the lyrics of these songs gives me a deeper understanding of Chinese music and culture.

In addition to poetry and music, I also like Chinese dances. I am fascinated by the unique cultural significance of Chinese dances, such as the dragon dance performed during the Chinese New Year to bring good luck. The strong appeal of these beautiful dances prompted me to start learning Chinese dances. With the help of my dance teacher, I learned fan dance and umbrella dance. By learning different types of dances, I can appreciate the more profound beauty and charm of Chinese dances.

Learning Chinese has also greatly enhanced my understanding of Chinese history. As a

直在阅读中文的历史文献。蒋介石的日记是我读过最有趣的文献之一。日记记录了他在战争期间对中国政治和经济状况的内心想法。蒋介石的日记，以及其他从未被翻译成英文的中文历史文献，让我对中国历史有了更深入的了解，也让我对过去中国公众人物的思想有了更细致的理解。

中文确实让我的世界变得不同。我深深感到我学习的是一种不同的、充满活力的文化。我会继续致力于学习中文，研究中国历史，以不断扩展我的世界。

student majoring in history, I am currently working on a thesis on Chinese monetary policy in the 20th century. In order to research this topic, I have been reading historical documents in Chinese. Chiang Kai-shek's diary is one of the most interesting documents I have read. The diary records his inner thoughts on China's political and economic conditions during the war. Chiang Kai-shek's diaries, along with other Chinese historical documents that have never been translated into English, have given me a deeper understanding of Chinese history and a more nuanced understanding of the thinking of past Chinese public figures.

Chinese language has made a difference in my world. I truly feel that I am studying a different and dynamic culture. I will continue to devote myself to learning Chinese and studying Chinese history to expand my world.

我的中文之路

作者：容英里　指导教师：刘锦城　圣母大学

> 那是我第一次感受到语言的力量，相同的语言可以让两个人的关系立刻变得很近。

我十岁开始学中文，可是这不是我自己的决定。我妈妈是一个华人，但她是在美国出生、长大的，所以她没有说中文的环境。我妈妈的爷爷奶奶很久以前从中国来到加州建造铁路。为了保留我们家族的中国传统，我父母想要他们的子女学中文。开始的时候，我特别讨厌学中文，一方面是因为中文太难了，我有点儿受不了，另一方面也是因为我的中文老师给我的压力。我的中文老师不但严格，而且“雄心勃勃”，她希望我可以成为我们学校中文项目的代表。简单地说，我们学校中文说得最好的学生要么是中国人，要么是在中国住过很长时间的外国人。其他美国学生的中文水平都不够高，没有办法参加 AP 中文和中国文化的考试。我的中文老师认为，如果她从四年级就开始帮我准备这些中文考试，那我就可以变成我们学校第一个没有中文背景却通过 AP 中文考试的学生。显然，老师的目标太高了，我觉得我永远都不可能达到。于是，老师给我的压力越大，我就越讨厌中文。

可是后来我竟然越来越喜欢中文，促成这个转变的原因是我第一次在课堂外体验到中文的用处。我妈妈是我上的国际学校的一名小学老师。我上八年级的时候，在我妈妈的教室外面遇到了一位中国新生的奶奶，她看起来很无聊，也有点儿紧张。我跟她说英文，可是她摇摇头，用中文告诉我，她听不懂。于是我开始

My Chinese Language Learning Journey

Author: Miles Roberts Instructor: Jincheng Liu University of Notre Dame

> That was the first time I truly understood the power of language, and how the same language can immediately make the relationship between two people very close.

I started studying Chinese when I was 10 years old, but this was not my own decision. My mom is of Chinese ancestry, but she was born and raised in the U.S. So she doesn't have any background speaking Mandarin. A long time ago, my mother's grandparents moved from China to California of the U.S. to work on the railroads. In order to preserve my family's Chinese heritage, my parents thought it would be best for their children to learn Chinese. When I first started, I absolutely hated studying Chinese. In one aspect, Chinese was simply too hard. I could not handle it. In addition, it was because my Chinese teacher put a lot of pressure on me specifically. She was not only very strict, but also "ambitious." This is because she hoped I would become a representative of the school's Chinese program. Simply put, the best Chinese speakers in my school were all either Chinese people or students that lived in China for a very long time. Of all the Americans studying Chinese, none of their levels were high enough, so there was no way to participate in AP Chinese Language and Culture. My teacher thought, if she could start preparing me to take AP Chinese from the fourth grade, I could become the first student to take the AP Chinese exam without any Chinese speaking background experience. Obviously, her goals were a little too lofty, and I thought I could never achieve them. Hence, the more pressure my teacher gave me, the more I hated Chinese.

But later on, I actually began to like Chinese more and more. What prompted this transition was my first experience of the usefulness of Chinese outside of the classroom. My

跟她说中文。没想到她完全听懂了我的中文。我跟她解释说，她孙子的老师是我妈妈，我妈妈是华人，可是不会说中文。这位老奶奶高兴地说：“太好了！我孙子的老师是华人，这让我感到很高兴。”她甚至高兴得拥抱了我。老奶奶很担心她孙子的英文水平太低了，听不懂老师、同学的话。我也安慰她说，不要担心，她的孙子又聪明又用功，相信他学英文会学得非常快。听了我的话，老奶奶轻松多了。那是我第一次感受到语言的力量，相同的语言可以让两个人的关系立刻变得很近。那时候我也发现我可以跟地道的中国人交流，而不只是跟我的老师。这次谈话也让妈妈知道我的中文比她想象的要好得多，妈妈也很为我骄傲。

我开始爱上中文，还因为我认识到通过学习中文，可以更了解中国文化和中

mother is an elementary school teacher at the international school I attended. In the eighth grade, I happened to meet the grandmother of a new Chinese student outside my mother's classroom. She looked very bored and a bit nervous. I started to speak to her in English, but she shook her head and in Chinese told me she did not understand. So, I started talking to her in Chinese, little did I know that she would completely understand what I said. I explained to her that her grandson's teacher will be my mother and that my mother is of Chinese ancestry, but does not speak Chinese. The grandmother happily replied, "That's amazing! I'm so happy that my grandson's teacher is of Chinese ancestry." She evenly excitedly hugged me! This is because the grandmother was worried her grandson's English proficiency was too low, and he would not be able to understand what his teachers and classmates said. I comforted her and said, "Don't worry. Your grandson is smart and hard-working. I believe he will learn English very quickly." Upon hearing my words, the grandmother relaxed a great deal. That was the first time I truly understood the power of language, and how the same language can immediately make the relationship between two people very close. From that point on I realized that I could communicate with authentic Chinese people, not just my Chinese teacher. This instance also made my mother realize that my Chinese was much better than she originally thought, and she was very proud of me.

My love for learning Chinese was also because I realized that through learning Chinese, I could better understand Chinese culture and Chinese people's values. It's often said, the key to learning a foreign language is to understand that country's culture. The longer I learned Chinese, the more I understood the meaning of that sentence. For example, when writing articles, I would often write "my family," "my school," and "my country." However, my Chinese teacher would always correct me and say "our family," "our school," and "our country." At first, I was very confused, why must I say "our school?" It was not until after my teacher explained it that I found out that this way of speaking reflects China's emphasis on "collectivism." They believe that their family, school, and country are everyone's, not just theirs. Everyone is a part of their "family."

At times, learning Chinese came with some difficulties. When I was in middle school, I lived in Vietnam. Vietnamese and Chinese are very similar with regard to some aspects. For example, in Chinese, the number 8 sounds like the number 3 in Vietnamese. Their

国人的观念。有人说，学外语是了解外国文化的一把钥匙。学中文的时间越长，我越觉得这句话有道理。比方说，我自己写文章的时候，我常常写“我的家”“我的学校”“我的国家”。可是，老师总是把它们改成“我们家”“我们学校”“我们国家”。起先，我觉得很困惑，为什么一定要说“我们学校”？后来，老师告诉我以后，我才了解到，这种说法可能反映了中国人重视“集体主义”，他们认为，家、学校、国家都是大家的，不是一个人的。在这些“家庭”里，每个人都是一分子。

学中文有时也会给我带来一点儿小困扰。上中学的时候，我住在越南。越南语和中文在有些方面很像。比如说中文的“八”听起来很像越语的“三”，他们的发音都是“Ba”。有一天，我在一家餐馆想点三碗牛肉河粉。可是点完以后，我开始怀疑我是不是点了八碗牛肉河粉。于是我开始担心起来，因为我带的钱不够买八碗牛肉河粉。不过，像这种小困扰，现在想想，也挺有意思的。这说明中文已经慢慢地变成了我生活中必不可少的一部分。

现在呢，中文课是我最喜欢的课，因为我已经知道我可以把课上学的中文用在课堂外。另外，中文课也给我很多机会深入了解中国传统文化。我觉得中国文化也是我生活中必不可少的一部分。我已经决定选择中文专业。我很感谢父母让我学中文，我也很感谢我的中文老师对我的帮助。我是美国人，可是有的人认为我看起来像一个中国人。最近，美国和中国的关系在很多方面都有很大的退步，可是我希望我可以改善中国和美国的关系。我爱美国，也爱中国，希望我的看法能影响别人，能为中美关系的发展做出自己的贡献。

pronunciation is exactly the same: "ba." One day I was at a restaurant and wanted to order three bowls of Vietnamese pho. But after I finished speaking, I began to wonder if I ordered eight bowls of pho, so I became worried because I did not have enough money for eight bowls of pho. However, now that I think about it, this small incident was very interesting, because it meant that Mandarin was slowly becoming an essential part of my life.

Now, Chinese is my favorite subject, because I know that I can utilize the Chinese I learn in class outside the classroom. In addition, Chinese class gives me many opportunities to deeply understand Chinese tradition and culture. I believe Chinese culture is an indispensable part of my life. I've already decided to make it one of my majors. I'm grateful to my parents for making me learn it. I'm also grateful to all the help I've received from my Chinese teachers. I'm American, but some people think I look Chinese. Recently, in many aspects, the Sino-U.S. relationship has regressed; however, I hope that I can help improve that relationship. I love America, and I also love China. I hope my views can help influence others and make my own contribution to the development of these two countries' relations.

学习中文对我的影响

作者：阮芳　指导教师：李昱　加州大学戴维斯分校

你也可以学习中文，不一定要是中国人，也不一定要是一个语言天才。

我姓阮，单名一个芳字，是“芳草连天碧”的芳，现在是加州大学戴维斯分校大四的学生，就读心理学专业。我是在越南出生，也是在越南长大的。

越南和中国是邻居，中华文化对我当然是影响很大的。我童年的时候，父母工作很忙，所以让外婆照顾我。我每天都在又旧又小的家里，跟外婆一起一边吃饭，一边看翻译成越南语的影视节目，比方说《封神榜》《神雕侠侣》《西游记》《还珠格格》等等。我当年看这些影视作品看上瘾了，看了一个又一个。有一天，我看电影连时间都忘了，结果上学都迟到了。对看过的影视节目，我当年有很多很多问题，可是不知道问谁。为什么清朝的男人得把他们的头发刮掉一半？为什么女孩儿得缠足？那些年，我对华人的风俗习惯、衣服着装、历史典故颇感兴趣。

再大一点儿后，我开始听中国音乐。有人跟我说：“没意思，你又听不懂汉语。”我就说：“听不懂看越南语字幕就行了。”周杰伦的歌曲我现在还很喜欢。每次去唱卡拉OK，一定选光良的《童话》！我还看金庸的小说和古典名著，比如《天龙八部》《红楼梦》，当然都是翻译版的。少年时代，我特别喜欢中国爱情电影，可惜看不懂，也听不懂中文。我等啊等，等了很久，就等着有人能把这些作品翻译成越南语。因为听不懂，我就迫切地想学习中文。可惜在越南学中文得花钱，我不想增加父母的经济负担，所以就忍痛放弃了学中文的打算。

The Impact of Learning Chinese on Me

Author: Phuong Nguyen Instructor: Yu Li University of California, Davis

> You don't have to be a Chinese or a language genius to learn Chinese.

My surname is Ruan (阮), and my first name simply has one character (芳, meaning: fragrant; flowers & grass), which is from "芳草连天碧" (meaning: the green grass stretches far to the sky). I am currently a senior at the University of California, Davis, majoring in Psychology. I was born and raised in Vietnam.

Since Vietnam and China are neighbors, Chinese culture certainly has a great impact on me. When I was little, my parents were occupied with work, so my maternal grandmother had to take care of me. Every day, in our old and small home, with my grandma I would eat while watching Chinese TV programs, which were translated into Vietnamese, such as *Gods of Honor, The Return of the Condor Heroes, Journey to the West, My Fair Princess*, and many more. I got addicted to watching these films and TV shows. One day, I was so focused on watching a movie and ended up being late for school. I had a lot of questions about the movies and the TV shows I watched, but I didn't know whom to ask. For example, why did the men during the Qing Dynasty have to shave half of their hair off? Why did women have to bind their feet? Back then, I was very interested in Chinese customs, clothing, and historical allusions.

When I grew older, I started listening to Chinese music. Some people would tell me, "It's not interesting. You don't understand the language anyway." To respond to this comment, I just said, "I can just read the Vietnamese subtitles." Until now, I still like Jay Chou's songs. Every time I go to karaoke, I always choose *Fairy Tale* to sing. In addition, I also read Jin Yong's novels and classical literature, such as *Demi-Gods* and *Semi-Devils* and *Dream of the*

16岁那年，我们一家移民到了美国。我惊喜地发现，在美国的高中，你不但可以学中文，而且还是免费的。我家人一心想让我学西班牙语，我的朋友们也都选了西班牙语课，当时只有我一个人选了中文课。大家都跟我说，汉字看起来很复杂啊，一定很难吧？我说，没事没事，只要我喜欢就不会觉得难。我的第一位中文老师是张老师。她教中文的方法有点儿奇怪，她教我们中文的第一个月里，我们连一页书也没有翻过。她只让我们练习听和说，不练习读和写。

Red Chamber, all of which are of course translated. When I was a teenager, I especially liked Chinese romantic movies, but unfortunately, I couldn't read or understand Chinese. As a result, I waited and waited such a long time for someone to translate these works into Vietnamese. For I couldn't understand it, I was eager to learn Chinese. However, sadly, in Vietnam, learning Chinese cost quite a bit of money. I didn't want to add more financial burdens to my parents, so I reluctantly gave up my plan to learn Chinese.

At the age of sixteen, our family immigrated to the United States. I was pleasantly surprised to find out that in American high schools, you could not only learn Chinese but also for free. My family wanted me to learn Spanish, and on top of that, all of my friends took Spanish classes. I was the only one who took Chinese classes. Everyone told me, "Chinese characters look so complicated. It must be difficult, right?" I said, "It's OK. As long as I like it, it won't be difficult."

My first Chinese teacher was Ms. Zhang. Her method of teaching Chinese was a bit strange, because we didn't even turn a page of the textbook during the first month of studying. She only made us practice listening and speaking, rather than reading and writing. She said that learning Chinese should be accomplished by listening and speaking first, then followed by reading and writing. Moreover, Ms. Zhang taught us that when you study a foreign language, should you not only study the language but also study the culture of that country. Therefore, she had us study history, took us to the Chinese Museum, and even let us make a dragon from clay. On the Mid-Autumn Festival, she shared a mooncake with us, and gave us red envelopes during the Chinese New Year. Because of Ms. Zhang, I felt that learning Chinese was so interesting. I started to like Chinese more and more, and my motivation grew bigger and bigger.

After learning Chinese for 2 years, I graduated from high school. However, unfortunately, my local community college doesn't offer Chinese classes. Two years later, after graduating from community college, I transferred to UC Davis and started learning Chinese again. Although I had not studied for two years and had forgotten a lot, I was fortunate to be accepted by Professor Li. She gave me a chance to continue my journey of learning Chinese.

她说，学习中文应该先听说，然后再读写。而且，张老师对我们说，你学外语的时候，不只是学语言，也应该研究那个国家的文化。所以她让我们研究历史，带我们去华人博物馆，让我们把黏土做成一条龙。中秋节张老师跟我们分享月饼，新年给我们发红包。因为张老师，我觉得学中文更有意义，更有动力，也更喜欢中文了。

我在高中学了两年中文就毕业去了社区大学，可惜社区大学没有中文课。又过了两年，我从社区大学毕业以后就转学到了加州大学戴维斯分校，又开始学中文了。虽然我两年没学，也忘了很多，不过很幸运地被李老师接纳，给了我一个机会，继续我学习中文的旅程。

我的中文水平现在虽然不太高，可是我觉得我现在比当年进步了很多。为了挑战自己，我还报名参加了一次中文演讲比赛，并在比赛中得了一等奖。我特别想对学习中文的同学们说，你也可以学习中文，不一定要是中国人，也不一定要是一个语言天才，只要你真的喜欢，有动力，每天都努力学习，一定有一天能流利地说好普通话！我们一起来学习吧！

Though my Chinese level isn't very high right now, I feel that I have improved a lot compared to the past. To challenge myself, I signed up for a Chinese speech contest, and got the first prize! I want to say, especially to those who are learning Chinese, that you don't have to be a Chinese or a language genius to learn Chinese. As long as you really like the language, are motivated, and study hard every day, one day you will be fluent in Chinese. Let's learn together!

买包子

作者：刘笑寒　指导教师：刘刚　卡内基梅隆大学

> 我想通过学习中文，了解中国文化和历史，并为自己有中国血统而骄傲。

我叫刘笑寒，是一名卡内基梅隆大学大三的学生，我主修统计及数据科学和中文双学历。很多人问过我为什么要学中文。我也从来没有想到我学中文的故事是从一次买包子的经历开始的。

我是一个华裔，出生在中国，一岁就来到了美国，在美国长大。2018 年的夏天，我和家人一起去北京旅行。这是我在 17 年里第二次去中国。虽然我从小就在家里和父母说中文，但是从来没有上过中文学校或正式地学习过中文。我不认汉字，更不会写汉字。从外表上看，我就像普通的中国高中生一样，但在文化观、社会观、语言等种种方面，我在中国就是一个外国人。

不知出于什么目的，可能是为了证明自己的汉语水平真的没有那么差，我准备给自己一个挑战——自己一个人去买五个包子。

战场——一个不起眼的包子摊，就在眼前。

我鼓足勇气，走到包子摊前。但是当我从模糊的玻璃窗外看到一个个方块汉字时，紧张、恐惧和尴尬刹那间吞没了我刚才所有的勇气。我用中文小声地问卖包子的阿姨："你好，包子都有什么馅儿的？"

卖包子的阿姨头也没有抬，说道："自己看，这里写着呢。"

我当然一个字也不认识，只好更胆怯地说："你能帮我念一下有什么馅儿的吗？"

Buying *Baozi*

Author: Xiaohan Liu Instructor: Gang Liu Carnegie Mellon University

> Through studying Chinese, I want to gain a deeper understanding of Chinese culture and history and be proud of my Chinese heritage.

I am Xiaohan Liu, a third-year college student studying Statistics & Data Science and Chinese at Carnegie Mellon University. Many people have asked me why I want to study Chinese. I also could have never imagined that my Chinese learning story would start from an experience of buying *baozi*.

I am a Chinese American who was born in China and grew up in the United States since one year old. During the summer of 2018, my family and I went to Beijing for a trip. In seventeen years, this was only my second time visiting China. Although I speak Chinese at home with my parents, I have never gone to Chinese school or learned the language formally. I did not know how to read Chinese, let alone how to write the characters. On the outside, I looked like a typical Chinese senior high student, but from social culture, social views, and language, I was an alien in China.

For some reason, perhaps to prove that my Chinese proficiency is really not that bad, I decided to give myself a challenge: buy five *baozi* by myself.

The battlefield, an inconspicuous *baozi* stand, was right in front of me.

I gathered up my courage and walked to the *baozi* stand. But when I saw the blocks of Chinese characters written on the hazy glass window, nervousness, fear, and awkwardness swallowed the courage I had a moment ago. In Chinese, I asked the auntie who sold *baozi*, "Hello, what types of fillings do the *baozi* have? "

阿姨匆匆忙忙地抬起头，看着我大笑起来。排队的人也都给了我很不耐烦的眼神。

阿姨指着玻璃上的汉字，回答说："别胡闹了。都写在那儿，自己看。"接着我身后的老头也喊了一声："给我来三个韭菜鸡蛋的。"

我当然一个字都看不懂，只好红着脸、忍着气，不得其所地指着摆在加热盘上的包子随便买了几个。我当时非常尴尬，也感觉特别生气。难道中国人都这么不友好，不愿意帮助别人吗？

The auntie did not even lift her head and replied, "See for yourself. It's written here."

Of course, I could not recognize any of the characters, so I asked more timidly, "Can you help me read what fillings there are?"

The auntie hurriedly raised her head, looked at me, and burst out laughing. Others waiting in line to buy *baozi* gave me an impatient look.

Pointing to the Chinese characters written on the glass, she said, "Don't mess around. It's all written there. See for yourself." An old man behind me shouts, "Give me three *baozi* with leeks and eggs fillings ."

I could not read a single character. Red-faced, confused, and holding back anger, I randomly pointed at a few *baozi* sitting on the heating plate. I was very embarrassed and also very resentful. Are all Chinese people so unfriendly and unwilling to help others?

After a few weeks when it came time to leave China, my experience of buying *baozi* no longer made me feel angry. I understood that the auntie refused to help me because she assumed I should be able to read Chinese from my appearance. On the other hand, I had unconsciously formed a generalization about all Chinese people's attitudes toward helping others.

I realized stereotypes and generalizations arise from these types of misunderstandings.

For example, even though English is my native language, there were always teachers and classmates from elementary school to high school who assumed I could not speak English. Due to the lack of understanding of Chinese society and culture, some people also form prejudice against Chinese people from news reports and media.

After this experience of buying *baozi*, I realized just how easy it is for us to misunderstand and make preconceived judgments or conclusions about people, especially when their backgrounds and cultures are different from our own.

At the same time, this experience also gave me the motivation to study Chinese. Although as a Chinese American, I had some understanding of China, because of the language barrier, I was an outsider to Chinese culture. Through studying Chinese, I want to gain a deeper understanding of Chinese culture and history and be proud of my Chinese heritage.

过了几个星期，到了要离开中国的时候，我已经不再为买包子的经历感到生气了。我明白那位阿姨可能是从我的模样判断，认为我应该认识汉字，所以才不愿意帮我，而我却不知不觉地以为她的行为代表了所有中国人对帮助别人的态度。

也许刻板印象和歧视正是来源于这样的误解。

比如，即使英语是我的母语，从小学到高中都会有老师和同学以为我不会说英语。同样，因为缺少对中国文化的了解，有的人也会通过新闻报道和其他媒体对中国人形成偏见。

有了这次买包子的经历后，我意识到我们多么容易误会别人，又是多么容易对人做出先入为主的判断，特别是当这些人的背景和文化与我们不一样的时候。

不过，这次买包子的经历也给了我学习中文的动力。虽然作为华裔，我对中国有一些了解，但是因为语言的障碍，中国文化对我来说比较陌生。我想通过学习中文，了解中国文化和历史，并为自己有中国血统而骄傲。

大学毕业后，我希望用统计和中文的双学历，在一个语言学习软件公司做数据分析，帮助外国人学好中文，并通过语言学习来促进中国和美国人民之间的友好交流与合作。

After graduating from university, I hope to use my degrees in Statistics and Chinese to work in data science at a company that develops language learning apps. In this way, I can help foreigners learn Chinese, and promote friendly communication and cooperation between Chinese and American people through language learning.

我的周末中文学校

作者：孙逊　指导教师：刘艳　杜克大学

> 中文课让我更能接受自己的双重身份，也让我更理解父母和家人的经历。

我出生在美国的马里兰州，罗克维尔市，五岁就开始上中文学校了。每到星期六下午一点半，爸爸妈妈就会开车带我去附近的中文学校上课。这是一所由当地华人办的周末中文学校，租用当地一所高中的教室上课。我现在已经记不清那时候我对中文学校的感受了，但是我肯定不是特别开心。幸运的是，我在中文班里交了一个新朋友，他的英文名叫 Danny，中文名字是邵丹宁。Danny 的妈妈就是我们的老师——徐老师。我从五岁开始学中文到十六岁从中文学校毕业，一直都是徐老师教的。徐老师因此成了我们家的好朋友，现在还跟我爸妈微信聊天儿，或者一起去旅游。我小时候在中文学校上中文课的时候，只想出去玩儿，不想在教室里上中文课。我非常羡慕那些星期六不用去上中文学校的孩子，尤其是外边天气好的时候。

不过，我的周末中文学校也有我喜欢的事情。学校会给学生和家长提供各种各样的课外文化和体育活动，比如画画儿、跳舞、武术等。学生上课的时候，爸爸妈妈就在体育馆里打羽毛球。当然还有老师教学生书法、画画儿什么的。所以中文学校算是当地华人社区的文化中心。我们这些孩子下课后也会到体育馆打篮球。我每星期都期待着跟中文学校的同班同学一起打篮球，因为在英文学校的篮球场上，很少有亚裔孩子的身影。

在我的全日制英文学校，那里也有中文课，但是我没有在那里上过中文课，

My Weekend Chinese School

Author: Henry Sun Instructor: Yan Liu Duke University

> Chinese school taught me to embrace my dual identity as a Chinese-American, and to appreciate my family's culture and life experience.

I was born in Rockville, Maryland in the U.S., and started attending Chinese school at weekends when I was five. Every Saturday afternoon at 1:30, my parents would drive me to the nearby Chinese school, a program operated by local Chinese people at weekends using rented classrooms from a local high school. While I can no longer remember my feelings toward Chinese school when I first started, I was likely not super optimistic. Luckily, I made a new friend in my Chinese class, whose English name is Danny and Chinese name is Shao Danning. His mom was actually our teacher, Mrs. Xu, and she taught me from the age of 5 all the way until I graduated from my Chinese school when I was 16. She even became a close friend of our family, and even today she talks with my parents on WeChat or takes trips with them. When I was young, I always wanted to go outside and play rather than sitting in Chinese class – I would always be jealous of other kids who didn't have to attend Chinese school on Saturdays, especially when the weather was nice.

However, my Chinese school had a major benefit. It provided all sorts of extracurricular activities and athletic options for both students and parents, such as drawing, dancing, and practicing martial arts. While we kids were in class, parents would be in the gym playing badminton. There were also teachers who taught calligraphy and drawing, of course. Thus, Chinese school was essentially a cultural center for the local Chinese community. My friends and I would also go to the gym to play basketball after our classes ended. I looked forward to playing basketball at Chinese school each week, because on the court at my everyday American school, it was rare to see many other Asian kids.

所以我跟其他同学的中文教育肯定有点儿不一样。我的周末中文学校非常强调中国文化和价值观。我学过的内容包括古典小说《三国演义》里面的故事，李白、杜甫、白居易的诗，中医的治病方法，还有孔子的《论语》等。我曾经背过："天行健，君子以自强不息。地势坤，君子以厚德载物。"但我对那些东西似懂非懂，不是特别喜欢。而我最喜欢学的东西就是中国烹饪。什么是中国的四大菜系，中国人的饮食习惯，饺子怎么包……这些我都非常感兴趣。当然我也很喜欢跟家人一起去中国餐馆大吃一顿。我是一个地地道道的吃货—— 中国吃货。

虽然小时候我在中文学校上了这么多年的中文课，但是我在家里不常跟父母

While my everyday American school also had Chinese classes, I never took them, so my Chinese education may more or less differ from my peers. My weekend Chinese school stressed teaching Chinese culture and values. I've learned about many such topics, including the stories from the classical fiction *Romance of the Three Kingdoms*, the poems of Li Bai, Du Fu, and Bai Juyi, the traditional system of Chinese medicine, and *The Analects of Confucius*. I have once memorized "As heaven maintains vigor through movements, a gentleman should constantly strive for self-perfection. Just like the earth, which is generous and peaceful, a gentleman should have ample virtue and accommodate all things." I didn't fully understand these sayings, thus not very fond of them. Instead, my favorite part of the curriculum was learning about Chinese cuisine. Be it the four great culinary traditions of China, the eating customs of Chinese people, or how to make dumplings, I loved them all. Of course, I also looked forward to eating at a Chinese restaurant with my family – I'm a true Chinese foodie.

Although I spent many years at Chinese school, I always used to avoid speaking Chinese with my parents at home. I often talked with them in "Chinglish", e.g., "I'm going to the 操场 to 打球". But now in college, as I noticed my Chinese proficiency declining, I've started to speak Chinese with my parents consciously. Fortunately, I managed a good score on my SAT and AP Chinese tests.

Whether I liked it or not, during all those years in Chinese school, I never seriously thought of dropping out. Maybe it's because I made some friends there, or because I knew my parents would never agree. Of course, if I hadn't learned Chinese, I would find it difficult to interact with my family, and would be surely disappointed in myself. Chinese school taught me to embrace my dual identity as a Chinese-American, and to appreciate my family's culture and life experience. While in class for everyday American school, I would often sit in the back row and seldom speak. However, in Chinese school, I competed for the front seat and often raised my hand to answer questions.

If I have my own kids one day, I would also encourage them to go to Chinese school, while not forcing them. However, I will be sure to pass on the aspects of Chinese culture my parents and Chinese

说中文。我经常会用 Chinglish 跟他们说话，比如，“I'm going to the 操场 to 打球”。我现在上大学了，开始有意识地多跟父母说中文，因为我能够感觉到我的中文在退步。还好，我考 SAT 和 AP 中文的时候发挥得还行。

我情愿又不情愿地上了那么多年的中文学校，从来没有认真地考虑过放弃。这有可能是因为中文学校里有我的朋友，也有可能是因为我知道爸爸妈妈肯定会坚决反对我退出。当然了，如果我不会说中文，跟家人交流就会很别扭，我也肯定会对自己很失望。中文课让我更能接受自己的双重身份，也让我更理解父母和家人的经历。我在全日制英文学校上课的时候，通常会坐在最后一排，很少发言，但在中文学校，我却抢着坐在前排，积极举手回答老师的问题。

如果我将来有了自己的孩子，我也会鼓励他们去上中文学校，不过不会逼着他们去。但是，我一定会把爸爸妈妈和中文学校教我的中国文化传承给他们。如果我是个父亲的话，我肯定更像一个中国父亲。当然，我希望我不会像某些家长那样一天到晚拉长着脸那么严肃！

school have given me. As a father, I'd definitely be more like a Chinese dad. I just hope I won't be as stern and strict as some parents!

一堂有关十二生肖的中文课

作者：李洪锴　指导教师：顾利程　西北大学

在今天的中文课上，老师给我们介绍了中国的十二生肖。老师说，生肖是中国传统文化的重要部分，由十二种动物组成。它们是：鼠、牛、虎、兔、龙、蛇、马、羊、猴、鸡、狗和猪。

生肖是中国传统文化的重要部分，由十二种动物组成。

关于十二生肖的由来，老师给我们讲了一个神话故事。当年，皇帝要选十二个跑得最快的动物给自己当卫士。皇帝说："明天一早，你们从你们的住处出发，十二个最早到我宫殿的动物就可以当我的卫士。"动物们听说了都非常兴奋，准备明天天一亮就出发。猫很想跑第一，可是它有一个爱睡懒觉的毛病，所以就拜托老鼠明早叫醒它，老鼠满口答应了。可是老鼠担心猫跑得比它快，所以第二天早上并没有叫醒猫，自己悄悄跑出去了。结果猫没有选上，从此跟鼠结成冤家。老鼠快跑到宫殿的时候，前面遇到了一条大河，老鼠过不去了，非常着急。这时候，牛跑过来了，要蹚水过河。老鼠很聪明，一下就跳到牛背上，跟着过了河。过河以后，牛停在那里甩干身上的水，老鼠趁机飞奔而去，抢先一步跑到了皇宫。这样，聪明的老鼠和勤劳的老牛获得了第一和第二。别的动物排在了后面。肥肥懒懒的猪最晚才到，所以排在了最后。所以最后形成了鼠、牛、虎、兔、龙、蛇、马、羊、猴、鸡、狗、猪的顺序。后来，人们用这十二种动物配

A Lesson about the Chinese Zodiac

Author: Thomas Li Instructor: Licheng Gu Northwestern University

In today's Chinese class, the teacher introduced us to the Chinese zodiac. The teacher said that the zodiac is an important part of traditional Chinese culture and consists of twelve animals. They are rat, ox, tiger, rabbit, dragon, snake, horse, goat, monkey, rooster, dog and pig.

> The zodiac is an important part of traditional Chinese culture and consists of twelve animals.

Regarding the origin of the Chinese zodiac, the teacher told us a fairy tale. Back then, the emperor wanted to choose the twelve fastest animals to be his guards. The emperor said to the animals, "Tomorrow morning, start from your home, and the twelve of you that arrive at my palace first can be my guards." The animals were very excited when they heard the news and prepared to depart at dawn. The cat really wanted to win first, but it had a habit of sleeping late, so it asked the rat to wake it up in the morning, and the rat agreed. But the rat was worried that the cat would run faster than him, so he didn't wake the cat up the next morning and ran out quietly by himself. As a result, the cat was not chosen and became an enemy with the rat from then on. When the rat was about to run to the palace, there was a big river in front of it. The rat couldn't cross it and was very worried. At this time, the ox ran over and wanted to wade across the river.

The rat was very clever, so he jumped onto the ox's back and followed him across the river. After crossing the river, the ox stopped there to shake off the water from his body, and the rat took the opportunity to gallop away, running to the palace first. In this way, the clever rat and the hard-working old ox won the first and second places. The other animals followed suit. The fat and lazy pig was the last to arrive, so that's

合十二个地支来记载年份，每一年出生的人，他的属相或者生肖就是这一年对应的动物，这就是“十二生肖”。

我是1994年出生的，所以我属狗。我的哥哥比我早生了两年，他属猴。我们班里有一个从越南移民来的学生告诉我们，在越南他们也有十二生肖，但是他们有鼠，也有猫，只是没有兔子。我开玩笑说：“那越南的猫一定原谅了越南的老鼠。越南猫不吃老鼠，只是把兔子吃了。”

老师解释道：“现在我们看到的这十二生肖，是在中国流传使用最广的一种，一些少数民族也有不完全一样的十二生肖。而且，世界上除了中国和越南以外，还有日本、印度、埃及、韩国、希腊、墨西哥等国家也有自己的十二生肖，有的

why it comes at the end of the zodiac. In the end, the order of rat, ox, tiger, rabbit, dragon, snake, horse, goat, monkey, rooster, dog and pig was formed. Later, people used these twelve kinds of animals to match the twelve Earthly Branches and record the year. The zodiac of a person born in each year is the animal corresponding to that year, and this is the "Chinese zodiac."

I was born in 1994, so my zodiac is the dog. My older brother was born two years earlier than me, so his is the monkey. In our class, a student who migrated from Vietnam told us that they also have zodiac signs in Vietnam, and their zodiac has the rat and the cat, but no rabbit. I joked, "The Vietnamese cat must have forgiven the Vietnamese rat. The Vietnamese cat doesn't eat the rat; it just eats the rabbit."

The teacher explained, "The twelve zodiac signs we see now are the most widely used ones in China, and some ethnic groups also have different zodiac signs. Moreover, in addition to China and Vietnam, Japan, India, Egypt, South Korea, Greece, Mexico and other countries in the world also have their own zodiac signs. Some are the same as China and some are different."

A classmate asked, "The twelve zodiac signs are all animals. We've learned 'dog' and 'cat' before, and they both have the '犭' radical in the characters. Why do only the animals like monkey, dog, and pig in the twelve zodiac signs carry the '犭' radical?"

The teacher replied, "This is because 'animal' describes a very broad category, including those that fly in the sky, those that run on the ground, and those that swim in the water... There are many types. Therefore, the Chinese characters that represent the names of animals also have different radicals, and '犭' is just one of them."

"You see, in the twelve zodiac signs, in addition to beasts with '犭' such as monkey (猴), dog (狗) , and pig (猪) , there are also birds with the radical '鸟', such as rooster (鸡). Snake (蛇) is a reptile, and similar to the names of many insects, it has the '虫' radical. In addition, the words '牛' (ox), '龙' (dragon), '马' (horse), and '羊' (goat) are all single-element characters, and they can also be radicals of other Chinese characters such as '牦' (yak), '牧' (herd) and '牡' (male) which all have '牛' as the radical, along with characters like '骑' (ride), '驾' (ride), '驶' (drive) which all have '马' as the radical...

跟中国一样，有的不一样。”

一个同学问道：“十二生肖都是动物，我们以前学了‘狗’和‘猫’，它们都有‘犭(反犬旁)’，为什么十二生肖里只有‘猴、狗、猪’有‘犭(反犬旁)’？”

老师回答道：“这是因为‘动物’是一个很广的概念，包括天上飞的、地上跑的、水里游的……有很多种类。所以，表示动物名称的汉字也有不同的偏旁，‘犭(反犬旁)’只是其中之一。

“你们看，十二生肖里，除了带‘犭(反犬旁)’的兽类，比如‘猴、狗、猪’，还有带‘鸟’字旁的飞禽类，比如‘鸡’。‘蛇’是爬行动物，跟很多昆虫的名称一样，它有一个‘虫’字旁。另外，‘牛、龙、马、羊’等字都是独体字，它们同时也可以是其他汉字的偏旁。比如‘牦、牧、牡’(牛字旁)，‘骑、驾、驶、驰、骋’(马字旁)……

“只有‘龙’，因为比较特别，也比较神圣，所以很少有跟它一类的东西，连它生的九个儿子都有不一样的名字，比如赑屃、饕餮、麒麟、狻猊……尽管这样，还是有几个不常用的汉字是‘龙’做偏旁的，比如‘聋、垄’……”老师边说边在黑板上写这些汉字。

同学们看到这些字，纷纷笑着说道：“这些字太酷了！就是不要考我们这些不常用的汉字啊。”

"Only the character for dragon (龙) is particularly unique because it's thought to be special and sacred, and there are very few things like it. Even its nine sons have different names, such as *bixi* (赑屃), *taotie* (饕餮), *kylin* (麒麟), *suanni* (狻猊)… Even so, there are still a few uncommon Chinese characters with '龙' as the radical, such as '聋' (deaf), '垄' (ridge)… " The teacher wrote these Chinese characters on the blackboard while explaining.

When the students saw these characters, they all laughed and said, "These characters are so cool! Just don't test us on these uncommon Chinese characters, please."

我为什么要学习中文

作者：孔禄　指导教师：于丽萍　华盛顿大学（西雅图）

> 所谓的“千里之行”并不是一个星期、一个月或者一年，而是一辈子。

老子曾经说过：“千里之行始于足下。”谁都熟悉这个说法，但是我怀疑是否所有的人都完全理解这句话想表达的真正意思。表面上，这句话的意思是只要你努力工作就能实现各种各样的目标。但实际上，这所谓的“千里之行”并不是一个星期、一个月或者一年，而是一辈子。在我看来，开始学中文成了我生活中的又一次“千里之行”，并且是一个前所未有的经历。本来，我以为掌握中文是一个“一蹴而就”的过程，但不久之后我就发现，要想达到“说得流利”的水平，需要一个“拾级而上”的过程。这让我反思当初我为什么决定开始学中文？我的动机是什么？事实是，学中文实际上并不是为了帮我找到工作，也不是为了面子，更不是为了提高社会地位，而是为了扩大我的视野，跟别人更深入地沟通。因此，我心甘情愿地埋头书海，一步一个脚印地朝着我的梦想前进。凭着我的努力，我相信我会自然地、慢慢地实现我的梦想。

首先，我认识很多会说外语的家庭和朋友。小时候，每当我看到他们使用别人的母语来交流的时候，我都羡慕不已。在我眼里，他们都展示出超强的能力！我惭愧！羡慕！嫉妒！恨！“为什么我不能这样？”所有的孩子都有超能力的梦想。我呢？我那时的梦想就是掌握全世界所有的语言。从我出生到二十几岁，虽然一直忙着读书，做实验，写论文，交朋友，做运动……但是我始终没有忘记小时候要学外语的梦想。我每次听到别人讲外语的时候，就再次想起了这些被遗忘

Why I Want to Learn Chinese

Author: Luke Khoury   Instructor: Liping Yu   University of Washington (Seattle)

Laozi once said, "a thousand-*li* journey begins with the first step." While it's true that everyone is familiar with this saying, I question whether they fully understand the meaning it's trying to express. On the surface, this quote states that as long as someone works hard, he can achieve any goal. But in reality, this so-called "a thousand-*li* journey" doesn't take one week, one month, or even one year of work, but rather a lifetime. From my view, starting to study Chinese became yet another "a thousand-*li* journey" in my life, an experience I had never experienced before. Originally, I assumed that grasping the language would be an overnight process, but not long after, I realized that wanting to reach a level of fluency would be a slow and deliberate one. All of this made me reflect why I originally decided to study Chinese, and what my motivations were. The truth is, studying Chinese wasn't for help in finding a job, wasn't for showing off, and wasn't for status-seeking, but rather, it was to expand my horizons and more deeply connect with others. Therefore, I jumped headlong into studies, and slowly worked toward my goal. Through my effort, I believe that I can naturally and slowly reach this dream.

This so-called "a thousand-*li* journey" doesn't take one week, one month, or even one year of work, but rather a lifetime.

To start with, I know many family and friends who can speak other languages. When I was young, every time I saw them use other people's native languages to converse, I felt so admiring. In my eyes, they were all showing superpowers! Shame, jealousy, and envy! "Why can't I be like this?" Every child has dreams of having superpowers. What about mine? At that time, mine was to be able to fluently speak all the world's languages. Up to my mid-twenties, even though I was busy studying, doing research, writing papers, making friends, and doing sports, I still didn't forget my childhood dreams of speaking a foreign language. And every time

的梦想。由于各种各样的原因，我一直在用各种借口来推迟学外语的计划。好在，有一天迫于无法忍受的内疚感，我决定开始学习一门外语。世界上有那么多种外语，我应该学哪个呢？思来想去，最终我决定学中文。这是因为我知道世界上有六分之一的人口说中文。如果我能和世界上六分之一的人口直接沟通，那该多了不起呀！

现在，我已经是一个快要毕业的化工专业的博士生了。我上博士一年级的时候，除了进行自己的科学研究以外，还决定开始学中文。不过，因为缺乏指导，我无法开始学中文的“千里之行”。情急之下，我购买了一个教中文的电脑软件。这个电脑软件固然让我熟悉了一点儿中文，但它无法帮我了解中文的复杂性。简而言之，要达到一个更高的中文水平，我需要接受正规的中文教育。有一天，我跟一位好朋友谈起关于我学中文的情况。他理所当然地建议我去上学校中文系的

I heard other people speaking one, I was reminded of these forgotten dreams. For a variety of reasons, I used every excuse to put off my plans to study a foreign language. Thankfully, forced through a feeling of regret, one day I decided to start studying one. The world has so many languages though, which one should I choose? Pondering back and forth, I finally decided to study Chinese. This is because I knew that one-sixth of the world speaks Chinese. If I could directly talk to one-sixth of the people on the earth, that would be amazing!

Now I'm a Ph.D. student in chemical industry, and I'm already quickly approaching graduation. During my first year of Ph.D., besides doing my scientific research, I also decided to start studying Chinese. However, because of a lack of guidance, I had no direction to start this "a thousand-*li* journey." So, in my anxiety, I purchased a Chinese teaching computer program. Even though this software admittedly made me more familiar with Chinese, it couldn't help me understand its complexity. To put it simply, if I wanted to reach a higher level of Chinese, I would have to receive formal education. So, one day, I brought up the state of my Chinese studies with a friend. And he suggested I attend some of the classes offered by the Chinese Department of the university. The moment I heard his suggestion, I instinctively objected! I came up with all sorts of reasons as to why I couldn't join the Chinese classes: "I don't have any time! Graduate students don't have classes with undergraduates! The Chinese classes at the University of Washington are just too hard!" Despite all of this, I still reflected on what he said for a long time. Later, I sensed that what he said was right. This is because all dreams worthy of pursuing are not easy to achieve. Therefore, in one autumn, I, a Ph.D. student with many undergraduate freshmen started the first-year Chinese language classes offered by the University of Washington.

Afterward, studying Chinese surely became "a one-thousand-*li* journey," and changed into a meaningful adventure. Even though every day I ran back and forth between research, friends, family, and studying Chinese, I found this lifestyle exciting. From 5:30 in the morning to late at night, from Monday to Sunday, from school to my apartment, I was earnestly studying and working. After class, in addition to doing Chinese homework, I also immersed myself in many activities to help learn, such as watching Chinese TV serials, studying Chinese history, reading Chinese books, and studying idioms, allusions, legends, to name a few. Four years went by in a

中文课。听了他的建议，我本能地反对！我想出了成千上万个不上中文课的理由：“我没有时间！研究生不跟本科生一起上课！华大的中文课太难了！”尽管如此，他所说的话，我还是考虑了很久。后来我觉得他说得有道理。因为所有值得追求的梦想都不是容易实现的。因此，有一年的秋季，我这个博士生跟许多本科新生一起，开始在华盛顿大学上一年级的中文课。

后来，学中文真的成了一个“千里之行”，而且成了一个很有意思的“旅行”。虽然我每天都奔波在科研、朋友、家庭和中文课之间，可是这样的生活方式让我激动不已。从早上五点半起床到深夜，从周一到周日，从学校到自己的公寓，我都努力工作和学习。课余除了做中文作业以外，我还沉浸在很多学中文的活动中，比方说，看中国电视剧，学习中国历史，看中文书，学成语，学典故，了解传说等等。四年一晃就过去了，我写了无数篇的文章，看了很多部电影，克服了各种困难，当然重要的是我还结交了很多中国朋友。这四年的学习即将告一段落，但这只是“千里之行”的一个起点。现在呢？我还在学，我一定不能自满。有的时候，我当然也想要偷个懒，“晒个网”，但是我绝不会放弃追求更高的标准。

我并不否认我走上了一条非主流的学中文的道路，但是这个经历让我非常有成就感。学中文真是一个特别有意思的过程，就像中国人常常说的：“书山有路勤为径，学海无涯苦作舟。”我始终相信“学无止境”，所以我还需要更加努力地学习中文。虽然我还会遇到各种各样的困难、各种各样尴尬的情况，但这些所谓的挫折将会变成一种经验。学中文无疑是一个“苦差事”，但它最终会丰富我的生活阅历。

flash, and I've written countless essays, watched many movies, overcome many difficulties, and importantly made many Chinese friends. These four years of studying are coming to an end, but this is only the starting point in my "a thousand-*li* journey." As for now? I am still learning, and certainly can't become complacent. Of course, from time to time I want to be lazy and just say "forget it all," but I won't give up pursing higher standards.

I can't deny that I've walked down an unconventional path to learning Chinese, but this experience has given me a great sense of accomplishment. Studying Chinese is such a compelling endeavor, just as Chinese people say, "The path through mountains of books can only be paved with diligence, and oceans of knowledge can only be crossed with hard work." I always believe that learning has no end point, so I still must study the language with even more effort. Even though I will encounter all types of difficulties and embarrassing situations, I will turn these so-called setbacks into learning opportunities. Studying Chinese undoubtedly is drudgery of sorts, but in the end, will enrich my life experiences.

我和中国的距离

作者：柯丽　指导教师：于丽萍　华盛顿大学（西雅图）

> 外公的故事让我明白了我家的历史也是中国历史的一部分。

我开始学中文，主要是想跟我外公说话。虽然他会说英文，但是我觉得跟他说中文可以让我们的关系变得更亲近。

我外公是在大陆出生，在台湾长大的。后来，外公移民到了美国。他在读研究生的时候遇见了我的外婆，外婆是美国人。他们从那时起就一直住在美国。我妈妈和舅舅都有中文名字，但是我出生的时候，外公觉得没有必要再给我起一个中文名字。虽然我们吃中国菜，喝中国茶，过中秋节和春节，但我们都不是中国国籍。妈妈、舅舅和外婆以前都学过中文。他们也喜欢用中文跟我的外公说话，加强他们跟我们家的中国背景的联系。所以学中文不但能帮助我理解我的中国家人，而且也让我理解我的美国家人。

童年的时候，我不太知道家里的故事。虽然我有中国家人，但是一般的人都觉得我的家人都是在美国或者欧洲出生的。我家的中国背景鲜为人知。我十岁才开始了解我家的历史。因为十岁那年，我们全家人跟外公一起回了一趟台湾。我们一起去参观他的中学，拜访他的老朋友。我吃到了很多我在美国常吃的中国菜。因此我明白了这些菜不但是我家常做的菜，也是台湾家庭常做的菜。我们去喝茶的时候，我才明白饭后喝茶不是外公一个人的习惯，而是中国人的习惯。通过这次旅行，我了解到我家的传统是从一个很丰富的文化来的。

因此，我选修外语的时候，选了中文。那一年我对自己的身份有了新的认同。

My Distance to China

Author: Lydia Crook Instructor: Liping Yu University of Washington (Seattle)

> My grandfather's story made me realize that my family's history is also part of China's history.

I mainly started learning Chinese because I wanted to be able to talk to my grandfather. Although he speaks English, I thought speaking Chinese with him could make our relationship closer.

My grandfather was born in Chinese mainland and grew up in Taiwan. Later, he immigrated to the United States. While pursuing graduate studies, he met my grandmother, who is American. Since then, they have lived in America together. My mother and uncle both have Chinese names, but when I was born, my grandfather decided there was no point in giving me one. Although we eat Chinese food, drink Chinese tea, and celebrate the Mid-Autumn Festival and Lunar New Year, we are not Chinese citizens. My mother, uncle, and grandmother have all studied Chinese and would also like to talk to my grandfather in Chinese to become closer to our family's Chinese heritage. Thus, learning Chinese can help me understand not only my Chinese family, but also my American family.

As a child, I didn't fully understand my family's history. Although I had Chinese relatives, most people thought my family was American or European. My Chinese background was little known. It wasn't until I was ten years old that I began to understand my family's history. When I was ten, my family went with my grandfather to visit Taiwan. We saw my grandfather's middle school and visited his old friends. I ate much of the same Chinese food I had eaten at my home in the U.S., which made me realize that it wasn't just food that my family cooked but food that families in Taiwan often cooked. When we drank tea, I finally understood that drinking tea after

我的变化有三点。第一，我开始学中文以后，慢慢地可以看懂街上的一些汉字，可以听懂一些中国人说的话了。第二，我跟家人去香港的时候，我的中文知识让我能更好地理解那个城市，因为我认识很多路标和招牌上的汉字。有一次，我爸爸想买一些茶叶，可是他看不懂汉字。我找到了他想去的茶庄，因为我在招牌上看到了“茶”字。借助我的中文知识，我可以用中文导航，这让我感到很骄傲。香港之行让我觉得学中文可以缩短我和中国的距离。第三，我了解了外公为什么离开大陆去了台湾。我的外公说，因为他的爸爸曾经在国民党军队中服过役，所以“文化大革命”的时候，他们就离开大陆去了台湾。外公的故事让我明白了我家的历史也是中国历史的一部分。因此，我觉得通过学中国历史，我可以知道我家的历史。

虽然我学中文的初衷是加深对家庭背景的了解，但是后来我的动力慢慢地改变了。我发现，中文比英文更加“诗情画意”。譬如在一部中文电影里，女主人

dinner wasn't just my grandfather's tradition, but was a Chinese tradition. Through this trip, I realized my family's traditions came from a rich culture.

Therefore, when I had to choose a language to learn, I chose Chinese. The first year of learning Chinese gave me a new relationship to my identity. This change came in three parts, the first being a gradual ability to read some of the Chinese characters around me and understand some of the Chinese language I heard. Secondly, while visiting Hong Kong with my family, my Chinese knowledge let me have a deeper understanding of the city because I was able to read a lot of Chinese characters on road signs and store windows. One time, my father was looking for a tea shop but couldn't read any Chinese. I was able to find the store because I recognized the Chinese character for tea. With my knowledge, I was able to use Chinese to navigate, which made me proud. This trip to Hong Kong made me realize that learning Chinese could close the distance between myself and China. The third part of my change was learning why my grandfather left the mainland for Taiwan. My grandfather told me that his father served in the Kuomintang army, so during the Cultural Revolution they left the mainland for Taiwan. My grandfather's story made me realize that my family's history is also part of China's history. Thus, I believe that through learning Chinese history, I can also learn my family's history.

Although my original intention behind learning Chinese was to deepen my understanding of my family background, my motivation slowly changed. I found that the Chinese language is more elegant than English. For example, in a Chinese film a female character affectionately says to a male character, "你根本不用说，你的眼睛已经告诉我了。" But the English subtitles translate it as "You didn't have to tell me. It's the way you look at me." This translation doesn't contain the same emotion as the Chinese sentence. Since I have learned Chinese, I was able to understand the sentence without translation and thus understand its original meaning. Through this experience, I better understood that my Chinese knowledge would let me understand the characters and themes present in Chinese films. My knowledge also helped me understand my own community. I often take a bus, and I hear Chinese conversations on the bus. I really like listening to them because I feel like it makes us connected. Since I don't look Chinese, they always assume I don't understand their conversations. I find this very funny, since having

公对男主人公含情脉脉地深情表白：“你根本不用说，你的眼睛已经告诉我了。”但是银幕上出现的英文字幕却是平铺直叙、毫无情感的一句“You didn’ t have to tell me. It’s the way you look at me.”英文字幕根本没有把中文原话所包含的情感翻译出来。幸亏我学了中文，听懂了这句中文原话，所以能够体会到其他美国人体会不到的真正内涵。通过这件事情，我深刻意识到，我的中文知识可以帮助我更好地了解了中文电影的人物和主题。我的中文知识也帮我了解了我的社区。我常常坐公共汽车，在车上听中国人用中文谈话。我很喜欢听他们说话，因为我感到我跟他们有关联。因为我看起来跟中国人不一样，所以他们都觉得我听不懂他们说的话。这让我觉得很好玩儿。学了中文以后我可以当“卧底”了。

学中文也让我了解了中国文化和历史。我想继续了解中国。高中二年级的时候，我和中文班的同学一起去过中国大陆。我们去看了丝绸之路，还去了很多不同的地方。虽然是跟团旅行，但是那次旅行让我加深了对中国人的理解。我觉得那次旅行让我想住在中国，想进一步了解中国人的生活。我现在打算去中国留学，毕业以后在那里继续住一年。我知道我的计划一定会变化，因为从开始学中文到现在，我已经变化了很多次。不过，我一想到未来就很兴奋，因为我知道中国将会一直伴随着我，在我的生活中起到重要的作用。

studied Chinese lets me be "undercover."

Studying Chinese also lets me understand Chinese culture and history. I want to continue to understand China. In my sophomore year of high school, I traveled with my Chinese class to Chinese mainland. We toured the Silk Road, visiting many different places. Although I went with a tour group, the trip deepened my understanding of Chinese people. I feel that trip made me want to live in China and improve my understanding of life there. I currently plan to study abroad in China, and live there for a year after graduation. I know my plan will change because I've already gone through much change since I started studying Chinese. However, I am excited at the thought of future since I know China will always be with me and be an important part of my life.

深情厚谊

Deep Friendships

导读

这一板块的十一篇文章都与友情和恋情有关。在《谁是亲妈》这篇文章中，西北大学的刘可阳同学通过四个情景，把自己在北京留学时认的中国干妈与美国亲妈相比较。在吃饭问题上，一个妈妈要他多吃多喝，担心他吃不饱，另一个妈妈是吃多少都随他；在晒黑不晒黑的问题上，一个妈妈千叮咛万嘱咐，要他用防晒霜，另一个妈妈一点儿都不在乎，认为晒得越黑越健康；在学习的问题上，一个妈妈在旁边端茶倒水，关怀备至，另一个妈妈则是不闻不问，任其发展；在交友问题上，一个妈妈一定要搞清楚对方是谁，另一个妈妈则是只问回来吃饭吗。可见一个妈妈问寒问暖，体贴入微，一切事务都要过问；另一个妈妈放手散养，让孩子有自己充分发展的空间。可阳面对亲生的美国妈妈和借宿家庭的中国妈妈，并没有厚此薄彼，尤其在描写中国妈妈时，那种不是亲人，却胜似亲人的感情传达得非常到位。设定四个相同的场景，比较两个人不同的反应，分析二者的区别，这种写作方法非常值得大家学习。

在《亦师亦友》一文中，斯坦福大学的彭兰如同学讲述了她在宜兰与小学生们结下的深厚友谊。小学生们开学第一天与作者见面，就提出了各种各样的问题：

“你有没有男朋友？”“没有。”

“为什么你想来宜兰？”“因为我想教你们英文，自己同时也想学中文。”

“你喜欢臭豆腐吗？”“不好意思，不太喜欢。”

“你的声音和 Siri 的很像！你是 Siri 吗？”“不好意思，不是。”

“为什么你的鼻子是这样的？”“什么‘这样’？”

“为什么那么……那么……那么大？”

Introduction

The eleven stories in this section are all related to friendship and romance. In the piece "Who Is My Biological Mother," Alec D'Alelio, a student from Northwestern University, compared the Chinese "mother" he met when he was studying abroad in Beijing with his actual American mother through four scenarios. When it came to eating, one mother always asked him to eat and drink more, fearing that he would not be full, but the other mother didn't mind how much he wanted to eat. One mother would always urge him to put on sunscreen while the other mother didn't care at all – the tanner he was, the healthier he looked. When it came to learning, one mother was very caring, serving tea and pouring water, while the other mother just not intervened him and let him take care of his own studies. When it comes to going out with a friend, one mother made sure to find out who he was meeting, while the other just asked whether he was going home for dinner. Overall, while one mother was considerate and showed much concern about him, the other mother chose to let go so that he had sufficient room for development. Through his writing, Alec remains fairly impartial and doesn't clearly favor one mother over the other. When describing the Chinese mother from his host family, he does a good job of narrating the strong bond he developed with her although they aren't blood-related. Setting four similar scenes and comparing the different responses of the two mothers is a writing technique that is quite worthy of further exploration.

In the story "Teacher and Friend," Lauren Barnes, a student who studies at Stanford University, describes the profound friendship she formed with elementary school students in Yilan. The primary school students met her on the first day of school and asked her various questions:

"Do you have a boyfriend?" "No, I don't."

"Why do you want to come to Yilan?" "So I can teach you all English, and I learn Chinese at the same time."

童言无忌，这段对话让我们感受到了当地孩子们的天真可爱。几乎不用任何描述，一群充满好奇心的孩子已经被带到了我们的面前，让我们怎能不喜欢上他们？可见这段对话的引用是非常成功的。

疫情暴发以后的三年里，美国留学生暂时不能去中国学中文，但是这并不能阻止他们继续与中国年轻人交朋友。在《我的中国笔友》一文中，北弗吉尼亚社区学院的文理爱同学通过网络，与远在中国的笔友结下了深厚的友谊。理爱与笔友的交流从轻松的话题开始，如学什么专业，家里有什么人，对什么感兴趣，小时候喜欢的糖等等。随后他们的话题慢慢转向了各自喜欢的电视剧，各种游戏。通过抖音，理爱给笔友唱歌，笔友给作者朗诵古诗。相当熟悉以后，他们的谈话慢慢地深入了。他们讨论两国之间的文化差别，贸易竞争，还有外交状况。虽然两国政府之间存在着巨大的分歧，但是两国的青年人认为双方应该保持沟通，保持友谊。理爱最后写道："虽然国家之间关系越来越紧张，但是我们的短信一向很温暖。……我们相信跨文化交流能改善人与人之间的关系，因为我们两个人的这条路已经走通了。"

在描写二人关系的发展过程时，理爱循序渐进，一步步从破冰，到热身，再到深入，最后升华。这种循序渐进的描述是值得大家学习的。

"Do you like strong-smelling preserved tofu?" "Sorry, not really."

"Your voice is very similar to Siri's voice! Are you Siri?" "Sorry, I am not."

"Why is your nose like that?" "Like what?"

"Why is it so… so… so… big?"

As the Chinese idiom goes, children's words carry no harm, and this conversation makes us feel the innocence and loveliness of the local children. Almost without any description, a group of curious children have been brought before us – how can we not like them? It can be seen that the quotation of this dialogue within the piece is very successful.

In the three years following the pandemic, American students studying abroad were temporarily unable to go to China to learn Chinese, but this did not prevent them from continuing to make friends with Chinese people. In the story "My Chinese Pen Pal," Raven Witherspoon, a student from Northern Virginia Community College, forged a deep friendship with a pen pal in China through the internet. Raven's communication with her pen pal starts with light topics, such as majors, family, interests, favorite sweets, and so on. Then, their topics gradually transitioned to their favorite TV series and games. Through TikTok, Raven sang to her pen pal while her pen pal recited ancient poems to Raven. After growing more comfortable and familiar with each other, their conversation slowly deepened. They discussed the cultural differences between the two countries, the trade competition, and the diplomatic situation. Although there are huge differences between the governments of the two countries, the young people of the two countries believe that the two sides should maintain communication and friendship. In the end, Raven wrote: "Although the relationship between our countries is becoming more and more tense, our texts are always very warm... We believe cross-cultural communication can improve relationships between people because we have already walked this road."

When describing the development process of the relationship between the two, Raven progressed step by step, from breaking the ice, to warm-up, to making further conversations, and finally to sublimation. This gradual process of narrative writing is definitely worth learning.

谁是亲妈

作者：刘可阳　指导教师：林秀玲　西北大学

> 我的中国妈妈虽然不是我的亲妈，但常常比我亲妈还亲。

一个人一般都只有一位妈妈，可是我有两位妈妈！

不是“亲妈”和“后妈”，而是一个美国妈妈，一个中国妈妈。

我在中国留学的时候，住在一个中国人的家里，他们对我像家人一样，于是，我就有了一对中国的爸爸妈妈。

我的中国妈妈对我像美国妈妈一样好，可是仔细想想，这两位妈妈还是有一些不一样的地方。下面，我就讲几个故事，说一说我这两位妈妈的不同，考一考大家，哪一位是我的亲妈？

第一个故事：吃饭的时候

第一个妈妈常这样说：“可阳，你瘦了！你要多吃饭！年轻人要多吃饭，才能长得又高又壮又健康！再多吃一点儿！都吃了！粒粒皆辛苦！粒粒皆辛苦！”

第二个妈妈这样说：“可阳，你要多吃蔬菜水果，最近又吃垃圾食品了吗？吃饱了就别吃了，剩下没有关系。”

你们说，哪一个是我亲妈？第一个还是第二个？

第二个故事：我从东南亚旅行回来

第一个妈妈这样说：“可阳！你晒黑了！不好看了！没有用防晒霜吗？”

第二个妈妈这样说：“可阳！你回来了我太高兴了！我可真想你啊。”

你们说，哪一个是我亲妈？第一个还是第二个？

Who Is My Biological Mother

Author: Alec D'Alelio Instructor: Hsiu-ling Robertson Northwestern University

> Even though my Chinese mother isn't my biological mother, I often feel even closer to her than I do to my biological mother.

A person usually only has one mother, but I have two mothers!

Not "biological mother" and "step-mother," but one American mother and one Chinese mother.

When I was studying abroad in China, I lived with a Chinese family. They treated me as if I was one of their family members, so just like that, I also had a pair of Chinese parents.

My Chinese mother treats me as nicely as my American mother, but after giving it some more thought, I realized that there are still some differences between the two. Next, I will share some stories and discuss the distinctions between my two mothers. Based on their responses in each scenario, can you tell which one is my biological mother?

The first story – At the Dinner Table

The first mother would often say: "Alec, you've lost weight! You need to eat more! Young people need to eat a lot to grow tall, strong, and healthy! Eat more! Finish it! Each grain of rice is from the sweat of farmers!"

The second mother would say: "Alec, you should eat more vegetables and fruits. Have you been eating junk food again recently? Stop eating if you're full; it's fine if there's still leftovers."

Who would you say is my biological mother? The first or the second?

The second story – After I Came Back from a Trip to Southeast Asia

The first mother would say: "Alec, you look so tan! You're not good-looking anymore! Did you forget to apply sunscreen?"

The second mother would say: "Alec! I'm so happy that you're back! I've missed you so much."

第三个故事：学习

第一个妈妈每天都要问我："今天学什么了？有没有不懂的地方？ 功课难不难？需不需要帮忙？"还常常坐在旁边看我做功课，一会儿拿来水果，一会儿又端来茶水，还不停问我："累不累？饿不饿？冷不冷？热不热？别太晚了，早点儿睡觉……"

第二个妈妈却觉得，学习是我自己的事，我应该自己安排好，有问题也要自己解决。我的房间她几乎从来不进来。

你们说，谁是亲妈？第一个还是第二个？

第四个故事：周末出去约会

第一个妈妈会问："你要去哪儿？去做什么？怎么去？跟谁一起？是男的还是女的？几点回来？带手机了吗？带钱包了吗？钱够不够？要爸爸送你接你吗？早点儿回来，晚上我做你最喜欢的菜！"

第二个妈妈只会问："回来吃饭吗？"

你们说，谁是亲妈？第一个还是第二个？

你们猜对了，第一个是我的中国妈妈，第二个是我的美国妈妈。虽然中国妈妈和美国妈妈有这么多不一样，但有一点是一样的，那就是全世界的妈妈都爱自己的孩子！我的中国妈妈虽然不是我的亲妈，但常常比亲妈还亲。

Who would you say is my biological mother? The first or the second?

The third story – Schoolwork

The first mother would ask me every day: "What did you learn today? Is there anything you don't understand? Is the homework difficult? Do you need help?" Often, she would sit next to me while watching me do my homework. From time to time, she would bring me fruit and tea, constantly asking me, "Are you tired? Hungry? Cold? Hot? Don't stay up too late, and make sure to go to bed early..."

The second mother would not say much. She believes that learning is my own business, so I should handle everything myself. If there's a problem, I should also solve it myself. She almost never comes into my room.

Who would you say is my biological mother? The first or the second?

The fourth story – Going out with My Friends on the Weekends

The first mother would ask: "Where are you going? What are you going to do? How are you getting there? Who are you going with? Boys or girls? What time are you coming back? Did you bring your phone? Wallet? Do you have enough money? Do you want Dad to take you there and bring you back home? Come home earlier, I'm cooking your favorite dish tonight!"

The second mother would only ask: "Are you coming home for dinner?"

Who would you say is my biological mother? The first or the second?

You guessed correctly, the first one is my Chinese mother, and the second one is my American mother. Although there are so many differences between the two, one thing is always the same. That is, mothers all over the world love their children! Even though my Chinese mother isn't my biological mother, I often feel even closer to her than I do to my biological mother.

亦师亦友

作者：彭兰如　指导教师：周小芳　斯坦福大学

感谢学生们让我跟中文结缘，祝福他们快乐和成功。

2019年的夏天，我一下飞机，就像到了一个全新的世界。中文字像海里的小鱼一样在我眼前游来游去，我都看不懂。我从来没学过中文，搭飞机去宜兰像搭上了一台时光机，上飞机前我是成人，下飞机时变成了一个需要牙牙学语的小宝宝。

这次我是作为福布莱特项目的英文助教来到宜兰。福布莱特项目是一项由美国政府推动资助的国际教育、文化和研究交流计划，世界上有150多个国家和地区参加。美国大学生去世界各地做英文助教是众多国际教育项目之一，而我有幸成为了他们中的一员。福布莱特项目安排了一辆巴士，把我和我朋友从台北机场送到宜兰。在巴士上，我一直透过窗户向外看，苍翠的山峦急速地掠过我眼前，甚至都来不及告诉我自己："兰如，你不在德州了。"

第一天在教室里，我的感觉从来没有如此复杂，胸有成竹却也很紧张，开心夹杂着一点儿忐忑。我对那天早上还有一些模糊的记忆，学校的英文老师陪我参观了整个学校。我记得我在美国的学校没有朝室外开的窗户，可能是因为有中央空调的原因吧。跟我在美国的学校不一样，在宜兰，每个教室都有朝室外开的窗户，每个老师一定要学会怎么开自己教室的窗户。这样才能保证教室内空气流通。那天早上一片忙乱的景象，来送孩子的家长骑着机车飞快地在校门口穿梭，老师为第一堂课做最后的准备，学生还有一点儿困。

Teacher and Friend

Author: Lauren Barnes   Instructor: Xiaofang Zhou   Stanford University

> I am grateful to my students who got me started in learning Chinese. I wish them happiness and success.

As soon as I got off the plane in summer of 2019, it was like I arrived in an entirely new world. Chinese characters swam in front of me like fish in the sea, all of which I couldn't understand. I had never studied Chinese. Getting on the plane to Yilan was like entering a time machine. Before boarding the plane, I was an adult, and after getting off the plane, I became a baby needing the simplest of Chinese.

I left the United States and came to Yilan to serve as an English teaching assistant with the Fulbright program. The Fulbright program is an international educational, cultural, and research exchange program funded by the United States government. More than 150 countries and regions across the world participate. American college students going to all parts of the world to serve as English teaching assistants is one of Fulbright's many international educational exchange programs, and I was fortunate to be chosen to be one. Fulbright had arranged a bus to take me and my friends to Yilan. On the bus, I stared out the window, watching the green hills quickly sweeping past me. I found no time to tell myself "Lauren, you're not in Texas anymore."

The first day in the classroom, I had very complicated feelings. I was confident, but also very nervous, excited and upset. I have a very blurry memory of that first day's morning. The school's English teacher took me on a tour of the entire school. I remember there are no windows facing outwards at my school in the United States, perhaps because of the central air-conditioning. Different from my school in the United States, every classroom in Yilan has windows facing outwards, and every teacher must learn to open the windows of the classroom.

下午第一堂课是五年级的。铃声响了，叮当叮当，我最后深呼吸，站在讲台上迎接学生们的到来。那时候，我什么都听不懂，但我看得出来他们对我很好奇。一位最勇敢的学生走到我身旁，流利地说道："Hello! I'm Vivian. Who are you?" 我们两个人开始聊天儿。Vivian 的英文很棒，她为其他同学做起了翻译。铃声又一次响了。外面的孩子们都涌进了教室。第一次有那么多水汪汪的眼睛好奇地看着我。因为是我当助教的第一天，我打算轻松一点儿，主要是自我介绍，然后让学生问我问题。这个计划很不错，学生问了我很多问题。

"你有没有男朋友？""没有。"

"为什么你想来宜兰？""因为我想教你们英文，自己同时也想学中文。"

"你喜欢臭豆腐吗？""不好意思，不太喜欢。"

还有一些更好笑的问题。

"你的声音和 Siri 的很像！你是 Siri 吗？""不好意思，不是。"

"为什么你的鼻子是这样的？""什么'这样'？"

"为什么那么……那么……那么大？"

This is the only way to allow air to circulate throughout the classroom. That morning was a busy scene. Parents were zipping around on scooters dropping their children off at the school gate, teachers were making the final preparations for class, and the students were still a little sleepy.

In the afternoon, the first class was for the fifth-graders. The bell rang, *ding dong ding dong*, and I took one last deep breath and stood on the platform in the front of the class to welcome my students into the class. At that time, I still didn't understand any Chinese, but I could tell the students were very curious about me. The bravest student walked right up next to me and said fluently, "Hello! I'm Vivian. Who are you?" We started to chat. Vivian's English was excellent, and she helped to translate for her classmates. The bell rang again. The students outside all entered the classroom. The first time standing in the front of the class, I saw many faces with limpid eyes curiously looking at me. Because it was my first day l as an English teaching assistant, I planned a more relaxing class. The most important part was self-introduction and allowing the students to ask me questions. This plan went off well and the students had many questions.

"Do you have a boyfriend?" "No, I don't."

"Why do you want to come to Yilan?" "So I can teach you all English, and learn Chinese at the same time."

"Do you like strong-smelling preserved tofu?" "Sorry, not really."

There were some even much funnier questions.

"Your voice is very similar to Siri's voice! Are you Siri?" "Sorry, I am not."

"Why is your nose like that?" "Like what?"

"Why is it so… so… so big?"

I really didn't know how to answer these kinds of questions, but I could intuitively tell myself I was going to like to teach these children quite a lot.

My life in Yilan was very full. Almost every day after finishing class, I would ride my scooter to attend Chinese class. My Chinese gradually improved, and I could start to chat with some of my students in Chinese. Some of my students would joke around with me, "Teacher, your Chinese handwriting isn't as ugly as the boys in our class is!" Other students would help

我真的不知道怎么回答这样的问题，但是我的直觉告诉我，我会非常喜欢教这些小孩子的。

在宜兰的生活非常充实，我差不多每天一下课，就骑车去上中文课。我的中文渐渐进步了，我开始能听懂一些学生的话，也尝试用中文跟他们聊天儿。有的学生会跟我开玩笑："老师，你的汉字没有我们班的男生那么臭啊！"也有的学生会当我的老师："老师，是'咖啡店'，不是'咖啡点'。"没过多久，我和他们的关系就越来越像朋友了。

两年的时间很快过去了，我离开的时候，孩子们都依依不舍，送了我很多礼物，我们都哭了。等新冠疫情过后，我打算回去看看这些孩子们。希望他们一切都好。我也希望我能不断提高我的中文水平。可能我下一次回到宜兰的时候，我的学生一听到我说中文就会吓一大跳。

2023 年 6 月 24 日，我再一次坐上了一辆开往宜兰的公车。我去那里看望好久不见的学生，参加他们的初中毕业典礼。与上一次不同，这次不是从台北来宜兰，而是从台中来宜兰。这是因为 2021 年从宜兰回到斯坦福大学以后，我发现我深深地爱上了中文。我决定攻读博士学位，准备做一名中国文学教授，把我对中文的热爱传播给更多的学生。因此我现在在台中的逢甲大学选修中文课程。

毕业典礼在学校的体育馆里举行。为了给学生们一个惊喜，我事先并没有告诉他们我来看他们。我悄悄地走向观众席的后排，当时学生们都没有注意到我，但是我在观众席上可以看到他们。当校长叫到他们的名字上台领取文凭时，我从远处一个个认出了他们。哇，几年不见，他们比以前高大丰满了不少。

毕业典礼结束了，体育馆里立刻充满了欢声笑语。学生们在接受家人和朋友的祝贺，与他们一起合影留念。我从后排座位悄悄地走了下来，怯怯地靠近我的学生。学生们见到我以后，表情都很复杂，好像不相信自己的眼睛。他们并没有像美国孩子那样大喊大叫着跑过来拥抱我，而是呆呆地站在那里不知所措。这时

me as a teacher, "Teacher, it's '咖啡店,' not '咖啡点.'" It was not long before our relationship seemed more and more like friends.

Two years went by quickly. When I left Yilan, the students were all sad to see me go. They gave me so many gifts, and we all cried. When the COVID-19 pandemic is over, I plan to return to see my students. I hope they're all doing well. I also hope I can continue to improve my Chinese. Maybe the next time I return to Yilan, I will shock my students when they hear me speak Chinese.

On June 24, 2023, I am once again riding a bus toward Yilan. This time, I am going to see the students I haven't seen in seemingly forever, to attend their middle school graduation ceremony. Unlike last time, I'm not coming from Taipei to Yilan, but rather from Taichung. This is because in 2021 after going from Yilan to Stanford University, I discovered I had deeply fallen in love with Chinese. I decided to pursue Ph.D. program in preparation to hopefully become a Chinese literature professor and share my love of Chinese to my students. As a result, I'm currently in Taichung at Feng Chia University taking more Chinese classes.

The graduation ceremony was held in the school gym. In order to surprise my students, I didn't tell them in advance I would be coming. I quietly took a seat in the back row to watch the ceremony. Since I was so far from the stage, my students couldn't see me, but I could see

我的头脑里闪过一个问题：“他们是不是不记得我了？”答案很快就来了。那个一向胆大的学生奥斯卡走了过来，请我在他的毕业礼服上签字。他对我说：“Lauren, can you sign my uniform?”这时其他学生也慢慢地靠近了我，腼腆地跟我说话。当年分别的时候他们还是小孩子，现在已经是少年了。有的学生比我还高大，但是显得比我还害羞。他们小声地请我跟他们拍照留念，然后就很快地跑去找他们的朋友了。看得出来，我的出现带给他们巨大的惊喜，但是他们好像刻意不表现出来。这时一个始终非常害羞的女生来到我的身边，悄声对我说：“老师，谢谢你来参加我的毕业典礼，我真很开心见到你。”

时间像闪电一样飞快地过去了。我曾经的学生已经长大，跟我记忆中的样子很不一样了。感谢学生们让我跟中文结缘，祝福他们快乐和成功。

them on the stage clearly. As the principal called out their names to receive their diplomas, I recognized my students one by one from a distance. In the few years I hadn't seen them, they had grown much taller and plumper.

At the end of the ceremony, the gym was filled with laughter. Students were receiving congratulations from their parents and friends and taking photos together with them. From the back row, I timidly walked closer to my students. As soon as they saw me, their expressions changed as if they couldn't believe their eyes. They didn't come yelling and hugging me like American students might do, but stood dumbfounded. I had one question in my mind: "Do they remember me?" My answer came quickly when a particularly brave student named Oscar said to me, "Lauren, can you sign my uniform?" Afterwards, other students slowly came toward me and chatted with me shyly. When I had left, they were still children. But they became teenagers when I came back. Even though some of them were even taller than me, they were still shyer. They quietly asked me to take pictures with them before quickly scuttering off to their small groups of friends. I could tell I really surprised them, but they seemed to try to hide their moods. A girl who had always been incredibly shy stood by my side and said, "Teacher, thank you for coming to see our graduation. I'm really happy I could see you."

Time flashes by. My students have already grown up and are quite different from the way they were in my memories. I am grateful to my students who got me started in learning Chinese. I wish them happiness and success.

学好中文，传递幸运

作者：余静佳　指导教师：于丽萍　华盛顿大学（西雅图）

> 我要继续学好中文，传递幸运，毕业以后去帮助那些跟我小时候一样需要帮助的人。

在我出生之前，我的养父和养母就开始申请领养一个中国孤儿了。我 11 个月的时候，我的养母和姐姐飞到了中国云南省昆明市，把我带回了美国的明尼苏达州。我的养父是中国香港人，养母是美国白人。领养我之前，他们已经生了一个儿子和一个女儿，就是我的哥哥和姐姐。我养父这边的家人都说广东话，他自己没教过我们说广东话，但其实非常重视我的中文学习。

刚刚上小学的时候，养父母就让我参加了我们学校开设的中文班，从此开始了我的中文学习。后来无论是上初中还是上高中，我都继续选修中文。这期间我还陆续参加了 HSK、AP 和 IB 的考试，并且取得了不错的成绩。这些中文课程和考试都给我大学的中文课打下了坚实的基础。从小学到大学，学习中文的过程让我交到了很多好朋友，而且还培养了我的领导能力以及勤奋学习的习惯。所以对我来说，学中文当然划得来，而且我现在回想起来仍然觉得当初学中文是我和父母做得最好的决定之一。

作为一个被美国人领养的中国女孩子，学中文、了解中国文化对我有着特殊的意义，因为这能让我更好地了解我的身份背景。从小到大，我已经去过八次中国，去过两次我小时候待过的孤儿院，去看过 2008 年的北京奥运会，还跟我八年级的同学一起到过北京和长春。通过这几次旅行，中国给我留下了非常深刻的印象，也让我深深地爱上了中国。

Learning Chinese Well to Spread Fortune

Author: Jingjia McIntosh-Yee   Instructor: Liping Yu   University of Washington (Seattle)

> I'll continue to learn Chinese well and spread the fortune. After I graduate from college, I hope to help people who are in similar situations where I was once.

Before I was born, my adoptive parents had already applied to adopt a Chinese orphan. When I was eleven months old, my adoptive mother and sister flew to Kunming in Yunnan Province of China to pick me up and brought me back to Minnesota in the U.S. My adoptive father is from Hong Kong of China, while my adoptive mother is a white American. They had already had a son and a daughter – my brother and sister.

My dad's side of the family all speak Cantonese. My dad has never taught us Cantonese himself, but he has paid much attention to my Chinese learning.

When I was just in elementary school, my parents enrolled me in my school's Chinese class, marking the beginning of my Chinese learning journey. Afterwards, whether in junior high school or senior high school, I continued to study Chinese as an elective course. During this time, I also took the HSK, AP, and IB exams, and scored well on each of them. The Chinese courses and exams I took had prepared me for Chinese classes that I would eventually take in college. From elementary school to college, learning Chinese has allowed me to make a lot of new friends, develop my leadership skills, and learn to focus on studying. Therefore, learning Chinese is worthwhile for me, and I fully believe that it has been one of the best decisions my parents and I have made.

As a Chinese adoptee by Americans, learning Chinese language and culture has been immensely important to me because it has allowed me to better understand my identity and background. As I've grown up, I have had the privilege of being able to go back to China

我现在是华盛顿大学的学生，主攻中文专业和国际关系专业。我从小就希望能去中国工作和生活。我清楚自己肯定会面临各种各样的困难，但是我会坚持下去。在我看来，这是我继续练习用中文的最好的机会。我很想在孤儿院工作或者在那里当义工，因为我想要回馈社会。我生活的目标就是帮助别人，所以我也可以在一个国际民间组织找一份工作，帮助那些需要帮助的人，尤其是中国一些偏远落后地方的人们。

新冠疫情期间大家都在网上上课，在网上上课有很多困难，特别是学中文。有时候，我觉得学中文简直太难了，真的想过要放弃。然而，我的父母鼓励我继续学习，并且要我把学中文放在第一位。他们认为只有这样，我才能在中国找到一份能充分发挥自己的专业特长的工作。我很感谢我的养父养母，因为在他们的帮助下，我开始学习中文，并且有了各种各样的工作机会。

我一出生就变成了一个孤儿，这对一个孩子来说是很不幸的。但是我的养父养母领养了我，把我看成是他们的亲生女儿。他们送我上大学，鼓励我学中文。所以现在我又会说英文又会说中文。我觉得我是一个很幸运的人，因此，我要继续学好中文，传递幸运，毕业以后去帮助那些跟我小时候一样需要帮助的人。

eight times. Some of the trips have included: going to my orphanage twice, watching the 2008 Beijing Olympics, and going to Beijing and Changchun with my eighth-grade classmates. These trips have not only greatly impacted me, but have also allowed me to cultivate a deep appreciation for China.

Currently, I am a student at the University of Washington, double-majoring in Chinese and International Relations. Ever since I was young, I have wanted to eventually live and work in China. Although I know this course may come with a lot of obstacles and difficulty, I will hold on, primarily because it would be the best way to continue to learn and practice Chinese. I would really like to work or volunteer at an orphanage, because I want to give back to the greater community. My goal in life is just to help other people, so I also aspire to work for some sort of international non-governmental organization to help those who need it, especially people in China's rural areas.

During the COVID-19 pandemic, most of our classes were online, which was fairly difficult when I was enrolled in Chinese language classes. There were multiple times where I thought of just giving up because it was too hard for me to learn Chinese. However, my parents encouraged me to continue and put Chinese learning in the first place. They believed that only in this way, could I find a job that brings my specialty into full play. Thanks to the help and endless support from my parents, I started my Chinese-learning journey, and had various work opportunities.

Shortly after I was born, I became an orphan, which was very unfortunate for a child. But my parents adopted me and have treated me as their own daughter. They encouraged me to go to college and pursue studies in Chinese. As a result, I'm able to speak both English and Chinese now. I consider myself to be extremely fortunate, so I'll continue to learn Chinese well and spread the fortune. After I graduate from college, I hope to help people who are in similar situations where I was once.

我的中国笔友

作者：文理爱　指导教师：谭大立　北弗吉尼亚社区学院

> 我们相信跨文化交流能改善人与人之间的关系。

我从中学开始学中文，那个时候我就产生了学习语言的兴趣。虽然中文对我来说真的是个挑战，但是我还是非常热爱中文课。很可惜，我的高中没有高级中文课，我上大学之后又参加了各种各样的活动，所以我没有时间学习中文。当我发现我快要把学过的中文忘掉时，就赶紧报名参加了一门校外中文课。

那门课又重新燃起了我对中国语言和文化的好奇。老师安排了一个中美交流项目：每个学生都会先收到一个中国学生的联系方式，与中国学生一起合作完成一些关于跨文化问题的作业和谈话。除了跟我一起完成作业的中国学生外，我还有一位特殊的笔友，我和他的认识方式跟别人不一样。有个学生跟我说，他的朋友很希望跟一位美国学生联系，但是找不到合适的对象。我们两个人的交流不是一个“作业”，所以我们可以一起放松地聊天儿，后来自然而然地成为了好朋友。认识他是一种缘分，我们交流的经历给我留下了很深的印象。

最初交流不太方便。我起床的时候他已经睡觉了，很难找到时间聊天儿。幸运的是，我从小是“夜猫子”，所以我们在美国晚上九点左右开始发微信，凌晨两点停止。不同的作息时间使我们第一次意识到彼此的文化不一样。到现在我们还是觉得很好笑，因为很多个晚上他都劝我早点儿睡觉。他说中国家长很重视睡

My Chinese Pen Pal

Author: Raven Witherspoon Instructor: Dali Tan
Northern Virginia Community College

We believe cross-cultural communication can improve relationships between people.

I began studying Mandarin Chinese since middle school, which sparked my early interest in language learning. Although Chinese was challenging, I truly loved the Chinese class. Unfortunately, my high school lacked higher-level Chinese language courses. After entering college, I became involved in various activities and had no time to study Chinese. I quickly registered for a Chinese class beyond my regular course schedule as soon as I noticed how quickly I was forgetting what I had once learned.

That class renewed my curiosity about Chinese language and culture. The professor organized a Sino-U.S. language exchange program: each American student received the contact information of a Chinese student, and they worked together to discuss and complete cross-cultural assignments. Aside from the students I completed assignments with, I also had another pen pal. The way he and I met was different from that of other students. One of my partners told me his friend really wanted to contact with an American student, but he was unable to find the right one. Since the interactions between the two of us were not based on homework or assignments, we chatted casually and became good friends. Meeting him was a certain kind of fate; our interactions have left a deep impression on me.

In the very beginning, communication was not very convenient. He was often already asleep as I was just waking up; it was very difficult to find time to talk. Luckily, I've been a "night owl" since I was a child, so we began to send WeChat messages around nine o'clock in the evening New York time and end sometime around two in the morning. We first became

觉对身体的好处，常常会督促孩子早点儿睡觉。我比他大三岁，但他却常常假装扮演我的家长——这也是我们常开的玩笑。

我们的谈话在开始时是轻松的。讨论的话题包括学习内容、家庭怎么样、对什么感兴趣？有的时候我们分享生活体验，比如小时候最喜欢的糖、亲手做的早餐等。有一天，我告诉他，我感觉学习压力非常大，他听了以后，问我喜不喜欢熊猫，然后发给我一大堆可爱的熊猫抖音视频。我非常清楚他这样做就是为了给我减压。我也尽力帮助他做一些事情。譬如，他说，他没有很多机会旅游，去过的地方不多。所以我们家庭旅游的时候，我就发给他不少附近的风景照片——漂亮农田和各种各样的动植物。我们用这样的方式来分享人生的快乐，分担彼此的困难。

conscious of our cultural differences because of these daily working and resting habits. Even now we find this funny because there have been many nights when he encouraged me to sleep earlier. He told me that Chinese parents pay particular attention to the health benefits of sleep, and often urge their children to sleep earlier. A common joke between us is that, although I'm three years older than him, he often plays the role of my "parent."

When we began talking, our conversations were very relaxed. Topics of discussion included the content of our studies, the conditions of our families, and our own interests. Sometimes we would share life experiences, for example, our favorite candy from childhood, the breakfast we made that morning, etc. One day I told him I was very stressed about school, and after hearing this, he asked if I liked pandas, and then he sent me TikTok videos about adorable pandas. I understood explicitly that he did so in order to relieve my stress. I also did my best to help him in similar ways. For example, he expressed he had few chances to travel, so I began sending him many photographs of the sights around me – lovely fields, and all kinds of animals and plants – whenever my family traveled. We used these methods to share with each other the joys and sorrows of life.

"Have you seen this TV show? I don't know if it's available in your country." "I found it! I really liked the first episode." "Have you ever learned to play Chinese chess?" "No, I haven't learned yet. But I can find the rules online. Once I understand the rules, we can play together." We talked about pop music and sent each other our favorite songs. He unexpectedly asked me to sing him a song in exchange for him reading aloud his favorite ancient poem. I sent him a recording of me singing "可不可以." We slowly became friends in this way, yet we never sent photos of ourselves. I believe we both enjoy slowly sharing our hobbies and other details of life, the kinds of details that can't be seen in a photograph.

We slowly ventured into new territory. His passion for history left a deep impression on me because we both realized the importance of history at a very young age. Both of us believe that we can draw lessons from history. When comparing our countries, we both acknowledged the existence of massive gaps between them: Chinese history and culture has persisted for thousands of years, while America has only existed for fewer than three hundred years. I explained a few things in detail: that white supremacy remains deeply entrenched in my country

“这部电视剧你看过吗？不知道在你的国家能不能找到？”“找到了！我很喜欢第一集。”“你学会下棋了吗？”“还没学过，但是在网上能找到规则，看懂了规则，我们就可以一起玩儿了。”我们聊了流行音乐，就发给对方最喜欢的歌曲。没想到他请我给他唱歌。他发给我他自己朗读的最喜欢的古诗。我发给他自己唱的《可不可以》。我们就这样慢慢地成为了朋友。虽然已经成为了朋友，但是我们一直没给对方发自己的照片。我认为，我们都很享受跟别人慢慢分享各自的爱好等细节，而这些细节是在照片中看不到的。

我们慢慢地踩出了新的土地。他对历史的热爱留给我很深的印象，因为我也很早意识到历史的重要性。我们两个人都认为“历史值得借鉴”。比较我们的国家，我们都承认二者之间存在着巨大的差别：中国历史是几千年来一直延续的，而美国只存在了不到三百年。我仔细地给他解释，内战以后在美国的“白人至上论”仍然根深蒂固，影响着一代又一代的美国人，特别是像我父母这种“跨种族”结婚的人。他认真地思考这些观念，然后跟我分享他对中国内战的理解，包括余光中的《乡愁》。

我们的谈话越来越深刻，我们提出了一些还没跟本国朋友讨论过的话题。他向我袒露他每天感受到的学习压力，向我诉说无法逃避的考试对他日常生活的影响。我则向他表达对美国的不满。譬如，我不但担心贫富差距每年都在加剧，而且认为政府提供的服务不足以解决人民贫困的问题。我们用这样既慎重又有同情的方式，多方比较中美生活。

我们认为我们的关系十分独特，不但在复杂情况之中开始，而且还笼罩在国际疫情之下。由于这些情况，我们花了很长时间讨论中美关系、贸易竞争，还有糟糕的外交状态。虽然国家之间关系越来越紧张，但是我们的短信一向很温暖。他每次聊天儿都问，弗吉尼亚感染率怎么样，我的家人日子过得好不好，有没有需要的东西。在美国一边无法控制死亡率，一边又发生“反对戴口罩”的抗议时，

even after the American Civil War, which still impacts the lives of generation after generation, especially for those like my parents who are in an interracial marriage. He earnestly considered these perspectives, then shared with me his understanding of China's Civil War, including a poem by Yu Kwang-chung entitled "Nostalgia."

As our discussions grew deeper and deeper, we broached topics we hadn't even discussed with friends in our own countries. He expressed the pressure he faces when studying every day, and shared his frustration with what he perceived to be the inescapable impact of test scores in his daily life. I in return expressed my frustrations with America; not only my concern that the gap between the poor and the rich is widening, but also my fear that the government's actions are not sufficient to remedy the issues of poverty experienced by our people. In this tentative and empathetic way, we compared our lives in the U.S. and China.

I believe that our relationship is completely unique; not only did it begin under complicated circumstances; moreover, it has remained shrouded under the impacts of the global pandemic. As a result of these circumstances, we've spent much time discussing the Sino-U.S. relationship, the trade war, and the concerning state of diplomacy. Although the

他安慰了我。我听说他的家乡河北省疫情得以控制，学校又开学以后，我给他发信表示祝贺。这些体验让我们感受到交流的温暖，也让我们更相信，即使是国际朋友，也可能发展出很深厚的友谊。

我们相信跨文化交流能改善人与人之间的关系，因为我们两人的这条路已经走通了。这个经验给我勇气来申请清华大学苏世民书院，一个通过国际合作培养全球未来领导力的项目，来学习如何更好建立坚实的跨文化关系。对笔友体验而言，我最终的目的是想保持一辈子的朋友关系，而且持续努力增强跨文化的理解与交流。

relationship between our countries is becoming more and more tense, our texts are always very warm. He frequently asks how the pandemic situation in Virginia is, how my family is doing, and if we have everything we need. He comforted me when we in the U.S. were experiencing both an uncontrollable COVID death rate and simultaneous anti-mask protests. I celebrated with him when I heard that his home province of Hebei was finally able to control the spread of the virus and his school was able to reopen. These personal experiences have allowed me to feel the warmth of our exchanges, and made me more firmly believe that even across borders one can develop profound friendships.

We believe cross-cultural communication can improve relationships between people because we have already walked this road. This experience gave me the courage to apply to Tsinghua University's Schwarzman Scholars Program, an international cooperation meant to develop global leadership in order to better establish and maintain cross-cultural relationships. As for my experience with my pen pal, my ultimate desire is to maintain a lifelong friendship, and to continue to work hard to strengthen intercultural understanding and exchange.

助人为乐，乐在心里

作者：柯洁西　指导教师：温晓虹　休斯敦大学

> 这件帮助中国人的事情让我更想学好中文。

我最喜欢的一个成语是“助人为乐”，意思是帮助别人是一种乐趣。我从小就喜欢帮助同学或者做义工。我常常会注意到有人需要帮忙，无论是在学习上帮同学解决数学问题，还是在生活中朋友有困难了，我都主动去帮助。我的专业是生物和中文，我想当一个医生帮助不同的病人，特别是从中国来的病人。虽然我没有去过中国，但是在今天的这个小世界，我居然有机会用我的中文帮助中国人！

我的第一份工作是在一家意大利餐厅。我找工作的时候，老板问我会什么语言。我告诉他英文、西班牙文，还有中文。于是我得到了这份工作！虽然这是一个意大利餐厅，但是常常有中国人光临。他们很多都不会说英文，我就成了他们的翻译和助手。常常是一些很简单的事，比如他们想用筷子吃饭，我就去给他们找筷子。有时候会回答一些关于饮食习惯的问题，更多的时候我会跟他们用中文聊一会儿天儿，让他们感到宾至如归。让顾客高兴是我的愿望，因为我特别喜欢开心的顾客。

有一次，一位中国老人匆匆忙忙地来到我们的餐厅。进来以后他好像在找人而不是要点餐。经理看见他那么着急，就去跟他打招呼，可是这位老人不会说也听不懂英文。经理于是把我叫过来，让我帮助他。我心里又高兴又有一点儿紧张。我上前跟他打招呼。原来他来我们餐厅真的不是为了吃饭，而是因为他迷路了。

It Is My Pleasure to Help

Author: Giselle Campos Instructor: Xiaohong Wen University of Houston

> Being able to help others makes me want to study Chinese even more.

One of my favorite idioms to use is "助人为乐," which means "find it a pleasure to help others." Since I was little, I enjoyed helping classmates and doing volunteer work. When I notice people who need a hand, whether it is a classmate struggling to solve a math problem or a friend who is going through a challenging time, I will take the initiative to offer help. My majors are Biology and Chinese Studies. In the future, I want to become a doctor helping various patients, especially the ones from China. Although I have never been to China, in today's small world, I have opportunities to use Chinese to help people.

My first job was at an Italian restaurant. When I looked for a job, the boss asked me what languages I could speak. I told him I could speak English, Spanish, and Chinese, and I ended up getting the job! Even though it was an Italian restaurant, there were often Chinese customers. Many of them could not speak English, and I would help them translate and assist them. It was simple things like if someone wanted to use chopsticks, I would help them get them. Sometimes I would answer questions about eating habits. Often, I would use Chinese to chat with them to make them feel at home. Making others happy is my wish, because I like happy customers a lot.

One time, an old Chinese man came to the restaurant in a hurry. After entering, he seemed like he was looking for someone. Seeing the anxious look on his face, the manager went to greet him. The old man only looked at him confused. He did not understand what the manager was saying. That was because the old man could not speak English. Therefore, the manager

他说他在这儿走了好久，但怎么也找不到回家的路了。他没有办法了，才来到我们餐厅，看看会不会有中国人能帮助他。我虽然不是中国人，但我能听懂他说的，而且我也学过中文的方位词和指路的句子。他问我，去奥格登大道应该走哪个方向？从这条街怎么走？虽然那条街我没去过，但我帮他查手机、看地图、指方向。我要把路线给他画下来，所以问他家的具体地址。但是这位中国老人说他也不知道地址，只是能认出他家附近的样子和他家的门。他本来打算叫出租车请司机开车转悠，直到他看到他所熟悉的路。但这时天已经黑了，恐怕他自己也看不

called me over to help him. In my heart, I was both happy and nervous. I went to welcome him and asked him what I could do for him. It turned out that he came to our restaurant because he was lost. He said he had been walking around here for a long time, but could not find his way home. All he wanted was to go home. Not knowing how to get back on his own, he came in to see if there was a Chinese person in our restaurant. Although I am not Chinese, I understood what he was saying and I have learned how to give directions in Chinese. The old man asked me which direction on Ogden Avenue to go, and where he should start walking. Even though I had never been to the street he mentioned, I still tried to help him check the map on my phone and point him in the direction he wanted to go. I planned to draw him the route to take, so I asked him if he could tell me the exact address of his house. However, the old man said he did not know the address either, but could only recognize his neighborhood and the door of his house. He told me he had planned to call a taxi and let the driver continue driving in the general direction of his home until he saw a familiar road. However, by this time, it was already dark, and I was afraid he would not be able to see the streets or his house clearly, and he would get lost again. I determined that the safer option was to contact his family. So, I asked for his son's phone number to reach him. After the phone rang a couple of times, his son answered. Hearing me talking to his son, the old man immediately became happy. I told him the restaurant's address, and his son said he was coming to pick up his father soon. This time I heard a sigh of relief from the old man.

This situation made me remember my great-grandmother. She often found herself in difficult circumstances because she spoke a different language from others. It is because of her that I know the importance of language. When people like my great-grandmother have trouble, having someone there to communicate with can make hard things a little easier. It is a pleasant thing if one's effort can make another's life a little easier! So, it gives me immense pride and joy to be able to do something for that old Chinese man because it felt like I was helping my great-grandmother.

Being able to help others makes me want to study Chinese even more. To improve my

清街道，看不清他家的门，会再次迷路。所以我决定直接跟他的家人联系。我们问他要了他儿子的电话号码，直接给他儿子打电话。因为已经是黑夜，这样做是最安全的。我给他儿子打电话，他儿子真的接电话了！这时我看到老人立刻开心起来。我告诉他我们餐厅的地址，他儿子说很快来接他的父亲。这时我听到这位老人长出了一口气。

这件事件让我想起我的曾外祖母，她经常会遇到麻烦，因为她说的语言跟别人不同。所以我知道语言的重要性。如果像我曾外祖母这样的人在遇到麻烦的时候，有一个人也会他们说的那种语言，并且乐意帮助他们，他们的生活可能就不那么困难了。因为一个人的努力可以让别人方便点儿，那真是一件让人很快乐的事情！所以我为那位中国老人提供了帮助，这给了我极大的自豪感和喜悦，因为这感觉就像有人帮助了我的曾外祖母一样。

这件帮助中国人的事情让我更想学好中文。为了提高中文水平，我特意去找中国人，跟他们交朋友，跟他们练习中文，同时也帮助他们提高他们的英文水平。我还学到了另一个成语——“举手之劳”。就是在别人感谢你的帮助时，可以说这个（当然说“不客气”也是可以的）。用我的中文帮助别人，真的让我乐在心里！

Chinese proficiency, I have made several friends from China. I would practice Chinese with them and, at the same time, help them improve their English. Through this, I also learned a useful Chinese idiom used when others thank you for your help; it means "it is no problem at all," (of course saying "you're welcome" is also good). It is a great pleasure for me to help others using my Chinese!

我的中国老朋友

作者：范贝琳　指导教师：温晓虹　休斯敦大学

> 世界又这样小，我要跟中国人交朋友的愿望就在我的家门口实现了！

我的中国老朋友叫李奕辰。他之所以是我的老朋友，不是因为我们认识了很多年，而是因为他比我年长很多。李先生没有什么头发，剩下的几根头发是银白色的。虽然在年初李先生掉了几颗牙齿，但他的笑容让人感到非常温暖。

我一直都记得我们是怎么认识的。那是2014年夏，我们搬到了新家。全家每个人都欢天喜地的，不仅仅是我和三个姐姐每个人都有了自己的房间，更因为这是我们在美国的第一个家！我们每天都忙着布置我们的房间，整理院子。有一天，突然有人敲门，我正纳闷儿谁会知道我们搬了家呢？一开门才发现，原来是隔壁的邻居。他看上去像一位亚裔，一位独居老人，上门向我们表示热烈欢迎。

第一次与这位邻居交谈时，我注意到他的英语很有限。我的父母也不会说流利的英语，但仍然尽力努力和邻居交谈。虽然我们肤色不同，语言也不同，但我们都是新移民。他走后我们开始猜他的母语是什么，越南语、日语、韩语……？我们心里一直在猜，但总不好意思问。日子一天一天地过去，直到我上了大学，又重新开始学起中文来，我忽然好奇地想，他可能是一个中国人。如果是，我的中文就有用了！

每隔一段时间，这位邻居就会敲开我们的门，给我们带来惊喜，比如他会送给我们燕麦片和亚洲梨。

My Old Chinese Friend

Author: Belén Fajardo Instructor: Xiaohong Wen University of Houston

Yet, we live in such a small world that my wish to become friends with a Chinese person came true right at my doorstep!

My old Chinese friend is called Yichen Lee. He is my old friend not because we have known each other for many years, but because he is much older than me. Mr. Lee doesn't have a lot of hair and the few hairs he has left are white. Although Mr. Lee lost a few teeth at the beginning of the year, his smile is still very warm.

I always remember how we met. It was the summer of 2014 when we moved to a new house. Everyone in my family was overjoyed, not only because my three sisters and I each had our own room, but also because it was our first home in America! We spent our days decorating our rooms and tidying up the yard. One day, we suddenly heard someone knocking on the door, and I wondered who knew we had moved in. I opened the door and found out it was the next-door neighbor! He looked like an Asian man, an elderly man who lived alone, and gave us a warm welcome at the door.

The first time I spoke with our neighbor, I noticed that his English was very limited. My parents did not speak fluent English either, but still tried their best so that they could talk with the neighbor. Although our race was different and we spoke different languages, we were both new immigrants. After he left, we started to wonder what his native language was. Vietnamese, Japanese, or Korean? We tried to guess but were too embarrassed to ask. Time flew by and it wasn't until I went to college that I started to learn Chinese again. Suddenly, I wondered if Mr. Lee might be Chinese. If so, my Chinese would be useful!

他说话不多，说几句话，就会笑着说：“对你的身体有好处！”

他来时常常带着他的小狗，小狗在他身后耐心地等待着。每次看到他的狗，我都很想去抚摸它。我爸爸告诉他，我很喜欢他的狗。邻居一听很高兴，就让我们抚摸他的狗。我问他狗的名字，邻居居然说它叫“女女”。我一听小狗的名字像是中文，就跟邻居说起中文来。他果然是中国人，因为他能听懂我的中文！那是我最高兴的一天，因为我终于有机会跟一个中国人用中文谈话了！他也很高兴，因为他没想到我会说中文！

Every now and then, our neighbor would knock on our door and surprise us with things like oatmeal and Asian pears.

He didn't talk much, but when he did, he would smile and say, "It's good for your health!"

Mr. Lee often brought his dog with him. When he came over to talk to us, his dog waited behind him patiently. Every time I saw his dog, I wanted to pet her, but was always scared to do so. My dad ended up telling Mr. Lee that I was fond of his dog. He was very happy to hear that and let us pet his dog. I asked him what the dog's name was and the neighbor replied saying her name was Nvnv. As soon as I noticed that the dog's name was Chinese, I spoke Chinese to our neighbor. Sure enough, he is Chinese because he could understand my Chinese! I was so glad finding this out because I finally had the chance to talk to a Chinese person in Chinese! He, too, was happy because he didn't expect me to speak Chinese!

Chinese, our common language, made it easier for me to become friends with our neighbor and shortened the distance between our family and the old man. There were times when I tried to talk to him in Chinese. For instance, when he came out to get the mail, when he was out walking, or whenever we met, we greeted each other in Chinese. Last spring, my father was diagnosed with cancer. After Mr. Lee found out, he showed special concern. When he came by our house, he sometimes spoke Chinese and then I became the interpreter. One evening, when my dad and I were out in the front yard, Mr. Lee came over to talk to us. Mr. Lee knew that the situation we were facing was tough. He asked my dad how he was doing with the treatments to fight off the cancer. Unfortunately, all my dad could say was that he was trying his best. Mr. Lee slowly nodded, sympathizing with my father's feelings.

That was when he said: "I have something for you! Wait for me right here."

My dad and I looked at each other in surprise, wondering what Mr. Lee had for my dad. After a few minutes, Mr. Lee came out with what looked like a bottle in his hands. "Here, these are vitamins that will help you get stronger. We immigrants have to take care of each other, you know," said Mr. Lee with a smile on his face. He began to tell us about his childhood in China and how he traveled to many different places when he was young. During our interaction, I

中文，我们的共同语言，让我和这位老人交上了朋友，也把我们全家和这位中国老人的距离拉近了。我找机会跟他聊天儿，比如他出来拿信或是在外边散步，见面时我们都用中文打招呼。去年春天，我父亲得了癌症，他知道后，特别关心。他到我家来，有时会说中文，我就成了翻译。一天晚上，我和爸爸在房子的前院，李先生过来和我们谈话。李先生知道我们所面临的情况很艰难。他问我爸爸在抗击癌症的治疗中表现如何。不幸的是，我爸爸只能说，他正在尽力。李先生慢慢地点点头，非常同情我爸爸的感受。这时他说："我有东西给你！请你在这里等我，在这里等我。"

我和我爸爸惊讶地看着对方，想知道李先生有什么东西给我爸爸。几分钟后，李先生从他家出来了，手里拿着一个瓶子。"给你。这些是一些维生素，可以让你变得更强壮。我们移民必须互相照顾，你知道的。"李先生笑着说。他开始向我们讲述他在中国的童年，以及他年轻时如何到许多不同的地方旅行。我将李先生说的中文翻译给我爸爸，然后把我爸爸说的西班牙语译成中文转告李先生。我爸爸和李先生分享了他们作为移民在美国所面临的许多困难，我们的谈话帮助我们更好地理解对方。我的中文把不同种族的人联系起来，这让我很高兴，也很自豪。

自从学习了中文以后，我一直都想去中国，想跟中国人交朋友。但是由于疫情，我这么多年的愿望一直还没有实现。让我没想到的是，我却跟我的邻居——一位中国老人，交了朋友！世界如此之大，我想去看看太平洋彼岸的中国，但太远了，我去不了。世界又这样小，我要跟中国人交朋友的愿望就在我的家门口实现了！

translated what Mr. Lee was saying to my father, and then translated what my father was saying in Spanish to Mr. Lee in Chinese. My father and Mr. Lee shared many of the same struggles that they faced as immigrants in the United States. Our conversations helped us understand each other more. My Chinese allowed people of different races to connect and have more friendship when they are together. This made me feel very happy and proud.

Since learning Chinese, I have always wanted to go to China, especially to try to make friends with Chinese people. However, because of the epidemic, my wish of so many years could not come true. What I didn't expect was that I would become friends with my neighbor – an old Chinese man! I wanted to travel across the Pacific Ocean to go to China, but it is too far for me to go since the world is so big. Yet, we live in such a small world that my wish to become friends with a Chinese person came true right at my doorstep!

拒绝他人的礼物

作者：詹家睿　指导教师：朱永平　圣母大学

中国古代有两个关于拒绝收礼的故事。

> 君子洁身自好。

从前有人送给郑国宰相一条鱼，郑国宰相并未接受。有人问郑国宰相："您平常喜欢吃鱼，为什么你不接受别人送的鱼呢？"郑国宰相回答道："正是因为我喜爱鱼，所以不接受鱼。接受赠送的鱼会丢失官职，失去俸禄也就没有鱼可吃了。"

曾子穿着很破旧的衣服在耕田，鲁国的国君派人去，要封给他一块土地，曾子坚决不接受。再送来，曾子还是不接受。使者说："这又不是先生您向人要求的，是国君送给您的，您为什么不接受？"曾子说："我听说，接受别人馈赠的人就会害怕得罪馈赠者；给了人家东西的人，就会对接受东西的人显露傲慢的神色。那么，就算国君赏赐我土地而不对我显露一点儿傲慢的神色，但我能不因此而害怕得罪他吗？"

郑国宰相和曾子都谢绝了他人赠送的礼物，但是除此之外他们的故事有什么异同呢？这两个故事虽然在明面上有很多相似的部分，不过我认为这两个故事的差别非常大。本文将要分析郑国宰相和曾子拒绝礼物的原因，同时还会把这两个故事跟两个伊索寓言做比较。

郑国宰相拒绝他人赠送的礼物有两个原因：第一是因为他拒绝腐败，他知道腐败是不道德的事情；第二是他不想因为接受眼前的礼物而失去职位和薪水。从经济学的角度来看，第二个原因是更重要的。他认为接受他人礼物是一种短期

Refusing Gifts from Others

Author: Margaret Rauch Instructor: Yongping Zhu University of Notre Dame

> A gentleman resists evil and avoids immorality.

There are two ancient Chinese stories about refusing gifts.

Once upon a time, someone gave the Chancellor of the State of Zheng a fish, but the Chancellor did not accept it. Someone asked the Chancellor of Zheng about this, saying "Sir, you usually like to eat fish. Why won't you accept the fish given to you?" The Chancellor of Zheng replied, "It is because I love fish that I do not accept the fish. Accepting a gift of a fish would mean that I would lose my official position. Without my government salary, I would have no fish to eat."

Zengzi was wearing shabby clothes and ploughing a field when a messenger from the ruler of the State of Lu arrived to grant him a piece of land. However, Zengzi firmly refused to accept it. When the message was sent again, Zengzi still did not accept it. The messenger said, "Sir, this is not something you asked others for, but something someone else has offered you. Why will you not accept it?" Zengzi said, "I have heard it said that one who accepts a gift will be afraid of offending the giver, and that he who gives will show arrogance toward him that receives. So, even if the king grants me land without expressing the slightest bit of arrogance toward me, can I not be afraid of offending him because of this?"

The Chancellor of Zheng and Zengzi both politely refused gifts from others, but how can their stories be compared beyond this? Although these two stories have many similarities on the surface, I think that they are actually very different. This essay will analyze the reasons why the Chancellor of Zheng and Zengzi refused gifts and compare these two stories with two of Aesop's Fables.

利益，而拒绝礼物是一种长期投资。虽然郑国宰相很聪明地拒绝了他人的礼物，不过他的理由是自私的。他希望得到最大的利益，根据这个原则，他才决定拒绝礼物。

郑国宰相的故事让我想到一个伊索寓言。一个樵夫不慎把斧头掉到了河里，找不到了。这是樵夫赖以生存的唯一工具，所以他在河边伤心地哭了起来。天神

The Chancellor of Zheng refused a gift from others for two reasons. The first is because he refused to be corrupt, knowing that corruption is an immoral thing. The second is because he did not want to accept the gift at hand only to lose his position and salary. From an economic standpoint, the second reason is most important. The Chancellor believed that accepting gifts from others was a short-term benefit, while refusing gifts was a long-term investment. Although the Chancellor of Zheng smartly refused others' gifts, his reasons were selfish. He hoped to achieve the greatest profit, and it was based on this principle that he decided to refuse the gift.

The Chancellor of Zheng's story reminds me of one of Aesop's Fables. A woodcutter accidently dropped his axe into a river and could not find it. This was the only tool the woodcutter relied on for his survival, so he cried in grief on the riverbank. The god Hermes happened to pass by and see this, so he asked the woodcutter why he was so sad. The woodcutter said that his axe had fallen into the river, so he had no way to cut firewood for a living. After hearing the woodcutter's story, the god Hermes said, "Don't worry. I'll go help you get your axe back." Upon saying this, Hermes dived under water. In a short time, Hermes came out of the water holding an axe made of gold and asked the woodcutter, "Is this axe yours?" The woodcutter replied honestly, "It is not mine." Hermes dived under the water again to look for the axe. This time, he dredged up an axe made of silver from under the water and asked the woodcutter, "Is this axe yours?" The woodcutter replied honestly, "It is also not mine." Hermes dived under the water once again. When he returned this time, he held the woodcutter's axe in his hand. The woodcutter said, "That's my axe! Thank you!" The god Hermes admired the woodcutter's honesty, so he returned the woodcutter's axe to him, while giving him the gold and silver axes as well.

To a certain extent, I think that the Chancellor of Zheng is very much like the woodcutter in the story from Aesop's Fables. Both of them are very honest, so they do not want what does not belong to them. Precisely because of this, they both secure future wealth. However, there is an important difference between these two stories: the Chancellor of Zheng knows that he will obtain more money in the future if he refuses the gift, but the woodcutter did not want what was not his despite not knowing if Hermes would help him find his axe or not. Thus,

赫尔墨斯恰好路过，就问樵夫为什么这么悲伤。樵夫说斧头掉到河里找不到了，他没有办法砍柴度日。赫尔墨斯说：“别着急，我去帮你把斧头找回来。”说完，赫尔墨斯就潜到了水底。不一会儿工夫，赫尔墨斯从水中出来了，手里拿着一把金子做的斧头，问樵夫：“这把斧头是不是你的？”樵夫诚实地回答：“那不是我的。”赫尔墨斯又潜到水底找斧头，他从水底捞出了一把银子做的斧头，问樵夫：“这把斧头是不是你的？”樵夫诚实地回答：“那也不是我的。”赫尔墨斯再次潜到水底，这次回来时，他手里举着樵夫的斧头。樵夫说：“这才是我的斧头！谢谢你！”赫尔墨斯很佩服樵夫的诚实，他把樵夫的斧头还给了他，同时还把金斧头和银斧头也送给了他。

我认为郑国宰相在一定程度上很像伊索寓言故事中的樵夫。他们两个都很诚实，所以他们都不要不属于自己的东西。恰恰因为这样，他们两个都保证了未来的财富。不过这两个故事有一个很重要的差异：郑国宰相知道如果他拒绝礼物，他将来会能得到更多的钱，但是樵夫不要不属于自己的东西，他不知道赫尔墨斯会不会帮助他找到自己的斧头。因此这两个故事都强调诚实的重要性，但是郑国宰相清楚眼前的利益与长远的利益不能相比，而樵夫却是根本不接受不属于自己的东西。

曾子不接受礼物的原因跟郑国宰相的原因不一样。因为如果郑国宰相接受他人的礼物，他就会失去长久的富贵，不过如果贫穷的曾子接受君王赠送他的一大片土地，他就会享有无尽的财富。如果曾子相信郑国宰相的财富最大化的道理，他就会接受君王赠给他的土地。不过，曾子却认为，如果他接受了礼物，他就会害怕送给他礼物的人，而送给他礼物的人也可能会看不起他。曾子不希望因为接受别人的礼物而受到别人的控制。对曾子来说，个人的独立和信誉是最重要的。

曾子的故事让我想到另一个伊索寓言。天神朱庇特结婚，邀请所有动物来参加婚宴，跟他一起庆祝。每个动物都带来了一份礼物送给朱庇特。蛇给朱庇特

both stories emphasize the importance of honesty, but the Chancellor of Zheng knows that immediate profit cannot be compared with long-term gain, whereas the woodcutter simply does not want to accept what does not belong to him.

Zengzi's reasons for not accepting the gift were different from the Chancellor of Zheng's. If the Chancellor of Zheng accepted the gift offered, he would lose wealth in the long run. However, if Zengzi who was poor accepted the large piece of land given to him by the king, he would enjoy inexhaustible wealth. If Zengzi believed in the Chancellor of Zheng's principle of maximizing wealth, he would have accepted the land given to him by the king. However, Zengzi believed that if he accepted the gift, he would fear the person who gave him the gift, and the person who gave him the gift might look down on him. Zengzi did not want to be controlled by others because he accepted their gifts. In Zengzi's opinion, personal independence and honor were of the greatest importance.

Zengzi's story reminds me of another one of Aesop's Fables. When the god Jupiter

带来了一朵玫瑰，不过朱庇特谢绝了蛇的礼物。朱庇特拒绝礼物的原因并不是因为他不喜欢蛇的礼物，而是因为他知道如果他接受了蛇的礼物，就会欠蛇一个人情。朱庇特不要欠不好的动物的账，因为欠人的账将来就会很难公正执法。

这个故事跟曾子的故事很相像。曾子和朱庇特因为类似的原因而谢绝了他人的礼物。他们都不要欠别人的人情账，也不要受别人的控制。不过这两个故事也有很大的差别：在伊索寓言中，送礼物者的社会地位很低下，而谢绝礼物的是天神；但在曾子的故事里，送礼的人是君王，而谢绝礼物的是平头百姓。对朱庇特来说，玫瑰是一件可有可无的东西；但是对曾子来说，君王赠送的一块土地可能让他一辈子衣食无忧。由此可见，曾子的人品是非常高尚的。

郑国宰相和曾子他们二人都拒绝了他人赠送的礼物，但是从道德上看，哪一个更值得我们敬重呢？虽然郑国宰相的选择也算是道德高尚，但是我认为他的目的是自私的，因此我不欣赏他的做法。相比较而言，我更敬重曾子。虽然某一件事会帮你积累财富或提高你的社会地位，但如果你需要牺牲你的名誉的话，你就不应该做。这就是君子洁身自好。

was married, he invited all the animals to his wedding feast. He invited each animal to come celebrate with him. Each animal brought a gift for Jupiter. The snake brought Jupiter a rose, but Jupiter declined the snake's gift. The reason that Jupiter declined was not because he did not like the snake's gift, but because he knew that if he accepted it, he would owe the snake a favor. Jupiter did not want to owe a debt to a bad animal, because owing debts to others would make it difficult for him to enforce the law justly in the future.

This story is very similar to Zengzi's story. Zengzi and Jupiter declined the gifts of others for similar reasons. They both did not want to owe favors to others or be controlled by others. However, there is also an important difference between these stories: in the story from Aesop's Fables, the gift giver's social status is low, while the person refusing the gift is a god. However, in Zengzi's story, the gift giver is a king, while the person refusing the gift is a commoner. From Jupiter's perspective, a rose is a dispensable thing; to Zengzi, the king's gift of a piece of land could give him financial security for the rest of his life. Thus, it can be seen that Zengzi's moral character was very noble.

Both the Chancellor of Zheng and Zengzi refused gifts from others, but which one is more deserving of our respect from a moral point of view? Although the Chancellor of Zheng's choice is morally upstanding, I think that his motives were selfish, so I do not admire his approach. In comparison, I respect Zengzi more. Although something will help you accumulate wealth or increase your social standing, you should not do it if it will cause you to sacrifice your reputation. This is how a gentleman resists evil and avoids immorality.

我的中国男朋友

作者：史秀雅　指导教师：顾利程　西北大学

> 有了中国男朋友以后，我每年能过两次“情人节”。

我叫 Sydney Smith，中文名字是史秀雅。我学汉语学了三年了，而我跟我的中国男朋友也交往三年了。现在大家明白我为什么努力地学汉语了吧。三年了，真是有许多甜酸苦辣。现在趁他不在，我给大家讲一讲我中国男朋友的优点和缺点吧，此外再介绍一下找中国男朋友的诀窍。

我的男朋友有很多优点和缺点。我还是先说一说他的优点吧。他的优点太多了，三天三夜也讲不完。我简单说三条吧。第一，他肯定比我以前的美国男朋友更爱我。有了中国男朋友以后，我每年能过两次“情人节”。二月十四日是美国的 Valentine's Day，这一天，我的中国男朋友会给我送花，送巧克力。七夕是中国情人相会的日子。我的男朋友也一定会带我出去吃饭，给我买礼物。所以农历七月初七这一天，我是美国女孩子里最得意的一个。

他的第二个优点是他很会做中国菜。跟他交往以来，我随时可以吃到地道可口的中国菜。他的拿手好菜是宫保鸡丁，真是又辣又香，吃了以后浑身是汗，完全可以抵御芝加哥冬天的狂风暴雪。我们不做饭的时候，还可以一起去地道的中国饭馆大吃一顿。我的男朋友很会点菜。他点出来的一桌菜荤素搭配，咸淡可口，还经济实惠。最突出的一点是，我们出去吃饭，他从来不要我付钱，他认为 AA 制有损他中国男子汉的英雄形象。这恐怕是我妈妈最喜欢他的一点。没有办法，我只好给他多买礼物，作为补偿。

My Chinese Boyfriend

Author: Sydney Smith　Instructor: Licheng Gu　Northwestern University

I've got to celebrate Valentine's Day twice every year since I have my Chinese boyfriend.

I am Sydney Smith. My Chinese name is Shi Xiuya. I have been studying Chinese for three years, and I have been dating my Chinese boyfriend for three years. Now you understand why I study Chinese hard. Three years have passed. I have mixed feelings about my Chinese boyfriend. While he is not around, let me tell you his strengths and shortcomings. On top of that, I will also share with you the tricks in finding a Chinese boyfriend.

My Chinese boyfriend has many strengths and shortcomings. Let me start with his strengths. He has countless strengths. Undoubtedly, my Chinese boyfriend loves me much more than my former American boyfriend. I've got to celebrate Valentine's Day twice every year since I have my Chinese boyfriend. February 14 is American Valentine's Day, when my boyfriend sends me flowers and chocolates. July 7 of Chinese Lunar calendar is the Chinese Valentine's Day. He takes me to a restaurant and buys me presents. I am the luckiest American girl on this day.

The second strength of my boyfriend is that he is very good at cooking Chinese dishes. Ever since I started dating him, I can always enjoy authentic and delicious Chinese food. My favorite dish is his Kung Pao Chicken. It is spicy and hot just right and it tastes great. After eating it, I sweat all over my body and feel hot enough to go outside and deal with the winter snowstorm in Chicago. When we do not cook, he takes me to a genuine Chinese restaurant. He knows very well what to order. They are always a balanced combination of vegetables and

他的第三个优点是他非常懂礼貌。他到我的家里来做客从来都不空手，总是带一些有中国特色的小礼物送给我的爸爸、妈妈。他进屋第一件事就是脱鞋，这让我那有洁癖的妈妈非常满意。他也从来不大大咧咧地叫我妈妈 Mary，叫我爸爸 John。他一定礼貌地称呼他们 Mrs. Smith，Mr. Smith，绝对是一个谦谦君子，所以我的爸爸、妈妈都非常喜欢他，接受他。

有了中国男朋友以后，我显得比以前幸福多了，所以别的朋友总是问我怎样才能找到一个中国男朋友。我的诀窍是，如果你喜欢的中国男同学生病了，你一定要去看望他。看他的时候，建议他“多喝热水，多休息”。你只要这么一说，他很快就会爱上你了。因为在中国他生病的时候，他的妈妈都是这样安抚他。现在他在美国，妈妈不在身边，你这么一说，他就把你当成他的妈妈了。每个人多少都有一些恋母情结哦。当然，学一点儿汉语也非常有帮助。这样你就能听懂他在说什么了。

meat. And they don't have to cost much. The most important part is he never allows me to pay my share. He thinks that going Dutch with his girlfriend damages his pride as a Chinese man. Maybe this is what my mother likes him most. To compensate that, I have to buy him a lot of presents.

The third strength of my boyfriend is he is always polite and courteous. Whenever he comes to visit me at home, he brings some Chinese gifts to my parents. He always takes his shoes off as soon as he comes into the house. This makes my mother, who is very fussy about cleanness, very happy. He does not call my mother "Mary" or call my father "John." He calls them "Mrs. Smith" and "Mr. Smith." A real gentleman. Therefore, my parents liked him and accepted him immediately.

Ever since I dated a Chinese boyfriend, I appeared happier than before, so people ask me ALL THE TIME how to find a Chinese boyfriend. Well, here is my secret method. Wait for the guy you like to get sick, and then visit him and tell him to drink more hot water and have a good rest. The moment you say those words, he will fall in love with you. When he fell ill back in China, his mother would always say that to him. Now he is in the U.S., and his mother is not with him. He is now taking you as his mother. After all, all men have more or less Oedipus complex. Of course, you will understand him better if you can speak some Chinese.

OK. I need to stop here. I hope you can find your own Chinese boyfriend as you wish. Oh wait, I forgot to talk about the shortcomings of my Chinese boyfriend. Well, of course he has shortcomings, some big shortcomings. First of all, due to the difference in language and culture, I sometimes don't understand what he said. Even though we've been dating for three years, some of his family still don't know that he has a girlfriend, much less that she is American. It looks like he may not care enough of me.

On the one hand, it looks like he does not care enough of me; but on the other hand, it looks he cares too much of me. He cares if I talk a little more to another male student. He would become unhappy and wears a long face. Therefore, when my Chinese language teacher needs to arrange us Chinese language partners to practice Chinese, I have to request to have a

好的，就讲这些吧。我希望大家能找到一个称心如意的中国男朋友。哎呀，我忘了还应该讲一讲我中国男朋友的缺点呢。他当然有缺点，有很大的缺点。首先，由于语言和文化的不同，有时候我不懂他在说什么。还有，虽然我们交往三年了，可是他有些家人还不知道他有女朋友了，更不知道这个女朋友是一个美国姑娘。他可能不太重视我吧。

我的中国男朋友一方面可能不太重视我，可是另一方面他好像又太重视我了。他的心思很重。他不希望我跟别的男生有过多交往。我如果跟哪个男同学接触多了一点儿，只是一点点啊，他就一脸的不高兴。没有办法，当老师给我们安排汉语语伴时，我只好要老师给我安排一个女生语伴。真不好意思。

这就是我的中国男朋友。当你决定是不是要找一个中国男朋友的时候，想想他们的优点和缺点哟。

female partner. I feel so embarrassed when I made the request.

Well, this is my Chinese boyfriend. When you consider dating a Chinese boyfriend, think about their strengths and shortcomings.

中国式相亲

作者：韩娜　指导教师：顾利程　西北大学

> 很多未婚青年的父母都会聚集在人民公园替孩子相亲，寻找合适的结婚对象。

在中国留学的时候，我和同学们利用假期一起去上海旅游。听说上海的人民公园很特别，那里有中国最有名的相亲角，是中国最大的征婚广场。从 2004 年开始，每逢星期六、星期天，从中午到下午五点，很多未婚青年的父母都会聚集在人民公园替孩子相亲，寻找合适的结婚对象。如今上海人民公园的相亲角已经享誉全球，所以我们几个美国同学决定到那里一探究竟。

我们到人民公园的时候，已经是下午两点了。虽然不知道相亲角在哪里，但是我们随着人流，很快就找到了。相亲角人头攒动，很多人在那里交谈着。我们看到不少五六十岁的家长坐在那里，为他们的孩子征婚。家长们把孩子的信息写在纸板上，随身带来。信息牌有的放在地上，有的挂在树和树之间的绳子上，有的贴在撑开的雨伞上。我们走近一看，发现上面写着征婚人的年龄、身高、学历、工作、资产。当然还有希望对方应该是什么样的条件，譬如希望有上海户口，有房有车，一米六五以上等等。这些家长坐在自己带的折叠椅上，紧挨着自己的信息牌，与感兴趣的人交谈。

我们虽然不是来相亲的，但是发现这个相亲角很有意思。对我们来说，可是一堂很好的中文阅读课。那些个人信息是很好的阅读材料。中文非常简洁，几十个汉字，就把自己是什么情况、想找什么样的人讲得非常清楚。但这不是一堂成

The Chinese-Style Blind Date

Author: Anna Sheehan   Instructor: Licheng Gu   Northwestern University

> The park is packed with parents gathering together in hopes of finding a suitable mate for their single children.

During my study abroad in China, my classmates and I took a trip to Shanghai on vacation. I heard there is the People's Park in Shanghai that is known for having a famous blind date corner, which is the biggest marriage square in China. Starting from 2004, every Saturday and Sunday from noon to 5 p.m., the park is packed with parents gathering together in hopes of finding a suitable mate for their single children. The blind date corner in the People's Park in Shanghai is now world-renowned, so a couple of my American classmates and I decided to take this opportunity to check it out.

When we arrived at the park, it was already 2 p.m. We didn't know where the blind date corner was located, but we soon found it after following the crowd. The blind date corner was full of people interacting with each other. Most of the people were parents in their 50s and 60s sitting there seeking suitable marriage partners for their children. The parents wrote their children's information on the cardboards and brought them along. These cardboards were displayed on the ground, hung on the strings between trees, or stuck on open umbrellas. When we approached, we saw the age, height, education, job, and wealth of the partner-seekers were written on the board. Some also wrote their expectations for the other side, for example, he/she should have Shanghai *hukou*, a house and a car, or should be over 1.65 meters in height. Those parents sat in their folding chairs next to their information cardboards, talking with the people they were interested in.

Although we were not there to seek partners, we found the blind date corner fascinating. To us, that was an excellent Chinese reading class as the various personal information were

功的中文听力课，因为很多时候他们在说我们听不懂的地方话。

我们听说中国男女比例失调，男多女少。所以我们以为物以稀为贵，男方会屈就女方，降低自己的择偶条件，对女方的条件不会太挑剔，但事实并非如此。他们的想法还是很传统、很保守。所有男方都是要求女方比男方年轻，健康漂亮，有稳定的工作。

很多时候，父母都是在孩子没有许可的情况下，背着孩子来人民公园相亲的。当然也有个别人亲自来这里相亲。在公园的一角，我们就看到几位家长围着

great reading materials. The information was concise and distinct. Everything was clearly explained in just dozens of characters. But that was not a good listening exercise for us, for the local people often spoke a dialect that we did not understand.

We learned that there is a great gender imbalance between the male and female ratio in China. We hypothesized that due to the scarcity of females, men would lower their partner matching criteria and be less picky. The reality was far from that, men continued to hold a traditional, conservative viewpoint. All men wanted the female partners to be younger, healthy, beautiful, and have a stable career.

The parents often came to the park without the knowledge or consent of their children. Of course, a few people came to seek a partner for themselves. In a corner of the park, we saw several families surrounding a young lady who had come to self-seek a partner. Out of curiosity, we walked over to eavesdrop. The lady had an informational cardboard next to her that read "Master's degree from an American elite university, a white-collar worker of an international company in Shanghai, owning a house in the suburb..." Then I heard a parent ask, "Lady, are you seeking for a husband for yourself? How old are you?" The lady replied, "Yes, I am, and I am 34 this year."

When they heard her age, the excitement suddenly left the parents' faces. They remarked that many of her excellent qualifications are disadvantageous because she is a woman. Her high qualification, education level, and age made it hard for someone to match her level. It was the first time I heard such remarks. How could someone be unpopular because of his/her excellency! We all felt indignant for the lady. After the parents left, we encircled her in an attempt to provide some comfort. With a sense of being wronged, she hurriedly left.

All of this reflects the bias of traditional ideas Chinese parents continue to hold toward women. Parents hope to find a future daughter-in-law who is young, beautiful, and filial. They are also deeply impacted by the traditional concept of "a woman's incompetence is a virtue."

Lastly, my classmates and I all sat down to discuss why there is no blind date corner in New York City Central Park. We believed it is due to the cultural differences between the East and West. In conclusion, American culture has the following differences: firstly, American parents do not focus so much on a child's marriage, as they believe it is the child's decision and

一位亲自征婚的年轻女士问话。出于好奇，我们也走过去旁听。那位女士身旁有一个信息牌，上面写着“美国名牌大学硕士，上海外企白领，郊区有房……”这时我听到一个家长问道：“姑娘，你为自己征婚啊？你今年多大？”那位女士回答：“是的，我今年34岁。”

一听到她的年龄，家长们的热情就没有了。他们说，她的优异条件作为一个女人反而是个缺点。因为她太优秀、学历太高、年龄也太大，没有男的配得上。这还是我第一次听到这种话，还有人因为太优秀而不受欢迎的。我们都很为这位女士感到不平。等这些家长离开以后，我们围住了她，努力想给她一些安慰。这位女士一肚子委屈，赶紧离开了。

这一切都反映出中国父母对女性仍抱着一种非常传统的看法。父母们都希望未来的儿媳年轻、漂亮、孝顺。他们还深受“女子无才便是德”的传统观念的影响。

最后，我们几个美国同学坐下来讨论为什么纽约的中央公园没有相亲角。我们认为这是中美文化差异造成的。总结起来，美国文化有如下不同：第一，美国的家长不太关注孩子的婚姻，认为那是他们自己的事情，应该自己解决；第二，美国孩子18岁以后就基本上独立，有了工作就早早搬出去独立生活，不希望父母为自己的婚事操心；第三，美国人性格外向，善于表达自己的感情，而且社交活动很多，喜欢谁就告诉对方“我喜欢你”，不用别人介绍，更不会需要父母介绍。

由于文化上的差异，所以美国是不会有相亲角的。

相亲角是中国城市的一个特色。改变老一辈中国父母的传统观念很难，相亲角这个社会现象也因此而存在下来。既然年轻人改变不了父母，就应该试着改变自己。中国年轻人应学会如何回击并表达他们的不满，掌握自己的人生。年轻人应该过好自己的生活，而不是按照社会设计的所谓幸福的标准行事。跟谁结婚和什么时候结婚是自己的事情，不是别人的事情，也不是父母的事情。自己要掌握好自己的幸福标准，尤其是终身大事——婚姻。

responsibility; secondly, once American children turn 18, they are independent and move out early when they have a job, so they do not want their parents to worry about their marriage; thirdly, Americans tend to be more outgoing, good at expressing emotions, and enjoy various social activities. If they like someone, they will communicate directly with "I like you," so they do not need assistance with an introduction, let alone have parents meddle in the affair.

Due to cultural differences, blind date corners do not exist in America.

Blind date corner is a specialty of Chinese cities. Changing older generational parents' traditional concept is difficult, therefore, blind date corners will continue to be a social phenomenon. Since young people cannot change their parents, they should learn to change themselves. Young Chinese people should learn how to fight back, express their dissatisfaction and control their own life. Young people should live their life in their own way, rather than live according to the socially designed standards of so-called happiness. Whom to marry and when to marry should not be anyone else, nor the parent's decision. One should master their happiness standards, especially in a lifelong event such as marriage.

他的父母是做什么的

作者：陶逸灿　指导教师：王炳匀　普林斯顿大学

> 可怜天下父母心。

美籍华人与中国人虽然同文同种，但是在文化上仍然存在着相当大的差别。最有趣的一个差别反映在对待孩子的婚姻问题上。从公园里父母为孩子打的征婚广告，到对孩子婚姻的期望，中国父母往往都会非常在意孩子对象的家庭背景。我不是说美国父母不在乎孩子跟谁在一起，而是在我看来，中国父母比美国父母更在乎孩子对象的人品和事业，更多地介入孩子婚前及婚后的生活。

美籍华人父母与中国父母的第一个不同是孩子多大才可以谈恋爱。在很多中国父母眼里，孩子高中毕业以前是不能谈恋爱的。我认为他们这样想有一定的道理。因为中国高中毕业前的高考是千军万马挤独木桥，所以家长们担心孩子一旦陷入恋爱，必然会影响学习，耽误高考。而美国父母并没有这样的担忧。在我的经历中，我遇到过很多美国父母鼓励他们的孩子早些开始谈恋爱，甚至早在初中的时候就开始谈恋爱。我记得去年三月份，我跟奶奶打电话的时候，她还嘱咐我和我的弟弟们别交女朋友。可是不到三个月，她突然改变了态度。虽然我觉得在这三个月里我没有什么明显的成长，但是在她看来，孩子高中一毕业就可以考虑未来的爱人了。

从中国父母的角度看，他们会觉得美国父母这样做并没有真正地为孩子着想；但是从美国父母的角度看，他们也可能觉得中国父母想要把孩子谈恋爱的时间严格地限制在一个时间段，也就是十八岁以后，是不现实的。在我看来，谈恋

What Do His Parents Do?

Author: Alexander Tao Instructor: Ben Wang Princeton University

Much sympathy to the hearts of parents across the world for the burdens they often carry!

Although Chinese Americans and Chinese people share the same language and race, there are still considerable cultural differences between the two groups. One of the most interesting of these differences is parental attitudes toward children about their marriage. From the common occurrence of marriage advertisement for children in parks of some China's large cities, one can see that Chinese parents are generally very concerned about the family backgrounds of their children's significant others. Now I'm not saying that American parents don't care who their children end up engaged to, but in my opinion, Chinese parents tend to care more about the characters and careers of their children's significant others. Generally, I also believe that Chinese parents are often more involved in their children's life before and especially after marriage compared to American parents.

The first big difference between Chinese-American parents and Chinese parents is their views on the appropriate age for dating. In the eyes of many Chinese parents, children should not engage in romantic relationships until they at least graduate from high school. I think there's certainly some merit to this line of thinking, as the college entrance exam in China, the *gaokao*, has such high-stakes attached to it. Parents are logically worried that once their children get into a relationship, it will inevitably affect their studies and negatively impact how they score on the *gaokao*. In my experience, American parents have much less of this sort of concern. I have met plenty of American parents, Chinese-American parents included, that have encouraged their children to start dating early, even as early as middle school. I remember last

爱是一个很复杂的过程，是随着一个人的成熟发育而自然发展的。所以如果一个孩子乖乖地听父母的话，十八九岁以前从来没有比较谈得来的异性朋友，那么这个孩子到了所谓适合谈恋爱的年龄，可能会有一些心理上的障碍。当然，这只是我一个在美国出生长大的男性华裔青年的想法。

最近发生在我身上的一件事也能说明中国父母与美国父母的不同。上个学期，我开始经常跟我一个在普林斯顿大学的中国留学生同学聊天儿（我们还没成为真正的男女朋友）。这个女同学的家人是中国广东人，她的父母就像我上面讨论的中国父母那样。我的这位朋友跟她父母的关系很好，所以她把我的很多事都告诉了她妈妈。这几个月来，她妈妈问了她很多关于我的问题。从我的父母是从哪儿来的，到他们的学历和工作成就，从我的专业，到我将来打算从事什么工作，甚至到我的身高，这些问题都问过。一个让我很好奇的事就是在这些问题中，她的妈妈从来没有问我叫什么。她妈妈不知道我叫什么名字，但是我父母的收入她大约能猜到。

March when I called my grandmother and her telling me and my three brothers to not have girlfriends and within the span of three months, changing her attitude. Even though I didn't think I underwent any significant maturation within those three months, from her point of view, the moment I graduated from high school it, became due time for me to start thinking about my future partner.

From the perspective of Chinese parents, some may feel that American parents aren't really thinking about their children's long-term well-being when they encourage their children to start dating so early; but from the perspective of American parents, they may also feel that Chinese parents in a way are trying to designate a strict time-period for their children's love lives. In my opinion though, love simply is not an easy thing. Learning to exist within the dynamic of a relationship is a complex process that must develop along with a person's maturity. Thus, if a child obediently listens to their parents and even goes as far as not having friends of the opposite sex until the age of 18 or 19, then there may be some psychological turmoil when they reach the so-called suitable age for relationships. Now of course, these thoughts are simply the ideas of a young Chinese American male born and raised in the United States.

An incident that happened to me recently also illustrates the difference between Chinese and American parents. Last semester, I started chatting a lot with a fellow student from China at Princeton (we weren't dating officially). This female classmate's family is Cantonese, and her parents are like the Chinese parents I have mentioned above. This friend of mine has a great relationship with her parents, so she told her mother a lot about me. Over the course of many months, her mother has asked her many questions about me. Questions such as where my parents are from, to their education background and work achievements. Questions about my major to what job I plan to do in the future and even my height were asked. One of the curious things to me, however, is that of these questions, her mother never asked what my name was. While her mom didn't know what my name was, she could roughly guess my parents' income.

At Princeton University, some of my Chinese teachers are also from China. When I

在普林斯顿大学，我的一些中文老师也是从中国来的。我跟她们讨论过这个事情。她们说这样的事情也曾经在他们自己的生活中发生过。其中的一位老师说，她在国内的爸爸等了一年以后才问她的男朋友叫什么名字。除了让我们大笑了半天以外，我觉得这样的事情确实能反映美国华裔文化与中国文化的差别。

虽然美国华人和中国人的文化有很多不同，但是他们有一点是完全相同的，那就是父母对孩子的爱。无论是美国华裔父母还是中国父母，他们只是想要他们孩子做最好的决定，过最幸福的日子。真的是可怜天下父母心啊。

discussed this situation with them, they also said things like this have happened in their own lives. One of the teachers said her father in China didn't ask her boyfriend's name until a year later. Besides making us laugh for a while, I think things like this really reflect differences between Chinese-American culture and Chinese culture.

Although there are many cultural differences between the Chinese Americans and Chinese people, there is certainly one thing in common, that being the love of each culture's parents for their children. Whether it be Chinese-American parents or Chinese parents, parents from both cultures only want their children to make the best decisions and lead the most fulfilling and happiest lives. Much sympathy to the hearts of parents across the world for the burdens they often carry!

“剩女”之我见

作者：林梦　指导教师：井茁　俄勒冈大学

如果一个女人选择过独身生活，或等待着爱的出现，这样的选择应该得到尊重。

在中国，27 岁还没结婚的女性被称作“剩女”。越来越多受过良好教育的女性保持独身成为一种普遍存在的社会现象。虽然很多女性都乐于独身，但是她们不得不面临来自方方面面的压力。媒体、家长甚至朋友都要求适婚女性早日结婚。从社会上这些对所谓“剩女”的负面评论来看，人们普遍认为她们缺少足够的魅力找不到对象。但实际上，这些女性往往是受教育程度和职业能力都非常好的人才。

在中国，男女性别失衡问题比较严重，适婚男性多于适婚女性，但是许多女性仍然没有结婚。此外，还没结婚的女性往往是受过良好教育的成功女性，是中国社会最鼓励结婚的人。但这并不意味着她们能轻易结婚。因为很多男性会选择年龄比自己小、学历比自己低的人结婚。因此，那些高学历的大龄女性只得选择过独身生活。现在越来越多的女性会专注于事业，而不是爱情。女性宁愿独身，等待着爱的出现，也不愿意嫁给自己不爱的男人。现在越来越多的女性不想为结婚而结婚。

虽然适婚男性比适婚女性多，但是男性并没有受到跟女性一样的不公平待遇。因为男性一般会选择比自己年轻的女性结婚，所以他们的可选范围比较大。女性一般会选择比自己年长的男性结婚，所以她们的可选范围比较小，而且更容易因尚未结婚而受到不当的责备。出于这个原因，许多女性讨厌被称为“剩女”——这一带有贬义的称号。“剩女”，顾名思义，就是被人挑剩下的女人，是

My Views on "Leftover Women"

Author: Alison Roden Instructor: Zhuo Jing-Schmidt University of Oregon

> If a woman chooses to be single or to wait for love, that choice should be respected.

In China, women who are still unmarried by the age of 27 are called "leftover women." This increasing number of educated women remaining single has become a pervasive social phenomenon. Although many women are happy to stay single, they have to face all sorts of pressure. The media, parents, and even friends expect marriageable women to get married as soon as possible. From the perspective of those in society who view these so-called "leftover women" negatively, they believe it is more so because they lack the necessary attractive qualities to find a partner. But in reality, these women are often very well-educated and talented professionals.

In China, gender imbalance between men and women is relatively severe. There are more marriageable men than women, and yet many women remain unmarried. In addition, these single ladies tend to be just the sort of well-educated successful women that are most encouraged by Chinese society to marry. But this doesn't necessarily mean they can easily get married. This is because many men will choose to marry someone whose age and level of education are lower than their own, therefore leaving these older, highly educated women with only one choice: a life of celibacy. Nowadays, more and more women choose to focus on their careers over love. Women would rather be single and wait for love than marry someone they don't love. Increasingly, women don't want to get married just for the sake of marriage.

Although there are more marriageable men than women, men do not receive the same kind of unfair treatment as women. Because men generally choose women younger than themselves to marry, they have a wider range of options. Women tend to marry older men, so they have fewer options and are more likely to be unduly blamed for not being married.

没人要的。有人可能会说这是因为她们不漂亮，或者太挑剔。“剩女”这个称谓暗示：如果一个女人不结婚，那她就是一个失败者。这是不公平的。实际上，结婚不一定是人们生活的唯一目标。

尽管女人可能乐于过独身生活，但是很多父母仍然会不遗余力地帮助自己的女儿找男朋友，他们会为女儿安排相亲，甚至自己到征婚市场上帮女儿寻找潜在的伴侣。这些父母认为女儿没有嫁出去是家里的耻辱，所以父母不愿跟女儿一起参加聚会，因为不愿让别人知道他们有一个年龄这么大还没结婚的女儿。有些父母深受“不孝有三，无后为大”的影响，把女儿选择过独身生活当作不孝敬老人。

“剩女”是一个充满歧视的称号。如果一个女人选择过独身生活，或等待着爱的出现，这样的选择应该得到尊重。女人不应该因为社会压力而结婚。在中国，这个观点已经在慢慢被接受，社会将越来越尊重女性的选择。我希望有一天，“剩女”的称号将成为过去。

For this reason, many women resent being called "leftover women" as it is a derogatory title. "Leftover women," as the name suggests, are women who were selected and then left behind, who no one wants. Some might even claim it's because they're not pretty, or too picky. The title "leftover women" implies that if a woman does not marry, she is a failure. This is not fair. In fact, getting married is not necessarily people's only goal in life.

Although these women may be very content to live a single life, many parents will still go to great lengths to look for boyfriends, arrange blind dates, and even go to marriage markets to find potential partners for their daughters. These parents view their unmarried daughter as a disgrace to the family and are therefore reluctant to go to parties with them because they don't want others to know they have a daughter who is still unmarried at such an age. Some parents are deeply influenced by the saying that "there are three ways to be unfilial and having no descendants is the worst," regarding their daughter's choice of celibacy as a sign of disrespect to her elders.

"Leftover women" is a label filled with discrimination. If a woman chooses to be single or to wait for love, that choice should be respected. Women should not have to marry because of pressure from society. In China, this perspective is already slowly being accepted, and society gradually begins to respect women's choices. My hope is that one day "leftover women" will become a term of the past.

血浓于水

Blood Is Thicker than Water

导 读

上一板块的文章写的是友情与恋情，这一板块的文章则写家人的亲情。家是一个人在外劳累一天后归来歇息的港湾，家人是鼓励你砥砺前行、可以依赖的坚实靠山。在《家力山大》这篇文章里，耶鲁大学的江慧楠同学深切地讲述了自己在这方面的体会。对于慧楠来讲，家，就是早晨六点妈妈一个人忙碌的厨房。家人起床以后，可以立即享受丰盛的早餐。家，就是下午三点放学回到家里与弟弟窃窃私语的卧室。当弟弟听说姐姐的同学把小组的工作都推给姐姐一个人，他立即给她现编现演说唱，批评指责对方，鼓励姐姐勇敢面对。家，就是晚上七点爸爸下班刚刚进门后倾听慧楠诉苦的门厅。爸爸立即给她出主意，叫她把小组的工作分配平均，通知每个人都要各司其职，共同完成小组的任务。所以对于慧楠同学来讲，家不是“压力山大”，而是“家力山大”。

与慧楠同学不同，布朗大学的张元佳同学却是从汽车里感受到了家人的深切关爱。在她的文章《在车里》的一开头，元佳同学就写道:“我一直觉得在车里的时候我才最能接近我的亲人。”元佳记得第一次为他人哭是她四岁准备回美国时，外婆送她去机场。马上就要离开那个疼她、爱她、抚养她四年的外婆了。元佳不知道再团聚是什么时候，所以非常伤心。到了美国以后，每个星期六早上，元佳坐在妈妈的身边，由妈妈开车带着她转战不同的战场。上完游泳课再去上中文课，上完中文课再去上绘画课。当元佳累得向妈妈发脾气时，妈妈从不抱怨，总是温柔地安慰女儿。妈妈知道这些活动会帮助女儿成为一个更全能、更优秀、更有毅力的人。有的周末，又是爸爸开车几个小时，送元佳去参加花样游泳比赛。原本寡言少语的父亲在车里好像立即换了一个人。他们一起听中国歌曲，聊发生在他

Introduction

The stories in the previous section were about friendship and romance, yet the stories in this section focus on family bonds. Home is a harbor where we can all return to rest after a long and tiring day spent outside. Family is a strong support system that protects us and encourages us to forge ahead – we can always rely on family. In the story "Pressure as Heavy as a Mountain and Family as Great as a Mountain," Eunice Kiang, a student from Yale University, described in detail her own experience in this regard. For Eunice, family was the kitchen where her mother was busy at six o'clock in the morning. After the family members got up, they could enjoy a delicious breakfast immediately. Family was the bedroom where she returned home from school at three o'clock in the afternoon and where she could whisper her complaints to her younger brother. When her brother heard that his sister's classmates had pushed all the group work onto her, he quickly made up a live rap for her, criticizing and blaming the classmates while encouraging her to have courage by standing up for herself. Family was the hallway where Eunice's dad listened to her complaints just after he got off work at seven o'clock in the evening. Dad immediately gave her an idea, telling her to distribute the workload of the group evenly so that everyone can perform their duties and complete their tasks. Therefore, to Eunice, family was not "great pressure" but rather "great strength."

Unlike Eunice, Amanda Zhang from Brown University felt the deep love of her family in the car. At the beginning of her story "In the Car," Amanda wrote: "Ever since I was young, it has always been in a car that I've felt closest to my relatives." Amanda remembered the first time she cried for someone else. This was when she was four years old and ready to return to the United States, and her grandmother took her to the airport. She was about to leave her grandmother, who had cared for her and raised her for four years. Amanda didn't know when the next reunion would be, so she was very sad that they had to part. After arriving in the United States, every Saturday morning, Amanda sat beside her mother, and her mother drove her to different "battlefields." After swimming class, she went to Chinese class, and after Chinese class, she had to go to painting class. When Amanda was so tired that she lost her temper, her mother never complained and instead comforted her daughter gently. Amanda's mother knew these activities would help Amanda

们周围的种种事情，在女儿面前展现出浓浓的父爱。

张元佳同学太累了对妈妈表示不满的方式是发脾气，但是西北大学王晓濛同学对待妈妈的办法就是一个字——哭。在《给妈妈的一封信》里，王晓濛同学写道："每一次您带我去打网球时，我就抱怨天气太热；带我去滑冰时，我抱怨溜冰场太冷。……我一学中文，就不停地哭，总是大喊大叫：'汉字太多了，发音太难了！'"但是妈妈没有放弃，仍然继续教女儿。如今晓濛已经长大成人，在大学里面继续选修中文，写下这一封信，对妈妈当年的良苦用心表达感激之情。在这封信的结尾，晓濛同学写道："小时候让您为我操碎了心。您一天到晚陪着我学这学那，一定很累，所以我现在从心底里感激您。"

与本板块的其他文章一样，这三篇文章都有很多可取之处。《家力山大》的作者巧妙地通过三个不同的时间和场所，即早晨六点的厨房、下午三点的卧室、晚上七点的门厅，展示她"全天候、无死角"地受到了全体家人的呵护。而《在车里》的作者则是通过三个不同场景彰显家人的关爱。在去机场的车里与外婆告别，在去中文学校的车里向妈妈发脾气，在去参加游泳比赛的车里与爸爸敞开心扉。在《给妈妈的一封信》里，晓濛同学小时候没有少流眼泪。而收到女儿晓濛的这封信以后，相信妈妈也会流出眼泪，但那应该是幸福的眼泪。一封能让妈妈流出幸福眼泪的信应该是一封值得你学习的信吧？

become a more well-rounded, excellent and persevering person. On some weekends, Amanda's dad would drive for several hours to send her to synchronized swimming competitions. The originally taciturn father seemed to be transformed immediately in the car. They listened to Chinese songs together, chatted about all kinds of things that happened around them, and he showed her deep fatherly love.

When Amanda Zhang was exhausted, she would express her dissatisfaction by losing her temper to her mother. However, Grace Wang from Northwestern University would react by crying. In "A Letter to My Mother," Grace wrote: "I still remember every time you took me to play tennis, I would complain that it was too hot outside; when you took me to go ice skating, I complained the ice rink was too cold... As soon as I'd start learning Chinese, I would not stop crying, always screaming and shouting: 'There are too many Chinese characters, and the pronunciation is too hard!'" But her mother did not give up and still patiently taught her daughter. Now that Grace has grown up, she takes Chinese as an elective in college, and she wrote this letter to express her sincere gratitude for her mother's hard work and dedication all these years. At the end of the letter, Grace wrote: "In my childhood, you have placed so much energy and dedication on me. You accompanied me all day long to learn this and that. It must have been very tiring. So truly from the bottom of my heart, I am grateful to you."

Like the other stories in this section, the three essays have a lot of aspects we can learn from when writing our own stories. The author of "Pressure as Heavy as a Mountain and Family as Great as a Mountain" cleverly used three sequential time and places, namely the kitchen at six o'clock in the morning, the bedroom at three o'clock in the afternoon, and the hall at seven o'clock in the evening to show the unconditional care and attention she received from her family. The author of "In the Car" showed her love for family through three different scenes: bidding farewell to Grandma in the car on the way to the airport, throwing a tantrum to Mom in the car to Chinese school, and opening her mind to Dad in the car on her way to a swimming competition. In "A Letter to My Mother," Grace shed a lot of tears when she was a child. After receiving this letter from her daughter, I believe Grace's mother would also start to shed tears, but they would be tears of happiness. After all, a letter that can make a mother shed tears of happiness should be a letter worth learning from, right?

我的多民族家庭

作者：邓凯　指导教师：顾利程　西北大学

> 在我的家庭里，不同肤色的人相亲相爱，和平共处。

每一个人都非常清楚自己是什么种族，是哪国人。现在请大家猜一猜，我是什么人？中国人？不对。非洲人？也不对。白人？黑人？印第安人？都不对，但是也都对！我的家庭背景比较复杂。我的身上有中国人的血统、非洲人的血统、英国人的血统，以及美国印第安人的血统。血统越复杂，人就越聪明，难道大家不觉得我是一个多民族的完美结合吗？

我妈妈是中国人，从小在哈尔滨长大的。我妈妈在黑龙江大学学习经济时，选了一门英语课。这门课由一位年长的美国女外教教授，助教是一个从美国来的英俊小伙子。这个年长的英语外教后来成为了我奶奶，而那个助教就是我爸爸。大家现在明白了吗？我的奶奶和爸爸是我妈妈的英语老师！我爸爸来自密歇根。他有一个很不一般的家庭。我爷爷是来自非洲的黑人，但是他身上有四分之一印第安人的血统。我奶奶一家来自英国，是比较典型的白人。我爸爸就是黑人和白人生的混血儿。

我的爸爸和妈妈一见倾心，双双坠入爱河，很快就结婚了。我就是他们爱情的结晶。小时候，我的家里每天都有黑人、白人、中国人、印第安人出出进进。他们虽然肤色不同，语言不同，文化背景不同，但是他们都深深地爱着我。我从小就明白，不管对方是什么民族，什么肤色，哪国人，你都要尊重对方，尊重所有的人。如果你尊重别人，别人也会尊重你。

My Multiracial Family

Author: Christopher Dungey Instructor: Licheng Gu Northwestern University

> In my family, people of different skin colors love each other and live together in harmony.

Everyone clearly knows what race and nationality he/she is. Now, I would like all of you to please guess what my nationality could be. Chinese? Incorrect. African? Also incorrect. White? Black? Indian? While these are incorrect, they are all also correct! As a matter of fact, my family background is rather complicated. I have Chinese, African, British, and American Indian lineage. The more complex the lineage, the smarter the person. Don't you think that I am the perfect blend of many ethic groups?

My mother is Chinese and grew up in Harbin, China. She went to Heilongjiang University to study Economics. There, she took an English class that was taught by an older American female foreign professor, and the teaching assistant was a handsome young man from America. The older foreign teacher became my grandmother, and the teaching assistant became my father. Do you understand now? My grandmother and father were my mother's English teachers! My father is from Michigan, and he has a quite unique family: My grandfather is a black man from Africa, but he is also a quarter Indian. My grandmother's whole family is from England, so they can be considered as typical white people. Of course, this means my dad is biracial.

My father and mother fell in love at first sight and soon got married; I am the crystallization of their love. When I was a child, black, white, Chinese, and Indian people would come and go from my home every day. Although they have different skin colors, speak different languages, and come from different cultural backgrounds, they all love me deeply. From a very young age, I understood that no matter what ethnicity, skin color, or nationality

在我的家庭里，不同肤色的人相亲相爱，和平共处。世界上不同的国家和民族也应该像我的家庭一样和平共处。但是现在世界还不太平，有的国家还在侵略别的国家，还有战争。我希望世界永远和平。

someone has, we should always respect each other. As long as you treat others with respect, they will also respect you.

In my family, people of different skin colors love each other and live together in harmony. I believe that like my family, different countries and nations in the world should also coexist in peace. However, the current world is not peaceful, with invasions and war between some countries. I hope that the world will always be peaceful.

我的日记本

作者：赵景熙　指导教师：闫玲　哥伦比亚大学

我四岁生日的那一天，妈妈送了我一份礼物——一个日记本。从此，每天睡觉前，我都会和妈妈坐在一起，写各自的日记。因为那时我还是一个上幼儿园的孩子，所以还没有能力写字。看着妈妈龙飞凤舞写下一段又一段的日记，我也时常胡乱写些没有意义的“草书”。我妈妈和幼儿园老师写字写得既快又漂亮，受她们的影响，我也尽量试着模仿她们的笔迹。由于我还无法记录自己想表达的内容，我的日记只能重复着我能写的“我爱你（I love you），我爱你，我爱你”一句话。我很沮丧，不满意地说：“我为什么不能写更多的字？为什么只能写一句‘我爱你’？”妈妈不禁笑起来，安慰我道：“好孩子，你很快就能学会写更多字了。现在呢，你想说什么，我就写什么，妈妈做你的记录员。”所以，刚开始的时候，是我说，妈妈替我写日记。后来慢慢地，就是我自己写日记了。

从小到大，我每天都坚持写日记，里面珍藏着我的感情、愿望和一些小诗。

从小到大，我每天都坚持写日记，里面珍藏着我的感情、愿望和一些小诗。我从小就不喜欢跟别人说话，说话的速度很慢（所以别人也不喜欢跟我说话），不能娓娓道来地讲故事。可是，用日记，我能清楚地表达自己的想法。上小学时，我非常喜欢自我反思，心事重重，一些小事情就会使我负疚不已。我会想：“我今天可能说错话了，做错事了，恐怕我的朋友不会再跟我来往了。”从上小学起，我每天做什么事都要挎着装有日记本的小包。如果出去忘了带日记本，我便会感到惴惴不安。即使我现在已经上了大学，在大学乐团里演奏的时候，我也常常在

My Diary

Author: Loa Cho　Instructor: Ling Yan　Columbia University

On my fourth birthday, my mother gave me a gift – a diary. From that day on, every night before bed I sat down with my mother, writing in our diaries together. Since I was only a child in kindergarten, I wasn't able to write words on my own. Envious of the beautiful cursive writing of my mother and my teacher in kindergarten, I often filled the pages with meaningless scribbles, only able to imitate their motions. The one phrase I was able to write was "I love you." "I love you. I love you. I love you." I would write over and over. Unsatisfied with my work, I would say to my mother, "Why can't I write anything else? All I can write is 'I love you!'" My mother burst out laughing and comforted my cries, "You'll be able to write many more words soon. For now, I'll write for you; I'll be your scribe!" So I started again, my mother writing for me the diary entry I spoke. Later, I gradually started to write my own diary.

I grew up, grew older, and I still continued to write in my diary every day. I wrote about everything and all of my ideas, from my feelings and hopes to short poems. Since childhood, I didn't like talking to others and my talking speed was quite slow (both reasons making others don't like to talk to me as well). I was never able to tell stories easily. But, using my diary, I could clearly express my thoughts. When I was in primary school, I was almost too self-reflective, treading through interactions with utmost care, all the little things giving me frequent pangs of guilt. I would think, "I said something by mistake today. I did something wrong today. I'm afraid that my friends won't play with me anymore." Wherever I went, my diary and my

I grew up, grew older, and I still continued to write in my diary every day. I wrote about everything and all of my ideas, from my feelings and hopes to short poems.

演奏间隙记录自己的感触与看法。如果哪天忘了带日记本，我便会因不能及时记录自己的灵感和想法而失落不已。

世界上很多人为他们自己认定的理念而奋斗。许多人面对令人困扰的问题时，期望能求助于宗教、亲友、书籍，或者上大学，读研究生，去寻求答案。知识渊博的人试图通过写书寻求答案。艺术家潜心艺术寻求答案。自然环境越来越恶劣，无家可归者的人越来越多，各类歧视越来越严重，贫富差距越来越大，世界越来越不和平。哪里都有不平等，如何消除不平等呢？有时候想起这些问题来，我发自内心地希望人人都能拥有博爱之心。我也意识到这个世界最需要的不是毫无意义的长篇大论；可能仅仅只需要一句话——“我爱你”，就是我四岁时在日记里写下的第一个句子。

self-reflection came with me since I was a primary school student. Leaving home without my diary would be a source of anxiety. Even now as a college student, when playing in a college band, I often record my feelings and opinions between performances. If I forget to bring my diary with me one day, I will feel lost since I am unable to document my inspirations and ideas in time.

Many people in the world fight for what they believe in. People turn to religion, relatives, friends, books, or a college degree to find answers. Scholars try to find answers by writing books. Artists pour their souls into their art to find an answer. The environment on earth is getting worse. There are more and more homeless people. Discrimination is becoming more and more serious. The gap between the rich and the poor is getting wider, and the world is becoming less and less peaceful. How can we live with this injustice and inequality? Sometimes, when I think of these issues, I sincerely advocate universal fraternity, and I realize what the world needs is not meaningless long speeches, but just a simple sentence – "I love you," the first sentence I wrote in my diary when I was four years old.

在车里

作者：张元佳　指导教师：汪洋　布朗大学

> 我在车里留下的温馨记忆和从长辈那里学到的人生知识，将永远伴随我，让我受益一生。

从小到大，我一直觉得在车里的时候我才最能接近我的亲人。说实话，汽车有时会是一个危险的大机器，随时可能出车祸。然而，对我来说，我们家房车那个裂开的皮座位，淡淡的汽油味道，车窗上留下的油滋滋的手印，以及我们用车窗上的雾气作为背景画的漫画，总能让我想起我的家人。

我记得第一次为一个人而哭是为了我的外婆——那个天天照顾我的外婆，天天和我说上海话的外婆，从小总是把好吃的留给我的外婆。我四岁的时候，准备离开上海回美国，外婆送我去机场。我和外婆分别后，还不知道再团聚是什么时候，我非常舍不得。在去机场的路上，我回想起：外婆用《两只老虎》这首歌教会我身体各个部位的名称；她培养了我对动画片《网球王子》的迷恋，以及对味千拉面、旺旺雪饼、家乐福的喜爱；在经济不宽裕的情况下，外婆会努力给我留下我最喜爱的东西……这一路上，我突然意识到原来外婆这么爱我。

我记得我第一次真正感到累了是在每个星期六：我要在早上六点练习花样游泳，九点上中文课，下午一点上绘画课。妈妈开车带着我转战不同的战场。在我累得发脾气的时候，妈妈从不抱怨，总是优雅地对待我的疲倦和脾气，因为她知道这些课外活动会帮我成为一个更全能、更优秀、更有毅力的人。她教我成语“乘风破浪、勇往直前、坚韧不拔、锲而不舍”，用它们来提醒我：“女儿，你

In the Car

Author: Amanda Zhang   Instructor: Yang Wang   Brown University

> The memories and the knowledge about life I learned from them will be with me for a lifetime.

Ever since I was young, it has always been in a car that I've felt closest to my relatives. To tell you the truth, the car is sometimes a dangerous machine that can crash at any time. But for me, the cracked leather seats, the smell of gas, and the remnants of oily hands and fingerprints from left-over rain drawings remind me of my family.

I remember the first time that I cried for someone: my grandmother. When I was 4 years old, I was in a car with my grandma, going away from Shanghai and to the airport for America. I knew that this car ride would be the last time I spent with my grandma, the one who took care of me and spoke Shanghainese to me every day, and who had always given me delicious food. She used the "Two Tigers" song to teach me about different body parts. She nurtured my fascination with the *Prince of Tennis* cartoon, and my love for Ajisen Ramen, Wangwang crackers, and Carrefour. Even in the case of economic hardship, my grandma would try her best to give me my favorite things. The car ride to the airport suddenly made me realize how much my grandma loves me.

I remember the first time that I was really tired was on every Saturday: I had synchronized swimming practice at 6 a.m., Chinese class at 9 a.m., and drawing class at 1 p.m. My mom drove me among all of these places, never complaining, always taking in my tiredness and grumpiness with grace, because she knew that these extracurricular activities would make me a more well-rounded, excellent and persevering person. She taught me the Chinese idioms for perseverance, such as "乘风破浪," "勇往直前," "坚韧不拔," "锲而不舍," as a way of saying "My daughter, you can do it! " While I sat in the car, rushing from one place to another, the car

一定行！”我坐在车里，从一个地方赶到另外一个地方，我逐渐意识到妈妈是多么爱我。

我记得我第一次觉得和爸爸很亲近，是一个周末爸爸开车送我去参加花样游泳比赛。去参加比赛，开车需要几个小时的路程。虽然爸爸紧张地工作了一周，已经很累了，但是他从不抱怨，像一个专职司机一样，随时可以开车送我去赛场。爸爸不是个健谈和善于表达情感的人，但在汽车里，他很放得开。我们在车里听张学友的歌，聊在我生活中发生的事情。有时候，爸爸会想到一个和中文有关的例子，他就用这个机会教我一些中国文化和词语。爸爸是一个冷傲的人，但却是一个非常关心我的人。现在在开车去布朗的路上，他依然表现出同样的耐心和温暖。坐在爸爸的车里，我意识到爸爸是如此地爱我。

大学生活马上就要结束了，这是我大学的最后一个学期。之后，我会毕业工作，进入社会。这次毕业典礼很可能是最后一次，外婆、妈妈、爸爸和我都在同一辆车上。幸运的是，我在车里留下的温馨记忆和从长辈那里学到的人生知识，将永远伴随我，让我受益一生。

rides made me gradually realize how much my mom loves me.

I remember the first time that I felt close to my dad. It was on a weekend when my father drove me to my synchronized swimming meet. It took us several hours to drive there. Although my dad had been working hard in the past week, he drove like a professional full-time driver and never complained about the drive. My dad isn't talkative or good at expressing his emotions, but in the car, he would come alive, listening to Jacky Cheung's songs and chatting with me about things going on in my life. Sometimes, my dad thinks of an example related to Chinese and uses it as an opportunity to teach me more about Chinese culture and words. My dad is a proud man, but also a deeply caring one, and even to this day driving to Brown, he still expressed the same patience and warmth. The car rides made me realize how much my dad loves me.

College life is coming to an end, and this is my last semester before I graduate and go off into the society. Graduation will most likely be the last time that my grandma, my mother, my father, and I take the same car. Fortunately, the memories and the knowledge about life I learned from them will be with me for a lifetime.

我与众不同的奶奶

作者：郭润瑶　指导教师：陈利砼　惠顿大学（伊利诺伊州）

> 这位与众不同的奶奶，让我在美国的童年受到了中国文化的影响。

每当我回想起童年，总是会想到奶奶给我家带来的温暖。在奶奶和父母的陪伴下，我在美国度过了一个“非典型”却很愉快的童年。我父母是第一代移民，工作非常辛苦。他们总是在太阳升起前就出门，直到天黑才拖着疲惫的身体回家。我父母不在家时，奶奶会代替他们照顾我们。在我记忆中，奶奶老是在家照顾我们几个像小猴子一样精力旺盛的孩子。奶奶在我家陪伴我们的时候，大多数日子都很平凡，但是很快乐。在我的童年，我从奶奶身上学到了很多，不仅是中国的语言，也有中国的传统文化，更有做人的道理。

为什么说我的童年因为奶奶而变得“非典型”呢？因为她与众不同，一点儿都不像我美国朋友的奶奶。第一个不同是她不会说英文。我父母的母语是广东话，但是为了练习英文，他们很少用广东话和我们沟通。由于奶奶只会说广东话，我们就只能强迫自己用广东话跟她交流。时间越长，我们的广东话就越好。试想一下，童年期间若不是有奶奶陪伴，我们弟兄姐妹几个很可能已经丢掉了广东话。我从高中开始正式学习中文，现在是大学三年级中文专业的学生，以后也希望从事服务华人社区的工作。我的广东话大大地帮助了我的中文学习。这一切都归功于奶奶在我小时候给我打下的良好基础。

奶奶不仅让我们接触到中国的语言，也让我们接触到与之相关的文化。其他

My One-of-a-Kind Grandma

Author: Jessie Guo　Instructor: Litong Chen　Wheaton College (Illinois)

> This unique grandma exposed my American childhood to the influence of Chinese culture.

Every time I reminisce about my early years, I can't help but recall the warmth my grandma brought to my family. As a result of the way my grandma and parents raised me, I had a somewhat unconventional yet joyful childhood. My parents were hard-working first-generation immigrants. They were always out the door before sunrise, only dragging their fatigued bodies home until it was dark outside. If my parents weren't home, my grandma would be the one to take care of us. As far back as I can remember, my grandma was always at my house looking after us overenergetic monkeys. Although most days were uneventful when she was with us at my house, they always passed by happily. I learned a great deal from her constant presence in my life, including how to speak Chinese, the traditional culture of China, but most importantly, valuable moral values.

Why do I claim that my grandma made my childhood unconventional? It's because she was completely different from the grandmothers of my American friends. Her lack of English language proficiency is the first distinction. Although Cantonese is my parents' native language, they primarily spoke English to us in order to practice their English. Because my grandma could only understand Cantonese, we had to force ourselves to speak it to converse with her. As a result, we naturally become more fluent in it over time. Thinking about it now, my siblings and I probably wouldn't have been able to speak a lick of Cantonese if it weren't for my grandma. I later began to study Chinese formally in high school, and I am currently a third-year Chinese major with the intention of finding employment within the Chinese community. I found that my knowledge of Cantonese has been a huge help in my learning of Mandarin. All

奶奶会从他们的手袋里拿出巧克力豆或者彩虹糖哄逗孙子孙女，而我的奶奶裤兜里却常有山楂饼。她告诉我们说，山楂饼生津开胃，是广东孩子最喜欢的零食之一。从甜甜的山楂饼中，我们也尝到了一丝传统的味道。奶奶还带领我们收集塑料袋，以备再用。奶奶说这是中国家长都会做的事情。

奶奶的与众不同还表现在她带我们做的事情。别的美国小朋友的奶奶会带他们出去玩儿，而我奶奶会带我们在后院种菜。奶奶刚来我们家的时候，我还很小。她到家后，立刻在房子外面走了一圈，后院引起了她的兴趣。我们住在郊区，那个时候后院除了草坪以外什么都没有。在我眼里，如果加一个白色的围栏，再加一些花儿和灌木，就是一个典型的美国后院，简单又完美。可是在奶奶眼中，这个院子有着不一样的潜力。接下来的日子里，奶奶每天都会戴上斗笠和手套出去

of this is a result of the strong foundation my grandma gave me as a child.

My grandma not only exposed us to the Chinese language, but also the culture associated with it. She was the type to carry haw flakes in her pocket while other grandmothers pulled out M&Ms and Skittles to offer to their grandchildren. She explained to us the benefits of haw flakes for boosting appetite and how they are a favorite snack among Cantonese children. As we savored the sweet flavor of the candy, we also got to taste hints of Chinese culture. In addition, my grandma showed us how to collect plastic bags for later use, explaining that this is a common habit among Chinese parents.

The way my grandma engages with us makes her unique as well. While other American children's grandmas would take them outside to play, my grandma would take us to the backyard to grow vegetables. I was very young the first time my grandma visited our home. When she first arrived, she took a walk around the house, and then the backyard piqued her interest. The only thing in the backyard at the time was grass because we lived in the suburbs. In my eyes, if you added a white picket fence and some flowers and shrubs on top of that, it could become a typical American backyard, simple and perfect. My grandma, however, saw that this yard had a different potential. In the days that followed, Grandma would put on a bamboo hat and gloves and walk outside every day to weed and turn the soil. We, as grandchildren, enthusiastically joined her in making holes in the ground and constructing roofs for each seed. She frequently yelled at us and shouted commands for us to follow. Perhaps we were constantly "stopping the world from turning," as she says in Cantonese frequently, and got in the way of her more often than not. But even though we couldn't fully comprehend what it meant at the time, we could see that her shouting and chiding couldn't hide the smile on her face.

Our backyard gradually transformed from ordinary to unique: from grass to a blooming garden bursting with little tomatoes that exploded in your mouth the moment you bit into them, winter melons bigger than my two-year-old brother, endless snow peas, and bitter melons that I still don't know how to appreciate to this day. Other grandmas might use fertilizer, but my grandma had her magical shrimp shell formula. As long as my grandma buried her magic formula deep into the soil, the vegetables were guaranteed to be fruitful. Each fruit that is bared is a symbol of the value of the sustained effort that it took to grow

除草，翻土。作为孙辈，我们很热情地陪她在土里挖洞，为每颗种子“盖房子”。她经常对我们大喊着，指导我们应该怎么做。也许我们像她常常用广东话说的那样——“阻止地球转”。虽然我们不能完全听懂，但我们能看到，她的喊声和呵斥声掩盖不了她脸上的笑容。

慢慢地，我们的后院从平凡变得独特；从只有青青的小草，到四处都有一咬就会爆炸的小番茄、比我两岁的弟弟还大的冬瓜、永远吃不完的雪豆和我到现在还不懂如何欣赏的甘味苦瓜。别的奶奶可能会用肥料，但我奶奶有她的虾壳魔法。只要奶奶把她的魔法与种子埋在地下，就一定会结出丰硕的果实。每一个成果都代表着值得投入的长期劳动。如果它长得特别大、特别甜、特别好，这种快乐的感觉就会放大十倍。对一般美国人来说，我们的后院长满了各种各样的野草；但对中国人来说，这些珍贵的植物是令人艳羡的。在我眼中，后院最重要的价值在于我和奶奶留下的回忆，以至于多年以后，当我在大学中国现代文学课堂上学到《落花生》这一课时，我第一个想到的就是我的奶奶。

生活中的大事小事，点点滴滴，让我看到了也许奶奶和其他人真的不一样，但这并不重要。重要的是，这位与众不同的奶奶，让我在美国的童年受到了中国文化的影响，让我看到了自己作为美国华裔的特殊身份。我带着这样的身份，向未来骄傲地出发。

it. This feeling of happiness will be multiplied tenfold if it grows unusually large, especially sweet, or particularly well. Our backyard looked like it was full of weeds to average American, but these precious plants are a source of envy to the Chinese. In my eyes, however, the most valuable asset of this backyard are the memories I made with my grandma, so much so that years later, when I learned of the story *Peanuts* while attending a Chinese literature class in college, my mind immediately thought of my grandma.

The big and small things in life, bit by bit, made me see that maybe Grandma stands out from the crowd, but it doesn't matter. The thing that is important is that this unique grandma exposed my American childhood to the influence of Chinese culture, allowing me to embrace my Chinese American identity. With this identity, I set out proudly toward the future.

外婆的感恩节大餐

作者：罗安玲　指导教师：汪洋　布朗大学

> 正是因为她的感恩节大餐，她对家庭每一个成员的照顾，我们一大家人才能团聚在一起，相亲相爱。

每年的十一月初，我外婆都会扎根在厨房里。她首先做可以放在冰箱里储存的食物：馅儿饼皮、甘薯面包和南瓜芝士蛋糕；感恩节的两个星期以前，她开始做胡萝卜汤和蔓越莓酱；感恩节一个星期以前，她把花儿、南瓜和蜡烛放在桌子上。感恩节的前三天，她从早上九点到晚上九点都在厨房里切萝卜，烤蘑菇，煮米饭，做土豆泥，然后把三百棵小洋白菜的叶子都剥下来。最后到了感恩节的早上，我外婆六点半起床，烤一只三十磅的火鸡。

据其他家庭成员讲，过去的四十五年里，我外婆每年都这样做感恩节大餐。每年二十五位家人，包括舅舅、舅母、许多表哥和表弟及他们的小孩儿，都开车几个小时到我外婆外公家一起庆祝感恩节。这时候，我们一起吃吃喝喝，说说笑笑。这真是我一年当中最开心的一天。大餐以后，外婆把所有剩下的菜放在各种各样的小盒子里，让大家带回去，确保每个人收到了自己最喜欢的菜。

我想，读到这里，你已经知道我外婆是一个什么样的人了。

外婆是一个做事很有条理、很细致的人，什么事情都做得井井有条。她做事讲究“精准”，而且她特别喜欢用列表制订很详细的计划。她有两个大大的活页夹，

My Grandmother's Thanksgiving Dinner

Author: Annabel Roth Instructor: Yang Wang Brown University

> It is because of her Thanksgiving dinner and her love for each member of the family, our large family get together and love each other.

Every year at the beginning of November, my grandma disappears into her kitchen. She starts off by making the things for the freezer – pie crust, sweet potato bread, and pumpkin cheesecake. Two weeks before Thanksgiving, she begins to make the carrot soup and cranberry sauce. One week before, she decorated the table with flowers, pumpkins, and candles. Finally, during the 3 days before Thanksgiving, my grandma is in the kitchen from 9 a.m. to 9 p.m. chopping turnips, roasting mushrooms, cooking rice, mashing potatoes, and taking the leaves off 300 Brussel sprouts. Finally, on Thanksgiving morning, my grandma wakes up at 6:30 a.m. to roast a 30 lb turkey.

According to other family members, my grandma has been cooking Thanksgiving dinner like this for the past 45 years. Each year, around 25 members of my family, including my aunts, uncles, and many cousins and their children, drive from hours away to celebrate together at my grandparent's house. Together we talk, laugh, and eat together, making this day my favorite of the whole year. At the end of the meal, as everyone is leaving, my grandma puts all the leftover food in all different sized boxes. She then

里面挤满了感恩节的食谱，而且在每个食谱上还有她多年来积累的手写小笔记。

外婆也是一个“霸道、专横”的人。我和家人都知道如果外婆在厨房里做饭，你一定得坐在旁边，不要碍她的事儿。如果你在她的厨房里做饭，一定得把锅和碗放回原处。

但是，我外婆也是我认识的最慈祥、最有爱心的人。为了自己的家人，她什么都愿意做。虽然她想要尝试做新菜，每年都在考虑把感恩节菜单做一些改变，但最终什么都没有改变，因为她要零失败，给每个家人做他们最喜欢的菜是她最重视的事情，她不想让她爱的人失望。

看着我外婆每年做感恩节大餐，我慢慢理解她怎么用做饭来表达她对家人的感情，她的爱就像她的饭菜一样厉害，天下无敌。正是因为她的感恩节大餐，她对家庭每一个成员的照顾，我们一大家人才能团聚在一起，相亲相爱。

passes it out to all my family members, making sure everybody gets to take home their favorite dishes.

I think that my grandma's Thanksgiving dinner perfectly illustrates who she is as a person.

My grandma is organized, meticulous, and methodical. She is precise, a planner, and big believer in making lots of lists. For Thanksgiving dinner in particular, she has 2 huge binders filled with recipes, each one covered in handwritten reminders and instructions that she has added over the years.

She is bossy. Everyone in my family knows not to get in my grandma's way when she is in the kitchen, and, if you cook something in her kitchen, you'd better put all the pots and bowls back exactly where you found them.

She is also one of the most loving and caring people I know, and someone who will do anything for her family. Even though she would rather experiment with new recipes and every year considers changing the Thanksgiving menu, she never does because she does not want to disappoint any of the people whom she cares about so deeply by not making their favorite food.

Watching my grandma cook Thanksgiving dinner every year, I gradually come to know how she uses food and cooking to demonstrate her boundless love toward my family. It is because of her Thanksgiving dinner and her love for each member of the family, our large family get together and love each other.

我的姐姐

作者：葛爱婷　指导教师：张虹　寇比学院

> 之所以姐姐对我影响很大，是因为她告诉了我怎样完全信任另一个人。

姐姐是我最好的朋友，她可以读懂我的心思。我姐姐叫卡罗琳，今年二十六岁，比我大四岁。有的时候，这四岁感觉很多，她是我的大姐姐；有的时候，我又感觉我们是双胞胎。很难用文字来描述我们的关系。不说话，我们就知道彼此在想什么，就好像我们只用脑子就可以沟通。我们互相照应，心照不宣。

记得小时候，我非常害羞。那时我们家常常去朋友家做客。父母的一个朋友说话的声音特别响亮，因此他说话常常把我吓得发抖。姐姐看到这个情况，就会保护我。如果这个大嗓门的朋友问我问题，姐姐就帮我回答。如果他太吵，让我感到焦虑，姐姐就跟我聊天儿，帮我分心。我没要求姐姐这样做，可她能读懂我的心思，主动这样做。

我和姐姐都很爱我们的家人，可是，参加家庭聚会的时候，外婆、外公、爷爷、奶奶有时候会说一些又荒谬又恼人的话题。他们讨论这样的话题时，我知道姐姐在想什么。我们都知道我们两个都很恼火。我们眼神接触，默默互相同情，默默地笑。私下，我们偷偷抱怨，评论我们的家庭。

2020 年因新冠疫情居家隔离的时候，我们都在父母家住。我们的父母很忙，因此，我跟姐姐分担了大部分家务。我们做饭，打扫，洗衣服，倒垃圾，去超市采购等等。我们都喜欢做这些事情。每天晚上，我们一起做晚饭。有的时候，我

My Sister

Author: Emily Glass Instructor: Hong Zhang Colby College

> My sister has had such a big influence on me because she taught me how to completely trust another person.

My sister is my best friend and she can read my mind. Her name is Caroline. She is 26 years old, four years older than I am. Sometimes, this four-year age difference feels a lot and she feels like my elder sister; but sometimes, I feel that we are twins. It is very difficult to find words that describe our relationship. Without talking, we know what each other are thinking, and it seems like we are telepathic. We are close to each other, and we often reach a tacit understanding.

As a child, I was shy. Our parents would often take us to a friend's house. One of these friends always spoke and laughed so loudly that it often made me shiver with fright. My sister saw this and protected me. If he asked me a question, my sister would help me answer it, and if his voice was too loud and made me anxious, my sister would chat with me as a distraction. I didn't ask her to do so, but she could read my mind and offered to do so.

Both my sister and I love our family. However, at family parties, our grandparents sometimes talk about some ridiculous and annoying topics. When they discuss such topics, I know what my sister is thinking. We know that both of us are annoyed. We make eye contact, silently sympathize with each other, and silently laugh. Privately, we complain and comment on our family.

Both my sister and I lived at our parents' house in 2020 when we were quarantined due to COVID-19. Our parents were very busy, so my sister and I did most of the housework. We cooked, cleaned the house, did laundry, took out the trash, went to the supermarket, etc. We both enjoyed these tasks for the most part, so it was not a problem. Every night, we would

们一边做饭，一边聊天儿。不过，也有的时候，我们什么话也不说，只是安安静静地一起做事。这是我一天中最惬意的时刻。我们做饭的时候，彼此都拥有读心术。我们不需要讨论谁做什么任务，就像一个人一样。我们两个都有各自不喜欢的任务，所以，不用任何沟通，我做她不喜欢的任务，她做我不喜欢的任务。这是一个轻松的过程。

我跟姐姐的关系建立在互相尊重的基础上。不过，我姐姐讨厌我流泪。不是因为我流泪的时候显得懦弱，而是因为我流泪让她非常难过，感觉无助。姐姐难过、感觉无助的时候，她会很生气。我小时候流泪时，姐姐不高兴，我还以为她在生我的气。可是现在，我知道她不是生我的气，而是感觉到了我的痛苦。她想帮助我，可是有的时候，她没有办法。她因我痛苦而生气，是因为她不能解决我的问题。姐姐那么爱护我，她对任何伤害我的事情都感到很生气。

有人能完全理解我，这让我感到很幸运。我们不需要解释彼此的行为、想法、情绪。我们直观地知道彼此为什么，做什么，怎么彼此支持。我非常感谢姐姐，我无法想象没有她的生活。之所以姐姐对我影响很大，是因为她告诉了我怎样完全信任另一个人。当我非常伤心、担心、感觉自己的生活没有掌控在自己手里的时候，姐姐就会出现在我身边。无论什么情况下，她都会支持我，这是最好的感觉。

cook dinner together. Sometimes we would cook and chat at the same time, but sometimes we said nothing and just did things together quietly. This was my favorite time of day. When we cook, we read each other's minds. We do not need to discuss who does what task; we function as a unit. We each have tasks we do not like, so, without asking, I do tasks she does not like, and she does tasks I do not like. It is an effortless process.

My relationship with my sister is based on mutual respect. However, my sister hates when I cry. Not because she thinks I'm cowardly when I cry, but because my tears make her feel sad and helpless. It makes her angry to feel this way. When I was little, I thought she was mad at me for crying. But now I realize she was not mad at me; she felt my pain. She wanted to help me, but sometimes, she could not. She was mad at me for being miserable because she could not solve my problems. She loves me so much that she gets mad at anything that hurts me.

I'm glad to know that someone completely understands me. My sister and I do not need to explain our actions, thoughts, and emotions to each other. We intuitively know why the other does what and how to support each other. I am very grateful to my sister. I cannot imagine life without her. My sister has had such a big influence on me because she taught me how to completely trust another person. I know she is there for me whenever I am sad, worried, and feel like my life is out of my hands. No matter what the situation is, she will support me. This is the best feeling.

我和哥哥争冠军

作者：吕迪克　指导教师：顾利程　西北大学

胜不骄，败不馁。

学校组织了一场乒乓球比赛。我过五关斩六将，打败了所有对手，最后一轮冠亚军争夺赛，跟我较量的竟然是我的哥哥。

作为华人，特别是受到爸爸的影响，我和哥哥都爱打乒乓球。我家的地下室里就有一张乒乓球台子。从小爸爸就教我和哥哥打乒乓球。为此爸爸还买了一台发球机，供我们训练使用。放学以后，我还经常请小朋友们到我家来打乒乓球。打得好些以后，我们还去一些俱乐部参加比赛。我和哥哥是我们州少年组的两个小球王，基本上没有什么对手。所以通常到决赛，就是我们小哥儿俩争夺冠军。平常比赛，我和哥哥有输有赢。但是今天我非常想赢这一场球。很多好朋友都来观看了，当然还有她也来了。

比赛开始了。我先发了一个高抛球。哥哥接了过来，我提拉了过去，哥哥又推挡了过来，回球有些高。我抓住时机，挥拍抽了过去，哥哥没有接住，我得了第一分。第二个球，我发了一个快球。哥哥挡了过来，我提拉了过去，非常转。哥哥回球高了，我大力扣杀了过去，又得了一分，二比零。换哥哥发球。哥哥发来的球很低，但是我总是能够找到机会提拉起来。这样我控制住了局面，先拿下了头两局。五局三胜，再赢一局，我就是冠军了。这时的我掩饰不住得意的心情。每当打了一个好球以后，还向有她的人群挥手。

第三局开始了。原以为可以轻而易举地赢球，但是不知怎么搞的，我抽过去

Competing with My Older Brother for the Championship

Author: Dick Lu Instructor: Licheng Gu Northwestern University

Don't be arrogant in victory, and don't get discouraged by defeat.

My school organized a table tennis match. After overcoming various obstacles and difficulties to defeat all my opponents, during the last round of the championships in the runner-up competition, my older brother happened to be my opponent.

As Chinese Americans who are greatly influenced by our father, my brother and I both love to play table tennis. We have a ping-pong table in the basement of our house, and my father taught my brother and me to play table tennis ever since we were young. For this reason, Dad also bought a table tennis machine to help with our training. After school, I would often invite friends over to my house to play some games. After improving, we also went to clubs to participate in competitions. My brother and I are considered as the table tennis champions in our state's junior team, and we basically have no opponents. Typically, when it comes to the finals, it's the two of us who are competing for the championship. Usually, my brother and I might lose or win. However, I really wanted to win this game today. Not only did many of my good friends come to watch, but of course, *she* came as well.

The game began. I started off by serving a high throw. My brother returned it, I pulled it back over, and my brother blocked it again but returned it a bit high. I seized the opportunity to smash. My brother couldn't return it, and I scored the first point. During the second shot, I served a fastball. My brother blocked it, and I returned it in a fast spin ball. My brother returned the ball high, and I smashed the ball vigorously to score another point: two to zero. It was now my brother's turn to serve. His serves tended to be low, but I could always find

的球，哥哥都挡了回来。不但时而轻、时而重，而且角度很大。我的回球不是落网，就是出界。八比十一，哥哥竟然扳回了一局。后来哥哥越打越好，我却越打手脚越软，完全处于被动挨打的地步。最后，我输了。

还好，她过来拥抱了我，安抚我说："胜不骄，败不馁。"对。暂时胜利了不能骄傲，失败了也不气馁。我要记住这个深刻的教训。

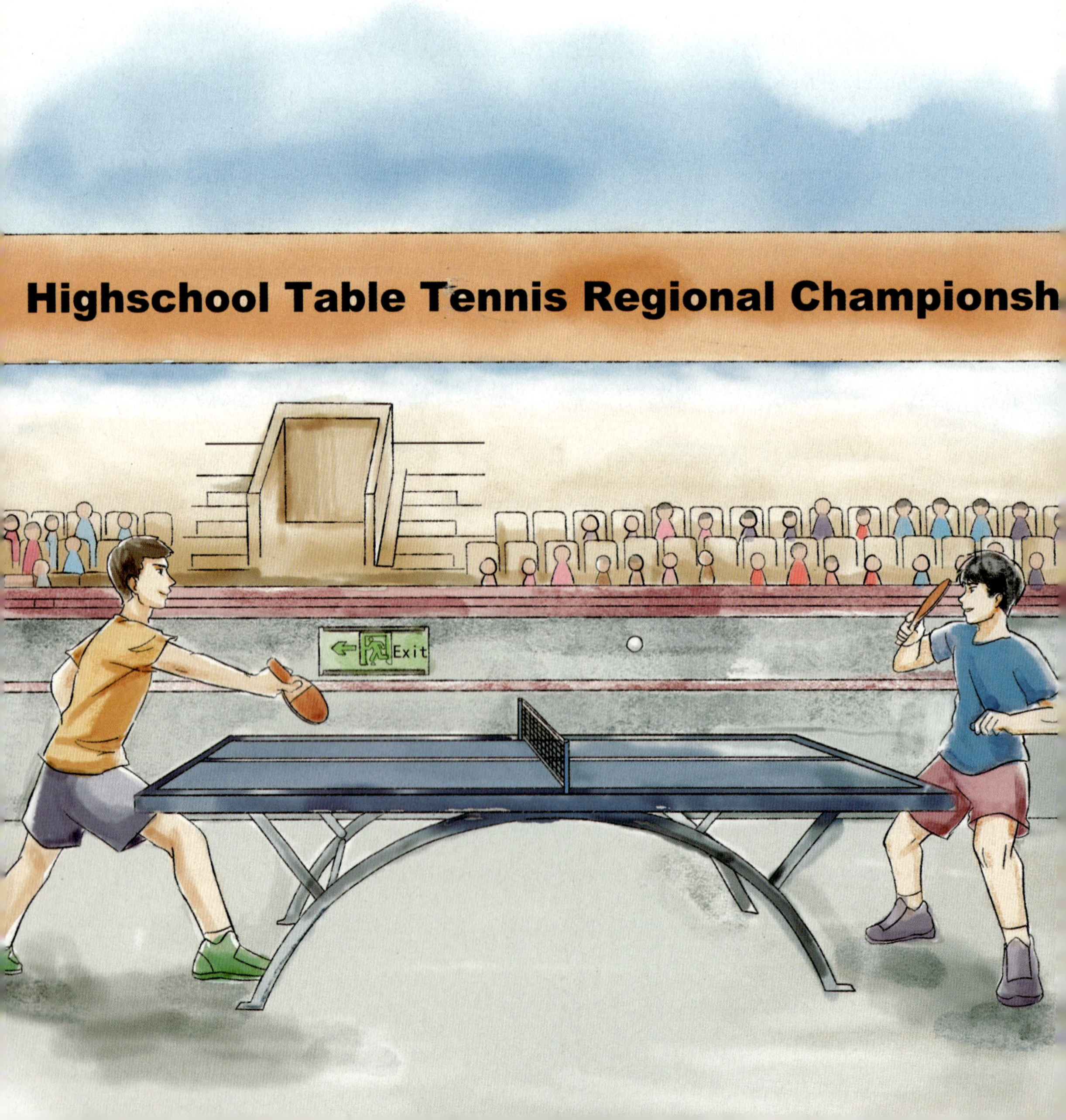

opportunities to pull it back up. Just like this, I got the game under my control and won the first two rounds. I only need three wins out of five, so I just had to win one more round to be the champion. In this moment, I couldn't hide my pride and elation. Every time I hit a good shot, I would also wave in triumph to the crowd, where *she* also stood and cheered for me.

The third game started. Although I originally thought that I could win easily, for some reason, my brother was able to block all my smashes. Not only were his returns sometimes forceful and sometimes light, but they also came from large angles. As a result, a lot of my returns would either go into the net or out of bounds. The score was eight to eleven, and my brother finally won a round. Later, my brother played better and better, but my hands and feet became weaker and weaker, putting me in a passive situation. In the end, I lost.

Fortunately, *she* came over and hugged me, comforting me, "Don't be arrogant in victory, and don't get discouraged by defeat." Indeed, we shouldn't be complacent when we win temporarily, and neither should we be discouraged when we lose. I will always remember this profound lesson.

三姐妹

作者：李乐伊　指导教师：汪洋　布朗大学

> 虽然我姥姥不常谈论她自己的故事，但是我觉得这些画儿是一种无声的交流。

我小的时候特别喜欢跟姥姥一起画画儿。她公寓的墙上有好多画儿，都是她自己画的。我自己家的房间里也有好多画儿，很多也是姥姥画的。姥姥画的画儿，有的是山水，有的是花草，有的是建筑。姥姥画的很多画儿都有一个我最喜爱的细节：总是有三个女孩儿，一起坐着，背对着我。我小的时候觉得她们就像我书里的人物。在我的想象中，这些女孩儿可能是精灵，可能是间谍，也可能在等我走进画儿里跟她们一起玩儿。

我姥姥不常告诉我她小时候的故事。我以为她一直都是成人。我想象不出来我姥姥小时候是什么样子。我总觉得，她出生的时候就已经是我的姥姥了。

我差不多八岁的时候，学校开始学第二次世界大战这段历史。下课以后我跑到我的妈妈面前，问她："你听说过二战吗？你听说大屠杀吗？"妈妈不知道应该笑还是应该哭，她说："对，我听说过。你在学校学了什么？"我告诉她我不敢相信犹太人受到那么多伤害。我们是犹太人，但是我不知道居然有人想杀我们。妈妈说："你知道吗？你姥姥就是一个大屠杀的幸存者。"我听了以后非常生气，说道："我快八岁了，你怎么一直都没告诉我这件事？你在等什么？！"

我妈妈让我坐下，给我讲了姥姥的故事。这个故事给了我非常强烈的冲击。

我姥姥六岁的时候，德军入侵了她家乡的小镇。差不多有三个月的时间，小镇的大门紧紧关闭，门边还有纳粹士兵把守，里面的犹太人都不能自由进出。有

Three Sisters

Author: Maya Azrieli Instructor: Yang Wang Brown University

> Although my grandmother doesn't often talk about her story, I think the paintings are a kind of communication on their own.

When I was young, I loved to draw with my grandmother. Many paintings were hanging on her apartment walls, all of which were her own. My room at home also had many paintings hung on the walls, many of which were painted by my grandmother. There were paintings of landscapes, plants, and buildings. In many of my grandmother's paintings, there is a detail that I loved: there are three girls, sitting together with their backs to me. When I was little, I thought of them like characters in my books. I imagined that these girls were elves, maybe spies, or maybe that they were waiting for me to come into the painting and play with them.

My grandmother didn't often tell me stories about her childhood. I believed that she had always been an adult. I couldn't imagine my grandmother as a child. I felt as though she had been born as my grandmother.

I started learning about the history of World War II at school when I was almost eight years old. After class, I ran up to my mom and asked her, "Have you heard of World War II? Have you heard of the Holocaust?" She didn't know whether to laugh or cry. She said, "Yes, I've heard of it. What did you learn at school?" I told her that I couldn't believe how the Jews had been hurt. We are Jewish, but I didn't know how anyone could want to kill us. She said, "Did you know that your grandmother is a Holocaust survivor?" I was immediately angry when I heard that, "I'm almost eight years old and you have never told me that? What were you waiting for?"

一天，有一个十七岁的男孩儿听到两个纳粹说话：“明天，纳粹打算杀死镇上所有的犹太人。”这个男孩儿马上把他听到的话告诉了其他犹太人，于是镇上的犹太人开始计划逃跑。

第二天一大早，为了让纳粹打开镇上的大门，犹太人放火把镇子烧了。在熊熊大火中，镇上所有的犹太人，包括我姥姥、她的父母和她的两个姐姐都趁机逃跑了。逃离小镇以后，我姥姥找到了她的爸爸和大姐，但是找不到她的妈妈和二姐，后来也一直没有找到。在以后的日子里，姥姥和她的爸爸、姐姐开始躲避纳

My mother sat me down to tell my grandmother's story. The impact that it had on me was profound.

When my grandmother was six years old, the German army invaded her hometown. For almost three months, the town gates were locked and guarded by Nazi soldiers. No Jews were allowed to enter or exit. One day, a seventeen-year-old boy overheard two Nazis speaking to each other. He learned that the next day, the Nazis planned to kill all of the Jews living in the town. The boy told the other Jews right away and they began to plan their escape.

粹的追捕。他们在树林里忍饥挨冻躲了两年，直到二战结束。

我悄悄地问妈妈：“姥姥的妈妈和二姐后来找到了吗？”“我们仍然不知她们发生了什么事，但是都认为她们或是被火烧死了，或是被纳粹杀死了。”妈妈伤心地答道。听到这些以后，我不知道该说什么，我们坐在那里沉默了许久。妈妈最终打破了沉默：“你看见姥姥的很多画儿里都有三个女孩儿吗？我觉得那是她跟她的两个姐姐。”

现在，在我大学宿舍里还有一张画儿，上面画的是三个女孩儿看着一条河。两个女孩儿坐着，一个站着。我常常想那三个女孩儿是不是我姥姥和她的姐姐。虽然我姥姥不常谈论她自己的故事，但是我觉得这些画儿是一种无声的交流。我想我不会问她画儿里的人是不是她们姐妹三人，我更喜欢想象在这些画儿里，她们三姐妹永远在一起。

Early the following day, the Jews set the town on fire in order to force the Nazis to open the town's gates. In the raging fire, all of the Jews in the town, including my grandmother, her parents, and her two sisters, took the opportunity to escape. Once free, my grandmother found her father and eldest sister, but not her mother and second eldest sister. In the days that followed, my grandmother, her father, and her eldest sister began to hide from the Nazis. They lived, starving and freezing in the woods, for two years until the end of World War II.

I quietly asked my mother, "Were my grandma's mother and second eldest sister found later?" "We still don't know what happened to them, but we think that they were either burned to death or killed by the Nazis," replied my mother sadly. I didn't know what to say and we sat in silence for a long time. My mother broke the silence, "Have you seen the three girls in Grandma's paintings? I think that they are her and her two sisters."

There is a painting hanging in my college dorm room now of three girls looking at a river. Two girls are sitting and one is standing. I often wonder if the three girls are my grandma and her two sisters. Although my grandmother doesn't often talk about her story, I think the paintings are a kind of communication on their own. I don't think I'll ask her whether the painting is of her and her sisters. I prefer to just imagine that the three of them are together forever in these paintings.

给妈妈的一封信

作者：王晓濛　指导教师：顾利程　西北大学

> 我从心里意识到，因为有您，才有今天的我。

亲爱的妈妈：

在西北大学的中文课上，老师让我回忆自己的童年，给妈妈写一封信，反思自己在童年时受到的教育。

一想起童年，我就想起您给我安排的日复一日的钢琴课、美术课、网球课、滑冰课……总之，您认为我小时候最好什么都学学，结果我小时候的时间被安排得满满的。我还记得每一次您带我去打网球时，我就抱怨天气太热；带我去滑冰时，我抱怨溜冰场太冷。无论您要我学什么，我不是抱怨，就是哭，特别是您要我学中文的时候。我一学中文，就不停地哭，总是大喊大叫：“汉字太多了，发音太难了！”我很快就不想学了，但是您还是坚持继续教我。

您很坚定地跟我说：“濛濛，当人们看到你的外表时，他们就会认为你是中国人，一定会说中文。”您说得很有道理，可是我小时候一点儿都不想当中国人，我只想当美国人，跟我的美国同学一样。对我来说，不会说中文，只跟您和爸爸说英文是一件很酷的事情。

小时候因为我非常不愿意学中文，每一次您教我都得花费好大的力气。每个周末，我一边哭，一边念中文课文。那时您总是耐心而坚定地坐在我旁边，陪着我学。这样一直坚持到我初中毕业。一个人的耐心和毅力不是无限的，终于有一天您无可奈何地跟我说：“濛濛，从此以后，中文你想学就学，不想学就不学了

A Letter to My Mother

Author: Grace Wang   Instructor: Licheng Gu   Northwestern University

> I have realized, from my heart, only because of you could I have become the person I am today.

Dear Mom,

In Northwestern University's Chinese class, the professor wanted me to recall my childhood, write my mom a letter, and reflect on the education I received as a child.

When I think of my childhood, I think of the piano lessons, art lessons, tennis lessons, ice skating lessons... you scheduled for me day after day. Basically, you believed I should learn a little bit of everything while I'm young. As a result, my time as a child was packed full. I still remember every time you took me to play tennis, I would complain that it was too hot outside; when you took me to go ice skating, I complained the ice rink was too cold. No matter what it was you wanted me to learn, if I didn't complain about it, I'd start crying about it, especially when you wanted me to learn Chinese. As soon as I'd start learning Chinese, I would not stop crying, always screaming and shouting, "There are too many Chinese characters, and the pronunciation is too hard!" Very quickly, I did not want to learn anymore, but you still insisted on continuing to teach me.

You firmly told me, "Grace, once people see your outward appearance, they will just assume you're Chinese and that you definitely can speak Chinese." What you said made sense, but when I was little, I did not want to be Chinese at all. I only wanted to be American, just like my American classmates. For me, not knowing how to speak Chinese, only speaking in English to you and Dad was a cool thing to do.

Because I really didn't want to learn Chinese when I was younger, every time you taught me Chinese, you had to spend a lot of effort. Every weekend, I would have tears streaming

吧。这是你自己的生活，我已经尽到了妈妈的责任，精疲力尽了。”当时听到这句话，我心里可高兴了，终于可以不学中文了。但是现在我长大了，进了大学，

down my face while I read the Chinese textbook passages. At that time, you would always sit next to me patiently yet firmly, accompanying me as I learned. This continued until I graduated from middle school. A person's patience and perseverance is not infinite. Finally, one day you told me helplessly, "Grace, from now on, Chinese is something you can learn if you want to. If you don't want to learn it, you don't have to. This is your own life. I've done my job as a mom, and I'm exhausted." At the time, when I heard this, I was so happy. I can finally stop learning Chinese. But now that I've grown up, entered college, and also have a better understanding of the world, I really wish you continued to teach me Chinese.

I really want to learn Chinese, understand Chinese culture, try Chinese food, and watch Chinese TV dramas. So in college, I chose to take a Chinese class, through which I've realized the importance of learning Chinese and inheriting my Chinese culture. I've also learned that being able to use Chinese when communicating with my family back in China is super important. That's why I regularly try to speak in Chinese with you now. The younger version of me could have never guessed I would be the person I am now. How did I not even like to eat Chinese food when I was younger?

In my childhood, you have placed so much energy and dedication on me. You accompanied me all day long to learn this and that. It must have been very tiring. So truly from the bottom of my heart, I am grateful to you. There's a saying in China, "Pathetic are the feelings of all parents under heaven toward their offspring." If I could have made my own decisions about my lifestyle and activities as a child, I would have definitely done nothing. When I was little, I didn't have any hobbies or interests. It was only because you took me to try volleyball that I discovered I actually really enjoy playing it. But it is never too late to make amends, only because of your perseverance for so many years, do I have the foundation I have now in Chinese, where I can further improve on my Chinese skills in college, and write this letter to you in Chinese. Your efforts have not been in vain. Your daughter Grace has grown up

也懂事了，我真希望当时您一直坚持教我中文。

我很想学中文，了解中国文化，尝中国美食，看中国电视剧。所以在大学里，自己选择上中文课。通过上中文课，我意识到学习中文、继承中华文化的重要性，也意识到能用中文与国内的家人沟通是非常重要的。所以现在我常常试着用中文跟您聊天儿。从前的我肯定都想不到我现在会成为这样一个人。我小时候怎么会连中国菜都不想吃呢?

小时候让您为我操碎了心。您一天到晚陪着我学这学那，一定很累，所以我现在从心底里感激您。所以中国有句话:“可怜天下父母心。”如果我小时候可以自己决定我的生活方式和学习安排，那我肯定就什么都不会干。我小时候没有什么爱好或兴趣，只是因为您陪我去试了试排球，我才发现我很喜欢打排球。亡羊补牢，为时未晚，因为您的多年坚持，我才能拥有较好的中文基础，现在在大学里能够进一步提高我的中文水平，用中文给您写这封信，您的功夫没有白费。您的濛濛现在长大了，懂事了。我从心里意识到，因为有您，才有今天的我。所以我要再一次感谢妈妈的养育之恩!

永远爱您的濛濛

3 月 8 日于芝加哥

now, and she's matured now. I have realized, from my heart, only because of you could I have become the person I am today. So I want to thank you, Mom, again for taking care of me all these years and raising me up!

Always love you, Grace

March 8, Chicago

给奶奶的一封信

作者：马书文　指导教师：陈靖文　弗吉尼亚大学

亲爱的奶奶：

您那么爱我，现在轮到我来回报您的爱了。

您好！

好久不见！我现在跟您距离太遥远了，想念您却见不到您，让我很难过。但距离挡不住我对您的思念，我想念您做的家常菜，想念您笑眯眯的脸和您的拥抱。

小时候，爸爸妈妈都忙工作，大部分时间都是您陪我度过的。我甚至误以为您就是我的妈妈。那时候，您每天早晨给我做饭，白天还要给我洗衣服，晚上我

A Letter to Grandmother

Author: Sean Martin Instructor: Jack Chen University of Virginia

> You love me so much, and now it's my turn to repay your love.

Dear Grandma,

Hello! It's been a long time since we last saw each other. I miss you but I can't see you, which makes me very sad. However, distance cannot stop my longing for you. I miss the home-cooked meals you made, your smiling face, and your hugs.

When I was a child, my parents were busy with work, so most of the time it was you who accompanied me. I even thought you were my mother. At that time, you made me breakfast every morning, washed my clothes during the day, and sang songs to me at night when I was afraid of the dark and wouldn't sleep. Listening to your singing, I always slept soundly. Although you were always busy with my affairs, you were happy every day, and I knew you also enjoyed my company.

I remember when we traveled to Japan together, we ate different Japanese dishes every day and visited different tourist attractions. The photos we took in front of the castle are still on my phone. When I miss you, I take them out and look at them. Seeing our smiling faces in the photos immediately makes me happy.

When I had to leave home for university, both you and I cried, and I really didn't want to leave you. During those early days at school, I had to call you every day to be able to have a good day. Gradually, because of more and more coursework, increasing exam pressure, and daily trivial matters taking up my time, I called you less and less. Please forgive me for that. I promise that as soon as winter break comes, I will come home immediately, give you a big

怕黑不肯睡觉，您就唱歌给我听，哄我睡着。听着您的歌声，我总是能睡得特别安稳。虽然您总是为了我的事忙碌，可是您每天都乐呵呵的，我知道您也喜欢我的陪伴。

记得一起去日本旅行时，我们每天都吃不同的日本菜，去不同的景点参观。我们在城堡前拍的照片现在还存在我的手机里。我想您的时候，就拿出来看一看。看到照片上我们的笑脸，我立刻就开心起来。

当我必须离家去上大学时，您跟我都哭了，我真舍不得您。刚到学校的那些日子，我每天都得给您打电话，才能安心过好一天。慢慢地，因为功课越来越多，考试的压力越来越大，生活中的琐事也占用了我的时间，我给您打电话的次数也变少了，请您原谅我。我保证，一放寒假我就立刻回家，给您一个大大的拥抱，陪您聊天儿、做饭。想到我的计划，我就很激动。您那么爱我，现在轮到我来回报您的爱了。

敬祝

安康！

孙女书文　　敬上

12 月 1 日

hug, chat with you, and cook for you. Thinking of my plan, I am very excited. You love me so much, and now it's my turn to repay your love.

Wishing you good health,

Sincerely,

Sean

December 1

家力山大

作者：江慧楠　指导教师：苏炜　耶鲁大学

在我的人生中，家仿佛一座大山，山上万物共生。

看完巴金的《家》之后，我不禁唏嘘小说里的“家”，跟我对“家”的看法天差地别。在小说里，祖父给孙子安排的婚姻，导致三弟觉慧失去了恋人。家长强迫老大觉新担起长子的责任，导致他失去了梦想。家人明明应该是最理解和支持自己的人，但是这样的家人却带给了高家三兄弟无尽的痛苦。对他们而言，家意味着束缚和压抑，无助和放弃。家，意味着压力山大。幸亏每当我想起我的家，脑海中会浮出一座晴朗无云、翡翠碧绿的大山。

家，就是凌晨六点，太阳还没升起来的时候，厨房里独自忙碌的身影。虽然还很早，但是她的头发已经梳好，围裙系得整整齐齐。这就是我的妈妈。她切菜、洗碗、炒蛋的声响，像是用锅碗瓢盆奏出的交响曲，响彻房间。妈妈每天早上像蚂蚁一样忙碌，但是也跟蚂蚁一样强大。她惊人的毅力与无私奉献的精神可以移山，可以填海。早晨七点，阳光慢慢洒进房，早餐的香味飘进卧室。暖金色的蛋黄便成为唤醒我和弟弟的晨光。当我们围着圆饭桌坐下，拿起叉子时，妈妈仍然在厨房里忙个不停。我无数次问妈妈：“为什么你那么早起来准备我们的早餐和午餐饭盒，自己却不过来吃？这样不累吗？”妈妈每次都微笑着回答：“做菜给心爱的人吃是一种幸福。只要你们健健康康，茁壮成长，无论有多忙，我都心甘情愿。”

Pressure as Heavy as a Mountain and Family as Great as a Mountain

Author: Eunice Kiang Instructor: Wei Su Yale University

> In my life, family is like a great mountain. On it, all sorts of things coexist.

After reading *The Family* by Ba Jin, I could not help but sigh, for the difference between "family" in the story and my view of family is as vast as the distance between the sky and earth. In the novel, the grandfather arranges a marriage for his grandson, causing the third brother Juehui to lose his lover. The parents force the eldest brother Juexin to take up the responsibilities of an eldest son, causing him to lose his dream. Family is supposed to be the people who understand and support oneself the most, yet it brings the three Gao brothers nothing but endless suffering. To them, "family" means restrictions and depression, helplessness and giving up. "Family" means "pressure as heavy as a mountain." Luckily, whenever I think of my family, in my mind there surfaces a sunny, cloudless, jade-green, and great mountain.

Family is the solitary silhouette busying about in the kitchen at six a.m. before the sun rises. Even though it is still early, her hair is already combed and her apron is already neatly tied. This is my mom. Her every move, be it chopping vegetables, washing dishes, or scrambling eggs, rings and clangs like an ant, agile and strong. She can remove mountains and fill up seas with her amazing perseverance and selfless dedication. At seven in the morning, when sunlight slowly spills into the house, the fragrance of breakfast drifts toward the bedroom. Warm golden egg yolks promptly become the morning sun that awakens me and my younger brother. By the time we sit down at the round table and grab our forks, our mom is still in the kitchen busying about nonstop. I asked my mom countless times, "Why do you get up so early to prepare our breakfast and lunchboxes, but do not come to eat yourself? Aren't you tired?" Every time, my mom replied with a smile, "Cooking for my loved ones is a kind of happiness.

家，就是下午三点，放学后开秘密会议的时候，卧室里亲切的身影。每当我被欺负，弟弟都会站在我这边。记得有一次历史课，班上的同学被分成了若干小组，而我的小组队友要我一个人把全组的作业完成。即使我不愿意，队友还是强人所难，我感到很无奈。但是，一踏进我们姐弟俩的房间，我从一脸乌云一转眼就变成了笑逐颜开，因为眼前出现了一张又可爱又顽皮的小狗似的脸庞。弟弟宣布道："他们竟敢欺负我姐姐？好，今天咱们两个的会议，让我来表演说唱！"我连书包都来不及扔，就在一张纸上潦草地写下"疯粉"来支援弟弟的表演。弟弟一边打节拍，一边说唱："同学要我姐，干全组的活儿。无聊透顶呀，都是大

As long as you are healthy and grow up quickly, no matter how busy I am, I will gladly do it."

Family is the familiar silhouette in the bedroom at three p.m., the time for After-School Secret Meeting. Whenever I get bullied, my younger brother always sides with me. I remember once, my history class was divided into groups, and my teammates wanted me to finish all of their work alone. Even though I was unwilling, my teammates still forced difficulty upon me, so I felt very frustrated. However, upon stepping into the room that we brother and sister shared, the storm clouds on my face dissipated into a glowing smile in the blink of an eye, because a face as cute and mischievous as a puppy's had appeared before my eyes. My younger brother announced, "How dare they bully my big sister? Alright, in today's meeting, let me perform a rap!" I did not even have time to throw aside my backpack before I scribbled "Crazy Fan" on a piece of paper to support my younger brother's performance. Drumming a beat, he rapped, "Classmates want Sister to be their slave. How stupid this is, lazy bugs and knaves!" At that moment, I ecstatically tore up my piece of paper, then could not resist hurling it at the ceiling and screaming with both thumbs up, "Awesome!" I was very thankful that he created lyrics especially for cheering me up. Even though I am not familiar with music, no matter how his performance is, I am still his most loyal fan. We have always supported each other, and he is always my best friend.

Family is the warm silhouette entering from the dark outside when a click resounds in the house at seven p.m. "Welcome home, Daddy!" He had not even removed his shoes yet when my younger brother and I charged at him and impatiently began summarizing everything that had happened that day at school. I exclaimed dejectedly, "My classmates want me to do the whole group's work all by myself. I'm screwed." My dad's eyebrows instantly frowned, then he said sternly, "How can your classmates take advantage of you like this? They're looking for an excuse to put you in a difficult situation, hoping that you'll make a mistake. Look at those who have succeeded throughout history. They experienced so many adversities and failures, but they would never give up. Instead, after falling, they would get up and run even faster. So, you must be strong and think of a solution to the problem, not hang your head." After listening to my dad, I firmly told my teammates that if they want to get a good grade, we must work together. Moreover, I took the initiative to distribute labor to each teammate. Ultimately, our group finished the assignment together and got the highest grade. Ever since I was little, my dad has shared many stories to teach me and my younger brother principles of life, like a huge tree

懒虫！”唱到这里，我疯狂地把纸撕碎，抛向天空，双手竖起大拇指呐喊：“太棒了！”我很感激弟弟特意为我创作歌词来逗我开心。虽然我不懂音乐，但是无论弟弟表演得怎么样，我都是他的铁粉。我们一直以来互相支持，而弟弟永远是我最亲近的朋友。

家，就是晚上七点，屋里发出咔嚓声的那一刻，从漆黑的门外进来的温暖的身影。“爸爸回来啦！”爸爸还没来得及脱鞋子，我和弟弟就向他冲过去，迫不及待地讲述当天在学校里所发生的一切。我沮丧地倾诉道：“小组里的同学要我一个人完成小组作业。我完蛋了。”爸爸眉头一皱，严厉地说道：“你的同学怎么可以这样欺负你？他们找理由为难你，就是希望你出错。瞧瞧历史上的成功人士，他们经过多少的挫折和失败。但是他们跌倒后绝不会放弃，反而爬起来跑得更快。所以你要坚强，想想办法解决问题，而不是垂头丧气。”听了爸爸的话之后，我坚定地告诉了小组队友，要拿高分的话，一定要一起合作。而且，我主动分配了每一个队友的工作。结果，我们小组一起完成了作业，并且得到了最高分。在我们成长的过程中，爸爸总会分享很多故事，教给我和弟弟人生的道理。仿佛森林中守护着小树苗的大树，传授长者积累的智慧。

正是如此，在我的人生中，家仿佛一座大山，山上万物共生。一年四季，在草丛最不显眼的地方，身材弱小的蚂蚁不求回报地付出，正是它们的辛勤劳作，维系了整个生态的平衡。在草丛中，两只兔子蹦蹦跳跳，亲热地玩耍，让彼此的日子永远不孤独而且充满欢乐。遇到敌人时，兔子会联手互相支持，一起扑上去反击敌人。在草丛上，透过茂密的树叶照进来的阳光，像是高高耸立的树有了明亮温和的眼睛。这双眼睛慈爱地照亮着兔子的世界，帮助它们洞察人生。即使有时候太阳会被遮住，无论是暴风雨、龙卷风，还是打雷闪电，家这座山仍然稳稳地处在我心中的第一位。我铭感五内，我的家不是“压力山大”，而是“家力山大”。

protecting saplings in the forest and imparting the accumulated wisdom of an elderly.

It is exactly so; in my life, family is like a great mountain. On it, all sorts of things coexist. At all seasons, in the most invisible corners of the grass, small ants give their all without expecting compensation to help all living things operate peacefully. Ants' hard work maintains the balance of the whole ecosystem. Amidst the grass, two bunnies prance around, enthusiastically playing together and filling each other's days with companionship and joy. Upon meeting an enemy, the puppies join forces with each other, bark incessantly in fury, and pounce to defeat it. Above the grass, the sunlight that filters through the thick foliage is as if the tall and erect trees have bright and gentle eyes. These eyes lovingly light up the bunnies' world and help them discover the meaning of life. Even if on some days the mountain loses its sunny weather, no matter if it is a rainstorm, tornado, or thunder and lightning, the mountain of my family will still firmly stand at the first place in my heart, because it is carved into my very soul that my family does not have "pressure as heavy as a mountain," but is "as great as a mountain."

我的外公鲁冠球

作者：倪雪睿　指导教师：顾利程　西北大学

> 他教给我的“决心、乐观、慷慨”，是送给我的最大的财富。

我对外公的最初印象可以追溯到妈妈第一次带我去外公的办公室。

当时外公不在，于是妈妈把我留在办公室便出门去找他，出门时还叮嘱我：“别乱碰办公室的东西。”妈妈出门后，我当然不停地到处摸索了起来，还在外公的办公桌后发现了一个小冰箱。大概是从外公那里继承了好奇的性格，我忍不住打开了冰箱，非常欣喜地发现冰箱里有一些巧克力。但欣喜很快便烟消云散，因为我感到背后有人。外公回来了，我被抓了个现行。我转过身来，脸上写满愧疚，却看到外公脸上灿烂的笑容，“你若不告诉妈妈和外婆我这里藏着巧克力，我就给你吃。”外公说道。这是我记忆中最美味的巧克力。

由于我在美国出生长大，中文不流利，外公经常会教我一些中文的表达，同时教给我做人的道理。外公教给我的第一个词是“决心”：要有从失败中学习的决心，而不是被打倒；要有想他人所不敢想的决心；要有为实现目标不分日夜努力的决心。外公常说，你可以是世上最聪明、最富有才华的人，但如果没有决心，你将难以为继。虽然外公出生在动荡年代并且曾经辍学，但他却孜孜不倦地工作，把每一次挑战作为机会，他生命中的每一分钟都充满了激情和能量。即便在外公生病住院期间，他仍然戴着眼镜，手中握笔，在文件上不停批注。外公

In Memory of My Grandpa Lu Guanqiu

Author: Shirley Ni   Instructor: Licheng Gu   Northwestern University

> The greatest wealth and legacy he left me is determination, optimism, and generosity.

The earliest memory I have of Grandpa was when Mama took me into his office.

Grandpa wasn't there at the time, so Mama left me alone in the office while she went to find him. "Don't touch anything in the office," she said as she left, so of course I touched everything, including a small fridge behind Grandpa's desk. I guess I inherited my curiosity from Grandpa. I opened the fridge, and to my great delight, I found some chocolate in it. However, my delight soon faded as I felt a towering presence behind me. Grandpa had returned, and I was caught red-handed. I turned around, guilt written upon my face, only to find a great smile written upon Grandpa's face. "I'll give you some chocolate if you don't tell your Mom or Grandma." he said. It was the most delicious chocolate in my memory.

Since I was born and raised in the U.S., I was not fluent in Chinese. Grandpa often taught me Chinese expressions and passed on lessons in life. The first word he has taught me is "决心," or determination. I need to have determination to learn from failures rather than feeling defeated, determination to pursue ideas bigger than people can conceive, and determination to work passionately day in and day out toward those ideas. Grandpa often said that you can be the most talented or smartest person in this world, but if you do not have the determination to work hard, then you will find yourself unable to move forward. Despite being born during challenging times and even dropping out of school, Grandpa worked relentlessly and viewed

不知疲倦、勤勉工作的决心给我留下了深刻的印象，从幼年起我就对外公充满了敬意。

外公教我的第二个词是“乐观”。外公就是我的“圣诞老人”。这并不只是因为他有个像圣诞老人一样的大肚子，笑容可掬的面庞，更是因为他乐观的天性。他总是第一个开玩笑，也常常第一个被自己的玩笑逗乐，我永远忘不了他那极具感染力的笑声和魅力超凡的激情，即使隔着世上最厚的墙，都能听到他充满活力的爽朗笑声。

外公教给我的第三个词是“慷慨”。他将对生活的热爱分享给每一个他遇见的人，帮助别人是他最大的快乐。我曾经多次听长辈们说过，在商务谈判过程中，外公总是首先考虑商业合作伙伴的利益，再考虑自家公司的利益。在商业合作上，他总是追求双赢的目的。从外公的身上，我也从小就学会了帮助我周围的人，并且从中享受巨大的快乐。我跟我的朋友们分享我的礼物，跟朋友们分享各种喜悦。

every challenge as an opportunity. He lived every moment of his life with this strong spirit and willpower. Even when ill, you would find him in the hospital with his glasses on, pen in hand, marking up pages and passing on notes. His tireless energy and industrious determination never failed to leave me in awe, and ever since I was young, I respected him immensely.

The second word Grandpa has taught me is "乐观," or optimism. Grandpa is my Santa Claus, not just because of his round belly and smiling expression, but because of his jolly nature. He was always the first to tell a joke and often the first to laugh at his own joke. I will always remember his dangerously contagious laugh and his charismatic passion. Even with the thickest wall in the world, you could still hear his vibrant and abundant laugh.

The third word Grandpa has taught me is "慷慨," or generosity. He shared his love of life with whomever he met, and his greatest joy was helping and enriching the lives of others. I heard from the elders many times that in business negotiation, Grandpa always put the interest of his partners ahead of that of his own company. He always sought for mutual benefit in business cooperation. I learned from Grandpa to help people around me and enjoy the great happiness from it. I often share gifts and joy with my friends. I am very happy when everyone is happy.

Grandpa lived a life that impacted and changed many people, and the greatest wealth and legacy he left me is determination, optimism, and generosity, which inspired me and shone through the darkest of times and lighted the way for me.

The last memory I have of Grandpa was when he was in the hospital. Despite the fact that he was heavily medicated, despite the fact that he had lost his Santa Claus belly, despite everything that was wrong with his body, he still wore the same great big smile he gave me in my first memory of him. There will be times where I face difficulties in life, and in those times, I will give a great big smile of my own as I challenge and tackle hardships head on. Grandpa can smile even in the face of death, and then surely his granddaughter can smile before challenges. I hope that someday I will be able to make him, up in heaven, be as proud of me as I am proud of him. With every step I take, I know he is watching me from the heaven and

大家都很高兴的时候，我也会感到无比的快乐。

外公的一生影响、改变了很多人，他教给我的“决心、乐观、慷慨”，是送给我的最大的财富，激励着我奋力前行，也让我能在困难的时候看到阳光和希望。

我对外公的最后记忆是他临终前在医院的时候，尽管他那时已经没有了圣诞老人的大肚子，身体到处都出现了问题，他脸上仍然挂着和蔼的笑容，就像我记忆中第一次见他时那样。我的人生也一定会有困难的时候，但我一定要像外公一样，用微笑去迎接挑战。外公能在死亡面前保持微笑，作为外孙女的我也能在挑战前保持微笑。我希望有一天，天堂里的外公能为我感到骄傲，就像我为他感到骄傲一样。我知道我走的每一步，外公都会在天上看着我，暗中帮助我，他的光芒从来就没有离开过我。

谢谢您，外公，我想念您，爱您，我知道您在天堂也一定会成功，您的笑声也一定会在那里久久回荡。

helping me secretly. His light has never left me.

Thank you, Grandpa. I miss you, I love you, and I know you are prospering and spreading your laughter up above in the heaven as well.

文化交流
Cultural Exchange

导读

同学们学习中文，接触中国文化，必然会感受到东西文化的撞击，也不免把两种文化拿来对比，这更是每一个生活在美国的华裔学生必须面对的一个问题。在《生活在两种文化中的我》一文的开始，西北大学的夏丽莎同学就写道："美国是我成长的地方，中国是我传统文化的来源地。"丽莎接着写道："但我却无法把自己完完全全看成是美国人，因为我的身体里永远流着华人的血液，我的父母是地地道道的中国人。我成长的过程中到处是中国文化、中国饮食、中国道德。"最终，丽莎发现自己是"中国和美国文化交织的产物"。"我的性格有中国人的含蓄，也有美国人的干脆；有中国人的细腻，也有美国人的大方；有中国人的传统，也有美国人的开放。"丽莎同学对两种文化的对比具体细腻，令人回味无穷。中西两种文化各有所长，各有所短，但是结合在丽莎的身上，可以说是一个完美结合，正可谓珠联璧合。这种总结分析对比的写作方法非常值得大家学习。

如果说生长在华人家庭里面的青少年有文化认同上的纠结，那么从小被美国白人领养的中国小孩子所面临的窘境，更会超过一般人的想象。在《我是哪国人》的这篇文章里，洛尤拉大学的民雨磊同学讲述了她上小学时发生的一个故事。一次班里举行用筷子比赛，班里的所有同学都期待雨磊得第一。这让她感到"紧张、尴尬，甚至恐惧"。无论她会不会用筷子，就因为她长着一张华人的面孔，同学们就都认为她筷子一定用得最好。当陌生人问她："你是从哪里来的？"雨磊真的不知道怎么回答才好。迷茫在两种文化之间很长一段时间之后，雨磊最后在老师和家长的帮助下明确了态度。她写道："我觉得我不只属于哪一个国家，哪一种文化。我喜欢我这里的家人和朋友，熟悉的环境，各种有趣的娱乐活动。我也

Introduction

When students learn Chinese language and encounter Chinese culture, they will inevitably feel the clash of Eastern and Western cultures, and they will also compare the two cultures; this is a problem that every Chinese student living in the United States must face. At the beginning of the story "Living in Two Different Cultures," Lisha Xia, a student from Northwestern University, wrote: "America is where I grew up and China is my traditional culture comes from." Lisha then explained: "I cannot see myself as completely American because I always have Chinese blood in my body. My parents are Chinese from the ground up. I grew up with Chinese culture, Chinese food, and Chinese morals." In the end, Lisha discovered that she was "the product of the intertwining of Chinese and American cultures... My character has Chinese subtlety and American directness, the Chinese delicacy and American generosity, the Chinese reserve and American openness." Lisha's detailed comparison of the two cultures is particularly memorable. Both Chinese and Western cultures have their own strengths and weaknesses, yet Lisha embodies the combination perfectly. The writing method of summary, analysis, and comparison is well worth learning.

If young people who grew up in Chinese families struggle with their cultural identity, then the predicament faced by Chinese children who were adopted by white people and came to the United States is beyond ordinary people's imagination. In the story "What Nationality Am I," Natalie Braga from Loyola University shared a story when she was in elementary school. There was once a chopsticks competition in her class, and all the students in the class expected Natalie to win the first place. It made her "nervous, embarrassed, and even scared." Regardless of whether she could use chopsticks or not, just because she had a Chinese face, all the students thought that she must be the best at using chopsticks. When a stranger asked her: "Where are you really from?", Natalie really did not know how to answer this question. After being confused between two distinct cultures for a long time, Natalie finally clarified her attitude with

想更多地了解中国的语言文化，风俗习惯，那片生我的土地上勤劳生活的人民。”在文化认同的探索过程中，雨磊同学从满眼迷茫到头脑清醒，从充满恐惧到坚定自信，终于走出低谷和混沌，明确了自己应有的立场。这种描写的方法是非常值得借鉴的。

人有脸，树有皮，中国人最讲究面子。达特茅斯学院的田百合同学对中美两国的面子文化进行了深刻的比较。在她的《我看面子》一文中，百合写道:“学习中文让我了解了中国的面子文化，同时也让我看到了中国和美国在面子文化上的不同。”在分析中国的面子文化时，百合指出:“中国的面子文化是公众文化。在公众面前，一个人的面子非常重要，所以别人会给你留面子，也会让你丢面子，当然也可以给你挽回面子。”这个意思就是不能当面指出一个人错了，要给那人留面子，否则那个人会觉得受到了羞辱。百合接着对比道:“与中国社会不一样，美国社会没有羞耻感文化，而有罪恶感文化。美国的面子是要讲清楚谁对谁错。如果你错了，即使承认错误会让你丢面子，你也应该承认错误。美国人认为，所有人都要为自己的过失承担责任，否则就是不绅士，那才被认为是丢面子。”

写一篇文章比较两个事物，首先要确定比较同样的东西，即苹果与苹果比，橙子与橙子比。百合同学这篇文章通篇比较的是中美的面子文化。没有厚此薄彼，但是却指出了二者的区别。这种写法值得向大家推荐。

the help of her teachers and parents. She wrote: "I often feel I do not just belong to a single country or a single culture. I love my family and friends here, the familiar environment, and all kinds of interesting activities. At the same time, I want to learn more about Chinese language, culture, customs, and the hard-working people from the place I come from." In the process of exploring cultural identity, Natalie went from being confused to sensible, from being fearful to confident, and she finally walked out of the low ebb and chaos, having clarified where she stands. This description is very worth learning from.

As the Chinese idiom goes, a person has a face, and a tree has bark, and the Chinese care about face (reputation) the most. Aurélie Temsamani, a student at Dartmouth College, made a profound comparison between the "face cultures" of China and the United States. In her story "My Understanding of Face Culture," Aurelie wrote: "Studying Chinese has allowed me to both understand Chinese face culture and analyze the differences between the face cultures of China and the United States." When analyzing Chinese face culture, Aurelie pointed out: "Chinese face culture emphasizes the public community, and within this community, maintaining face is incredibly important. Community members, therefore, can grant others face, can cause others to lose face, and can help others regain lost face." This means that you can't point out an individual's mistakes in public. Rather, you must save face for that person to prevent them from feeling humiliated. Aurelie then continues: "Unlike Chinese culture, American culture is not a shame-based culture, rather it is a guilt-based culture. The goal of face culture in the U.S. is to determine who is right and who is wrong. If you are wrong, you must admit your mistakes, even if it might cause you to lose face. Americans believe that everyone must take responsibility for their own errors, and if you refuse to, you lose face and are considered impolite."

To write an essay comparing two things, you must first make sure you are comparing the same thing; that is, apples to apples, and oranges to oranges. Throughout her story, Aurélie compares the face culture of China with that of the United States. There is no preference for one over the other, but it effectively points out the differences between the two. This style of writing is recommended to everyone.

我是哪国人

作者：民雨磊　指导教师：陈红　洛尤拉大学

> 生活不可能一帆风顺，但我要学着自己接纳自己。

记得在中学的一次中文课上，班里组织了一次用筷子夹东西的比赛。不知为什么，大家都在喊："我们组想要 Natalie，她一定能帮我们赢！"我感到很高兴，但更觉得紧张、尴尬，甚至恐惧，因为我自己知道我用筷子的技术不比班上的任何同学好。但我告诉自己，这不是去参加奥运会或者世界杯，我不应该害怕。虽然我们组的成绩并不突出，但是这次活动还是很有意思，而且给我留下了深刻的印象。

这个活动让我思考一个问题，为什么我看起来像一个中国人，但不会用筷子？我不但不会用筷子，而且对中国的语言文化也知道得很少。为什么？因为虽然我出生在中国，可是在我一岁的时候，我的美国爸爸妈妈就领养了我，把我从中国带到了美国。和很多同龄的小朋友一样，家里不吃中国菜，吃饭都是用刀叉。我喜欢看迪士尼、好莱坞的影视片，听流行音乐，看各种球赛。虽然我也努力学习中国语言文化，了解了一些传统节日的历史、十二生肖的说法，但我觉得很多东西离我还是很遥远。

有时碰到陌生人，他们会问："你是从哪里来的？"我真是不知道如何回答这个问题。我觉得我不只属于哪一个国家，哪一种文化。我喜欢我这里的家人和朋友，熟悉的环境，各种有趣的娱乐活动。我也想更多地了解中国的语言文化，风俗习惯，在那片生我的土地上勤劳生活的人民。

What Nationality Am I

Author: Natalie Braga Instructor: Hong Chen Loyola University

> These experiences are not easy, but I am learning to accept myself.

Once during middle school Chinese class, a chopsticks competition was organized. For some reason, everyone was shouting, "Our team wants Natalie! She will help us win!" I was happy they believed in me, but I was also nervous, embarrassed, and even scared, because I knew my chopsticks skills were no better than any of my classmates. However, I told myself this was no Olympics or World Cup; I should not be afraid. Although the results of our group were not outstanding, this activity strongly resonated with me for years after.

This activity caused me to deeply reflect on myself. Why do I look Chinese, yet I cannot even confidently use chopsticks? Not only did I have poor chopsticks skills, but I also knew very little about Chinese language and culture. Why? I knew the reason was that I was born in China, but my American parents adopted me at one year old and brought me to the U.S. I was raised like all of my American peers; every day I eat American food with forks and knives. I developed typical American teen interests: watching Disneyland and Hollywood movies, listening to pop music, and watching various ball games. Although I have continuously worked hard to learn Chinese language and culture, including the history of traditional festivals, and the zodiac, I feel a lot of things still very far away from me.

Sometimes strangers come up to me and ask, "Where are you really from?" I still do not know how to answer this question. I often feel I do not just belong to a single country or a single culture. I love my family and friends here, the familiar environment, and all kinds of interesting activities. At the same time, I want to learn more about Chinese language, culture, customs, and the hard-working people from the place I come from.

作为一个生在中国、长在美国的亚裔女孩儿，我知道我要面对来自各方面的挑战，有时是歧视和偏见。生活不可能一帆风顺，但我要学着自己接纳自己。我就是我，要勇敢地迎接机会，面对挑战。中美文化都有吸引我的地方，我会继续努力学习和探索。希望有一天我们可以真正消灭种族歧视，人人平等互爱。我会继续享受我的兴趣爱好——棒球、音乐，同时也要学好中文，练好筷子功夫，随时准备参加筷子比赛。

As an Asian American, I know I have to face all kinds of challenges, including prejudices and discriminations. These experiences are not easy, but I am learning to accept myself. I am who I am, and I will face both these challenges and opportunities. Chinese and American cultures remain special and interesting to me, and I will continue to learn and explore both. I hope that racial discrimination will be eliminated one day, and everyone enjoys equality and loves each other. I will continue to enjoy my hobbies: baseball and music while studying Chinese and practicing my chopsticks skills. And from now on, I will be ready for a chopsticks competition at any moment.

邓丽君的音乐

作者：开罗　指导教师：闫玲　哥伦比亚大学

> 聆听着邓丽君迷人的歌声，我自己常常会思绪万千，沉浸于怀旧中。

直到现在，我仍然清楚地记得，三年前第一次听到邓丽君的歌声时那种奇妙的感受。那时的我正在昆明留学。在一个阴冷的早晨，中文老师提着锈色的录音机走进了教室，说道："我们今天要学唱一首歌。大家先听听。"说着她就按下了录音机的播放键。

老师给我们放的是邓丽君的《甜蜜蜜》。虽然说出来令我有些不好意思，但是我不得不承认：第一次听到这首歌曲的时候，我真的是无法欣赏，也无法领悟。毕竟，中国与美国的音乐文化完全不一样。邓丽君是著名的华语歌手，但是她的名字对美国人来说却并不熟悉。最后，在老师的带领下，我们一遍又一遍地跟着学唱，一直唱到熟悉得能倒背如流。虽然我们都是五音不全的人，但在熟读成诵之后，我们也体会到了大声唱歌所带来的喜悦之感。从此以后，我越来越喜欢唱邓丽君的歌，唱得也越来越好，从中还学到了不少中文。

一晃三年了，我现在仍然喜爱邓丽君的音乐。甚至把她的歌词当作判断我中文水平的一个标准；每当我的中文进步可观时，我总会再听一首邓丽君的歌，看看自己是否能有新的理解和领悟。自从开始学唱邓丽君的歌曲之后，我意识到音乐是学习语言的宝贵资源之一。

在聆听邓丽君歌曲的过程中，我也有了许多刻骨铭心的经历。去年我看了一部中国电影《芳华》。这部电影中恰好也有一个听邓丽君歌曲的情节。这是一部

The Music of Teresa Teng

Author: Carlos Goodwin Key Instructor: Ling Yan Columbia University

> Listening to the sweet sounds of Teresa Teng's music today, I myself often become lost in a myriad of thoughts and immersed in the nostalgia of days past.

Even now I can still clearly remember that day three years ago, the first time I ever heard the song of Teresa Teng, and the marvelous feeling it brought me. At that time I was studying abroad in Kunming. On one gloomy morning, our Chinese teacher entered the classroom carrying a rusty tape cassette. "Today we're going to sing a song. Everybody takes a listen first." Saying this, she pressed the play button.

The song that our teacher played for us was Teresa Teng's "甜蜜蜜," which translates to something like "Sweet like Honey." Although it pains me somewhat to say so now, I must admit that at the time I first heard this song, I was utterly unable to appreciate it, nor was I able to comprehend it. After all, the musical cultures of China and the U.S. are entirely different. Teresa Teng is a renowned Chinese singer, but to Americans, she is all but unknown. But in the end, under our teacher's leadership, we followed her in singing the song for repetition after repetition until we had it memorized. Although we are all but tone-deaf as far as singing was concerned, after reciting the song to the point that we knew it by heart, we also came to experience the joyful feeling that singing loudly brings. After this, I began to enjoy singing the songs of Teresa Teng more and more, gradually singing them better and better, and in doing so learning a meaningful amount of Chinese as well.

Three years have passed in a flash, and I still find myself in love with Teresa Teng's music. I even use her lyrics as a sort of standard by which to assess my own Chinese language ability; each time there is a noticeable improvement in my Chinese, I will always listen to a Teresa

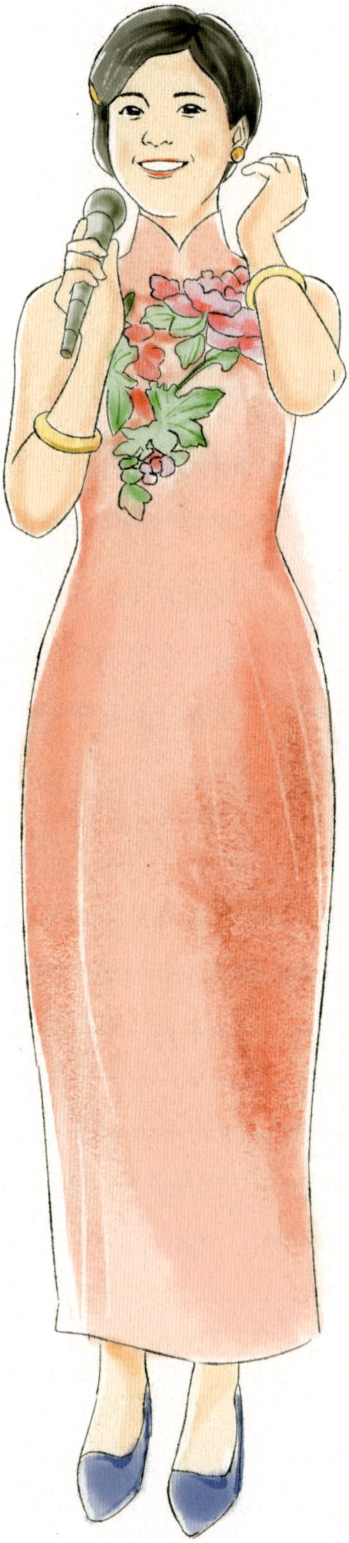

关于二十世纪七十年代中期军队文工团生活的电影。那个场景是：文工团的一位女兵来到男战友的寝室，男战友正在如醉如痴地独自聆听邓丽君的《侬情万缕》，对女兵的到来毫无察觉。女兵对男战友说道："我都洗澡回来了，你还在听。"男战友若有所思，缓慢地说道："太好听了！……每句词都往心里钻。"女兵听后，咯咯地笑了起来，问道："是不是觉得是对你一个人唱的？"男战友停顿了一下，回复道："是。"

这个场景让我想起了自己当时第一次学唱邓丽君歌曲的经历。我完全能理解男兵的感受。聆听着邓丽君迷人的歌声，我自己常常会思绪万千，沉浸于怀旧中。有的时候我泪流满面，而有的时候我不禁莞尔。在酒过三巡的深夜中，我偶尔会突发兴致要站起来，旁若无人地独唱一首邓丽君的《甜蜜蜜》。描写如此微妙的情感，我用英文尚且无从说起，何况是用我的初级中文。然而表达无法诉说的情感，不就是音乐独一无二的魅力吗？

Teng's song to see whether I have gained any newfound understanding of its meaning. And ever since beginning to learn Teresa Teng's music, I've realized that music is a precious resource for language learning indeed.

In the process of listening to Teresa Teng's music, I've also had many experiences that made a mark on my heart. Last year I watched a Chinese movie named "芳华," or *Youth*. This movie just so happened to have precisely such a scene portraying how it feels to listen to Teresa Teng's song. The film takes place in the 1970's, following the lives of a military performance troupe. In the scene, one of the female soldiers enters the dormitory of her male comrade to find her friend listening to Teresa Teng's song "浓情万缕" in a seemingly infatuated haze, so immersed that he doesn't even notice her enter. The woman jokingly says to him, "I've showered and come back, and you're still here listening." The man responds slowly, lost in thought: "It's incredible… every line pierces my heart." The woman chuckles, "You feel like she's singing just to you, don't you?" After a pause, he merely replies, "Yes."

This scene reminds me of my first experience of singing Teresa Teng's songs. I can totally understand the male soldier's feelings. Listening to the sweet sounds of Teresa Teng's music today, I myself often become lost in a myriad of thoughts and immersed in the nostalgia of days past. Sometimes my face fills with tears, and sometimes I cannot help but smile. During late nights of heavy drinking, I am sometimes even overcome by the sudden urge to stand up and chant a few lines of "甜蜜蜜" as if I were the only person in the room. Even in English I am not sure how to accurately describe the subtle feelings her music incites in me, to say nothing of what I might be able to express in my rudimentary Chinese. But then again, to express that which cannot be put into words… is this not precisely what makes music so enchanting?

生活在两种文化中的我

作者：夏丽莎　指导教师：林秀玲　西北大学

我觉得这种多族群的认同，让我的生活变得多姿更多彩，更加美丽，更加有趣，也让我更快乐。

我是美籍华人。美国是我成长的地方，中国是我的传统文化的来源地。我对这两个国家有着非常独特的认同。

到目前为止，我差不多都是在美国生活，我对美国的种种习惯、行为举止、幽默感、食物、体育活动、生活条件，甚至美国的政治都有一定的了解。但我却无法把自己完完全全看成是美国人，因为我身体里永远都流着华人的血液，我的父母是地地道道的中国人。我成长的过程中到处是中国文化、中国饮食、中国道德。我的家庭背景有着“红烧肉的味道”。从小到大，我大部分的回忆是黄色的。我的童年充满中国歌曲、中国电视，以及回国探亲的经历。我跳过中国的民族舞蹈，也上过中文学校，就连我的教养也是中国的。从小我就被教导要孝敬父母，尊敬长辈，做人要谦逊，更要有道德涵养。

随着年龄的增长，我也逐渐发现我身上的许多特征是中国和美国文化交织的产物。从小到大，我一直没有完全走出华人圈。最近，我给自己一些机会去跟其他国家的人交流，却发现跟他们交流，确实没有跟华人交流那么自然，那么舒服。比如说，我的美国朋友对中国文化的了解不如我深刻，对

Living in Two Different Cultures

Author: Lisha Xia　Instructor: Hsiu-ling Robertson　Northwestern University

> I think this multi-ethnic identity makes my life more colorful, more beautiful, more interesting, and happier.

I am a Chinese American. America is where I grew up and China is where my traditional culture comes from. I have a unique identification with these two countries.

Having lived in the United States for almost all my life so far, I have some knowledge of American habits, mannerisms, sense of humor, American food, sports activities, living conditions, and even American politics. Yet I cannot see myself as completely American because I always have Chinese blood in my body. My parents are Chinese from the ground up. I grew up with Chinese culture, Chinese food, and Chinese morals. My family background has a "flavor of the pork braised in brown sauce." Growing up, most of my memories are yellow. My childhood was filled with Chinese songs, Chinese TV shows, and visits to my family back home. I danced Chinese folk dances, went to Chinese school, and even my upbringing was Chinese. From a young age I was taught to be filial to my parents, to respect my elders, to be modest, and to cultivate moral character.

As I grew older, I also came to realize that many of the characteristics in me were the product of the intertwining of Chinese and American cultures. Since I was a child, I have never fully stepped out of the Chinese community. Recently, I have given myself some opportunities to interact with people from other countries, only to find that interacting with them is

中国文化的热爱也不如我浓厚。但我知道，跟不同族群的人相处，我必须自我调适。在这同时，我开始了解，我不一定需要通过“华人”的身份才能跟我身边的人沟通。放下“华人”的身份，我还是可以与他人有共同的话题，可以跟他们有很好的交流。这样的“两国认同”对我的成长，只有好处，没有坏处。我想当一个拥有两种身份的人：一个是尊重中国文化和历史的华裔，我想努力学习中文，想更深入了解中国文化；另一个是继续以美国方式生活的美国人。在我的身上有这两个不同的标志，对我而言，它们都同样重要。它不但能提高我经验层面的深度和广度，也会使我的世界观变得更丰富。

总之，我的家庭教养是中国式的；而学校与社会环境的教化是美国式的。我的性格有中国人的含蓄，也有美国人的干脆；有中国人的细腻，也有美国人的大方；有中国人的传统，也有美国人的开放。我觉得这种多族群的认同，让我的生活变得多姿更多彩，更加美丽，更加有趣，也让我更快乐。

not as natural and comfortable as interacting with Chinese people. For example, my American friends don't know Chinese culture as profound as I do, and their love for it is not as strong as mine. But I knew that I had to adapt myself to get along with people of different ethnic groups. At the same time, I began to understand that I didn't necessarily need to be "Chinese" to communicate with the people around me. I can still have common topics with others and communicate well with them without being "Chinese." This "bi-national identity" has only helped me and caused no harm in my growth. I want to be a Chinese person who respects Chinese culture and history, and I want to study Chinese and learn more about Chinese culture; and I want to be an American who continues to live in the American way. Having these two different strains in my body, they are both equally important to me. Not only will they increase the depth and breadth of my experience level, but they will also enrich my worldview.

In short, my family upbringing is Chinese; and my school and social environment upbringing is American. My character has the Chinese subtlety and American directness, the Chinese delicacy and American generosity, the Chinese reserve and American openness. I think this multi-ethnic identity makes my life more colorful, more beautiful, more interesting, and happier.

美式快餐在中国

作者：裴丽　指导教师：刘羽　迪保罗大学

> 尽管快餐文化在中美之间存在着差异，但快餐公司在这两个国家蓬勃发展，并为其他行业提供了成功的模式。

快餐业已成为全世界的一大产业。快餐始于20世纪20年代的美国，后来发展到其他国家，在世界各地蓬勃发展。在美国境外开设的美式快餐店通常做得很好，因为它们会调整菜单，以适应当地人的需求和饮食偏好。中国也对美国快餐敞开了大门。正因为如此，快餐在中国变得流行起来。然而，中国人对快餐的看法和接受方式与美国人大不相同。

在美国，“白色城堡”是第一家快餐店。白色城堡于1921年开张，至今仍在经营。今天，白色城堡在美国中西部最常见，在中西部以外的地区只有不到100家。在美国，快餐被视为美国人生中不可或缺的一部分。上至达官贵人，下至平民百姓，时不时都去吃快餐。人们普遍认为，每个人都至少吃过一家快餐店，因为在任何时候都至少有一家快餐店在你家附近。当长途驾车穿越偏远地区时，通常唯一可以吃的就是快餐。虽然快餐在美国人的饮食中一直占有重要地位，但快餐以廉价和不健康著称，并且可能是美国人肥胖问题的一个主要原因。很多人甚至说快餐可以致人死亡，因为它非常不健康。

与之相比，中国的快餐文化和观念非常不同。

中国第一家美式快餐店于1987年开业，这是一家肯德基。自开业以来，肯德基在中国已成为最受欢迎的快餐连锁店之一，目前在中国拥有8000多家分店。在肯德基之后，更多的美式快餐店在中国开业，包括1990年的麦当劳、1999年的星巴克和2016年的Taco Bell墨西哥卷饼。在中国，美式快餐很受小朋友欢迎，

American Fast Food in China

Author: Paige Fullman Instructor: Yu Liu DePaul University

> Despite the differences in fast-food culture between China and the U.S., it's really gratifying that fast-food companies thrive in both countries, and offers a successful model for other businesses.

The fast-food industry has become a major industry all over the world. Fast food started in the United States in the 1920s and later spread to other countries, flourishing all over the world. American fast-food restaurants that open outside the U.S. usually do well because they adjust their menu to suit local needs and dietary preferences. China has also opened its doors to American fast food. Because of this, fast food has become popular in China. However, Chinese people view and accept fast food very differently compared to Americans.

In the United States, "White Castle" was the first fast-food restaurant. White Castle opened in 1921 and is still in operation. Today, it is most common in the American Midwest, with fewer than a hundred locations outside the Midwest. In America, fast food is seen as an integral part of American life. Up to the dignitaries, down to the common people, everyone eats fast food from time to time. It is widely believed that everyone has eaten in at least one fast food restaurant because at any given time there is at least one fast-food restaurant around you. When driving long distances through remote areas, often the only food you can eat is fast food. Although fast food in American people's diets has always played an important role, it is notoriously cheap and unhealthy, and may be one of the main reasons of Americans' obesity problem. Many people even say that fast food can kill people because it is very unhealthy.

In contrast, the fast-food culture and concept in China are very different.

因此，爸爸妈妈会选择麦当劳、必胜客等快餐店为孩子举办生日聚会。这样的情形在美国很少见到。尽管中国人对快餐的看法不同，但越来越多的美国快餐连锁店在中国开业。这都归功于中国的对外开放。

中美快餐最大的区别就是价格。我相信这是由于起初人们对陌生的西方食物的迷信导致的。当西方产品首次在中国上市时，价格非常昂贵，因此它们被视为身份的象征。尽管制作快餐的成本很低，但美国公司仍然将价格定得很高，以保持其食品的身价。随着中国经济的快速发展，尤其是餐饮行业的快速发展，世界各地的美食纷纷进入中国，美式快餐的价格变得更加亲民，现在已经被大部分中国人所接受。

尽管快餐文化在中美之间存在着差异，但快餐公司在这两个国家蓬勃发展，并为其他行业提供了成功的模式，这仍然是一件可喜可贺的事情。希望中式快餐店也能打入美国，打入全世界，给世界人民带来新的味道。

The first American fast-food restaurant in China opened in 1987, a KFC. Since its opening, KFC has become one of the most popular fast-food chains in China and currently has more than 8,000 branches. After KFC, many American fast-food restaurants have opened in China, including McDonald's in 1990, Starbucks in 1999, and "Taco Bell" in 2016. In China, American fast food is very popular with children, so parents will choose fast-food restaurants such as McDonald's and Pizza Hut to host birthday parties for their children. Such a situation is rarely seen in the United States. Although Chinese people have a different perception of fast food, more and more American fast food chains are opening in China. This is all due to China's opening to the outside world.

The biggest difference between Chinese and American fast food is the price. I believe this is due to people's curiosity to unfamiliar Western food at first. When Western products were first introduced in China, they were very expensive, so they were seen as a status symbol. Although the cost of making fast food is low, American companies still set prices high to keep their food products worthwhile. With the rapid development of China's economy, especially the rapid development of the fast-food industry, food from all over the world has entered China. The price of American fast food has become more affordable and has now been accepted by most Chinese people.

Despite the differences in fast-food culture between China and the U.S., it's really gratifying that fast-food companies thrive in both countries, and offers a successful model for other businesses. I hope Chinese fast-food restaurants can also enter the United States and into the world, to bring a new taste to people around the world.

中美早餐

作者：华山　指导教师：刘羽　迪保罗大学

> 如果你想度过美好的一天，你可以从一顿美味的早餐开始。

民以食为天，一日三餐中的早餐格外重要。中国人和美国人也不例外，他们都认为早餐是非常重要的。不管是在中国文化里，还是美国文化里，人们都说，如果你想度过美好的一天，你可以从一顿美味的早餐开始。只是美国人和中国人早餐的食物有所不同。

中国的早餐因地区而异，但是最常见的中式早餐有豆浆、油条、馒头、豆花儿、面条儿和米粉。这里我将介绍几种受欢迎的传统中式早餐。

在中国，大多数人喜欢很方便的早餐食品，因为早餐一般没有时间悠闲享用。尤其是对学生、上班族和农民来说，每一天都要早早起床，开始繁忙的一天。因此，很多人在去上学或上班的路上，去早点摊吃早餐。馒头大概是最方便的早餐食品。馒头是一种简单的面食，它很容易让人吃饱。中国人也喜欢在早上吃稀饭。稀饭是一种大米做的流食。很多人喜欢就着咸菜一起吃稀饭。还有一种很受欢迎的早餐是油条。油条的颜色有点儿像美国的甜甜圈，但不是一个圈，而像一根小棍子，而且油条不甜，是咸的。人们常常喜欢一边吃油条，一边喝豆浆。豆浆是一种用黄豆

Chinese and American Breakfasts

Author: Rahsaan Liddell Instructor: Yu Liu DePaul University

> If you want to have a good day, it should start with a great breakfast.

People regard food as their prime want, with breakfast being of particular importance. Chinese and American citizens are no exception, as they both believe that having breakfast is very important. People in both Chinese culture and American culture say that if you want to have a good day, it should start with a great breakfast. The only difference is that breakfast food in China is different from that in the U.S.

Breakfast in China varies from region to region, but the most common Chinese breakfast dishes consist of soy milk, fried dough sticks, steamed bread, bean curd, noodles and rice noodles. Here I will introduce several popular, traditional Chinese breakfasts.

In China, most people prefer breakfast food that is quick and convenient, because typically, Chinese people have very little time to enjoy breakfast in a leisurely fashion. This holds particularly true for students, office workers and farmers, as their busy days typically begin with an early rise. As a result, many people go to storefront counters to purchase and on occasion quickly eat breakfast on the way to school or work. Steamed bread is probably the most convenient breakfast food in China. It is a simple wheaten food that fills you up quickly. Chinese people also enjoy eating porridge in the morning. Porridge is a

磨制成的饮料。很多人把油条浸在豆浆里吃，味道很特别。虽然中国人平时很看重全家一起吃饭的氛围，但是常常因为早上时间不够，很多人的早餐一般都是自己快速解决。

在美国，很多家庭常常一家人一起吃早餐。家人们可以讨论当天的活动安排。美国人早餐喜欢吃培根和鸡蛋。鸡蛋的做法有很多种，例如炒蛋、水煮蛋，还有煎蛋。和中国人不太一样的是，美国人很少在早餐时吃蔬菜。相反，他们喜欢吃很多肉食，如熏肉、香肠、牛肉饼等。另外，薯饼也是很受美国人欢迎的早餐食品。大部分美国人早上都喜欢喝咖啡、牛奶或者橙汁。

中国人和美国人都相信吃早餐很重要，但是两个国家的饮食文化不同，吃的食物也不同。中国人的早餐，乳制品少一些，牛奶、奶酪、黄油和酸奶不是必需品。中国人的早餐更清淡、更健康。而美国人的早餐有更多肉、更多高蛋白。很多美国人早餐吃得太多，因此容易长胖。

kind of fluid made of rice. Many people enjoy their porridge served with pickled vegetables. Another popular breakfast in China is the fried dough stick. Its color is comparable to that of an American doughnut, but instead of it being round like a doughnut, it is elongated. This dish is not sweet like a doughnut, but in fact has a salty flavor. People often like to eat fried dough sticks while drinking soy milk. Soy milk is a beverage made from soybeans. Many people prefer to dip fried dough sticks inside a bowl of soy milk, which produces a special taste. Although Chinese people value the atmosphere of eating together with the whole family, typically there is not enough time in the morning to dine as a family, so many people eat breakfast very quickly by themselves.

In the United States, many families often eat breakfast together as a family. Families often use this time to discuss activities for the day. Many Americans love to have bacon and eggs for breakfast. There are many ways that the eggs are prepared, such as scrambled eggs, boiled eggs, and fried eggs. Unlike Chinese, Americans rarely eat vegetables for breakfast. Instead, they often enjoy eating meats, such as bacon, sausage, beef patties, etc. In addition, hash browns are also a popular breakfast food for Americans. Most Americans like to drink coffee, milk, or orange juice in the morning.

Both Chinese and Americans believe that eating breakfast is important, but the two countries have different food cultures and eat different foods. For Chinese breakfast, dairy products such as milk, cheese, butter and yogurt are not essential and rarely consumed. Chinese breakfasts are lighter and healthier. Americans have more meat and high-protein food for breakfast. Many Americans eat so much for breakfast that it is easy for them to gain weight.

欢迎光临

作者：白美玲　代君　萧爱美
指导教师：齐润清　科罗拉多大学

成都人学习工作之余，大多喜欢来茶馆儿一边喝茶一边聊天儿，看表演，打麻将。

各位游客，欢迎光临！我们是美玲、代君和爱美。我们都是您的导游。今天我们要给您介绍一下成都的特色休闲方式：泡茶馆儿。

我们的参观从一家很热闹的茶馆儿开始。您看，右边有人在赏花，左边有人在采摘新鲜的水果，后边有人在享受室外清新的空气。成都人学习工作之余，大多喜欢来茶馆儿一边喝茶一边聊天儿，看表演，打麻将。

来，我们往前走。现在，您可以看到有一个人在掏耳朵。虽然这项服务听起来有点儿奇怪，但是很多人觉得掏耳朵让他们感觉飘飘欲仙，我鼓励您也试一试。在这里，我们能看到一整排竹桌竹椅，您可以坐上去试一试，很舒服。天气好的时候茶馆儿里常常座无虚席。幸运的是我们现在能找到一些空位。您看，茶馆儿的桌子和椅子是用竹子做成的，非常漂亮。因为竹椅比普通椅子矮一点儿，还有靠枕和坐垫，所以无论坐着还是半躺着都很舒服。坐下以后，您可以点杯茶或点个小吃，比如辣辣的豆花儿或者成都馄饨。如果点茶，您会体验到特别有趣的服务：服务员会用传统的长嘴茶壶把热水倒入放着茶叶的茶碗里。倒茶前，您可以看到带着长长茶嘴的茶壶在服务员身边上下飞舞，然后壶嘴远距离对准茶碗，从壶嘴喷出一道水柱，沿着抛物线，一滴不漏地注入您的茶碗。此时的服务

Welcome

Author: Mei White　Tyler Daniels　Abbey Shaw

Instructor: Runqing Qi　University of Colorado (Boulder)

After much hard work and studying, many people in Chengdu enjoy coming to the teahouse to chat, watch performances, and play mahjong as they drink tea.

Welcome, everyone! Our names are Mei, Tyler, and Abbey, and we'll be your tour guides. Today we are going to introduce you to a pastime that is characteristic of Chengdu: teahouses.

First off, we'll start at this lively teahouse. Take a look around – on the right, you can see some people enjoying the flowers; on the left, you can see other people picking fresh fruit; and behind us, you can see people taking in and appreciating the refreshing atmosphere. After much hard work and studying, many people in Chengdu enjoy coming to the teahouse to chat, watch performances, and play mahjong as they drink tea.

Alright, let's move on. Right now, you can see a person getting his ears cleaned. Although this service may seem a bit strange, many people think ear cleaning makes them feel great, and I encourage you to try it. Here, we can see a row of bamboo tables and chairs that you may go sit and try. Bamboo chairs are very comfortable. When the weather is nice, the teahouse will often have no empty seats. Fortunately, now, we can find some empty seats.

员简直就像身怀绝技的武林高手。长嘴壶茶艺不但具有观赏性，也具有很强的实用性。滚烫的沸水在流经又细又长的茶嘴后，温度会自然降低，这样最适合泡茶。

在这里，您也可以参加其他的娱乐活动，包括打麻将、听评书、看川剧等等。其中，我们尤其推荐川剧，因为川剧是中国西南地区的传统戏曲之一。川剧有五种特色声腔：高腔、昆腔、胡琴、弹戏、灯调。川剧高腔的音调比其他剧种高得多。川剧的变脸表演也十分有特色。演员用手一晃，头一摇，他的脸就会变成另外一个人物的脸，而且还能连续变出六七个不同人物的脸。中文里面的所谓“翻脸不认人”，是不是就是指的这个？有的川剧演员还能口吐火焰，那也是一绝，这个节目最好是在晚上看。如果您想去看川剧，我们可以给您打折的票！川剧表演十分令人惊叹，我们强烈推荐您去看看。

好了，我们的茶馆儿之旅到此结束。现在是自由活动时间，请随意尝试这里的各种休闲活动。请大家两小时后回到这里集合，然后我们会去参观下一个景点。

As you can see, the teahouse chairs and tables are made of bamboo and are very beautiful. Because bamboo chairs are a bit shorter compared to regular chairs and have back and seat cushions, they are very comfortable, no matter if you're sitting or reclining.

After getting seated, you can order a cup of tea or a snack, such as spicy bean curd or Chengdu wontons. If you order tea, you will experience a particularly interesting service: the waiter will use a traditional long-mouthed teapot to pour hot water into a tea bowl with tea leaves. Before the tea is poured, you will see the long-spouted teapot flying up and down around the waiter. Then, the spout is aimed at the teapot from a distance and a stream of water is sprayed out, following a parabolic shape, into your teapot without a single drop spilled. The waiter, at this time, resembles a martial arts master with unique skills. The long-spouted teapot is not only ornamental, but also very practical. After the boiling water flows through the long, thin spout, the water temperature naturally decreases, which is most suitable for making tea.

Here, you can participate in other leisure activities, including playing mahjong, listening to *pingshu* (storytelling), and watching Sichuan opera. Amongst the aforementioned, we recommend the Sichuan opera in particular because those are one of Southwest China's traditional operas. Sichuan opera has five distinctive tunes: *gaoqiang*, *kunqiang*, *huqin*, *tanxi*, and *dengdiao*. The pitch of the *gaoqiang* style is much higher than the other styles. The face changing performances in Sichuan operas are also distinctive. The actor covers his face with his hands, then the face painting will become that of another character in less than a second. He can also change into the faces of six or seven different characters in a row. Does the Chinese saying "翻脸不认人" (literally: turn face and nobody recognizes; this is a Chinese saying, which implies "turn against an old friend") point to this? Some Sichuan opera actors can breathe fire, which is also unique. It is best to watch this performance at night. If you want to watch Sichuan opera, we can give you discounted tickets! Sichuan opera is so amazing that we strongly recommend you go watch it.

Alright, we have reached the end of our teahouse tour. Now it's free time to do as you like; please feel free to try all the leisure activities. We will reconvene here in two hours then head to the next scenic spot.

中国饭圈文化之我见

作者：尤丽佳　指导教师：鲍莹玲　印第安纳大学（伯明顿）

在中国，“饭圈”是指同一个明星的粉丝通过微信群和贴吧聚在一起形成的团体。

在中国，“饭圈”是指同一个明星的粉丝通过微信群和贴吧聚在一起形成的团体。它的运作有两条标准：“花钱”和“花时间”。花钱就是购买跟这个明星有关的产品，粉丝会用真金白银支援他们的偶像艺人——“爱豆”，购买其代言的产品、周边产品。在花时间方面，粉丝会通过打榜、控评、骂战等方式来支持他们的爱豆。“打榜”是粉丝通过投票，让他们喜欢的爱豆在各种榜单上的排名上升。因此，如果看到负面评论，粉丝会对评论进行举报以删除负面评论。相反，如果看到正面评论，他们会对评论进行回复、点赞，让更多人看到，这就是“控评”。

饭圈文化对中国社会有着一定的积极影响。这一代年轻人平常很孤独，而饭圈提供了一个开放的平台来让他们追逐偶像，并让他们跟偶像的其他粉丝建立良好关系。在追星之余，粉丝通过这些虚拟关系建立陪伴和友谊。从经济角度来讲，我们不能低估饭圈文化的消费力。这些粉丝购买他们爱豆代言的所有产品和周边产品，有助于宣传爱豆作品，让他们获得更多利润，提高他们的影响力。

不过，我认为饭圈文化给年轻人带来的更多的是消极影响。有一些“无脑”粉丝用“不花钱就不是真粉”对饭圈的其他人进行洗脑，号召粉丝为爱豆消费，把普通粉丝转化成真粉。因此，许多粉丝在不知不觉中养成了打投（打榜和投票）

My Opinion on "Fan Community" Culture in China

Author: Linda You Instructor: Yingling Bao Indiana University (Bloomington)

In China, a "fan community" refers to a group of fans who admire the same star/idol get together through WeChat and post bar. It operates on two criteria: "spending money" and "spending time." In terms of spending money, fans will buy products and merchandise that are endorsed by their idols. In terms of spending time, fans will support their idols through "hitting lists," controlling comments, and "scolding wars." "Hitting lists" means that fans vote to increase the ranking of their favorite idols on various lists. For instance, if there are negative comments under the idol's page, fans will report and delete them. On the contrary, if they see positive comments, they will reply and like them so that more people can see it. This is what "control comments" means. "Fan community" culture has some positive influence on Chinese society. Because this generation of young people often feels lonely, the "fan community" provides an open platform for them to support their favorite idols and establish good relations with other fans. In addition to supporting their idols, fans can also build friendships through these virtual interactions. Looking at this from an economic point of view, we cannot underestimate the consumption power of "fan community" culture. These fans buy all the products and merchandise endorsed by their idols, which helps promote idols' works and ultimately helps them obtain more profits and increase their influence.

In China, a "fan community" refers to a group of fans who admire the same star/idol get together through WeChat and post bar.

However, I think the "fan community" culture has a more negative influence on young people. Some "brainless" fans will use the threat of "you are not a real fan if you do not spend money" against other fans to brainwash them. They call on the fans to consume for their idols,

的习惯，为爱豆投票冲榜单、买周边产品成为了他们生活的重心，影响了他们的正常生活。

我对粉丝的极端行为感到震惊，例如“敌对”粉丝团体之间的诽谤和人肉搜索，严重破坏了互联网生态，影响了年轻人的身心健康。我认为，不仅粉丝需要为他们的不当行为负责，爱豆也是如此。因此，政府应该加强对饭圈乱象的监管，当爱豆做错事时，政府需要干涉，让他们承担相应的责任。

so as to prove themselves to be real fans. Therefore, many fans have unknowingly developed the habit of ranking and voting. Voting for idols and buying their products have become the central focus of these fans' lives, and this has a huge impact on their everyday lives.

I am shocked by the extreme behaviors of these fans, such as the slander and cyber manhunt incidents that occur among hostile fan groups. These have drastically destroyed the ecology of the internet and affected the physical and mental health of many young people. In my opinion, not only do fans need to be held responsible for their misbehavior, but idols as well. Therefore, the government should work hard to strengthen the supervision of the chaos that runs within "fan communities." In a case where an idol does something wrong, the government needs to intervene and let them bear the appropriate responsibilities.

我看面子

作者：田百合　指导教师：吕俞辉　达特茅斯学院

世界上无论哪一个国家，都有自己的面子文化，但是各个国家的面子文化好像又有很大的不同。学习中文让我了解了中国的面子文化，同时也让我看到了中国和美国在面子文化上的不同。

到了中国，就按照中国的面子文化行事；到了美国，就按照美国的面子文化行事。这才叫有面子。

在中国，面子文化非常重要。如果你去中国而不懂中国的面子文化，你就很有可能在不知不觉中得罪别人，在跨文化交流中犯错误。在中国，受别人的尊重是一件非常重要的事情。中国的面子文化是公众文化。在公众面前，一个人的面子非常重要，所以别人会给你留面子，也会让你丢面子，当然也可以给你挽回面子。譬如，你去参加一个宴会迟到了，主人如果要给你留面子，就会等你，同时陪大家先喝茶、聊天儿。如果主人想让你丢面子，就会按时开饭，等你到时，大家已经吃一半了，这样你就会很没面子。如果主人想要帮你找回面子，等你来了之后，就会让后厨再多上几道菜，并且告诉大家，你迟到是为大家处理一件事情去了，这就为你保住了面子。让人丢面子就会得罪人，所以我们说话办事都要小心谨慎，为他人的面子着想。在中国，大家都注意遵守面子文化的行为规则，尽可能不在公众面前批评一个人，让这个人丢面子，下不来台。对领导和地位高的人更是要注意，不要当众让领导没面子。

美国的面子文化与中国的面子文化很不一样。因为美国的文化比较强调自己，

My Understanding of Face Culture

Author: Aurélie Temsamani Instructor: Yuhui Lyu Dartmouth College

Every country around the world has its own unique "face" culture. Studying Chinese has allowed me to both understand Chinese face culture and analyze the differences between the face cultures of China and the United States.

> Instead of adhering to one culture or the other, however, it is essential to adopt the norms of Chinese face culture when in China, and American face culture when in America. Doing so exemplifies having face.

In China, face culture is exceedingly important. If you go to China and do not comprehend Chinese face culture, you are likely to unknowingly offend others and make cultural blunders. Getting respect from others is very important in China. Chinese face culture emphasizes the public community, and within this community, maintaining face is incredibly important. Community members, therefore, can grant others face, can cause others to lose face, and can help others regain lost face. For example, if you arrive late to a dinner, the host can help you maintain face by delaying the meal, asking others to drink tea and chat while waiting for you to arrive. If the host wishes to make you lose face, on the other hand, he will begin the meal on time, forcing you to arrive in the middle of the meal and eat half-empty dishes. If the host wants to help you regain face, once you arrive he might request that additional dishes be brought from the kitchen and inform other guests that an important matter kept you from arriving on time. Causing someone to lose face can be highly offensive, so in Chinese culture people must speak cautiously and consider other peoples' face. In China it is crucial to abide by the behavioral norms of face culture and rarely criticize others in public, so as not to cause them to lose face. It is especially important to pay attention to the face of leaders and high-

别人不会在乎给你留面子还是让你丢面子。与中国社会不一样，美国社会没有羞耻感文化，而有罪恶感文化。美国的面子是要讲清楚谁对谁错。如果你错了，即使承认错误会让你丢面子，你也应该承认错误。美国人认为，所有人都要为自己的过失承担责任，否则就是不绅士，那才被认为是丢面子。

我刚刚到中国的时候还不太理解中国的面子文化，所以犯了很多错误。那

status citizens, as it is a grave mistake to cause them to lose face in public.

Face culture in the United States is highly different from that in China. Because American culture emphasizes the individual, others care less about helping you save face or causing you to lose face. Unlike Chinese culture, American culture is not a shame-based culture, rather it is a guilt-based culture. The goal of face culture in the U.S. is to determine who is right and who is wrong. If you are wrong, you must admit to your mistakes, even if it might cause you to lose face. Americans believe that everyone must take responsibility for their own errors, and if you refuse to, you lose face and are considered impolite.

When I first arrived in China, I did not quite understand Chinese face culture and therefore committed many errors. At that time, I had only studied Chinese for two years, and had never heard of Chinese face culture. I mistakenly assumed that Chinese face culture and American face culture were identical, which led me to unintentionally offending my Chinese teacher. One day in Chinese class, the teacher incorrectly wrote an English word on the white board. Acting according to American face culture, I raised my hand and informed him that he wrote the word incorrectly. The teacher then corrected his error, however I later realized that my teacher was incredibly embarrassed by my actions, and all his following classes did not go well. Once I learned more about Chinese face culture, I realized that correcting a teacher in public causes him to lose face and is tremendously embarrassing. Rather than correct his mistake in public, China's face culture dictates that I should inform him of his error privately after class. In the United States, notifying a teacher that he has made a mistake is a common occurrence, and is not considered a big deal. When in China, however, it is important to abide by Chinese culture, and I should therefore have not embarrassed my teacher in public.

I believe that Chinese face culture and American face culture each have their own merits and faults. Chinese face culture is advantageous in that it demands that everyone respect one another, and be cognizant of one another's face. This type of public, community culture therefore keeps a harmonious social environment. Chinese face culture, however, also has its defects. Due to the face culture, everyone is incredibly concerned about maintaining their own face and the face of others, causing issues in conflict situations, such as at work. People are unable to correct their coworkers' mistakes in the moment, and if a leader makes the wrong decision, his subordinates cannot make criticisms or suggestions. This inability to correct

时我刚刚在美国学了两年中文，对中国的面子文化一无所知，错误地以为中国的面子文化与美国的面子文化一样，所以无意中冒犯了老师。有一天上中文课，老师在白板上把一个英文单词写错了。我当时就傻乎乎地举手，告诉老师，他的英文单词写错了，应该这样写。老师虽然改了过来，但是后来我发现，老师非常非常不好意思，后面的课都没有上好。后来在中国了解了更多的中国面子文化以后，我才意识到，当众纠正老师的错误让老师很没面子，让老师很尴尬。我完全可以课后悄悄告诉老师错在哪里。在美国，告诉老师他写错了字是一件常见的事情，没有什么了不起。但是既然到了中国，就要遵守中国的文化，不要让老师当众出丑。

我认为中国的面子文化和美国的面子文化都有自己的长处和短处。中国面子文化的长处是，所有人都要尊重别人，为别人的面子着想，这样的公众文化能维持和谐的社会环境。中国面子文化的短处是，大家都太顾忌面子而耽误工作。为了保全面子，一个人工作出了差错不能当面批评；为了保全面子，领导的决定即使错了，手下的人也不能提出批评建议，这就会影响工作的效率。美国面子文化的长处是，大家在工作的时候可以畅所欲言，发现了什么问题，无论是谁的问题都可以直接提出来，所以问题可以很快解决，暂时丢掉的面子也可以很快挽回来。美国面子文化的短处是，美国人太强调自己的看法，不考虑他人的感受，常常让人下不来台，很尴尬。两种文化比较起来，好像中国文化太注重对方的面子，有什么想法不直说，让人捉摸不定。而美国文化太不重视对方的面子，有什么想法直接当众说出来，容易让对方下不来台，丢尽面子。中美两个面子文化各有长短，各有利弊，不能说哪一个更好。应该是到了中国，就按照中国的面子文化行事；到了美国，就按照美国的面子文化行事。这才叫有面子。

mistakes can lead to decreased efficiency. America's face culture, therefore, is beneficial in that it emboldens everyone to speak freely and bring up problems that they detect. This allows problems to be rapidly solved, increasing the efficiency of workflow, and the temporarily lost face can be regained soon. In foregoing public face culture, however, American face culture overemphasizes individual opinions and doesn't place enough consideration on the feelings of others. People are often embarrassed when they are corrected, and American culture does not protect their face. When comparing Chinese and American face cultures, I believe that Chinese face culture assigns too much stress on maintaining the face of others, so that individuals become unable to express their opinions directly and their attitudes are elusive. American face culture, in contrast, does not pay enough attention to the face of others, and individuals often speak their minds even knowing that it will greatly embarrass the other party and make them totally lose face. Each of Chinese and American face cultures holds its own strengths and weaknesses, and it is impossible to say that one face culture is superior to the other. Instead of adhering to one culture or the other, however, it is essential to adopt the norms of Chinese face culture when in China, and American face culture when in America. Doing so exemplifies having face.

和而不同

作者：康书文　指导教师：李恺　欧柏林学院

> 恰恰因为我们之间有些“不同”，我们的世界才能五彩缤纷。

几年前，我离开家乡加州，来到一个很远的地方，感受到了一种强烈的文化冲击。

这个地方比较古老，这里的人日常生活节奏缓慢，跟我的家乡不太一样。比如说，没有人在乎谁赢了星期天的橄榄球比赛，也没有人对电影明星的私生活那么感兴趣，即便是这里的年轻人也不熟悉现在美国电视上有什么时髦的音乐。

一般来说，这里的人不如加州人吃得那么多，不像加州人那么高大，当然，也没有加州人那么胖。同时，他们的衣着服饰也比较随意、自然。他们从不浪费水和其他自然资源。

这里不少人都很关心时事，会在你面前批评美国政府的政策，批评资本主义。公开告诉你，他们主张搞社会主义。总的来说，我觉得这里和这里的人有点儿与众不同。

这到底是哪里？你差不多已经知道答案了吧？

我在这里学习世界上使用人数最多的语言。因为在这里有很好的学习条件。不仅有不错的老师，也有很好的练习这种语言的环境和机会。

哈，我想你已经猜出来了。这里就是地处美国俄亥俄州的欧柏林学院！

历史悠久的欧柏林学院不仅教会了我说中文，而且帮助我开阔了视野，有了新的人生观。在欧柏林读了几年书以后，我又有幸去中国继续学习中文。还没到中国时，我有一点儿紧张，以为在中国会面对更大的文化冲击。但是让我想不到

Harmony in Diversity

Author: Stephan Campbell Instructor: Kai Li Oberlin College

> It is precisely because there are some "differences" between us that our world can be colorful.

A few years ago, I left my home state of California. After arriving at a place far from home, I felt a strong cultural shock.

This place is relatively old, and people here have a slow-paced lifestyle, unlike my hometown in California. For example, no one cares about who wins Sunday's football game, and no one seems too interested in the private life of movie stars. Even the young people here are not familiar with the trendy music played on American television nowadays.

Generally, people here don't seem to eat as much as Californians, and they're also not as tall as Californians. Of course, they're certainly not as fat as Californians either. At the same time, their clothing and apparel are more casual and natural. They never waste water and other natural resources.

A lot of people here are very concerned about current events and will criticize the policies of the U.S. government and capitalism in front of you, telling you publicly that they advocate socialism. All in all, I think the people here are a little bit different.

Where could this be? You almost know the answer already, don't you?

I am here to learn the language spoken by the largest number in the world because there are great learning conditions. Not only are there good teachers, but there is also a good environment and plenty of opportunities to practice the language.

Ha, I think you've guessed it. This is Oberlin College in Ohio, U.S.A.!

Oberlin College has a long-standing history, and it not only taught me to speak Chinese, but also helped me broaden my horizons and gain a new outlook on life. After a few years of

的是，到了中国，竟然没有那么不适应。恰恰相反，我居然多多少少有了几分仍然身在欧柏林的感觉。

这时我才深深地感受到，人们太容易关注世界的不同之处，关注我们自己与他人的不同。而事实上，我们的世界相同之处更多，我们与任何其他人的共同之处更多，我们更应该注意的是我们的“同”，而不是我们之间那少得可怜的“异”。

当初我之所以只注意到欧柏林和加州的种种不同，是因为我那时眼界狭窄，经历不够。当我来到中国，与中国人交上朋友以后，我看到中美之间竟有这么多相同。是因为我已经开阔了眼界，有了更多的知识与经验。

孔子说：“和而不同。”我们虽然有些不同，但是我们的相同远远多于不同。恰恰因为我们之间有些“不同”，我们的世界才能五彩缤纷。更重要的是，因为相同，因为“和”，我们的世界才能够和谐平安！

studying at Oberlin, I was fortunate enough to go to China and continue my Chinese studies. I was a little nervous before I got to China as I thought that I would have to face an even bigger cultural shock. But what surprised me was that when I arrived in China, I actually didn't feel so uncomfortable. On the contrary, I somehow felt like I was still at Oberlin.

This was when I deeply felt that it was too easy for us to focus on the differences in our world and how we're different from others. In reality, our world has much more in common, and we have even more in common with other individuals; we should pay more attention to our "similarities" instead of the pitifully small number of "differences."

Back then, the reason why I only noticed all the differences between Oberlin and California was that I was narrow-minded and didn't have enough experience. When I came to China and made friends with Chinese people, I saw so many similarities between China and the U.S. This is because I have expanded my world view, gaining more knowledge and experience.

As Confucius said, "a gentleman gets along with others, but not necessarily agrees with them." Although we're all a bit different from one another, we're much more alike than different. It is precisely because there are some "differences" between us that our world can be colorful. More importantly, because of "harmony," our world can be harmonious and peaceful!

尊重的重要性

作者：高瑾瑜　指导教师：孟多思　伊利诺州立大学（芝加哥）

> 尊重别人就是尊重自己。

在这个学期，我们了解了许多不同的中国文化和社会的方方面面。中国有很多不同的社会习俗，有些很简单，有些很复杂。比方说，用筷子吃饭，过年的时候吃鱼，老人给晚辈发红包，这些都是比较简单的习俗。但是，如果你没有关于中国文化的背景知识，你会发现有些习俗很复杂。接下来，我想要讨论一个很重要的中国习俗——社会尊重。

虽然别的国家也强调尊重，但是我发现中国的尊重非常有特色。在中国社会里，尊重长辈是一件非常重要的事情。我认为这种社会习俗可以改善社会关系。虽然人与人之间都有不同程度的尊重，但是中国人把对长辈的尊重看成重中之重。中国人尊重长辈表现在各个方面。比方说，在饭桌上，一家人一定要请长辈坐首席。长辈坐下以后，别人才可以坐下；长辈拿起筷子，别人才可以拿起筷子；长辈开始吃饭，别人才可以开始吃饭。人们见到长辈要主动问好鞠躬，让长辈走在前面。长辈老了退休以后，晚辈有义务照看长辈，养老送终。

在美国传统中，你很难找到这种尊重。比如，在美国，老人生活不能自理了以后，大部分情况下会被送进养老院，最多到了周末家人过来探望一下。据说有这样一个笑话，说是晚辈向长辈承诺："等你老了，我送你去好一点儿的养老院。"这在中国是不可想象的。另外，对祖先的纪念和祈祷是中国重要的文化特质，儒家、佛教、道教都是这样的主张，祖先在每个家庭中也是非常重要且

The Importance of Respect

Author: Valeria Gogunska   Instructor: Duosi Meng   University of Illinois (Chicago)

To respect others is to respect yourself.

During this semester, we were able to explore various different aspects of Chinese culture and society. There are many different societal customs in China: some are very simple, while others are much more complex. For example, eating with chopsticks, eating fish during the Chinese New Year, and elders giving red envelopes to the younger generations are relatively simple customs. However, if one has no background knowledge about Chinese culture, one will find that some of these customs are very complicated to understand. With this in mind, I would like to discuss a very important Chinese custom – social respect.

Although other countries also emphasize the importance of respect, I find that respect in China is very distinctive. In Chinese society, respecting one's elders is very important. I believe that this social custom can greatly improve social relations. Although there are different levels of respect among people, Chinese people regard respect for their elders as a top priority. Chinese people respect their elders in all aspects of life. For example, at the dinner table, the family always implores the elders to sit at the head of the table. After the elders sit down, others may sit down; when the elders pick up their chopsticks, others can pick up their chopsticks; when the elders start eating, others start eating. When one greets their elders, they should take

受人尊敬的。

在中国，好的学习成绩和一份好工作会被人们盛赞，你所做的一切都是在回报父母在你童年时为你所做的一切。中国父母常常给孩子灌输的理念是：小时候要好好读书，长大才能找到一份体面的工作，将来才有能力照顾老人。也就是长辈抚养晚辈，晚辈赡养长辈。尊重长辈的习俗也适用于学校。在中国的学校，学生很尊重老师。中国非常重视教育，对老师也更尊重，把老师看作引导年轻人走向成功的引路人。在中国有这样一个说法："一日为师，终身为父。"这个说法美

the initiative to say hello and bow, along with letting their elders walk in front. After the elder generations retire, the younger generations are obliged to take care of their elders until the end of their lives.

In American tradition, this kind of respect is hard to come by. For example, in the United States, when the elderly become unable to take care of themselves, they are often sent to nursing homes, where family members will come visit them on weekends at most. There is a joke that is often said by the younger generations to their elders as a promise: "Once you are old, I will send you to a better nursing home." This sort of joke is unimaginable in China. In addition, commemorating and praying to one's ancestors is an important cultural aspect held by Confucianism, Buddhism, and Taoism. Ancestors are extremely important and widely respected by every family.

In addition, good academic performance and a successful job are widely praised in China, and everything you do is to repay in gratitude everything that your parents did for you in your childhood. Chinese parents often emphasize the importance of studying rigorously in order to find a good job that is able to support the elders in the future. In this sense, the elders support the younger generations so that one day they are able to support them in return. The idea of respecting one's elders also extends to the context of schools. In Chinese schools, students respect their teachers very much. China attaches great importance to education and the teachers that enable it to flourish, thinking of teachers as guides that lead young people to success. There is a common saying in China: "A teacher for a day is a father for a lifetime." While this statement may sound exaggerated to Americans, many people in China hold this opinion. By contrast, classrooms in U.S. middle schools and high schools are very noisy and chaotic, and students lack such respect for teachers. Because of this, I think the relationship between students and teachers in the U.S. is not as good as that in China.

Respect also extends between people in daily life. If you respect me, I will respect you. If you save face for me, I will save face for you too. When you hit someone, don't hit his face; when you speak of someone, don't speak of his shortcomings. These ideas of respect are the concepts that are advocated by Chinese society. The government outlines laws to protect its people, while society follows social norms that maintain social order. If you don't respect

国人听起来可能觉得不可思议，但是在中国很多人都抱有这样的观念。相比之下，美国中小学的课堂非常吵闹、混乱，学生缺乏对老师应有的尊重。因此，我认为美国学生与老师之间的关系没有中国那么好。

在中国，人们互相尊重。如果你敬我一尺，我一定敬你一丈。你给我留了面子，我也要给你留面子。打人不打脸，揭人不揭短。这些都是中国社会推崇的人与人之间的尊重。政府有保护人民的法律，而社会有维护社会秩序的道德规范。如果你不尊重别人的话，别人也可以不尊重你。尊重别人就是尊重自己。中国社会推崇的人与人之间的尊重，不但有助于巩固家庭关系，而且有助于维护社会关系的和谐、幸福。尊重是维系中国五千年社会和谐文明的基石。

others, others will disrespect you. To respect others is to respect yourself. The respect that is advocated by Chinese society not only helps strengthen family relations, but it also helps maintain harmonic and happy social relationships. Respect is the cornerstone of China's 5,000-year-old maintenance of a harmonious society.

高考啊，高考

作者：曹安然　指导教师：顾利程　西北大学

寒窗苦读十余载，一朝高考定乾坤。

每年，世界各地的高中生都面临着申请大学的挑战，他们都在忙着准备申请材料，继续人生的下一个阶段。尽管有这种共同的经验，但世界各地的学生申请大学的过程却有所不同。通过比较中国和美国学生在申请大学过程中的差异，我们可以深入了解中国高中生和美国高中生在申请大学过程中面临的不同压力。

在中国，全国数以千万计的高三学生在每年六月份准备参加大学入学考试，也称为高考。高考持续 10 个小时，通常需要三天的时间。高考评估学生的语文、外语（通常是英语）、数学、物理、历史、化学、地理、生物、思想政治等科目的能力。如果是报考艺术院校，还会有额外的专业考试。由于高考分数是中国大学录取学生的唯一标准，中国学生为了考试而努力学习。高考分数将决定学生被录取到哪个档次的大学。此外，高考每年只进行一次，这使得考试变得更加艰苦和关键。收到高考成绩和大学发放的录取名额后，学生就可以参考大学历年录取分数，填报自己喜欢的大学。从历史上看，中国几千年前就拥有了统一考试的传统。分数面前人人平等，无论出身贵贱，学生都可以通过统一考试改变自己的命运。所以在今天的中国，高考是考生家庭中最大的一件事情。寒窗苦读十余载，一朝高考定乾坤。

与中国学生的大学申请过程相比，美国大学的申请流程就复杂多了。美国最

Oh, *Gaokao*

Author: Annie Cao Instructor: Licheng Gu Northwestern University

Students will study hard for a dozen years, but the result of the *gaokao* determines everything.

Every year high school students around the world face the challenge of applying to college to progress to the next stage of their lives. Despite this common experience, the process itself is different for every student. By comparing the differences in the college application process between students in China and the United States, we can gain a deeper understanding of the pressures students from these two countries face when they apply to universities.

In China, tens of millions of senior high school students every June prepare to take the college entrance exam, also known as the *gaokao*. The *gaokao* lasts for ten hours across the span of about three days. The exam assesses students in the areas of Chinese, foreign languages (usually English), math, physics, history, chemistry, geography, biology, politics, etc. Seniors applying to art schools may face additional exams. Since the *gaokao* score is the sole criteria for admission to Chinese universities, students in China study strenuously for the exam. *Gaokao* scores determine which universities students have a chance to be admitted to. Additionally, the exam is only conducted once a year, which makes the test even more tough and critical. After receiving their *gaokao* scores, students can check the universities they are eligible to apply to. Historically, China's tradition of utilizing unified examinations began several thousand years ago. In the face of the standardized scoring system, everyone is equal. Regardless of their background, students can ideally change their fate through their *gaokao* performance. In China today, the *gaokao* is one of the most important events for families with children. Students will study hard for a dozen years, but the result of the *gaokao* determines everything.

Compared to the college application process in China, the application process for

接近中国的高考是 SAT 和 ACT 的标准化考试，但这些考试在学生被美国大学录取中所占的分量与中国高考有很大的不同。SAT 和 ACT 分数对美国学生申请大学，不如高考对中国学生那么重要。SAT 和 ACT 的考试时间为 4 个小时，测试学生的阅读、写作、英语和数学能力（ACT 还包括一个科学部分）。并且，学生可以在同一年里参加多次考试。然而，这些考试成绩只是美国大学录取学生时所需申请资料的一部分。除了 SAT 或 ACT 成绩以外，美国高中生还要提交高中成绩单、学生论文，两份任课老师的推荐信，以及学生参加课外活动的清单。学生还有机会申请由校友进行的面试。有些学校还要求学生回答一些附加的问题，譬如说你为什么要申请我们学校。

American universities is much more complex. The closest equivalent to the *gaokao* in the United States is the standardized SAT and ACT tests, but these tests hold a different weight than the *gaokao* in determining a student's chances of admission into college. SAT and ACT scores carry less weight in the overall application process for American students than the *gaokao* does for Chinese students. The SAT and ACT are about 4 hours long and contain reading, writing, English and math skills sections (the ACT also includes a science section). Students can also take the test multiple times in the same year. However, SAT and ACT scores are only one component of the application profile that American universities evaluate. In addition to these test scores, American high school students are also required to submit high school grade transcripts, student essays, two letters of recommendation from teachers and a list of extracurricular activities they have participated in. Students also have the option to apply for interviews conducted by college

总体来看，美国大学不仅考虑学生的课堂成绩和考试成绩，还考虑成绩不能反映的素质。比如，由于美国学生在选择高中课程方面有更多的自由，大学也会评估他们课程的难度，以确定学生是否在挑战自己。此外，通过评估学生参加课外活动的情况，大学可以了解学生的兴趣和爱好，以及他们在俱乐部中的领导能力。学生论文和面试还可以让大学在个人的层面上更加了解学生。通过这些附加的评判标准，美国大学希望更好地了解学生的个性和性格。对美国大学来说，优秀的学习成绩和考试成绩并不足以保证学生被录取。

中国人口众多，还是一个发展中国家。由于文化传统与经济发展的原因，只能采取现行的高考制度。它可能不是一个完美的制度，但是它是一个现在唯一可行的制度。美国的高考制度貌似更加复杂全面，可是它也有一个很大的弊病。那就是没有考虑到巨大的贫富差距。美国富裕的家庭通常居住在好学区，有钱送孩子上资源丰富的中小学，并花钱送孩子参加补习班，雇人帮助学生包装大学申请材料。而比较穷的家庭可能负担不起这些费用，甚至有些家庭还需要孩子从小打工补贴家用。考虑到这些因素，家庭资源稀缺的孩子的确处于劣势。因此，中美两国的文化历史不同，经济发展及人口规模不同，两国的高考制度自然不同。二者之间没有优劣之分，只有哪种制度更适合自己的国情。无论申请过程如何，申请大学对所有高中生来说都是一个压力山大的过程。在这个人生的关键时刻，当大学根据不同的标准评估学生时，美国和中国的高中生都希望以最好的方式展示自己，成功走进自己最心仪的大学。

alumni. Some universities also have supplemental essays, asking students to answer additional questions like why they are choosing to apply to a specific school.

In general, American universities focus not only on a student's class grades and test scores but also consider qualities that grades do not reflect. For example, because American students have more freedom in selecting high school courses, colleges may also evaluate the difficulty of their courses to assess whether students are challenging themselves academically. Furthermore, by accounting for students' extracurricular activities, colleges can also learn about their interests, hobbies, and leadership abilities. Along with application essays and interviews, these additional criteria allow colleges to better understand the personalities and characters of applicants. For American universities, good academic performance and high test scores are not enough to guarantee student admission.

China has a large population and is still a developing country. Due to the country's cultural traditions and economic development, Chinese universities can only adopt the current *gaokao* system. It may not be a perfect system, but it is the one that is currently relied on. The American college application process seems to be more complex and comprehensive, but it also has crucial drawbacks, particularly when it comes to the disparities created by wealth inequality. Wealthy families in the United States usually live in good school districts and have the financial resources to send their children to well-funded elementary and middle schools, enroll them in tutoring classes, and hire professionals to help students assemble their college applications. Families with fewer financial resources may not be able to afford these expenses, and some children may even need to work to support their families. Given these factors, it is clear to see how families with fewer resources may be at a disadvantage when it comes to the college application process. Therefore, due to the vast differences in the cultural histories, economic development and population sizes of China and the United States, the college application processes in the two nations also naturally differ. There is no clear superior system, only options that are most suitable for each country. Regardless of the process itself, applying to college can be a stressful experience for all high school students. At such a critical moment in life as students are being evaluated, high school seniors in both China and the United States hope to showcase their strengths in the best possible way to be admitted to their dream universities.

中国茶文化

作者：陈凤嫣　指导教师：陈慰君　俄勒冈大学

对中国人来说，茶不仅仅是一种饮品，更代表了中国文化的博大精深。

众所周知，茶在中国文化中扮演着非常重要的角色。茶有着几千年的悠久历史，几千年来，一直伴随在中国人身边，人们对茶越来越热爱，不仅自己享用，还让它走向了全世界，让更多的人了解到茶文化。

在中国，不同的地区有着不同的茶文化，而最出名的地区之一要数四川成都。从清朝开始，成都的茶馆儿就遍布大街小巷。这首先是因为成都是中国历史上最早进行茶叶交易的地方。在古代中国的西南和西北地区，有一个茶马交易的贸易交通网络，叫“茶马古道”，成都作为茶马古道上最重要的城市，对当时的经济发展以及日后的文化变迁都起着非常重要的作用。由于西藏等地属高寒地区，人们需要摄入高热量的脂肪来抵御寒冷。然而过多的脂肪在体内不容易分解，茶叶恰恰能够分解脂肪，所以当地人对茶叶有着大量的需求，于是四川生产的茶叶开始大量销往这些地区。茶马古道就这样产生了，这也使得成都的茶文化越来越繁荣。

成都的茶文化发达还与当地人习惯慢节奏生活有关。成都人喜欢“坐茶馆儿”，茶客们可以看川剧、看闲书、摆龙门阵，或者打麻将，茶馆儿因此充满着生活气息。在现代生活中，随着经济的迅速发展，成都的茶馆儿也成为了很多生意人重要的工作场所。如此轻松的氛围有助于大家进行交流并促成合作。

除此以外，广东也是茶叶的消费大省。由于广东气候比较潮湿炎热，而喝

Chinese Tea Culture

Author: Aria Chen Instructor: Weijun Chen University of Oregon

As is known to all, tea plays an essential role in Chinese culture. It has thousands of years of history and has been part of Chinese people's life. People are increasingly passionate about tea. They not only enjoy it on their own, but also introduce it to the world, letting more people know about Chinese tea culture.

For Chinese people, tea is not only a drink, but also a symbol of profound Chinese culture.

In China, tea culture varies by region, and one of the most famous regions is Chengdu, the capital city of Sichuan Province. Since the Qing Dynasty, Chengdu has had teahouses all over its streets, mainly because it's one of the earliest cities to trade tea in Chinese history. In

茶可以止渴解暑，所以人们逐渐养成了喝茶的习惯。广东的茶文化与成都的茶文化截然不同。广东人习惯从早上开始喝茶，并把茶带入了饮食文化中。广东的早茶是用各式各样的点心搭配一壶热茶，既暖胃又去腻，有利于消化。对广东人来说，早茶不仅仅是休闲活动，还是现代社会中重要的生活方式之一。

对中国人来说，茶不仅仅是一种饮品，更代表了中国文化的博大精深。每个地区不同的茶文化代表着当地的文化特色，也推动着时代的进步。茶将不同年龄段的人都联系在一起，也在国际上得到越来越多的认可和支持。

the southwest and northwest regions of ancient China, there was a tea-horse trade network, called "Tea Horse Road." Chengdu, as the most important city on the Tea Horse Road, played a critical role in the economic development and cultural change at that time. Because Xizang and nearby areas belong to the alpine region, people needed to consume high-calorie heavy foods to ward off the cold weather. It's hard to break down the fat if too many high-fat foods are consumed, so people had a large demand for tea in order to help the body break down fat more quickly. Therefore, a large amount of tea produced in Sichuan began to be sold to these regions, making Chengdu's tea culture become more prosperous, and the Tea Horse Road was formed as a result.

The development of the tea culture in Chengdu is also related to the slow-paced life of the locals. People in Chengdu like to "sit in a teahouse," a lively place where they can watch Sichuan opera, read books, chat with friends, or play mahjong. With the rapid economic development in modern society, Chengdu teahouses have also become an important place for many businessmen. The relaxed atmosphere in teahouses is beneficial in facilitating communication and cooperation between business parties.

In addition, Guangdong is another major region of tea consumption. Because the climate in Guangdong is relatively humid and hot, and drinking tea can quench thirst and relieve heat, people have gradually developed the habit of drinking tea. However, the tea culture in Guangdong is completely different from that in Chengdu. Cantonese people used to drink tea in the morning and have brought tea into food culture, forming the Cantonese brunch – *zaocha*. *Zaocha* serves a variety of dim sum with a pot of hot tea, which warms the stomach and relieves the greasiness for digestion. *Zaocha* is not only a leisure activity for the Cantonese, but also an important lifestyle in modern society.

For Chinese people, tea is not only a drink, but also a symbol of profound Chinese culture. Tea culture in each region represents local cultural characteristics, as well as promotes social progress. Tea has been fostering connection and friendship among people of all ages, and it is now gaining increasing international recognition and support.

中美女性的审美标准

作者：阮嘉香　指导教师：张天璐　威斯康星大学（麦迪逊）

两个国家的审美标准都源于人们对更高社会地位的追求。

为什么我要讨论“中美女性的审美标准”呢？我是在美国出生和长大的，看美国电视剧或者杂志的时候，我看到里面的美国女人都长得很像，比如说她们的皮肤都是小麦色的，她们总是化着浓妆。上了大学以后，我跟很多中国女孩儿接触，发现她们喜欢的样子和美国人不太一样。比如，我的中国朋友喜欢买偏白的粉底液，但是我的美国朋友只买小麦色的粉底液。

我们先看看中国的女性审美标准吧。提到中国的审美标准，我首先想到的是“一白遮三丑”。中国人追求白肤色。除了白肤色以外，中国人也喜欢大眼睛、双眼皮、瓜子脸。中国人“以瘦为美”，意思就是瘦的样子是最美的。

那美国的女性审美标准有什么特点呢？大多数的美国人喜欢小麦肤色，洁白的牙齿，纤细的腰肢，丰满的胸部、臀部和嘴唇，还有浓妆。这些特征都凸显了女性的成熟之美。

为什么中国和美国会有这两种不一样的女性审美标准呢？我们先来看中国。从历史角度来看，以前穷人要在农田里干活儿，风吹日晒，皮肤黝黑；而有钱的人则待在家里，不用干活儿，皮肤白皙。所以肤色白对应的是较好的经济状况和较高的社会地位。从社会角度来看，中国人喜欢大眼睛和双眼皮。因为大眼睛

Chinese and American Beauty Standards

Author: Kristine Nguyen

Instructor: Tianlu Zhang University of Wisconsin-Madison

> These two countries' beauty standards both originate from society wanting higher social status.

Why do I want to discuss Chinese and American beauty standards? I was born and raised in America. When watching American shows or reading magazines, I saw that American women look very similar. For example, they all have tanned-tone skin and always wear heavy makeup. When I began college, I became close with many girls from China and found their beauty standards are not the same as American women's beauty standards. For example, my Chinese friend prefers to buy foundation that is fairer, but my American friends only buy foundation that is tanner in color.

Let's first look at the beauty standards of Chinese women. When mentioning Chinese beauty standards, I first think of an idiom "A white complexion is powerful enough to hide seven faults." Chinese people chase after fair skin. Besides fair skin, Chinese people also like big eyes, double-fold eyelids, and a "melon-seed" shaped face. Chinese people "take thinness as beauty," believing having a thin figure is the most beautiful.

What are the characteristics of American women's beauty standards then? Most Americans like tanned skin,

常常给人一种像小女孩儿一样单纯天真的感觉，所以很多中国人喜欢大眼睛的可爱女人。

我们再来说说美国。从历史的角度来看，以前美国人外出旅行并不容易。去海边或者热带岛屿度假的人，往往被晒出小麦色皮肤。所以小麦色的皮肤对应的是有能力外出旅行的经济能力。除此之外，很多美国人都觉得小麦色皮肤看起来很健康。从社会的角度来看，美国人喜欢整齐洁白的牙齿，也是因为这样显得人很健康。更重要的是，想要有整齐洁白的牙齿你肯定要花很多钱，所以如果你有整齐洁白的牙齿的话，你一定很有钱。

最后，我来反思和总结一下。了解不同国家的审美标准有什么意义？第一，我更深入地了解了美国和中国的文化。比如说，美国女性认为美是健康、性感和成熟。中国女性认为美是年轻、可爱。两个国家的审美标准都源于人们对更高社会地位的追求。

我也在想，我自己的审美标准是什么？因为我的父母是亚洲人，我在美国出生、长大，中美两国女性的审美标准，我都接受。比方说，我喜欢皮肤健康自然的样子，也喜欢整齐洁白的牙齿，这是美国的女性审美标准；我也喜欢大眼睛和可爱的女孩儿，这是中国的女性审美标准。

你的审美标准是什么呢？你觉得你的审美标准跟中国人的更像还是跟美国人的更像呢？

pure white teeth, a slim waist, a full chest, posterior and lips, and heavy makeup. These features all highlight mature women's beauty.

Why do China and America have these different beauty standards? Let's first look at China. From a historical perspective, in the past, poor people had to work on the farm, sun-drenched and dark-skinned. On the other hand, the wealthy stayed at home; not needing to do any labor, they had fair skin. Therefore, having fair skin corresponded to a better economic condition and higher social status. From a societal perspective, Chinese people like big eyes and double-fold eyelids because big eyes often remind others of the feeling of a young girl's innocence; therefore, a lot of Chinese people like cute women with big eyes.

Let's talk about America again. From a historical perspective, it was not easy for Americans to travel in the past. People who vacation to the beach or tropical islands, tend to be tan. Therefore, tanned skin corresponded to the economic ability to travel. Besides this, many Americans believe tanned-skin looks healthier. From a societal perspective, Americans like straight, pure white teeth because they look healthier as well. Furthermore, it costs a lot to have straight, pure white teeth, so if you have straight, pure white teeth, you must be wealthy.

Lastly, I will reflect and summarize my thoughts. So, what is the point of understanding different countries' beauty standards? First, I was able to gain a deeper understanding of American and Chinese culture. For example, American women believe that beauty is healthy, sexy, and mature. Chinese women believe beauty is young and cute. These two countries' beauty standards both originate from society wanting higher social status.

I also think about my own beauty standards. Because my parents are Asian, and I was born and raised in America, I accept both Chinese and American beauty standards. For example, I like healthy and natural skin, and also like straight, pure white teeth. These are American women's beauty standards. I also like cute girls with big eyes, which are from the Chinese women's beauty standards.

What are your beauty standards? Do you think your beauty standards are more similar to the Chinese's or the American's?

中国古代算学

作者：柯文宇　指导教师：梁霞　华盛顿大学（圣路易斯）

中国的算学基于某些具体问题，发现解决方案以后，再试图寻求通解。

首先，我来比较一下中国算学跟希腊算学。一般来说，希腊的数学注重以公理为基础来发展数学的概念。比如亚里士多德的演绎法，从一般的笼统的信息里推理出一个具体的结论。与此相比，中国的算学基于某些具体问题，发现解决方案以后，再试图寻求通解。这就是所谓的归纳法，也就是从具体的例子出发，然后推出一般规律的结论。这两种方法虽然不同，但都很重要。

中国古代算学主要使用两种计算工具。第一种是算筹。算筹是一种十进制的计算工具，使用的是小木棍，起源于商朝的占卜。第二种计算工具是算盘。汉代中国算盘的雏形就已经出现了，后来在宋代和明代又有进一步改进。珠算可算是中国非物质文化遗产的一个重要部分。在北宋名画《清明上河图》中，药师的账簿上就摆着一个算盘。

从周朝开始，人们就留下了很多有关数学的记录。周代的《周礼》所记录的六艺包括礼、乐、射、御、书、数，而且当时的数学可分为九数，其中两个是方田和均输，都是为了解决非常实际的问题。孔子就曾经接受过这方面的教育。

汉朝最重要的数学教科书是《算数书》和《九

Ancient Chinese Arithmetic

Author: Aaron Kirkland Instructor: Xia Liang Washington University (St. Louis)

First, I would like to talk about the comparison between Chinese arithmetic and Greek arithmetic. In general, Greek mathematics emphasizes developing mathematical concepts based on axioms. This is Aristotle's deductive reasoning, which is to infer a specific conclusion based on general and broad information. In contrast, Chinese arithmetic is based on certain specific problems, and a general solution is only found after a particular problem-solving approach has been identified. This is known as inductive reasoning; that is, starting from specific examples and then deducing general laws. While these two approaches are different, both are very important.

Chinese arithmetic is based on certain specific problems, and a general solution is only found after a particular problem-solving approach has been identified.

There were mainly two calculation tools in ancient China. The first one is called counting rods, which is a decimal calculation method using small wooden sticks that originated from the divination of the Shang Dynasty. The second calculation tool is the abacus. The prototype of the Chinese abacus appeared in the Han Dynasty and was further refined in the Song and Ming dynasties. The abacus can be regarded as an important part of China's intangible cultural heritage. In the famous painting from the Northern Song Dynasty Along the River During the Qingming Festival, there is an abacus on the top of the pharmacist's account book.

Starting from the Zhou Dynasty, people have left many records about mathematics. The Six Arts documented in the book *Rites of Zhou* from the Zhou Dynasty included rites, music, archery, chariotry, calligraphy, and mathematics. At the time, mathematics could be divided into nine

章算术》。有意思的是，《九章算术》自从公元 1 世纪成书一直到清朝都受到人们的重视与承认，可是《算数书》直到 1983 年才在湖北省张家山被考古学家发现，虽然它早在公元前 2 世纪就已经成书。这两本书里所包括的内容基本上是一样的，包括开平方、开立方、算术应用、正负数，甚至还包括一次方程式和二次方程式等。《九章算术》有几个额外的主题，因此《算数书》可能是《九章算术》的母本。《九章算术》中记载的很多的算法都是数学界最早出现的，比如著名的高斯消元法，早在《九章算术》中就有记载，比欧洲人早了 1500 年！

接下来，我们讨论圆周率的历史。汉代以前数学家用了圆内接的正六边形来

chapters, two of which were on the topics of measurements and fractions, which were both used to solve practical real-world problems. Confucius was also educated in this regard.

The most important mathematics textbooks in the Han Dynasty were *Book on Numbers and Computation* and *The Nine Chapters on the Mathematical Art.* Interestingly enough, *The Nine Chapters on the Mathematical Art* has been valued and recognized by the public since it was written in the 1st century AD until the Qing Dynasty, while the *Book on Numbers and Computation* was not discovered by archaeologists in Zhangjiashan, Hubei Province until 1983, even though it was written all the way back in the 2nd century BC. The content covered in these two books is basically the same, including square root, cube root, application of arithmetic, positive and negative numbers, and even topics such as linear and quadratic equations; however, *The Nine Chapters on the Mathematical Art* covers some additional subjects, so the *Book on Numbers and Computation* might be the parent book of *The Nine Chapters on the Mathematical Art.* Many algorithms in *The Nine Chapters on the Mathematical Art* are the earliest examples of mathematics to be discovered. For instance, Gaussian elimination was documented in this book, which was only invented by Europeans 1,500 years later!

Next, let's discuss the history of pi. Before the Han Dynasty, mathematicians used a regular hexagon inscribed in a circle to approximate the value of pi, and the number was 3. But later, Liu Xin of the Western Han Dynasty used a certain algorithm to get 3.1547; historians do not know which specific algorithm he used. Approximately a hundred years later, Zhang Heng approximate pi as 3.1622. Then, another one hundred years later, Liu Hui in Wei-Jin Period invented the so-called circle cutting technique. This was a very wonderful algorithm as it further improved the calculation of pi.

The pinnacle of the calculation of pi in Chinese history was Zu Chongzhi from the Song and Qi Dynasties. He found that pi was between 3.1415926 and 3.1415927, which was the best approximation of pi in the world for the next 1,000 years!

Jia Xian of the Northern Song Dynasty invented the triangle for calculating the binomial

逼近圆周率，得数为3。但是后来西汉的刘歆用了某一个算法得到3.1547，历史学家至今还不知道他用的是哪一个算法。大约一百年以后，东汉的张衡算出了近似值为3.1622。然后再过一百年，魏晋的刘徽发明了割圆术。这是一个非常精彩的算法，使得圆周率计算的准确率得到了进一步的提高。

中国历史上圆周率计算的巅峰是南朝宋、齐时期的祖冲之。他推算出圆周率在3.1415926和3.1415927之间，这是接下来的一千年中全世界最精确的数值！

北宋人贾宪发明了表示二项式系数的三角形，此发现在南宋数学家杨辉1261年所著的《详解九章算法》一书中出现，现称为杨辉三角。而法国人帕斯卡（Pascal）到了17世纪才研究出同样的三角形，比中国人落后了600年。

coefficients, this was compiled into *Detailed Solutions to Nine Chapters on the Mathematical Arts* by Yang Hui, a mathematician in the Southern Song Dynasty, in 1261. The result is known as Yang Hui's triangle today. Pascal from France did not discover the same triangle until the 17th century, almost 600 years later.

昔为今用

The Past Guides the Present

导 读

模仿昔日名篇的框架，填入新内容，写出自己的文章，这种做法被认为是一个提高写作水平的好方法。本板块收录的十二篇文章都与过去名人名篇的框架有关，但是内容都是讨论当下的事物。所谓照猫画虎，就是这个道理。读者不妨看看下面的两个范例。

布朗大学的康凯文同学的《算了吧先生传》很明显是脱胎于胡适先生的名篇《差不多先生传》。在凯文的笔下，一个什么事情都得过且过的“算了吧先生”被勾画了出来。去找工作面试，当然应该西装革履，但是“算了吧先生”觉得太麻烦，最后竟然穿着一件T恤衫就去面试了。他的这副打扮与正襟危坐的考官们形成了鲜明的反差。“算了吧先生”当然没有得到这份工作，但是他却安慰自己道：“反正我本来就没有那么喜欢这份工作，算了吧。”“算了吧先生”没有找到工作，却找到了一个他非常中意的女朋友。人家约他去一家高档餐厅吃饭，他这次原本想打扮一下，换上漂亮的衣服再去。临走的时候又嫌换衣服太麻烦，就对自己说：“算了吧，衣服不重要，我喜欢你就够了。”在高档的餐厅里，穿着随便的他与穿着得体的女朋友显得那么格格不入。可想而知，女朋友只好弃他而去。胡适先生笔下的“差不多先生”做什么事情都马马虎虎，认为差不多就行。他因为粗心大意做买卖赔了钱，最后又糊里糊涂看错了医生，丢了性命。无独有偶，凯文笔下的“算了吧先生”因为大大咧咧没有找到工作，又丢了女朋友，这二位可谓是一对难兄难弟。

在林语堂先生的《中国究有臭虫否》这篇散文中，他引用了十种典型人物的十种不同答案。他们是：辜鸿铭、爱国者、哥伦比亚博士、帝国主义者、西方传

Introduction

Imitating the framework of ancient famous literary works, filling in new content, and writing your own pieces are considered a good way to improve your writing skills. The twelve stories in this section are all related to the framework of renowned pieces from the past, but the content is correlated to modern occurrences. This coincides with the Chinese idiom that goes: Drawing a tiger using a cat as a model. Readers may wish to look at the following two examples.

"The Story of Mr. 'Forget It'" is written by Kevin Kang of Brown University and is clearly born out of Mr. Hu Shi's famous work, "The Story of Mr. Nearly." In Kevin's pen, a man who can muddle through everything, known as Mr. "Forget It," is outlined. When going for a job interview, of course you should wear a suit and leather shoes, but Mr. "Forget It" thought it was too troublesome and ended up wearing a T-shirt. His attire was in stark contrast to the interviewers sitting upright in professional attire. Obviously, Mr. "Forget It" did not end up getting the job, but he comforted himself: "I didn't like that job that much anyway. Forget it!" Mr. "Forget It" did not find a job, but he found a girlfriend that he cared about a lot. When she invited him to an exquisite restaurant for dinner, he originally planned to dress up and put on nice clothes. However, before going out, he felt that changing clothes was too cumbersome, so he told himself: "Forget it," believing that "clothes weren't important." He thought "If I liked you enough, then forget the rest." In the restaurant, he looked extremely out of place in his casual clothes when compared to his well-dressed girlfriend. Therefore, it was conceivable that his girlfriend chose to break up with him. Mr. Hu Shi's Mr. Nearly does everything so-so, thinking that "almost is enough." He lost money because of his careless business transactions, and in the end, he saw the wrong doctor in a daze and lost his life. Coincidentally, the Mr. "Forget It" in Kevin's story failed to find a job and lost his girlfriend because of his carelessness – the two characters can be considered as brothers suffering in the same boat.

In Mr. Lin Yutang's essay "Do Bed Bugs Exist in China," he quoted ten different answers from ten typical characters. They are: Gu Hongming, patriots, Dr. Columbia, imperialists,

教士、中国外交官、国民党党部、道士与和尚、胡适及论语派中人。由于他们的立场不同，回答当然不同。抓住了这篇文章的精髓，西北大学的陈焕斌写出了他的习作《先救谁》，更是把林语堂先生的幽默调侃继承了下来。“老婆和老妈同时落水，你会先救谁呢？”在这个千古之问面前，焕斌给我们挑选了十位古今中外典型人物。他们是：周幽王、爱德华八世、孟子、爱因斯坦、屈原、达尔文、刘备、牛顿、深圳某男及纽约某男。周幽王选择救老婆褒姒。为了博得褒姒一笑而烽火戏诸侯，最终丢了江山。同样不爱江山爱美人的爱德华八世也选择救老婆，因为他的老妈反对他迎娶辛普森。遵循孝道的孟子自然要救他的老妈，在他的眼里，当然是万恶淫为首，百善孝为先。与之相反，爱因斯坦要先救的是老婆。“每一次跟老婆耳鬓厮磨时，我觉得时间过得飞快。而每一次听老妈絮絮叨叨时，我觉得时间过得很慢。我发现时间不是绝对的，而是相对的。”看到老婆和老妈掉进水里，悲观极致的屈原纵身一跳，跟着老婆和老妈一起沉入了水底。看到老婆和老妈掉进水里，进化论的创始者达尔文决定谁也不去救。他认为适者生存，会等着看她们二人谁能自己爬上岸来。今天的深圳某男在这个问题面前左右为难。老妈的养育之恩，没齿难忘，美貌如花的爱妻更是割舍不掉。与之相比，纽约某男倒是态度明确，跳进水里先去救他的老婆了。

焕斌的十个人物正好五中五洋，中西对比。凸显了古今人物的个性，展示了东西文化的区别。这篇幽默散文的写作方法非常值得大家学习。

Western missionaries, Chinese diplomats, Kuomintang party headquarters, Taoist priests and monks, Hu Shi, and members of *The Analects*. Due to their different stances, their answers to the same question would obviously be different. Grasping the essence of this essay, Calvin Chen of Northwestern University wrote his piece "Whom to Rescue First," which inherits Mr. Lin Yutang's satirical writing style. "If your wife and mother fell into the water at the same time, who would you save first?" When faced with this question, Calvin selected ten renowned historical figures from all over the world. They are: King You of the Zhou Dynasty, Edward VIII, Mencius, Einstein, Qu Yuan, Darwin, Liu Bei, Newton, a man from Shenzhen, and a man from New York. King You of the Zhou Dynasty chose to save his wife Baosi. To make Baosi happy, he made fun of the dukes by faking fire but ended up losing the whole empire. Edward VIII also didn't love his country, but preferred a beautiful woman instead. So, he also chose to save his wife as an act of defiance because his mother opposed him marrying Simpson. Mencius, who followed filial piety, naturally wanted to save his mother. In his eyes, "Lust is the greatest of all evils, and filial piety is the greatest of all virtues." On the contrary, it was his wife that Einstein wanted to save first. "Whenever I share affectionate moments with my wife, I notice that time flies. However, every time I hear my mother ramble on and on, I find that time passes very slowly. Time is not absolute, but relative." Seeing his wife and his mother both had fallen into the water, Qu Yuan, who was extremely pessimistic, plunged into the water with them. Darwin, the founder of the theory of evolution, decided not to save anyone. He believed in the survival of the fittest and wanted to wait and see which of the two could climb ashore by themselves. A man from Shenzhen today is in a dilemma when faced with this question. His mother's kindness in nurturing him is memorable, yet his beautiful wife is even more unforgettable. In contrast, a man in New York had a clear attitude and jumped into the water to save his wife first.

Calvin's ten characters contain five Chinese people and five foreigners, clearly showing the contrast between Chinese and Western morals. His piece highlights the personalities of ancient and modern characters, thereby revealing the distinctions between Eastern and Western cultures. The writing method of this humorous prose is very worth learning from.

算了吧先生传

作者：康凯文　指导教师：汪洋　布朗大学

> 做事情不求善始善终，中途遇到困难就以“算了吧”来宽慰自己。

有一种现象席卷了现代的年轻人，那就是做事情不求善始善终，中途遇到困难就以“算了吧”来宽慰自己。这类人对什么是成功，什么是失败，模糊不清，对什么应该做，什么不应该做，无所谓。世事难料，对一切不明了的情况，还是“算了吧”！

这一类人就统称叫“算了吧”先生。他无处不在，随时随地可见，他是街上的叔叔，是骑自行车的小姑娘，或是在街角卖菜的大妈。他甚至有可能就是你。也许，他也就是我。天气变暖，得找出夏天的衣服了。哎，算了吧，懒得找！天气冷了，该找出冬天的衣服了。哎，还是算了吧！在寒冷的天气仍然轻松穿T恤也是一种风格。本来我想继续给你多介绍介绍“算了吧”先生的其他行为。哎，但算了吧，你懂的……

“算了吧”先生在寻找他一直想要的一份工作机会。他为这份工作的面试做了大量的准备工作。他知道，如果他得到这份工作，会令他的父母感到自豪。对“算了吧”先生来说，这可是一件十分重要的事情。“算了吧”先生对自己的能力也充满了信心。当他信心满满地走进面试考场的时候，却发现别人都是西装革履，而自己却忘了穿西装。想想算了吧，也许西装并不重要，西装和T恤衫有什么区别呢？“算了吧，我努力地准备了其他的东西，应该对自己的表现充满自信。”于是他就穿着一件T恤衫去面试了。一个星期过去了，他接到的通知是自己被

The Story of Mr. "Forget It"

Author: Kevin Kang Instructor: Yang Wang Brown University

Not to persevere to the end – when things are difficult to solve, they proudly proclaim "forget it!" to console themselves.

There's a phenomenon endemic amongst the contemporary young folk, that is, not to persevere to the end – when things are difficult to solve, they proudly proclaim "forget it!" to console themselves. The delineation between what's success and what's failure becomes ambiguous; what ought to be done is left undone, and left and right are rendered indistinguishable. These people are ambivalent about everything, letting things go!

This subset of people is collectively called Mr. "Forget it." He's everywhere – he's the uncle hollering on the street, the little girl biking around the block, or the corner store auntie selling vegetables like she always does. Perhaps, he's even you. Or maybe he's even me. When the weather gets hot, he mutters, "forget it," and is too lazy to find summer clothes. When the weather gets cold, he is too lazy to find winter clothes. Wearing a T-shirt in the coldest weather is cool! In fact, I had wanted to tell you more about him, but forget about it. There's more to know...

Mr. "Forget it" got the opportunity to interview for a job he had always aspired to do. As a result, he began preparing for it. He knew that if he got the job, it would inevitably make his parents proud. To Mr. "Forget it," it was a very important thing. Confident in his abilities, Mr. "Forgot it" walked into the interview only to forget to dress in formal attire. Forget it! Perhaps it was not important. Wearing a suit or a T-shirt doesn't

拒了。“算了吧”先生叹了口气说：“反正我本来就没有那么喜欢这份工作，算了吧。”

大学毕业已经一年多了，“算了吧”先生因为遇事总是算了吧，所以还没找到一份像样的工作。“算了吧”先生安慰自己说：“这些公司和打工的生活方式可能真的不适合我！”偶然有一天，“算了吧”先生遇到了一位他特别喜欢的女孩儿。在他眼里，这个女孩儿是完美的，但是，“算了吧”先生没有一份体面的工作，女孩儿约他出去旅游，他说：“算了吧，就在家里吧。”女孩儿让他穿上整洁干净的衣服跟她去见朋友，他说：“算了吧，衣服不重要，我喜欢你就够了。”算了吧，算了吧……很多次“算了吧”之后，女孩儿再也忍不住，叹了一口气，说：“算了吧！我们分手吧！”当他听到女朋友的这个决定时，“算了吧”先生悲痛欲绝。他苦闷了两天以后，安慰自己道：“还是算了吧！反正我也无能为力。”他付出了一切，为什么她要分手。但他不知道的是，要是自己细心一点儿，认真一点儿，遇事不要总是“算了吧”，就不会失去那个女孩儿了。“哎，算了吧。后悔有什么用呢？还是算了吧。”“算了吧”先生这样安慰自己。

make a big difference, right? "Forget it! I'm well prepared, so I should be confident in myself," he huffed. So he went to the interview wearing a T-shirt. A week passed, and he was rejected. Mr. "Forget it" sighed and thought to himself rather quietly, "I didn't like that job that much anyway. Forget it!"

Over one year after graduation, Mr. "Forget it" hadn't found a job because he was constantly forgetting about things. He muttered to himself, "These companies and the 9-to-5 lifestyle are probably not for me!" By chance, Mr. "Forget it" met a girl he particularly liked one day. In his eyes, she was perfect, but Mr. "Forget it" was still unemployed. This girl was insistent on going out for a trip together; he thought "forget it" and remained at home. This girl asked him to wear neat and clean clothes to meet friends with her; he thought "forget it," believing clothes weren't important. He thought: "If I liked you enough, then forget the rest, forget the rest!" The girl also couldn't put up with him any longer, so she sighed and retorted, "Forget it then! Let's break up!" Upon hearing this news, he was devastated: "I think it's better to forget it after all… There's nothing I can do about it." He had given everything, but why did she want to break up? But had he known to be slightly more careful, a little more serious, not always "forgetting it," he wouldn't have lost her. "Forget it! It's no use crying over spilt milk." Mr. "Forget it" comforted himself.

先救谁

作者：陈焕斌　指导教师：顾利程　西北大学

“如果老婆和老妈同时落水，你会先救谁呢？”在西北大学的高级汉语课上，顾利程教授向大家抛出了这千古一问。下面是古今中外人士给出的不同答案。

> “如果老婆和老妈同时落水，你会先救谁呢？”

周幽王：如果老婆和老妈都掉水里了，寡人当然要先救老婆了。为了逗老婆一笑，寡人烽火戏诸侯，连江山都不要了，连小命都不要了。再说寡人的那个老妈，在立太子的时候偏向弟弟，害得寡人差点儿坐不上王位。褒姒，寡人来救你了！

爱德华八世：跟周幽王一样，我也是先救老婆。至于我那女王老妈呀，那就算了吧。当初为了阻止我和我心爱的辛普森女士结婚，她骂我“不爱江山爱美人，不负责任，破坏王室形象”。反正我已经让位给我那结巴弟弟，对老妈没有责任了。什么？辛普森是一个离过婚的女人？你们中国人太在乎这些了。不理你们，我去救老婆了。

孟子：我从小死了老爸，全靠老妈一手含辛茹苦把我抚养成人。为了让我上进，老妈搬了三次家，最后搬进了最好的学区房，所以我才成名成家。老婆和老妈落水，我当然是先救老妈了。所谓万恶淫为首，百善孝为先嘛。老婆死了我还可以再找一个，老妈却只有一个啊。世上只有妈妈好！老妈，儿子来了！

爱因斯坦：跟孟子不同，我要先救的是老婆，而不是老妈。你们知道我是怎么研究出相对论的吗？每一次跟老婆耳鬓厮磨时，我觉得时间过得很快。而每

Whom to Rescue First

Author: Calvin Chen　Instructor: Licheng Gu　Northwestern University

"If your wife and mother fell into the water at the same time, who would you save first?" Professor Licheng Gu asked his advanced Chinese class at Northwestern University this renowned question. The following are the different answers Chinese and Westerners have responded with throughout history into the modern days.

"If your wife and mother fell into the water at the same time, who would you save first?"

King You of the Zhou Dynasty: If both my wife and mother fell into the water, I would obviously save my wife first. To make my wife Bao Si happy, I made fun of the feudal lords by faking fire. For her, I gave up the throne, and eventually my own life. That's not to mention that my mother even wanted my younger brother to become the prince back in the days, almost preventing me from taking the throne as a king. Bao Si, I'm coming to save you!

Edward VIII: Like King You in China, I would also save my wife first. As for my mother, the Queen, just forget about her. Back in the days, in order to prevent me from marrying my beloved wife Ms. Simpson, she would scold me and affirm that "Loving beautiful women more than your country is a sign of irresponsibility, and you will ruin the image of the royal family." Either way, I've already given up my throne to my stammering brother, so I have no more obligations toward my mother. What? Simpson is a divorced woman? You Chinese people just care too much about these trivial things. Whatever, I'm going to go save my wife.

Mencius: My father died when I was very young, and my mother single-handedly raised me through her dedication and hard work. In order to motivate me to learn, my mother moved three times until we found a house in the best school district, and that's how I became famous and started a family. If my wife and mother both fell into the water, I would definitely save my mother first. As the proverb goes, "Lust is the greatest of all evils, and filial piety is the greatest

一次听老妈絮絮叨叨时，我觉得时间过得很慢。我发现时间不是绝对的，而是相对的。这就是我的相对论。所以，爱老妈是相对的，而爱老婆是绝对的。老婆，我来了！

屈原：这个世界太黑暗了，活着也没有什么意思，不如都死了干净。沧浪之水清兮，可以濯吾缨，沧浪之水浊兮，可以濯吾足。投身于河水当中倒是一个挺

of all virtues." If my wife were to die, I can find another one, but I only have one mother. My mother is the best person in the world! Mother, your son is coming!

Einstein: Unlike Mencius, I would save my wife first, not my mother. Do you know how I discovered the theory of relativity? Whenever I share affectionate moments with my wife, I notice that time flies. However, every time I hear my mother ramble on and on, I find that time passes very slowly. Time is not absolute but relative. That is my theory of relativity. Therefore, loving my mother is relative while loving my wife is absolute. Wife, I'm coming!

Qu Yuan: The world is full of darkness, and there is no purpose in staying alive, so dying is a better choice. When the water is clear, I can wash my tassels, and when the water is turbid, I can wash my feet. Plunging into the river seems like a good resort. Wife, Mother, you both are very clairvoyant! I will die with both of you.

Darwin: The real world is brutal, and natural selection tells us that the strong will win over the weak, and only the fittest can survive. If my wife and mother drown because they can't swim, it is because nature has eliminated them due to their weakness. They can only blame themselves as those who are weak can't be saved. With the theory of evolution, everyone is created equal. Without environmental or external interference, let's see if my wife or mother will be able to climb ashore independently.

Liu Bei: Brothers are like hands and feet, while a wife is like clothing. If you lose your clothes, you can just buy new ones, but if you break your limbs, they won't be able to grow back. As long as my brothers don't fall into the water, I don't care about anyone else. Wife, Mother, what a tragic death! Oh no, my life is so miserable and painful without you!

Newton: Wife, Mother, why are you so careless! I'm coming to save you! Hold on, I need to do some calculations first. My wife is 20 meters away from the edge of the river, while my mother is 10 meters away. The water depth is approximately five meters, and the gravity of the Earth is…Ah, I figured it out at last! Hey, where did you both go?

A man from Shenzhen, China: A mother gave birth to a son. They are bonded together by heart and flesh, and the mother is worried whenever the son has to travel long distances. I've read the 24 Filial Exemplars a lot of times, so how can I not save my mother? Hold on, hold on. One day spent together as husband and wife means eternal devotion, and a hundred days of marriage is as deep as the ocean. Not only does my wife have to assist me and teach our children, but she is also as beautiful a flower, so how can I not save her? Who should I actually

好的归宿。老婆、老妈，你们真是有先见之明啊！我和你们一起去赴死吧。

达尔文：这是一个现实的世界，丛林的法则是弱肉强食，适者生存。如果老婆和老妈因为不会游泳而溺死，这正是因为她们羸弱而被大自然淘汰。这只能怪她们自己，因为弱者是救不得的。在进化论面前，人人平等。在没有外界干扰的情况下，看看老婆和老妈谁能自己爬上岸吧。

刘备：兄弟如手足，老婆如衣服。衣服丢了还可以买新的，手足断了可就长不回来了。只要二弟、三弟没有掉进水里就行了，其他人我就都不管了。老婆、老妈，你们死得好惨啊！呜呼，我的命好苦啊！

牛顿：老婆、老妈，你们怎么这么不小心啊！等一等，我来救你们了！慢着，我得先计算一下。老婆正处于离河边 20 米的距离，而老妈则处于离河边 10 米的距离。水深大约 5 米，地球引力是…… 啊，我算出来啦！我算出来啦！欸，你们人都到哪里去了？

深圳某男：娘生儿，连心肉，儿行千里母担忧。二十四孝我读了很多遍了，怎能不救老妈呢？！等一下，等一下。一日夫妻百日恩，百日夫妻似海深。我的老婆相夫教子，美貌如花，我怎能不救老婆呢？我到底应该先去救谁呢？让我再想一想吧。

纽约某男：这是一个很实际的问题。老妈已经是风烛残年，没有几年活头了，还不如早些去找我死去的老爸。而我的老婆风华正茂，要给我抚养三个读书的小孩儿，每天还要给我洗衣做饭，打扫房间。更重要的是，我还没有给她买人寿保险呢。我决定了，先去救老婆了！

以上十种不同的态度不代表我本人的观点，读者千万不要告诉我的老妈，更不要告诉我未来的老婆哟。

save first? Let me think about this some more.

A man from New York, U.S.A.: This is a very practical question. My mother is already in her declining years, so she does not have many years left in her life and may as well go find my long-dead father earlier. On the other hand, my wife is in her prime and must help me raise three children who are currently in school. She also has to do the laundry, cook, and clean the rooms for me every day. More importantly, I haven't bought her life insurance yet. I've decided that I'm going to save my wife first.

The ten different perspectives listed above do not reflect my personal beliefs or opinions, so readers need to make sure that they don't tell my mother. Moreover, they definitely can't tell my future wife!

天生我材必有用

作者：王煜雯　指导教师：顾利程　西北大学

“天生我材必有用”是我妈妈跟我分享的一句很有意义的话，我也认为这句话很重要。这句话出自唐代诗人李白的诗——《将进酒》。“天生”是说我们的存在都是天意。“我材”指的是我自己的才能，我们都是各个方面的人才。“必有用”是说不管我们有什么样的才能，我们的存在肯定会对社会有用处。这句话意味着每个人来到这个世界上都是有意义的，都可以为社会做贡献。虽然我们可能现在不知道，但如果我们努力地寻找，我们肯定可以找到让我们发光的独特才能。我感觉这句话无论在什么时代，都可以作为很多人上进的动力。

> 每个人来到这个世界上都是有意义的，都可以为社会做贡献。

李白写这首诗的时候，他正处在人生的低谷，生活得不如意，觉得自己的才能没有人赏识。所以他想鼓励自己，无论别人承不承认你的才能，你还是可以找到在世界里的角色。这句话很适用于我现在的情况，所以我能理解李白的心情。大学正是描绘自己人生美好蓝图的地方。但是，我经常感觉我做什么都做得不够好，不知道自己为什么要上大学，为什么要努力地读书学习。我更不知道将来应该做什么，是否能做出一番大事业。但是李白的这句话让我安心。坚信“天生我材必有用”这句话，我只需要多去探索，就能找到让我充实的生活目的。虽然我可能在科学方面不擅长，但是我发现我可以努力做好我喜欢的，比如说经济和数学。

Everybody Is Good for Something

Author: Elizabeth Wang Instructor: Licheng Gu Northwestern University

"Everybody is good for something" is a meaningful phrase that my mother shared with me, and I also believe it is very important. This phrase comes from a Tang Dynasty poet Li Bai's poem "Bring in the Wine." The first part of the phrase, "born of the world's will," refers to the fact that each person's existence is meaningful. The second part, "my talent," is showing that each person has a unique talent. The last part, "must have a use," is saying that, no matter what our talent is, our existence will benefit society somehow. This saying reflects the belief that every person on this planet has a purpose and can make some contribution to society. Although we might not know yet, as long as we explore, we can definitely find the talent that allows us to shine the best. I feel that this saying can become the motivation of many people, no matter what era they are in.

Every person on this planet has a purpose and can make some contribution to society.

When poet Li Bai wrote this poem, he was at a low point in his life and did not feel like he was living the way he wanted to. He felt that he was unable to fully display his gift. So, he wrote this poem to encourage himself that, no matter if others acknowledge your skills or not, you will still be able to find your role in this world. This saying is very applicable in my current situation, so I can really understand Li Bai's experience. College is exactly the time when you are trying to discover what you want to do in life. However, I often think that whatever I do, I don't do well enough. I don't know why I am in college, or why I need to work hard and study. Even more, I don't know what I will do in the future, and whether or not I can have a successful and impactful career. However, Li Bai's poem reassures me. Following the motto "Everybody is good for something," I only have to explore more, then I will be sure to find a fulfilling purpose

更重要的一点是，一个人的才华不仅仅是天生的，后天培养也很重要。我们年轻人应该利用现在的宝贵时光，在学校里，在社会上，利用各种机会培养自己的才能，为社会服务。当今，人工智能科学、环境保护科学、材料科学和生命科学，这些新兴科学将大大改善人们的生活，所以需要大量具有这方面才华的人才。我们可以把自己培养成这方面的人才。

我相信现代人也能从这句话获得激励，特别是自卑的孩子。我希望这句话可以安慰不知道自己长处的人，可以鼓励他们不要拿自己的弱点和别人的强项比，而是专心培养自己更擅长的东西，成为对社会有贡献的人。

in life. Although I may not be that good at science, I can work hard to excel in subjects I like, such as economics and math.

Even more importantly, one's special ability is not only given to them by the world, but also honed throughout life. We youngsters should take advantage of our bright youth, and take advantage of opportunities in school and the real world to improve our gift and contribute to society. Today, artificial intelligence, environmental conservation, materials and life sciences are set to rapidly change people's life. Thus, we need a large number of talents specialized in these fields. We can specifically develop our abilities in these fields.

I believe that our current generation can obtain encouragement from this saying, especially self-abased youth. I hope that this saying can comfort those who do not yet know their talent, and encourage them to not compare their own weaknesses with others' strengths. Instead, they should focus on sharpening their skills in things they are good at, and become people who can assist in the progressive development of our society.

万事开头难

作者：王睿轩　指导教师：顾利程　西北大学

中国有句话："万事开头难。"这句话的意思是开始一项新活动通常会极具挑战性，事情开始之后，往往会变得更顺利。我父亲总跟我和弟弟讲这句话，无论是批评我们（"你为什么要放弃？万事开头难！"），安慰我们（"不是最好的也没关系！万事开头难。"），甚至说服我们（"尝试这个还为时不晚！万事开头难。"）。我是听着这句话长大的，它帮助我度过了很多困难的时期。

> 开始一项新活动通常会极具挑战性，事情开始之后，往往会变得更顺利。

开始一项活动可能有很多不同的困难。首先，计划一项活动就很有挑战性。比如说，如果一群朋友想要聚会，人们都认为最难的一步是做计划。每个人都得在同一时间有空，并且能够在同一个地点会面。其次，第一次学习一项技能、一门课程也很有挑战性。比如，学习钢琴一开始是非常难的：得学会正确的技巧，还要学会识谱。如果活动太难的话，人们可能会早早放弃。

这句话对我来说非常重要，因为它适用于我生活的方方面面。对我来说，一个典型的例子是乒乓球。我花了这么多年的心血，才在这项体育活动中取得一些成绩，可是很多次我都想放弃。但父亲总是反复对我说："万事开头难。"这句话甚至可以适用于写这篇文章。开始写文章很困难：得先选择一个主题，考虑格式，等等。但是一旦一切都计划好了，我发现写文章挺容易的。

这句话也适用于学校的各种事务。在学校上一门新课程，比如高等数学课，

Everything Starts Hard

Author: Eric Wang Instructor: Licheng Gu Northwestern University

In China, there is a saying: "Everything starts hard." It means that starting a new activity is often extremely challenging. This is also to say that after things begin, they tend to progress smoother. My father would always repeat this saying to my younger brother and I, whether it's to scold us ("Why did you give up? Everything starts hard!"), comfort us ("It's okay to not be the best! Everything starts hard."), or even persuade us ("It's not too late to try this! Everything starts hard."). I grew up hearing this quote, and it has helped me through a lot of difficult times.

> Starting a new activity is often extremely challenging. After things begin, they tend to progress smoother.

Starting a new activity can have many different challenges. First, planning the activity can

一开始往往会很困难。学生首先必须从根本上理解数学公式，但之后，用这些公式解决问题就容易多了。跟一位陌生的教授开始新的学习也很有挑战性，因为不同的教授有不同的习惯和教学方式。“万事开头难”帮助我在学习遇到困难时继续前进。

我从小到大都很舒服地陪在父母身边，当我被西北大学录取后，是否要选择远离家乡去求学，这让我犹豫了很长时间，毕竟我从来没去过伊利诺伊州。我刚刚从弗吉尼亚来到西北大学的时候，人生地不熟，办什么事情都很艰难。但是想着爸爸常常跟我说的“万事开头难”，我克服了种种困难，坚持了下来。现在我庆幸自己选择离开了从小长大的家乡，来到西北大学，来到芝加哥，闯荡出了一片新天地。所以当我和朋友们谈起他们的困难时，我会跟他们说“万事开头难”。

be difficult. For example, if a group of friends wanted to get together, it is commonly known that the hardest step is planning. Everyone must be available at the same time and be able to meet at the same location. Second, learning a skill or partaking in a course for the first time is also challenging. For example, learning to play the piano is incredibly hard at first: one must learn the proper technique along with how to read music notes. People may give up on the activity early on if it's too hard.

This phrase is so important to me because it applies to so many aspects of my life. For me, a main example is table tennis. It took me so many years of training to achieve some success, and along the way I've wanted to quit multiple times. But my father would always repeat to me: "Everything starts hard." This saying can even be applied to writing this essay. Starting an essay is difficult: one must choose a topic, consider the format, etc. But once everything is planned out, I find that writing the essay itself is easy.

This saying is also applied in every setting in school. Taking a new subject in school, such as the higher match class, tends to be hard at first. Students must first fundamentally understand the math formulas, but afterwards, applying these formulas in problems is much less difficult. Learning from a new professor also has its challenges because different professors have different habits and ways of teaching. "Everything starts hard" has helped me push forward through difficult times in school.

I grew up comfortably with my parents since I was a child. After being accepted into Northwestern University, I was hesitant to choose to leave home. After all, I had never been to Illinois. When I first came to Northwestern University from Georgia, I was unfamiliar with the place, and it was very difficult to do anything. But I thought of what my father would always say, "Everything starts hard." I overcame these difficulties and persisted. Now I am glad that I chose to leave my hometown for Northwestern University, for Chicago, exploring a new world. So, when I talk to my friends about their troubles, my first word of advice to them is "Everything starts hard."

柔与刚

作者：何意　指导教师：朱永平　圣母大学

> “柔弱胜刚强”，但是“柔弱”必须有时间，必须有耐心。

“天下莫柔弱于水，而攻坚强者莫之能胜。”老子的这句话恰如其分地赞赏了水的力量。从中国的石林到美国的大峡谷的形成，水在大自然中的超凡力量得以充分体现，为人类提供了水胜石头的确凿证据。这些名胜古迹虽然很美丽，但是需要经过漫长的岁月才能呈现出来。因此，“柔弱胜刚强”，但是“柔弱”必须有时间，必须有耐心。有些人办事没有足够的耐心，做什么事情都急于求成。在我看来，这些人没有领悟到老子的思想真谛。中国有两个著名的成语故事，“揠苗助长”和“祸福相依”。这两个成语故事的精髓是中国古典文化的一部分。本文将讨论老子的思想在现实中的意义，特别是“柔弱胜刚强”怎么在中医里体现的。

在《揠苗助长》中，农夫干预禾苗的自然生长规律，其后果是显而易见的。他拔禾苗的做法也可以算是“刚强”的做法，而让禾苗自己生长可以算是无为的、柔和的做法。“刚强”的做法让禾苗马上死掉。因为农夫没有耐心，强迫禾苗按照他的意志快速成长，结果是欲速则不达，禾苗死了。“揠苗助长”说明了刚强做法的缺点。

值得注意的是“柔弱胜刚强”也存在于道教的理念里。老子就说过：“有无相生，难易相成，长短相形……”因为一个东西存在，它的反面也存在。因为人们了解一件事情，他们也可以理解它的反面。只要有“柔弱”就有“刚强”，只要有

Gentleness and Strength

Author: Chloe Hemm Instructor: Yongping Zhu University of Notre Dame

Gentleness is victorious over strength, but this gentleness requires time. It requires patience.

"There is nothing on earth that is softer or gentler than water. Yet, of all the hardest and strongest things, there is nothing that can defeat it." Laozi's words aptly praise the strength of water. From the Stone Forest in China, to the Grand Canyon in the United States, many natural wonders clearly exemplify the extraordinary capabilities of water, providing humanity with evidence for the power of water over stone. Although such scenery is beautiful, it is only after years and years of transformation that it is able to reach its current form. In this way, the "gentle" force of the water surpasses the "strong" rigidity of the rock. Gentleness is victorious over strength, but this gentleness requires time. It requires patience. Some people do not have this patience in various aspects of our lives. They do everything with a sense of urgency and become anxious only for results. From my perspective, these people fail to grasp the essence of Laozi's teachings. Here, we can reference two well-known Chinese idioms, "pulling the sprout up to help it grow" (a phrase likened to "haste makes waste") and "fortune and misfortune are intertwined." The stories and core meanings behind these phrases are a part of classical Chinese culture with meaningful connections to ongoing realities. This essay discusses Laozi's ideology, specifically how Chinese medicine embodies the concept of "gentleness" surpassing "strength."

We can first discuss the story of "pulling the sprout up to help it grow" (揠苗助长). In this story, a farmer interferes with the natural growth of a seedling by attempting to pull it up. The consequences are obvious. In this case, the farmer's actions may be regarded as a

“刚强”就有“柔弱”。这两个方面相互抗衡，互相依存；依靠对“柔弱”的理解而理解“刚强”，依靠对“刚强”的理解而理解“柔弱”。

这些来自道教的理念对中医有着深刻的影响。一来，要了解“柔弱”在中医中的用途，要先理解中医基础原理。中医最重要的概念是“气”。这个“气”是指能使人体器官发挥机能的动力。脏腑和经络都靠它，所以气也算是生命的营养。气分为阴和阳，两个部分是相反的，但互相存在，都是生活的原动力。阴和阳都是必要的，相反的力量才能找到平衡，否则，人体就会失去平衡，出现症状。

中医用几个范畴解释人体出现的问题，比如“寒/热”“内/外”等。根据《黄帝内经》，中医有八种治疗方法：“汗、吐、下、和、温、清、补、消”。八种方法不同，但是目的相同，即恢复人体内的阴阳平衡。需要注意的是，这些恢复平衡的方法不是激烈的，也不是马上见效的。中医治病的思想，强调预防性保健。如果人们坚持锻炼，保持阴阳平衡，他们就能过上健康长寿的生活。这个过程，即使需要医生的帮助，也要少用过激的干预。为病人诊断病情的时候，医生先考虑病人的整体情况，然后决定怎么帮助他康复。这个就需要医生有整体观念和耐心，他不能随便选择一个“刚强”的手术或什么“虎狼之药”。相反，

strong, unyielding approach, whereas letting the seedling grow up naturally would have been a gentle, passive approach. The strong approach led to the seedling's immediate death. Because the farmer did not have patience and tried to force the seedling to grow faster according to his own will, he could not achieve the desired result. In the end, the seedling died. This story is a testament to the shortcomings of a strong, unyielding approach.

It is worth noting that the concept of "gentle" surpassing "strong" is also present in Taoist philosophy. As Laozi said, "Having and lacking produce each other; difficulty and ease complete each other; long and short shape each other..." Because one thing exists, its opposite also exists. Because people can understand one thing, they can also understand its opposite. Only if "gentle and weak" exist, can there also be "hard and strong." Only if "hard and strong" exist, can there also be "gentle and weak." These two principles are in direct opposition, yet each mutually depends on the other. We must rely on our understanding of gentleness to understand strength. We must rely on our understanding of strength to understand gentleness.

These Taoist principles have profound influences in traditional Chinese medicine. To understand the applicability of "gentleness," one must first understand the basic concepts of traditional Chinese medicine. This begins with the most central component, *qi*, the vital energy within human body. The internal organs and energy channels, or meridians, in the body all depend on this force to function, so *qi* is also regarded as the nourishment for life. It is divided into *yin* and *yang*, two opposing yet interdependent parts. Each is essential and must exist in balance with the other. Otherwise, the body becomes out of balance and presents various symptoms of illness.

Traditional Chinese medicine uses several categories to explain the potential issues in human body. These include, hot or cold, inner or outer, as well as many others. According to *The Classic of Internal Medicine*, China's earliest classic work on medicine, there are eight types of treatment methods: sweating (汗), vomiting (吐), purging (下), harmonizing (和), warming (温), clearing (清), tonifying (补), and eliminating (消). Each method is different, but they all have the same goal: to restore the body's balance of *yin* and *yang*. It is important to realize that

他应该选择用“柔弱”的方法，让患者在整体上恢复平衡，从而使身心得到全面治疗。

美国人说“医学”时一般指的是现代医学。虽然西方世界和东方世界拥有自己独特的文化，但是一方不能只相信现代医学的“对抗疗法”，另一方不能只相信传统医学的“顺势疗法”。对抗疗法和顺势疗法，就像“阴”和“阳”，也像“柔弱”和“刚强”，并不是同样的，然而需要互相帮助。在今天全球化过程中，我们可以看到多种文化逐渐融合，不过这将是一个漫长的过程。

如果人们做事情过于“刚强”，大自然的规律就会被打破，世界就会失去平衡。与之相反，如果人们采取“柔弱”态度处理事务，事情就会循序渐进。采用柔和的方法时，人们就会感觉比较轻松，就会有机会考虑过程的每一步，避免犯错。当然，有时候用过激的治疗是必要的。但是，总体来说，过激治疗更有可能会带来副作用，而温和地处理病痛最终会彻底解决问题。每种情况都需要人们考虑怎么保持最自然的状态。维持柔弱和刚强的和谐应该是我们的最终目标，这不仅体现在我们对待病痛的问题上，也应该体现在处理所有的事务中。

these restorative methods are neither aggressive nor immediate. Instead, traditional Chinese medicine emphasizes the preventive aspects of health. If people exercise consistently and keep the balance of *yin* and *yang*, they can live long and healthy lives. Even if a doctor's help is needed, the least aggressive preventive treatments should be used when possible. When diagnosing patients, doctors must first view the patient as a whole before determining the proper treatment plan. This requires both a holistic mindset and patience. They cannot simply choose the "strongest" method, whether that be performing an aggressive surgical operation or prescribing potent medicine. On the contrary, doctors should choose the "gentle" method. In this way, they can help the patient return to a balanced state, giving the mind and body comprehensive treatment.

Generally speaking, Americans use "Western medicine" to refer to modern medicine. Although Western and Eastern worlds have their unique cultures, one side cannot only trust in modern allopathic methods while the other only trusts in traditional homeopathic methods. Homeopathic and allopathic approaches, just like *yin* and *yang*, and like "gentleness" and "strength," are certainly not the same. Yet, they are interdependent. In today's globalizing world, we can see multiple cultures' distinctive qualities merging together in a similar way. This is a gradual process with no finite end.

If people approach tasks in an excessively "hard and strong" way, the laws of nature would be broken and the world would lose balance. On the other hand, if people adopt a "soft and gentle" approach, many things can be dealt with one step at a time. When adopting the gentle approach, people can be in a relaxed state of mind to consider every step of a given process and avoid mistakes. Of course, "strength" is firmer than "gentleness" and sometimes using the firmest, most aggressive approach is necessary. However, when considering the full picture, the most aggressive treatments also have the highest possibility of unwanted side effects, while gentler approaches can ultimately resolve ailments comprehensively. Every case requires careful consideration to determine how the most natural balanced state can be preserved. Maintaining the harmony between gentleness and strength should be our ultimate goal. This not only applies to the way people treat diseases, but also extends to the way we can live out every aspect of our lives.

余桃之罪

作者：曹宇森　指导教师：梁霞　华盛顿大学（圣路易斯）

外表美是暂时的，内心善才是永恒的。

春秋时期，卫国国君宠爱年轻英俊的弥子瑕。一次弥子瑕与卫君游桃园，他吃到了一个桃子，发现非常好吃，就把吃剩的半个桃子让给卫君吃。卫君一尝，果然好吃，就夸他吃到好东西不自己独吞，贡献出来给君王享用。多年后，弥子瑕色衰爱弛，失宠于卫君，卫君居然指责弥子瑕当年让他吃自己剩下的桃子，属大不敬，所以治了他的罪。

这个故事是在说爱美之心人皆有之。一个人的美色有时可以暂时掩盖他的过失，但是报应早晚会到的。这种事情不但在中国古代有，在现代西方社会也有。比如下面两个例子。

2018 年，佛罗里达发生了一起恶性车祸。一位年轻妈妈带着她 1 岁大的女儿在斑马线上过马路时，被一辆正在马路上疯狂飙车的汽车撞上。妈妈当场死亡，一天后，小女儿也因抢救无效去世。

事件发生后，18 岁的肇事司机海林被判入狱 24 年。海林不服判决，认为 24 年的刑期太过分了，于是提出上诉。因为海林长得太帅了，社交媒体上开始出现许多支持他的声音。当地的电视台、报纸、网站等各类媒体上都是支持海林的评论，呼吁法庭减轻他的刑罚。甚至许多来自世界各地的留言者纷纷发布破碎的心形表情，或者对这刑罚表示不满。一些对海林感兴趣的支持者就像一群疯狂的粉丝，有人在网上发布海林中学时期帅气的照片；有人半夜打电话给海林的妈妈，鼓动她为海林上诉；有人花钱给海林在社交媒体上拉拢大批的支持者，油管上的

The Crime of a Leftover Peach

Author: Ethan Cao Instructor: Xia Liang Washington University (St. Louis)

> Beauty on the outside is temporary, but goodness on the inside is forever.

During the Spring and Autumn Period, the Duke of Wei was quite fond of his young and handsome minion called Mi Zixia. Mi Zixia once visited a peach farm with the Duke. He took a few bites of a peach and found it very delicious, so he offered the leftover half of the peach to the Duke. The Duke tasted it, and agreed that it was indeed delicious, so he praised Mi Zixia for not eating up the good food and dedicated it to the Duke. Many years later, Mi Zixia's handsomeness faded, and he fell out of favor with the Duke. The Duke suddenly felt angry and started blaming Mi Zixia for making him eat his leftover peach, which was a great disrespect to the Duke. Mi was subsequently chastised and punished for his offense.

This story tells us that everyone admires beauty, such that a person's beauty can sometimes temporarily cover up his faults, but the retribution for his or her wrongdoing will come in due course. These kinds of things happened not only in ancient China, but also in modern Western society. Let's look at the following two examples.

In 2018, a horrifying car accident occurred in Florida, in which a young mother and her 1-year-old daughter were crossing the street when a car that was racing wildly on the road plowed into them. The mother died instantly; the baby died a day later after unsuccessful rescue.

After this accident, Cameron Herrin, the 18-year-old driver, was sentenced to prison for 24 years. Herrin refused to accept the ruling and appealed, claiming a 24-year sentence was too harsh a punishment. As Herrin is very handsome, voices of support began appearing in waves on social media. Pages of reports from local TV stations, newspapers, websites, and other

听证会录像更是使他成了国际名人。看着海林英俊的照片和影像，粉丝们变得越来越可怕，越来越失去理智。有些人在社交媒体上跟踪他的家人和朋友的账号。粉丝们不断地打电话到监狱，让监狱的工作人员忙不过来。甚至有黑客进入监狱的计算机系统，让监狱的工作无法正常进行。

另一个例子是服装名模米克斯的故事。米克斯原先是一个街头帮派成员，因为非法持有枪械，被判刑 27 个月。他入狱时拍的相片太帅了。当警察局把他的相片贴到脸书上后，一天之内吸引了许多女性网友的关注。米克斯也因此被许多模特经纪公司看中，很多公司迅速和他签约。米克斯服刑结束后，摇身一变，成了知名的服装男模特。

海林和米克斯都是因为长相帅气而吸引了大众的注意，即使他们做了天大的坏事，那些人还是支持他们，甚至用各种方式来为他们脱罪。但是，青春靓丽不会永驻，当他们靓丽的外表随着时间的流逝而消失时，喜欢他们、支持他们的人们也会消失。当人们不再喜欢他们时，他们就会像弥子瑕一样，被大家攻击。外表美是暂时的，内心善才是永恒的。

media were full of comments supporting Herrin, calling on the court to reduce his sentence. Even commenters from around the world posted broken-hearted emojis or expressed their displeasure with the punishment. Some supporters interested in Herrin were like a group of crazed fans. Some people posted handsome photos of Herrin in middle school on the internet; some telephoned Herrin's mother at midnight to instigate her to appeal; some spent money for Herrin to amass a huge following of supporters on social media, and videos of the hearings on YouTube made him an international celebrity. Herrin's handsome pictures and videos made, fans acted increasingly scary and beyond reason. Some stalked the accounts of his family and friends on social media. Fans kept making phone calls to the prison, completely occupying prison staff. Hackers even hacked into the prison's computer system, hindering the prison staff's work.

Another example is the story of fashion model Jeremy Meeks. Meeks, a former street gang member, was sentenced to 27 months in prison for illegal possession of a firearm. His prison mugshot was so handsome that when the police station posted his photo on the Facebook page, within a day it attracted the attention of many women online. Meeks was also scouted by many modeling agencies and many companies quickly signed him. After serving his sentence, Meeks became a well-known male clothing model.

Herrin and Meeks both attracted public attention because of their handsome looks. Even when they did something terrible, people still supported them and even utilized various methods to exonerate them. However, youth and beauty will not last forever. When their handsome appearance is lost with the passage of time, the people who like them and support them will also disappear. When people don't like them anymore, in due course their wrongdoings will be discussed or they will be attacked, like what happened to Mi Zixia. Beauty on the outside is temporary, but goodness on the inside is forever.

海潮与浮云

作者：孙韵棻　指导教师：顾利程　西北大学

> 不要因为小小的成功就沾沾自喜，也不要因为暂时的失败而气馁。

2019 年在中国留学期间，我有幸到海滨小城秦皇岛旅游。在领队老师的带领下，我们来到了孟姜女庙。听说这就是传说中那个哭倒长城的孟姜女的庙，我们大家都非常兴奋。我们刚刚来到了庙前，老师就指着一副对联对我们说："这副对联很有意思，你们仔细看看，看得懂吗？会不会念？"我顺着老师的手抬头望去，只见对联是蓝底金字，右联竖着写着十个大字"海水朝朝朝朝朝朝朝落"，左边当然也是竖着写着十个大字"浮云长长长长长长长消"。

作为一个还在学习中文的学生，我觉得这副对联有些奇怪。怎么右边的对联一行十个字里面竟然只用了四个不同的汉字，其中的一个"朝"字竟然重复使用了七次；而左边的对联也是一样，一行十个字也是只使用了四个不同的汉字，其中"长"字也是重复使用了七次。这几个汉字我虽然都学过，可是还是不知道怎么念这副对联，当然更不懂是什么意思。早有准备的老师告诉我们说这副对联应该这样念：

hǎi shuǐ cháo　zhāo zhāo cháo zhāo　cháo zhāo luò
海水朝，朝朝朝，朝朝，朝落。

fú yún zhǎng cháng cháng zhǎng cháng zhǎng cháng xiāo
浮云长，长长长，长长，长消。

Tides and Clouds

Author: Isabelle Sun Instructor: Licheng Gu Northwestern University

Don't get complacent because of small successes, and don't get discouraged by temporary failures.

When I studied abroad in China in 2019, I was fortunate to travel to Qinhuangdao, a small coastal city in Hebei Province. Under the leadership of our teacher, we came to Lady Meng Jiang Temple. We were all very excited when we heard that this was the temple built after the legendary Lady Meng Jiang from the ancient stories, who wept bitterly until the Great Wall collapsed. As soon as we arrived at the temple, the teacher pointed to a couplet and told us, "This couplet is very interesting. Look carefully, can you understand it? Can you read it?" I followed the teacher's finger and looked toward the couplet in gold characters on blue background, with the right side written vertically in ten large characters "海水朝朝朝朝朝朝朝落." Of course, there were also ten large characters written vertically on the left side "浮云长长长长长长长消."

As a student who was still studying Chinese, I found this couplet to be a bit strange. I wondered why the right side used only four different Chinese characters in a line of ten characters, and the characters "朝" was used repeatedly seven times; the left side was the same – only four Chinese characters were used in a line of ten characters, among which the character "长" was also used seven times. Although I've learned all these Chinese characters, I still didn't know how to pronounce this couplet, and of course I didn't know what it meant. The teacher, who had been prepared for a long time, told us that this couplet should be read like this:

然后，老师给我们讲道，这副对联的意思是海水天天涨潮，涨起来还会落下去；而浮云总是在流动，有时飘走了，有时又飘回来了。这副对联利用中国汉字一字多音，一字多义的特点，生动描绘了海潮涨落，浮云长消的自然景象。老师又告诉我们，在古汉语里，“朝”与“潮”两个汉字是通用的，“长”与“常”两个汉字也是通用的。一个“朝”出现在句子里面到底是代表“朝阳”还是代表“潮水”要取决于上下文。这副对联的作者故意使用了“朝”和“长”这两个多音多义的汉字，跟我们做了一个文字游戏。老师说，当“朝”字代表“潮水”时，应该添上一个三点水，而“长”字代表“经常”时，应写成“常”，所以今天写起来应该是这样：

hǎi shuǐ cháo zhāo zhāo cháo zhāo cháo zhāo luò
海 水 朝， 朝 朝 朝， 朝 朝， 朝 落。

fú yún zhǎng cháng cháng zhǎng cháng zhǎng cháng xiāo
浮 云 长， 长 长 长， 长 长， 长 消。

Then, the teacher told us that this couplet means that the tides of the sea rise every day, and when they rise, they will also fall; while the floating clouds are always flowing, sometimes they float away, and sometimes they return. This pair of couplets uses the characteristics of Chinese characters with multiple sounds and multiple meanings, vividly depicting the natural scene of the ebb and flow of sea tides and clouds. The teacher also told us that in ancient Chinese, the two Chinese characters "朝" (zhāo, meaning "morning sun" and "潮" (cháo, meaning "tide") are mutually exchangeable, and the two Chinese characters "长" (zhǎng, meaning "grow") and "常" (cháng, meaning "often") are also mutually exchangeable. It depends on the context whether a certain character that appears in a sentence means "morning sun" or "tide." It is the same case with "grow" and "often." The author of this couplet deliberately used the two Chinese characters "朝" and "长," which are polyphonic and polysemous, to play a word game with us. Furthermore, the teacher shared that when the word "朝" means "tide," the Chinese radical representing "three water droplets" should be added to the character, and when the word "长" means "often," it should be written as "常," so today the characters would be written as:

海水潮，朝朝潮，朝潮，朝落。

浮云长，常常长，常长，常消。

Although writing in modern Chinese leads to the same exact meanings as what was written in ancient Chinese, it is far less interesting to write in modern Chinese than in ancient Chinese.

The teacher informed us that this couplet has a profound meaning. If the unpredictable happens, we should take it lightly. Don't get complacent because of small successes, and don't

海水潮，朝朝潮，朝潮，朝落。

浮云长，常常长，常长，常消。

虽然用现代汉语来写与用古汉语来写寓意是完全一样的，但是如果用现代汉语来写就远不如古汉语那么有趣了。

老师说这副对联是有着深刻的寓意的。如果不可预测的事情发生了，要泰然处之。不要因为小小的成功就沾沾自喜，也不要因为暂时的失败而气馁。该急流勇退时就要急流勇退。世间一切都有它的自然规律。大海能涨潮，也一定会落潮，云飘走了，还会再飘回来。这种随遇而安的平和心态深深打动了我，对中国古人的景仰之情，油然而生。

get discouraged by temporary failures. When it's time to retreat, retreat bravely in the rapids. Everything in the world has its natural laws. The sea can rise and the tide must also fall; the clouds will float away and come back again. I was deeply moved by this kind of peaceful mind, and my respect and admiration for the ancient Chinese stemmed from this unique experience.

古典文学的魅力

作者：苏菲　指导教师：史中琦　哥伦比亚大学

文学博大精深，对现代社会的影响颇大。

很多人觉得古典文学艰涩难懂，必须费很大力气才能读懂，所以古典文学在当代社会并不流行，尤其是在年轻人中。为什么我们要被禁锢在古人的创作里？而不是去室外享受灿烂的阳光和新鲜的空气呢？真实的生活远比文字里的历史更有吸引力。即使是在古典文学研究领域，对于作品的文学性分析，也常常由于过分解读而被诟病。

但是古典文学对我来说，有着超乎寻常的魅力。与现代文学的直白不同，古典文学往往更注重在字里行间表达含蓄内敛的深情。古典文学不浮华，作者能够用通俗的语言说明深刻的道理，他们对事物的本质和人生意义的描写也参差多样。因此，在浩瀚书海中，读者总能

The Charm of Classical Literature

Author: Sophie Ann Bryant Instructor: Zhongqi Shi Columbia University

> Literature is extensive and profound, and has a significant impact on modern society.

Many people think that classical literature is difficult to understand and requires a lot of effort to comprehend, so it is not popular in modern society, especially among young people. Why should we be trapped in the creation of ancients instead of going outside to enjoy the bright sun and fresh air? Real life is far more attractive than written history. Even in the field of classical literature research, the literary analysis of works is often criticized for over-interpretations.

But for me, classical literature has an extraordinary charm. Unlike the straightforwardness of modern literature, classical literature often pays more attention to expressing implicit and restrained affection between the lines. Classical literature is not ostentatious as the authors can explain profound truths in popular language, and their descriptions of the essence of things and the meaning of life are also varied. Therefore, in the vast sea of books, readers can always find something that expresses their hearts. What I love the most is when I accidentally come across a sentence or paragraph that I admire and resonate with while reading classical literature. This incomparable feeling cannot be obtained by reading modern literature. Reading classical literature is also like having a dynamic conversation with the author. Through reading, we can establish a rapport with an author who lived centuries ago, and we can even understand a completely different outlook on world.

The eternal themes explored in classical literature include: love, friendship, and war; social progress won't cause these themes to lose their dominant relevance in our lives. Only by studying our predecessors' thoughts and looking at current life and society through the perspective of an outsider can we truly face reality and objectively evaluate human behaviors

够找到一部写出他们心声的作品。我最爱在阅读古典文学作品时偶然读到一个自己欣赏的句子或段落，这种无与伦比的感觉是阅读现代文学作品无法获得的。阅读古典文学作品还可以与作者进行充满活力的对话。通过阅读，我们可以跟一位活在几个世纪前的作者建立默契，甚至了解一种完全不同的世界观。

古典文学探索的永恒主题包括：爱情、友谊和战争，这些主题并不会因为社会进步而失去在生活中的主导地位。以前人的思考为参照，跳脱出我们的现状，以局外人的身份来看待现在的生活与社会，才能真正地面对现实，使我们能够客观地评价人类的行为和特征。因此，阅读古典文学能够培养分析问题的能力、共情能力以及更广阔的世界观。观察不同的写作风格和语言的演变，将使我们能够更深入地了解我们自己的语言。从更好的阅读者，成长为更好的作者和沟通者。这些能力在当今的社会不可低估。

综上，文学博大精深，对现代社会的影响颇大。因此，我们不能把古典文学束之高阁，而是应该鼓励年轻人多多尝试，找到适合自己阅读的古典文学作品。

and characteristics. Thus, reading classics helps us develop our analytical skills and empathy while adopting a broader worldview. Observing the evolution of different writing styles and languages will allow us to gain a deeper understanding of our own language, from being a better reader to improving as a better writer and communicator. These abilities cannot be underestimated in today's society.

To summarize, literature is extensive and profound, and has a significant impact on modern society. Therefore, we should not just leave classical literature on the shelves. Instead, we should encourage young people to explore and read classic works that are suitable for them.

美国历史上的排华法案

作者：马筠淇　指导教师：顾利程　西北大学

> 我们更要了解历史，珍惜现状，不让历史重演。

1882年5月6日是美国文明史上最丑恶、最黑暗的一天。就在这一天，美国国会正式通过了美国历史上第一个限制禁止外来移民的法案——《关于执行有关华人条约诸规定的法律》（就是人们常说的“排华法案”），从而导致了大规模的排华暴乱，成百的华人在暴乱中被歹徒杀害、打伤，无数华人财产被掠夺，房屋被烧毁。

排华法案的产生，有其深刻的历史背景。

1872年，加州最大的银矿快要枯竭了。消息传来，股市大跌，银行倒闭，工厂关门，大批工人失业。恰在那时，加州的主要铁路完工，一万两千多华人也同时遭殃，步入了失业大军。为了生存，华人不得不接受又脏又累、工资又低的工作。工厂主看中了这一点，他们常常雇用这些不懂英文的特殊华工去顶替罢工的工人，从而使工会与华人之间种下了怨恨的种子。全美联合工会的一份传单里这样鼓动道：“美国人和亚洲人的种族差异是永远无法消除的，我们白人一定要运用法律或武力赶走亚洲人。”排华浪潮就这样在美国掀起来了。

由于华人不是美国公民，所以华人没有选举权。无论民主党还是共和党都以牺牲华人的利益来换取选票。因为国会中没有议员肯为华人争取权益，所以排挤华人的法案很容易通过。

The Chinese Exclusion Act in American History

Author: Angela Ma Instructor: Licheng Gu Northwestern University

> We must understand history, cherish the status quo, and prevent tragic history from repeating itself.

May 6, 1882 was the ugliest, darkest day in the history of American civilization. On this day, the U.S. Congress formally passed the first bill in U.S. history that restricted and prohibited foreign immigrants: "The Law Concerning the Implementation of the Provisions Relating to the Chinese Treaty" (often called the Chinese Exclusion Act). This caused large-scale anti-Chinese riots, during which hundreds of Chinese were killed and injured by gangsters, countless properties were plundered, and many houses were burned down.

The emergence of the Chinese Exclusion Act has its profound historical background.

In 1872, the largest silver mine in California was running dry. When the news came, the stock market plummeted, banks collapsed, factories closed, and a large number of workers lost their jobs. At that time, the main railway in California was completed, and more than 12,000 Chinese people also suffered at the same time while joining the army of unemployment. In order to survive, the Chinese had to accept dirty, exhausting, low-paying jobs. The factory owners took a fancy to this, and they often hired these special Chinese workers who did not understand English to replace the strikers, thus planting the seeds of resentment between the union and the Chinese. A pamphlet of the United Labor Union of the U.S. encouraged: "The racial differences between Americans and Asians will never be eliminated. We white people must use the law or force to drive out Asians." Just like this, the wave of Chinese exclusion was set off in the U.S.

Since the Chinese were not American citizens, they did not have the right to vote. Both the Democratic Party and the Republican Party sacrificed the interests of the Chinese in

排华法案第 1 条就列举了华人的过失："华工的到来给一些本来宁静的地区带来了不安全因素。因此，10 年内禁止任何华工来美。"第 14 条规定："任何法院不得批准华人入籍。"

排华法案直到 1943 年才被废除。在这漫长的 61 年里，在美华人以超强的毅力忍受着各种不公平的待遇。今天华人的社会地位与当年相比，已经有了很大的变化。众多优秀华人的身影已经出现在美国的主流社会。但是痛定思痛，我们应该从排华法案中吸取教训，不要忘记那段历史。华人应该积极参加投票选举，主动与其他种族沟通，掌握舆论工具，树立积极形象。当然，我们更要了解历史，珍惜现状，不让历史重演。

exchange for votes. Because no member of Congress was willing to fight for the rights of the Chinese, it was easy to pass the bill to exclude the Chinese.

Article 1 of the Chinese Exclusion Act lists the condemnations on the Chinese: "The arrival of Chinese laborers has brought unsafe factors to some originally peaceful areas. Therefore, any Chinese laborers are prohibited from coming to the U.S. within 10 years." Article 14 stipulates: "No court shall approve Chinese naturalization."

The Chinese Exclusion Act was not repealed until 1943. During the 61 long years, Chinese people in the U.S. have endured all forms of unfair treatment, reflecting their exceptional perseverance. The social status of the Chinese today has changed a lot compared to that back in the days. Many outstanding Chinese figures have appeared in the mainstream society of the U.S. Recalling past pain as a warning for the future, we should learn from the Chinese Exclusion Act and not forget that period in history. The Chinese should actively participate in voting, actively communicate with other races, master the tools of public opinion, and establish a positive image. Of course, we must understand history, cherish the status quo, and prevent tragic history from repeating itself.

中国成语的哲理

作者：孔禄　指导教师：于丽萍　华盛顿大学（西雅图）

> 中国成语是从人们丰富的生活经历中总结出的经验。

俗话说，读万卷书不如行万里路。读书与旅行这两个过程都有益，但在对中国文化缺乏深刻理解的情况下，读书与旅行之间就不会发生显著的联系。所以，学习中文时，大家不但必须学习语言，而且要了解语言背后的文化。学习中文而不了解中国的历史和文化，就像海洋没有沙滩。同时，学习中文而不理解中国的历史和文化实际上是一种教育的缺憾，使人失去了获得智慧的机会。在了解中国文化的过程中，我认为中国成语起到了连接语言和文化的桥梁的作用。因为相当一部分的成语反映了传统的中国文化，所以真正掌握成语并且适当地使用成语能够帮助我们表达比较复杂的思想。因此，这也能体现我们对中华文化和历史的尊重。因为学习成语让我更进一步地思考中国的语言和文化，所以在这篇文章里我将分享给我印象最深刻的三个成语。

我要分享的第一个成语是“塞翁失马”。表面上，生活是一件很简单的事，但这所谓的“简单”实际上常常存在于幻觉中。因此老百姓往往用“塞翁失马”这个成语来形容“一件结果尚不清楚的事情”。这个成语讲的是边塞的一个老头儿丢了一匹马，但是他没有因为失去马而过分难过。后来，老头儿的马突然回来了，所以他的儿子激动万分，决定骑马出去玩儿。但儿子骑马时发生了意外，他的腿被摔折了。尽管如此，老头儿仍然很乐观。有一天，战争爆发了，当地的政府开始招募新兵，但是，由于儿子的腿受伤了，无法参战，躲过了战争。从失去一匹

Philosophy in Chinese Idioms

Author: Luke Khoury Instructor: Liping Yu University of Washington (Seattle)

> Chinese idioms originate from the rich experiences, trials, and tribulations of people's lives.

It has been said that the wisdom gained from reading 10,000 books does not compare to that of traveling 10,000 *li*. It is true that reading and traveling both have many benefits, but when lacking deep knowledge about Chinese culture, it's hard to find any significant connection between the two. So, when studying Chinese, not only do you have to study the language itself, but you also must understand its cultural backdrop. To learn Chinese without understanding its history and culture is like an ocean with no sand. Similarly, it can reflect an educational insufficiency which deprives students the opportunity to gain wisdom throughout the process. In my case, I found that studying Chinese idioms brought forth a bridge between language and culture. And because large portions of the idioms reflect traditional Chinese culture, I was able to grasp their concepts, and use them to help me express more complex ideas. Therefore, it embodies our respect for Chinese culture and history. Because studying these idioms allowed me to further examine the language and culture of China, in this essay I will share the three ones which left me the deepest impressions.

The first idiom to share is "Sai Weng losing his horse." On the surface, life is quite simple, but these so-called "simplicities" often end up being illusory. Because of this, common folk will often say "Sai Weng losing his horse" to describe situations where the outcome is still unclear. What this idiom describes is an old frontiersman who lost his horse but wasn't ever too bothered by the situation. Afterwards, his horse came back, and his son excitedly decided to go enjoy himself and ride it. However, while riding, his son got into an accident and broke

马到捡回一条命，这个聪明的老头儿一直保持冷静。这个故事让我们明白：虽然生活的变迁很容易令人悲观失望，但是我们面临的大多数困难也许会有出乎意料的结果。

第二个给我留下深刻印象的成语是“盲人摸象”。表面上，这个故事讲的是一些盲人一起摸一头大象。因为大象很大，而每个盲人只摸到了大象的一小部分，所以盲人们对大象是什么样子众说不一。实际上，这个成语表达的意思是：即使看同一件事情，大家的想法也可能截然不同，甚至会因此而产生隔膜。最后，“盲人”对持不同看法的人也会越来越不宽容。从这个成语中，我还明白了一个道理：即使是最显而易见的道理常常也不能让一些“盲人”信服。

his leg. Despite this, the old man was still very optimistic. One day, a war had started, and the government was drafting solders. Due to Sai Weng's son's broken leg, he was unable to be drafted and escaped the war. From losing his horse to saving a life, the wise Sai Weng was able to keep his composure. This story makes me realize that even though the vicissitudes of life can easily leave people pessimistic and disappointed, many of the challenges we face can also have unexpected outcomes.

The second idiom that gave me a deep impression was "blind men touching an elephant." On the surface, this tale simply talks about blind men touching an elephant. And because the elephant is so large, each of them is only able to touch a small part of it, and consequently all disagree on what the elephant looks like. In fact, this idiom means that even if we all see the same thing, everybody probably has wildly different opinions, sometimes to the extent of causing unfamiliarity and division. And finally, these "blind men" begin to have less and less tolerance toward differing points of view. I've also learned one main idea from this idiom: even the most obvious and well thought out principle often can't convince "blind men" to change their mind.

最后一个成语是“覆水难收”，它的意思是我们无法改变或者挽回过去发生的事情。我们会不可避免地纠缠一些过去的事情，这很容易使人深陷其中，迷失方向。“覆水难收”提醒我们，让过去的事情过去吧，过分地纠结过去是不值得的，我们仍有能力去面对现在和未来。我喜欢“覆水难收”这个成语，因为它让我获得更多生活的恩典和美好。

中国成语是从人们丰富的生活经历中总结出的经验。学习成语能让我们获得古老的知识和智慧。这样我们可以用历史上有名的典故和思想来丰富我们自己的生活。现代社会在不断发展和进步，我们不仅要学习最新的思想，也不能忽视古老的传统，特别是有着五千年文明的传统。

The last idiom is "spilled water can't be picked up," meaning that we have no ability to change or redeem what has happened. We all unavoidably dwell on something in the past, and it's very easy to cause people to immerse themselves in the troubles and lose their way. "Spilled water can't be picked up" reminds us to let bygones be bygones, and that overthinking the past isn't much worth it. Rather, we have the power to face the situations of the moment and the ones yet to come. I like this idiom because it gives beauty and grace to my life.

Chinese idioms originate from the rich experiences, trials, and tribulations of people's lives. To study them, in turn, allows us to gain some of their knowledge and wisdom. In this way, we can all use the famous allusions and thoughts in history to enhance our own life. Modern society is ceaselessly advancing and moving forward. Not only should we study new trains of thoughts and ideas, but we can't forget the ancient traditions, especially the traditions of 5,000 years' civilization.

我是一杯“奶茶”

作者：邵威　指导教师：苏炜　耶鲁大学

> 我可以从老派与新派的文化中，旧习俗与新思想中，自由地挑选我所喜欢的，用于我自己的生活中。

读老舍的小说《黑白李》，我们在讨论“老派”和“新派”的话题。

“老派”和“新派”，这对词语隐含了不可避免的冲突，包括：传统与现代的冲突，保守哲学与进步理论的冲突。也许这对词语还暗示了交接，就像将火把从老一辈传递到新一代。虽然这个想法的确有道理，但是我自己认为：老派和新派并不是那么非黑即白的关系。我认为老派和新派的关系并不是战争，也不是交替，它们之间的关系更像老朋友之间的交流。老派和新派是相互联系的，并且两者对政治制度、文化和人民的价值都至关重要。

在政治制度上，老派和新派的关系有点儿复杂，但最终两方面都对社会的平衡和稳定起着重要的作用。比如说，美国的政治制度现在很有争议，因为保守的共和党人和激进的民主党人无法配合。当然，这个制度的效率是很低的，如今大半的新闻报道都是讲党派关系导致的政治失败。但是在美国多元的社会里，这不一定是个缺点。按照美国最早的传统价值，共和党人重视个人的自由，尊重保守的文化和习俗；另一方面，共和党所谓的对手民主党，重视平衡与社会进步。在美国，人们的政治取向大概两方均分，代表“老派”和“新派”的两党需要互相交流，听取和采纳对方有价值的观点，才能保护民众的权利，创造一个更周全、更富有同情心的国家。

I Am a Cup of "Milk Tea"

Author: Eric Youshao Instructor: Wei Su Yale University

Reading Lao She's novel, *Black Li and White Li*, we are discussing the topic of "old school" and "new school."

> I am free to choose from old and new cultures, old customs and new ideas, whatever ideas I'd like to incorporate into my own life.

The pair of words "old school" and "new school" implies inevitable conflicts, including: the conflict between tradition and modernity, and the conflict between conservative philosophy and progressive theory. Perhaps the pair of words also suggests a bridge of connection, like passing a torch from the old generation to the new generation. Although there's a certain level of truth behind this idea, I personally believe that old school and new school can't be described in terms of black and white. I think the relationship between the two is neither about war nor alterations. The relationship between them is more like an exchange between old friends. Fundamentally, the old school and new school are interconnected, and both are vital to the political system, culture, and values of the people.

In terms of politics, the relationship between the old school and new school is a bit complicated, but ultimately, both sides play an important role in maintaining societal balance and stability. For example, the political system in the U.S. is currently very controversial because conservative Republicans and radical Democrats don't get along. Of course, the efficiency of this system is very low, and most of the news reports today is about political failures caused by partisanship. However, this isn't necessarily a disadvantage in America's pluralist society. According to the earliest traditional values in the U.S., Republicans value individual freedom and respect conservative culture and customs; on the other hand, the so-called opponent of the Republican Party, the Democratic Party, values balance and social progress. In the U.S., people's

在文化制度上，“老派”和“新派”共同存在，会创造一种平衡，让民众更好地体会两边的优缺点。为了说明我的观点，我们来看一下茶文化。在我的日常生活中，虽然东方的老派长辈很重视茶文化，但是新派的年轻人并不那么欣赏喝茶。看来文化冲突是不可避免的。但实际上，这两种文化相结合并创造出来一个不中不西、不老不新的饮料——奶茶。饮料的核心——茶，仍然是“老派”的，但已进行了革新，以反映新时代的要求。在奶茶的例子里，老派和新派相得益彰。这种交流与合作的结果，使茶的吸引力扩散到了国际上，扩散到了不同年龄的广大民众中。这个例子表示老派和新派可以合作，互相贡献，创造一个更独特的文化。

对我自己来说，我的华裔美国人的身份，可以视为是老派和新派的交集。虽然我父母移民到美国来的时候，他们只带了一个行李箱和少量现金，但是他们的内心带着老派的思想。于是，我的童年有点儿传统老派的味道，我的父母经常向

political orientation is divided equally between the two parties. The two parties representing the "old school" and "new school" need to communicate with each other while actively listening to and adopting each other's valuable views in order to protect the rights of the people and create a more inclusive nation filled with compassion.

In terms of cultural systems, the co-existence of "old school" and "new school" will create a balance and allow the public to better understand the advantages and disadvantages of both sides. To illustrate my point, let's look at tea culture. In my daily life, although the old oriental elders attach great importance to tea culture, the young people of the new school do not appreciate tea drinking as much, so it might seem like cultural clashes are inevitable. However, the characteristics of two cultures have been combined to create a drink that is neither strictly Chinese nor Western, neither old nor new – milk tea. The core of the beverage, tea, is still "old school," but has been revamped to reflect the demands of the new times. In the case of milk tea, the old school and new school complement each other. As a result of such exchange and cooperation, the appeal of tea has spread internationally and to people of different ages. This example shows that old school and new school can collaborate and contribute to each other, creating a more unique culture.

For me, my Chinese-American identity can be viewed as an intersection between old school and new school. Although my parents immigrated to the U.S. with only a suitcase and a small amount of cash, they carried old-school thinking at heart. Therefore, my childhood leaned toward the traditional and old-fashioned side. My parents often told me about their culture and ideas, such as filial piety and the belief that "everything is inferior; only learning is valuable." At the time, I really didn't understand these concepts. While being influenced by traditional Chinese culture, I pursued my studies in the U.S. Surrounded by American classmates, I worked hard to remember new American ideas about things like individual choice and freedom. In my teenage years, I could always feel the conflict between old school and new school. On some nights, I'd have old school dreams in Chinese; while on other nights, I'd have new school dreams in English. For many years, I've believed that the conflict between Eastern and Western cultures, the boundary between our ancestral homeland and our new home in America, would never be resolved. Like the American political system, I felt as if my identity and dreams were divided

我讲述他们的文化和思想，像孝顺，像“万般皆下品，唯有读书高”，这些观念我当时真是半懂不懂。在受到中国传统文化熏陶的同时，我在美国读书上学。在美国同学的包围下，我努力地记住美国人关于个人选择和自由之类的新观点。在我的少年时代，我随时能感受到老派与新派的冲突。虽然有些夜晚，我会用中文做老派的梦，而在另一些晚上，我会用英语做新派的梦。多年以来，我一直认为：东西方文化，祖先的故乡和美国的新家之间，冲突永远无法解决。像美国的政治制度一样，我感觉我的身份和梦想，被分为不相容的两个方面。

慢慢地，我终于意识到：我内心的老派与新派的冲突是可以避免的。我的确不是传统的中国人，但也不是真正的美国人。我做梦的时候，总会有英文和中文混合在一起。我可以从老派与新派的文化中，旧习俗与新思想中，自由地挑选我所喜欢的，用于我自己的生活中。我认为“奶茶”的隐喻很恰当——我就是一杯“奶茶”。虽然我来自老派的中国文化家庭，但是我遇见新派的美国社会和现代的西方世界，才开始真正地活泼起来。即使在我祖先最疯狂的梦想中，他们也不会想象出珍珠奶茶中的“波巴”（珍珠），或我现在生活的自由和权利。我盼望我的祖先会为我们对老派传统的更新而感到自豪，并对新派的未来感到乐观。

into two incompatible sides.

Gradually, I finally realized that the conflict between the old school and new school within me can be avoided. Indeed, I'm not a traditional Chinese, but I'm not a real American either. When I dream, there is always English and Chinese mixed together. I am free to choose from old and new cultures, old customs and new ideas, whatever ideas I'd like to incorporate into my own life. I think the metaphor of "milk tea" is very appropriate – I am a cup of "milk tea." Although I come from an old-school Chinese cultural family, it was only when I encountered the new-school American society and modern Western world that I began to truly feel alive. Even in the wildest dreams of my ancestors, they would not have imagined the "*boba*" (pearls) in bubble tea, or the freedom and rights I live with now. I look forward to my ancestors being proud of our renewal of old school traditions and optimistic about the future of the new school way of thinking.

桃花源后记

作者：董安琪　指导教师：吕珏　普林斯顿大学

> 顺其自然，既来之则安之，才是他应该遵从的生活方式。

阳光暖暖地洒在软软的草地上，每走一步都能留下一个浅浅的脚印。粉色的花瓣从树上温柔地飘落，一阵阵轻风带来的是桃花的清香，宛如仙境。然而，在这个宛如仙境的地方却有着一幅与此处格格不入的景象。

一个身着渔人服饰的男人四处奔跑，嘴里一遍又一遍地念着："记号呢？在哪里？"此人满头大汗，蓬头垢面，看起来像是在疯狂地寻找着什么东西。突然，他看到了一个山洞。洞口好像透着若隐若现的光，仔细听的时候，隐隐约约能听到孩子的嬉笑声。渔人眼中透着痴狂，原本疲惫不堪的身体也仿佛瞬间充满了力量。他拼尽全力地向山洞奔跑，将手伸到最长，仿佛这样便能离山更近一点儿。随着时间的流逝，他与山的距离不断缩短。然而当他离洞口只有一步之遥的时候，一切回归黑暗。

渔人睁开眼睛，从床上突然坐起，手还保持往前伸的姿势。他旁边睡着的妻子被他的动作吓醒了。看着丈夫的样子，妻子叹了一口气。她为丈夫擦了擦汗，柔声道："相公可是又做了关于桃花源的梦？不是说让你忘了那个地方吗？虽然我理解当今世道大乱，处处都是战争，但是一直沉浸在一个幻想的世界里逃避现实，也不是长久之计啊！"

The After Story of the Peach Blossom Spring

Author: Angel Dong Instructor: Jue Lu Princeton University

> Going with the flow, and accepting things as they come, that was the way of life he shall follow.

The sun shined warmly on the soft grass, and each step seemed to leave behind a faint footprint. Blush pink petals floated down gently from blossoming trees, and each breeze brought with it the sweet scent of peach blossoms, as if it was a fairyland. However, within this peaceful scenery lay an incompatible sight.

A man dressed like a fisherman ran around frantically, muttering under his breath again and again, "The mark, where's the mark?" He seemed to be looking for something, with his face covered in a combination of sweat and mud. Suddenly, he saw a cave in the distance. A soft glow illuminated the cave entrance, and from within came the faint sound of children's laughter. Seeing this, the fisherman's eyes lit up with craze, and his exhausted body was filled with energy once again. He ran as fast as he could toward the cave with his arms outstretched, as if that would make him a little closer to the entrance. He quickly approached the cave, but just when he was a step away from his destination, the world around him suddenly went dark.

The fisherman woke up from his sleep and sat up from his bed abruptly, his hands still in an outstretched position. His sudden movement woke up his wife sleeping next to him, and she sighed as she dabbed away his sweat with a nearby towel. "Did you dream of the peach blossom spring again? Didn't I tell you to forget about that place? I understand that the world is rather chaotic right now with all the wars going on, but you can't just keep hiding in your imaginary world forever!" she chided softly.

"I've already repeated this many times, but the peach blossom spring is real, so is

渔人怒道：“我说了很多遍了，桃花源是真的！里面的小村子也是真的！太守的人找不到，是他们无能！我一定会找到桃花源，然后献上它，升官发财！”言罢，渔人便夺门而出，又去寻找桃花源了。

妻子已经见怪不怪，只是叹了一口气，默默地去取自己的绣花材料。自从丈夫一个月前打鱼回来，便一直念着什么人间仙境桃花源。他甚至还告诉了太守，希望用桃花源谋个一官半职。可是无论太守派了多少人去找，传说中的桃花源依然无迹可寻，官府也就放弃寻找了。

从此，丈夫便没日没夜地寻找这个桃花源，连鱼也不打了，仿佛着了魔一

the village in it! The only reason why the government officials can't find it is that they're incompetent! Just wait and see. I will find the peach blossom spring and become a rich official!" the fisherman replied angrily. After his outburst, the fisherman stormed out of the house and left in search of the peach blossom spring.

The wife, already used to her husband's erratic behavior, only sighed in resignation before going to gather her embroidery supplies. Ever since her husband returned from a fishing trip a month ago, he's been obsessed with some mysterious "peach blossom spring." He even alerted government officials, hoping his so-called discovery could bring him glory and riches. However, no matter how many people the government sent in search of the peach blossom spring, it remained nowhere to be found. Eventually, the government gave up.

And so, the fisherman took the matter into his own hands. He became so infatuated with searching for the peach blossom spring that he neglected his job. For the past month, the family's living expenses have come out of their savings and the little income the wife brought in with her embroidery work. However, the savings were quickly running out as well as the food supply, and the wife's embroidery work failed to bring in any sufficient income. The household was holding on by only a thread.

The wife became very weak because of long-time overwork. One day, early in the morning, the wife was preparing breakfast for her family. "Mother, I am still hungry, can I have some more?" her little son asked as he peered up at her. The wife looked over at the empty rice jar and hesitated. Despite the food supply running low, the child was still at an age where he was growing, how could she deprive him of food? In silence, she poured what little food she had in her bowl into his. She had already been rationing food portions for days in an attempt to make the food supply last longer.

This scene was what the fisherman saw when he returned home. He noticed his wife and son had become much thinner than what he remembered. There were also dark circles under his wife's eyes and bruises on her hands. Suddenly, it dawned on him that he had made a huge mistake. The reason why he wanted to look for the peach blossom spring was that he wanted to give his family a better life with his newfound riches. But he had neglected his duties while looking for the peach blossom spring, causing his family to suffer instead, it was truly madness!

般。近日来，一直都是靠妻子熬夜刺绣和之前的积蓄维持生活。可是家里的食物和积蓄即将耗尽，绣品也卖不了多少钱，很快就要撑不下去了。

妻子因为长期过度劳累，身体非常虚弱。一天早晨，妻子正在为家人准备早餐。“娘亲，孩儿很饿了，可否多给些粥啊？”只有几岁大的小娃娃眨着亮晶晶的大眼睛，看着他的母亲。妻子为难地看了一眼空空如也的米缸。孩子正是长个儿的年纪，妻子于心不忍，默默地将自己本就少得可怜的粥全给了孩子。妻子为了让家里所剩不多的食物能多吃几天，已经限制了孩子好几天的饭量了。

这就是渔人一回来看到的情形。他愣在了门边，看着妻子和孩子日渐消瘦的身体，又看着妻子眼下的淤青和伤痕累累的双手，渔人忽然醒悟。他想找到桃花源、当官，不就是想让妻子、孩子过上好日子吗？如今他为了寻找桃花源而导致家里没有收入，害得妻子、孩子受苦，真是本末倒置，荒谬至极！渔人此刻大梦初醒，也顾不上吃饭了。他马上带上了钓鱼的器材，准备好好儿地钓几条大鱼来补偿家人。

渔人在小舟上等候鱼儿上钩，静静地坐在河中央。他顺着小舟轻轻地摇摆，借用此时的安静来思考。渔人看着波光粼粼的水面，豁然开朗。当初找到桃花源的时候，并不是刻意为之，而是无意之举。他对桃花源的执念给身边的家人带来了许多的伤害。古人云“祸莫大于不知足，咎莫大于欲得”，果真如此。渔人深感愧疚，桃花源之所以是人间仙境，人们安居乐业，正是因为那里的人们内心朴实。在那里，人们不受外界干扰，生活简单而快乐。若是让外界闯入，便不再是那个纯粹的桃花源了。

或许，渔人出来之后再也找不到它的原因，正是因为他在欲望与贪婪之间忘了自己原本最干净的样子。这样的他，怎么可能找到桃花源呢？渔人悟到了，自然的规则本就是要顺从的。就如同落水之人，顺则浮，挣则溺。凡事都有它的自然规则，若是强求或挣扎，可能会越陷越深。顺其自然，既来之则安之，才是他

Having come to his senses, the fisherman immediately set off on a fishing trip in hopes of making it up to his family, even forgetting to eat.

Soon, the fisherman was sitting on a boat in the center of a lake, waiting for fish to take the bait. The boat swayed gently, and he used the peacefulness of the moment to think. He gazed at the sparkling blue water, fully enlightened. When he first found the peach blossom spring, it was by chance and not intentionally. His infatuation with the peach blossom spring had brought upon his family many sorrows. As Laozi once said, "There is no misfortune greater than being discontent and no fault greater than desire." It was truly so, and the fisherman felt very guilty. The reason why the peach blossom spring was a fairyland where people lived happy lives was that the people there were kind and content. In the peach blossom spring, people were not affected by the outside world, and life was simple yet filled with joy. If the outside world was allowed to contaminate the peach blossom spring, it would no longer be the same.

Perhaps the reason why the fisherman could no longer find the peach blossom spring after he left was that he had been blinded by desire and greed and forgotten what he was originally like. How could someone like him find the peach blossom spring? The fisherman understood now that one must obey the rules of nature. It was like a person who fell into deep water. They would float if they abided, and sink if they resisted. All that was in life had its natural tendencies; if one forced themselves against those tendencies, they would likely sink deeper and deeper. Going with the flow, and accepting things as they come, that was the way of life he shall follow.

Having let go of his obsession, the fisherman felt as though a great weight had been lifted from his shoulders. His body felt relieved and light. He kept the fattest fish from his harvest and sold the rest. With fish, grains, and money in hand, he happily returned home and handed the fruits of his labor to his wife. When night fell, the family gathered for dinner. Watching his wife and son happily enjoy a tasty meal, the fisherman truly understood the joys of being content.

One day, the fisherman fell fast asleep on his boat while on a fishing trip. In his slumber, he seemed to smell a faint aroma of peach blossoms. He opened his eyes to see a familiar

应该遵从的生活方式。

放下了执念，渔人感觉如释重负，全身轻松。他留了最肥美的那条鱼，便把剩下的鱼都卖了。他带着鱼、谷米和钱，开开心心地回家交给妻子。夜幕降临时，渔人看着妻子、孩子快乐地吃饭，真正体会到了知足常乐的道理。

时光流逝，有一天渔人在钓鱼的时候，在小舟上睡着了。迷迷糊糊之中，仿佛闻到了淡淡的桃花香。睁眼一看，又是那熟悉的桃花林。在半睡半醒之中，渔人分辨不出桃花林是真实的还是梦中的，不过他也不在意。渔人往桃花林的方向笑了一下，以示告别，便回家了。家中，妻子端来香喷喷的饭菜，孩子拉着他玩耍。一家人坐在一起吃饭，欢声笑语，其乐融融，不就是世外桃源那般最美好的样子吗？

forest made up of peach blossom trees. The fisherman was unable to tell if the vision was a dream or reality in his semi-conscious state, but he did not pay much attention to it. He smiled at the peach blossoms as a sign of farewell and headed back home. At home, his wife brought plates of delicious food to the table, and his son called on him to play together. A happy family sitting around the dinner table, the air filled with laughter and joy, isn't this the paradise of the peach blossom spring?

有感而发
Reflections

导 读

本板块的十三篇文章都是同学们读完一部作品以后写的读后感，或者是看一部电影以后写的观后感。

读完中国寓言故事《愚公移山》以后，圣母大学的高美睿同学写道："刚刚读《愚公移山》的时候，我确实觉得愚公很笨。但是仔细思考以后，我意识到他的做法有一些很值得敬佩的地方，也能理解为什么他最终赢得了山神的赞扬和帮助，搬走了两座大山。"在讲到这篇文章的现实意义时，美睿认为世界上需要更多像愚公一样的人。面对地球变暖这个山一样大的问题，"我们应该学习愚公移山的精神，为了我们的后代，敢于挑战自己的极限，从现在做起，从我们做起，解决全球变暖的问题。一个人是渺小的，但是只要我们坚持下去，世界上越来越多的人会被感动，加入我们保护地球的行动。他们就是我们的山神。"美睿的读后感写得非常有水平。先是分享寓言的真实意义，然后又引申到它的现实意义。这一点非常值得学习。

阅读完《西游记》以后，中北学院的高亮亮同学发现书中的几个主要人物恰好代表我们人类的不同方面。唐僧是人类正面性格的代表，他善良、有同情心、有耐心。八戒是人类负面形象的代表，他自负、爱欺负人、贪吃、好色。悟空代表人类的大脑，他有着火爆的脾气和冲动的性格。沙僧是一个坚强、冷静的角色，正好和悟空互补。白龙马虽然很容易被读者忽视，但它是整部小说的重要组成部分。它自始至终任劳任怨，"肩负着人类沉重的行囊，沿着主人指引的方向砥砺前行。没有白龙马的默默奉献，主角们就无法发挥自己的潜力。"亮亮对书中人物的分析非常到位。观察书中的五个主角，我们会发现我们每个人都可能会有唐

Introduction

The thirteen essays in this section are all reflections written by students after reading a literary work or watching a movie.

After reading the Chinese fable story *Yugong Removed the Mountains*, Marie Gerges, a student from University of Notre Dame, wrote, "My initial reaction to this story was that Yugong was indeed quite foolish. However, after carefully contemplating the story, I realized that Yugong's actions have serval admirable qualities. I can also understand why he ultimately earned the praise and assistance of the mountain gods and removed the mountains." When discussing the practical significance of this story, Marie believes that the world needs more people like Yugong. Faced with the enormous problem of global warming, she states, "We should learn from the spirit of Yugong and challenge ourselves to make the world safe for our descendants, starting from now and starting with our own actions. One person's actions may be insignificant, but through one person's example, many people around the world can be moved to protect the Earth. The protectors of the Earth are our mountain gods." Marie's reflection is very well-written. She first shares the true meaning of the fable and then extends it to its real-life significance. This aspect is well worth learning from.

After reading the Chinese novel *Journey to the West*, Jorge Navarro Jr., a student from North Central College, discovered that several main characters in the book represent different aspects of humanity. Tang Monk represents the positive characteristics of humanity as he is kind, sympathetic, and patient. Pigsy represents the negative image of humanity as he is arrogant, likes to bully others, and is gluttonous and lustful. Monkey King represents the human brain, characterized by a fiery temper and impulsive nature. Sandy is a strong and calm character who complements Monkey King. Although the White Dragon Horse is easily overlooked by readers, it plays an important role throughout the entire novel. "It works tirelessly from the start to the end, carrying the heavy luggage of human beings on

僧的善良、八戒的自负、悟空的冲动、沙僧的冷静、白龙马的任劳任怨，只不过是因人而异，因环境而异。所以亮亮才建议美国学生都要读读《西游记》。

通过观看三部中国电影，即《新女性》《红色娘子军》和《杜拉拉升职记》，弗吉尼亚军事学院的吴敏同学分析出了中国女性社会地位的变化。1935 年拍摄的《新女性》中的女主角叫韦明。她原本要凭着自己的能力教书、写作，做一个不依附男人的新女性。但是在那个男权社会里，韦明碰得头破血流，最后只能自杀。1961 年拍摄的《红色娘子军》中的女主角叫吴琼花。她受尽地主南霸天的欺凌。后来党代表洪常青救了吴琼花，并送她去参加了红军。在洪常青的耐心教育下，吴琼花飞速成长，最后带领红军消灭了南霸天。与三十年代的新女性相比，六十年代新女性的社会地位已经有了很大的提高。她们在男性的帮助下取得了很大的进步。2010 年拍摄的《杜拉拉升职记》中的女主角叫杜拉拉。杜拉拉在一家国际大公司工作，有很多想法，能力很强，很快引起了上司的注意，并且在爱情和工作之间取得了平衡。吴敏分析道："跟《新女性》不一样，杜拉拉对她的生活有更多的掌控。跟《红色娘子军》也不一样，杜拉拉不需要男性的鼓励和帮助。"通过对这三部电影的分析对比，吴敏同学成功地展示了中国妇女社会地位的变化。她的这篇《中国电影中的新女性》非常值得大家一读。

his shoulders and forging ahead in the direction guided by his master without complaint. Without the silent dedication of the White Dragon Horse, the protagonists would not be able to realize their potential." Jorge's analysis of the characters in the book is extremely accurate. By observing the five main characters, we will find that everyone may have the kindness of Tang Monk, the arrogance of Pigsy, the impulsiveness of Monkey King, the calmness of Sandy, and the selfless dedication of White Dragon Horse. It is simply the individual differences and environmental influences that make them distinct. Therefore, Jorge recommends that American students should read *Journey to the West.*

After watching three Chinese movies, namely *New Woman, The Red Detachment of Women*, and *Go Lala Go!*, Lauren Wolf, a student from Virginia Military Institute, analyzed the changes in social status of Chinese women. In the 1935 movie *New Woman*, the protagonist is Wei Ming. She has wanted to rely on her own abilities to teach and write, becoming a new woman who doesn't depend on men. However, in the male-dominated society back in the days, Wei Ming faces severe obstacles and ultimately resorts to suicide. In the 1961 movie *The Red Detachment of Women*, the protagonist is Wu Qionghua. She endures the oppression of the local tyrant Nan Batian. Later, the Party Representative Hong Changqing saves Wu Qionghua and sends her to join the Red Army. Under Hong Changqing's patient guidance, Wu Qionghua grows rapidly and eventually leads the Red Army to defeat Nan Batian. Compared to the new women of the 1930s, the social status of new women in the 1960s has significantly improved, and they make great progress with the help of men. In the 2010 movie *Go Lala Go!*, the protagonist is Du Lala. Du Lala works in a multinational company, overflowing with ideas and energy. She quickly catches the eyes of her superior, and finds a balance between her love life and career. Lauren analyzes, "Unlike the characters in *New Woman*, Du Lala has more control of her life. And unlike the characters in *The Red Detachment of Women*, Du Lala does not need the encouragement and assistance of men." Through the comparative analysis of these three movies, Lauren successfully demonstrates the significant changes in the social status of Chinese women. Her essay, "The Roles of Women in Chinese Movies," is highly recommended to everyone.

愚公移山

作者：顾文迪　指导教师：林秀玲　西北大学

“愚公移山”强调的是一种锲而不舍、持之以恒的精神。

“同学们好，现在我们开始上课。”王老师一进我们的教室，就像往常一样这么说道。“昨天布置大家阅读中国古代寓言《愚公移山》，现在我们讨论这个故事。你们谁先发言？”

这是清华大学对外汉语教育中心暑期三年级班的汉语课。坐在课堂里面的是我们八个来自美国西北大学的留学生。为了今天的讨论，昨天晚上我认真读了好几遍《愚公移山》，觉得这个故事非常有意思。故事里的愚公是一个老人。他家门口有两座大山，挡住了出门的路，他决定带领家人把两座山移走。有个人看到愚公带领全家挖山，就嘲笑道：“您都这么大岁数了，山这么高，您怎么能把它们搬走呢？”愚公回答道：“我虽然老了，但是我的子子孙孙会永远挖下去，一直到把山搬走。”愚公的决心感动了上天，就帮助愚公把两座山搬走了。听到老师的问话，我们几个同学互相看了一眼，好像是在商定谁先发言。“老师，我先说吧。”不用看，一听那洪亮的声音，就知道是麦克又抢着先发言了。

“我不觉得愚公做的事情值得提倡。既然山挡住了他家的路，出门很不方便，他就应该搬家，而不是搬山。是人家山先在那里，然后他才在山前盖了房子。中国人不是讲究先来后到吗？再者说，搬家多么容易呀。租一辆 U-Haul 卡车，哦，对了，是租一辆马车，一天就可以搬到没有大山挡路的地方去了。搬山得需要多

Yugong Removed the Mountains

Author: Wendi Lulu Gu Instructor: Hsiu-ling Robertson Northwestern University

"Hello everyone, let's start class now," Professor Wang said as he entered our classroom. "Yesterday, I assigned everyone to read the ancient Chinese fable *Yugong Removed the Mountains*, and today we will discuss the story. Who would like to speak first?"

> The story emphasizes a spirit of determination and perseverance.

I'm at a summer Chinese class for third year college students at Tsinghua University's Center for Teaching Chinese as a Foreign Language. Sitting in the classroom are eight of our international students from Northwestern University. In preparation for today's discussion, I carefully read through the text several times the night prior. I found this story to be very interesting. In this story, Yugong is an old man. Two big mountains blocked the road in front of his house. So he decided to remove the mountains and enlisted the help of his family. When another man saw Yugong and his family digging the mountains out, he laughed and said, "You are so old and the mountains are so big. How can you remove them?" Yugong replied, "Although I am old, my children and their children will keep working on it till the job is done." But soon Yugong's determination moved the god in the heaven, who used his powers to help Yugong remove the two mountains. After hearing the teacher's question, several of us glanced at each other, trying to decide who should speak first. "Professor, I can go first." I didn't even have to look to know that it was Mike's loud voice, always rushing to speak first.

"I don't think what Yugong did is worth advocating. If the mountains blocked his way, making it inconvenient for him to leave his house, he should move out himself instead of removing the mountains. The mountains were there first, and then he built a house in front of the mountains. Don't Chinese people honor the phrase 'first come, first served?' Besides, it's so

少人力物力呀？不划算！”麦克一边说着，一边摊开双手，摇着他那长着一头乱发的大头。

“我也觉得搬山不好，”这时坐在我左边的玛丽也摇着头说话了，“愚公不能为了一家人的利益就移山填海，那是破坏生态环境！如果把山搬走，山上的熊猫怎么办？长颈鹿怎么办？海里的鱼虾怎么办？海豚怎么……”

“对不起，玛丽，愚公的家在中国的北方，那里山上没有熊猫。长颈鹿生活在非洲，那时还没有来中国呢。”坐在我右边的杰克最受不了玛丽的啰唆，打断了玛丽那可能是很长、很长的单子。我们都知道玛丽在美国就是动物保护协

easy to move out. Just rent a U-Haul truck; oh yes, rent a wagon and you can move out within a day to a location where there are no mountains blocking the road. It takes so much human labor and resources to remove a mountain. It's not worth it." Mike said as he spread his hands and shook his big head with messy hair on it.

"I also don't think it's good to remove the mountains," Mary to my left, said shaking her head. "Yugong shouldn't remove mountains for the sake of his family – that would be destroying the ecological environment! If the mountains were all dug up and moved away, what would happen to the pandas on the mountains? What about the giraffes? The fish and shrimp in the sea? The dolphins…"

"Sorry, Mary, but Yugong's house is in the northern part of China, where there are no pandas in the mountains. Giraffes lived in Africa, and they didn't come to China at that time," Jack, to my right, said, irritated by Mary's comment. Mary is an activist for the Animal Protection Society in the U.S. It was time to stop her from talking. Jack said casually, in a very American manner, "I think everyone should enjoy freedom. This is a natural right. If an old man in his eighties wants to dig up a mountain, that's his own business, so we should just let him dig. It's not like he can dig up much anyway. No one should object." As he said this, Jack proudly glanced around the room, but when he met with everyone's disdainful looks, he immediately changed his attitude and said: "OK, maybe I don't oppose Yugong's removing the mountains, but I oppose his making his children and grandchildren remove the mountains with him. Think about it – if our grandfather forced us to do the same thing with him for the rest of our lives, who would be able to stand it?!"

Later, there were a few other classmates who shared their own reasons for opposing Yugong's decision to remove the mountains. The more I listened, the more I felt embarrassed for my American classmates. I mean, how can we measure the behavior of a Chinese person from 4,000 years ago using our American values today, without even understanding the moral of the story? I sat there staring at the floor, lost in thought, as the voices of my classmates gradually faded away from me. My classmates definitely didn't thoroughly read the fable *Yugong Removed the Mountains* last night. If they read it several times, they should be able to realize the true meaning of *Yugong Removed the Mountains*. The story emphasizes a spirit of determination

会的积极分子，现在不能让她再往下说了。杰克显得很宽容，用美国人那惯有的腔调说道："我认为，人人都应该享受自由。这是天经地义的权利。一个八十多岁的老人要去挖山，那是他自己的事情，让他去挖嘛。反正他也挖不了多少。别人不必反对。"说到这里，杰克得意地向四周瞟了一眼，但是当他看到大家都多少显示出不屑的神情时，立即改变了他的态度，说道："我不反对愚公搬山，但是我反对他让他的孩子，让他的孩子的孩子都跟着他去搬山。想想如果我们的爷爷强迫我们跟他一样一辈子做一件事情，谁会受得了？！"

后面还有几个同学提出他们各自反对愚公搬山的理由。我越听越为我的美国同学感到不好意思。天啊，我们怎么能如此不求甚解，用美国人今天的价值观去衡量四千年前一个中国人的行为呢？我坐在那里望着地板，陷入了深思，同学们的声音渐渐地离我越来越远。昨晚我的这些同学肯定没有好好读《愚公移山》这个寓言故事。如果多读几遍的话，就应该能悟到"愚公移山"的真正意义。"愚公移山"强调的是一种锲而不舍、持之以恒的精神。搬山看起来是一件不可能完成的任务，但是只要我们踏踏实实，一步一个脚印，每天都坚持做下去，就有可能完成任务。山没有变，任务没有变，但是你周围的情况在变，你的条件在变。你的同事、你的邻居、你的国人同胞都可能会支持你，加入你的队伍。科学技术在变，你的工具在变。那么这个看起来不可能完成的任务就有可能完成。如果你没有"愚公移山"的精神，什么也不敢做，没有坚持到底的决心，当然肯定什么也做不成。在故事的结尾，愚公的精神感动了上天，帮助他把山搬到应该去的地方。所以愚公没有真的把山搬走，没有破坏环境，更没有强迫子孙做他们不想做的事情。我们为什么要在这里指责一个四千年前、充满智慧的中国老人呢？别人虽然叫他"愚公"，其实他是"大智若愚"，是一个真正的智者。对待其他国家的文化习俗，我们要设身处地地思考为什么是这样。我们不能用美国人的标准衡量

and perseverance. Although removing a mountain may seem like an impossible task, as long as we remain grounded, take one step at a time, and keep doing it every day, it is possible to complete it. While the mountains and task won't change, the situation around you is always changing. Your colleagues, neighbors, and fellow citizens may all support you and join you in your endeavors. Science and technology are changing, and your tools are changing. Therefore, circumstances can make anything seemingly impossible possible. If you don't have the unwavering spirit of Yugong, you would cower from challenges and be unable to persevere to the end. At the end of the story, Yugong's strong spirit touched the god in the heaven, who helped him to remove the mountains to where it should go. So, Yugong didn't actually destroy or remove the mountains, and neither did he damage the environment or force his descendants

世界上的一切。不能刚刚知道一些皮毛就品头论足，说长道短。

“文迪，大家都说了，请你也说一说对《愚公移山》的看法吧。”王老师突然叫我的名字，把我从沉思中拉了回来。我抬起头，微微一笑，说道：“我同意大家的意见。没有什么可以补充的了。”

接着我把眼光又投向了地板。大夏天的，我才不想给我这些同学上课呢。这个任务，还是交给可怜的王老师吧。

to do things against their will. Why are we out here denigrating an old Chinese man from 4,000 years ago, who was full of wisdom? Although others call him "Yugong" (which translates into "Foolish Man"), I would actually argue he is the real man of wisdom, so wise that he seems like a fool to others. When dealing with the cultural customs of other countries, we should put ourselves in their shoes. We cannot measure everything by American standards, nor can we take the story too literally.

"Wendi, everyone has shared their thoughts already. Please share your perspective as well." Professor Wang suddenly called my name, pulling me back from my deep musings. Smiling to myself, I looked up and said, "I agree with everyone. There's nothing much to add."

Then, I turned my eyes to the floor again. In the hot summer, I didn't want to take the time to teach my American classmates this lesson in Chinese culture. Let's leave this task to poor Professor Wang.

愚公移山有道理吗

作者：高美睿　指导教师：朱永平　圣母大学

在山一样的困难面前，愚公没有退缩或者放弃，而是坚定不移地朝着既定目标走下去。

《愚公移山》里的愚公尝试做一件不可能做到的事：挖平他家门口的两座大山。可是对愚公来说，似乎有另外一个更容易解决问题的办法——搬家。这个故事今天给我们提出了很多问题。愚公是不是真的很愚笨，缺乏基本的常识？难道他真的不知道两座山有多么大吗？还是他有一些不被他人知晓的、不能搬家的理由？

刚刚读《愚公移山》的时候，我确实觉得愚公很愚笨。但是仔细思考以后，我意识到他的做法有一些很值得敬佩的地方，也能理解为什么他最终赢得了山神的赞扬和帮助，搬走了两座大山。首先，他非常重视家人的意见。在决定挖山以前，他向他的家人征询意见，问他们愿意不愿意跟他一起挖山。经过家人的讨论、同意之后，他们才开始挖山。所以说，愚公没有搞一言堂，他是民主的。当智叟嘲笑他的时候，愚公承认，在山被挖平以前，他可能早就死了，但是对他来说，只要他孙子的孙子的孙子有一天出门不必翻山越岭，他现在的努力就是值得的。前人栽树，后人乘凉，这不说明愚公很无私吗？最重要的是，愚公表现出了一种不怕困难的精神。在山一样的困难面前，愚公没有退缩或者放弃，而是坚定不移地朝着既定目标走下去。愚公和他的孩子以及邻居努力挖山时，智叟只会嘲笑他们，却不提出什么解决问题的建议来。后来，山神被愚公锲而不舍的精神感动，

Is Yugong Who Removed the Mountains Actually Wise?

Author: Marie Gerges Instructor: Yongping Zhu University of Notre Dame

Yugong in the story *Yugong Removed Mountains* attempted to do something that cannot possibly be done: flatten the two mountains in front of his house with a mere shovel. As far as Yugong is concerned, there appears to be an easier solution to his problem: moving to a new house. This story poses many questions to readers today. Is Yugong truly foolish, lacking basic common sense? Is it possible that he does not comprehend the size of the mountains? Or are there reasons unknown to the readers that prevent Yugong from moving to a new house?

> In the face of challenges as great as mountains, Yugong did not retreat or lose hope. Instead, he firmly resolved to work toward his goal.

帮助愚公搬走了两座大山。

我觉得世界上需要更多像愚公一样的人。《愚公移山》让我想起了现在全球变暖的问题。很多人认为全球变暖现在还没有造成什么大问题，所以没有必要改变我们今天习以为常的生活方式，应该继续使用化石能源，应该继续吃我们一日不可或缺的牛肉。还有很多人虽然承认地球变暖了，但是认为这个问题比山还大，根本解决不了，那就像智叟一样什么都不做吧。这都是不对的。我们应该学习愚公移山的精神，为了我们的后代，敢于挑战自己的极限，从现在做起，从我们做起，解决全球变暖的问题。一个人是渺小的，但是只要我们坚持下去，世界上越来越多的人会被感动，加入我们保护地球的行动。他们就是我们的山神。

My initial reaction to this story was that Yugong was indeed quite foolish. However, after carefully contemplating the story, I realized that Yugong's actions have several admirable qualities. I can also understand why he ultimately earned the praise and assistance of the mountain gods and removed the mountains. First, Yugong greatly valued the opinions of his family members. Before beginning to dig, Yugong convened with his family, asking them whether they would be willing to join his project. Only after discussion and receiving the approval of his family did Yugong begin digging. Thus, it can be said that Yugong did not run a one-man show and was democratic in his approach. When a supposedly wise man in the village mocked Yugong, he admitted that he would probably be dead by the time the mountains were flattened. According to Yugong, his hard work would be worthwhile if his descendants could one day go out without traversing the mountains. As the Chinese saying goes, "One generation plants the trees in whose shade another generation rests." Is Yugong's attitude not quite selfless? Most importantly, Yugong demonstrated a sort of willingness to endure suffering bravely. In the face of challenges as great as mountains, Yugong did not retreat or lose hope. Instead, he firmly resolved to work toward his goal. While Yugong, his children, and his neighbors were diligently digging, the wise man simply laughed at them and offered no advice. Later, the mountain gods were moved by Yugong's indefatigable efforts and helped Yugong relocate the two mountains.

I believe that the world needs more people like Yugong. This story called to mind our current global warming crisis. Many people believe that because global warming has not caused any major issues yet, there is no need to change our current way of living. According to this logic, we should continue utilizing fossil fuels and eating meat without restraint. There are also many people who acknowledge that global warming is taking place, but believe the issue is unsolvable. Thus, like the wise man in the story, they decide to do nothing at all. I believe the perspectives of these two groups are mistaken. We should learn from the spirit of Yugong and challenge ourselves to make the world safe for our descendants, starting now and starting with our own actions. One person's actions may be insignificant, but through one person's example, many people around the world can be moved to protect the Earth. The protectors of the Earth are our mountain gods.

《漫话缠足》读后感

作者：魏查德　指导教师：李可宁　密歇根大学

《漫话缠足》是一个网络上的互动故事，一个历史科普作品，它通过以对话为主的叙述方式来让读者了解缠足这个历史现象。作者卢薇薇是一位刚从密歇根大学硕士毕业的中国研究者，精通宋史。因为我本人很喜欢中国历史，也想更多地了解这个复杂的历史现象，所以我对这个故事很感兴趣。

这个小故事展示了当时的社会对女性的严格要求。

《漫话缠足》总共有三篇，通过穿越时空，让读者回到三个时代，包括清末民初、明末清初和两宋之交。每篇都有一个女主角，以此来推动故事的发展，展现她缠足的经历。

因为故事很长，所以到现在为止，我只读完了明末清初这部分。在这部分里，女主角叶蕙绸是一个七八岁的女孩儿，她出身于一个高贵的南方家庭，她的父母也很重视女儿的教育。蕙绸是老二，她还有一个姐姐和一个妹妹。姐姐妹妹都非常优秀，但是蕙绸自己不太喜欢读书，也不想缠足。故事里的第一个冲突就涉及开始缠足的时候蕙绸跟她两个姐妹的关系。一个重要的情节是，有一次蕙绸的妹妹在一群大人面前朗诵诗歌，她的表现比蕙绸好得多，这让蕙绸很丢脸。从此以后，蕙绸下决心要好好读书，也决心配合缠足，这样才不会落后于她那两个优秀的姐妹。这个小故事展示了当时的社会对女性的严格要求。

读《漫话缠足》之前，我对缠足的所有知识都是从课本上学来的，只知道

Impressions after Reading *Talking about Foot Binding*

Author: Chad Westra   Instructor: Kening Li   University of Michigan

Talking about Foot Binding is an interactive online story and a work of popular history. Through dialogue-based narrative, readers gain an understanding of the historical phenomenon of foot binding. The author, Lu Weiwei, is a researcher of China who, versed in the history of the Song Dynasty, recently graduated with a Master's degree from the University of Michigan. My interest in this story arose out of my enjoyment of Chinese history and my wish to better understand this historical phenomenon.

This small episode demonstrates the strict requirements placed on females during this period.

By way of time travel, readers can go back to the three historical periods which *Talking about Foot Binding* covers in its three periods, including the late Qing and early Republican period, the late Ming and early Qing period, and the transition from the Northern to Southern Song. Each period has a main female protagonist from whose perspective the reader drives forward the story, unfolding her

它是违背人性的。然而，这个故事使用第一人称的视角，让我好像进入了那个时代背景下，自己可以体验到女性在当时社会的经历和想法。作者对缠足过程的生动描写，使我对故事里被迫缠足的角色产生同情之心，譬如有仆人用布条把蕙绸的脚紧紧缠住的时候。

这个故事的写作风格也很好，作者以现代汉语为主要叙述语言，同时融入很多古代汉语的语体特色。这样的风格有一个好处，就是这个作品不像古代汉语作品那么难读懂，但是又充满中国传统文化的韵味。我发现这种风格其实经常出现在现代汉语中，很多历史题材的电视剧也会用这种风格。所以我觉得《漫话缠足》的内容不但读起来很有趣，而且了解它的风格还对我的中文能力的提高有实际的帮助。

foot binding experience.

Because it is a long story, up to this point I have only read the section on the late Ming and early Qing. The main character in this part is Ye Huichou, a seven-to-eight-year-old girl born to a noble southern family whose parents prioritized female education. She is the second child and has an older and younger sister. Both of her sisters are extremely impressive; Huichou, however, is not very interested in her studies, nor does she want to undergo foot binding. The first conflict in the story arises when Huichou is going to start binding her feet and concerns her relationship with her sisters. An important plot point occurs when, while reciting poetry in front of a group of people, Huichou is embarrassed because her younger sister's performance greatly outdid her own. From this moment on, Huichou resolves both to study diligently and to bind her feet in order not to fall behind her outstanding sisters. This small episode demonstrates the strict requirements placed on females during this period.

Before reading *Talking about Foot Binding*, my knowledge about foot binding came from textbooks and all I knew was that the practice violated human nature. However, because this story uses the first-person narrative perspective, it seems as if I had entered the historical period's environment, providing a sense for myself of the experience and thinking within that society. The author's vivid depiction of the foot binding process makes me sympathize with the characters in the story who experience foot binding, such as the moments when a servant uses strips of cloth to tightly bind Huichou's feet.

The story also has a great writing style. While taking modern Chinese as the primary language base, the author at the same time infuses many characteristics from ancient Chinese language. The advantage to this type of style is that it is not so hard to read as a work of ancient Chinese, yet it still manages to be filled with the flavor and charm of traditional Chinese culture. In fact, I have come to realize that this style frequently appears in modern Chinese, such as in the many historical dramas one can find on TV. Therefore, I not only find the content in *Talking about Foot Binding* fascinating to read, but also believe that understanding its writing style has been a substantial aid for improving my Chinese ability.

我从《西游记》学到的

作者：高亮亮　指导教师：孙金爱　中北学院

《西游记》可以帮助美国学生更多地了解中国人看世界的视角和自我提高的方法。

《西游记》能够成为中国四大名著之一，其中一个重要的原因是因为它对儒教、佛教和道教的理解和诠释，反映了中国人的心态和文化，让很多中国人有共鸣。我觉得这样一本重要、有趣的书，美国人也应该读一读。下面我分享一下我的阅读经历和想法。

首先，我发现吴承恩用他的方式所写的人物都有不同的含义。比如他用唐僧师徒四人代表人类精神的一部分，这样我们可以更好地了解自己。另外，用相互补充的二分法来分析人物，可以很容易地理解他们。无论你学习什么角色，他们都展现出人类的不同特点。孙悟空代表人类的头脑。他表现势不可挡的脾气和冲动。世界上很多人都有思想，可是他们不能都公开表达或者行动。但是孙悟空有能力表现出这些想法。

从我的角度来看，唐僧是人类正面性格的代表，他善良、有同情心、有耐心。可能是他对佛教的信仰帮助他提高了自我修养，提高自我修养是每个人都应该追求的。

相反，猪八戒是人类负面性格的代表，他自傲、爱欺负人、贪吃、好色。虽然猪八戒有很多缺点，但是他不断实现自己的目标，代表了人类可以通过帮助他人变得更好。

What I Learned from *Journey to the West*

Author: Jorge Navarro Jr. Instructor: Jinai Sun North Central College

> *Journey to the West* can help American students learn more Chinese ways of seeing the world and improving themselves.

Journey to the West has earned its place among the four Chinese classics. One of the most important reasons is its understanding and interpretation of Taoism, Buddhism, and Confucianism, which reflects the mentality and culture of Chinese people that they can resonate with. I believe such an important and interesting book should also be read by Americans. Below I share my reading experience and thoughts.

First of all, I found that the characters in the novel created by the author Wu Cheng'en represent different categories of people. For example, he used Master Tang Monk and his three disciples to represent aspects of the human spirit, so that we can better understand ourselves. Additionally, by placing these characters into complementary dichotomies, they become easy to understand. Regardless of the characters you observe, they all express different human characteristics. Disciple Monkey King represents the human mind. He displays an unstoppable temper and impulsiveness. Many people in the world have thoughts that they do not overtly express or act upon, but Monkey King has the ability to manifest them.

From my point of view, Tang Monk is the representation of the positive character capable of human beings. He is kind, compassionate, and patient. Although it may be that his belief in Buddhism helps him reach his own cultivation, this kind of self-improvement should be what everyone should pursue.

因此，唐僧是自我完善的代表，而猪八戒体现了人类可以不断进步。

沙悟净是一个坚强、冷静的角色。就像猪八戒和唐僧的二分法一样，沙悟净正好和孙悟空互补。沙悟净没有孙悟空表现出的欲望或者固执己见。恰恰相反，他表现出忠诚和谦虚，而且只要有正确的方向，他就能坚持并且获得成就。我觉得沙悟净表现了人类只要坚持正确的方向就可以实现伟大的目标。

最后，“白龙马”可能是最容易被忽视的角色，但它是让整个故事完整的重要组成部分。白龙马看起来代表被他人驱使的动物，但是它体现了人类最原始的意志。它可以自始至终任劳任怨，无所求，只是肩负着人类沉重的行囊，沿着主人指引的方向砥砺前行。没有白龙马的默默奉献，主角们就无法发挥自己的潜力。

总体来说，我认为《西游记》传达的最重要的信息是不同性格和品质的人怎么在一起工作，了解这一点可以帮助我们提高自己的行动力和决策力。这就是为什么我认为《西游记》是一个出色的寓言故事，它可以帮助美国学生更多地了解中国人看世界的视角和自我提高的方法。

Adversely, disciple Pigsy is the negative representation of human character. He is arrogant, deceitful, gluttonous, and lustful. Despite his many flaws, he continues to achieve his goals, which represents that human beings can become better by helping others. Therefore, while Tang Monk represents the self-improved state, Pigsy is the representative of continuous improvement of human beings.

Disciple Sandy is a strong, but reserved character. Just like the dichotomy between Pigsy and Tang Monk, Sandy is Monkey King's complementary character who is the exact opposite of him. He doesn't have the arrogance or stubbornness shown by Monkey King. On the contrary, he has shown loyalty and humility, and given the right direction, he can persevere and achieve great things. I think Sandy shows that human beings can achieve great goals as long as they stick to the right direction.

Finally, while the White Dragon Horse may be the most overlooked character, it is an integral part of the story. It seems to represent animals that are driven by others, but it embodies the most primal energy and willpower humans need. It works tirelessly from the start to the end, carrying the heavy luggage of human beings on its shoulders and forging ahead in the direction guided by its master without complaint. Without the silent dedication of the White Dragon Horse, the protagonists would not be able to realize their potential.

Overall, I think the most important message of *Journey to the West* is how people with different personalities and qualities work together, and understanding this can help us improve our own ability to act and make decisions. That's why I think *Journey to the West* is an excellent story that can help American students learn more Chinese ways of seeing the world and improving themselves.

助我成长的《红楼梦》

作者：孟露菲　指导教师：孙金爱　中北学院

> 《红楼梦》虽然是一部古典名著，却依然能穿越时空，引领我们每个人学会如何过好自己的一生。

我在大学四年级的时候读了《红楼梦》，直到今天它都对我有很大的影响。作为一名美国学生，这本书让我第一次接触到中国古典文学，并很快产生了深刻的共鸣。《红楼梦》，作为中国的“四大名著”之一，是 18 世纪曹雪芹所著，它描写了古代贵族生活和小说中各种人物错综复杂的经历，充满了中国哲学思想，也展现了很多古代文化。读完《红楼梦》以后，我才明白为什么这部作品直到今天在中国还经久不衰。

故事开始于《女娲补天》的神话，一块失落的石头因为无法用来补天而被抛弃在青埂（“情根”的谐音）峰下。一位僧人和一位道士发现了它，他们听完石头的故事以后，就决定带它到人间去看看。石头忘记了自己原来的身份，投胎到一位叫“贾宝玉”的少爷身上，经历了家族的繁华、衰败，还有感情的纠葛。从这个故事中，每个读者都可以通过宝玉命运的起伏和对生命的感悟，加深对世界的理解。而对我来说，这部作品最有影响力的地方就是它把道家、儒家和佛家思想融合在具体的故事中，帮助我理解中国的哲学和价值观。这让我大开眼界，开始从三种不同的思想去理解人生意义。

故事发生在一座大的府邸和一个叫“大观园”的地方，宝玉在这园里与姐妹和朋友一起度过童年。大观园象征着理想的世界，没有规矩，可以让年轻的宝玉

Dream of the Red Chamber, a Book that Helps Me Grow

Author: Laurel Murphy Instructor: Jinai Sun North Central College

> I think this is the very reason *Dream of the Red Chamber* is considered a classical Chinese masterpiece and has been able to travel through time and space to guide each of us to lead better lives.

In my senior year of college, I read an influential novel called *Dream of the Red Chamber*. As an American student, this was my very first encounter with Chinese classical literature, and I immediately felt a deep connection. Written in the 18th century by Cao Xueqin, *Dream of the Red Chamber* is known as one of China's "Four Great Classical Novels." It is filled with Chinese philosophical thought and ancient culture, depicting the life of aristocrats in the Qing Dynasty and the intricate experiences of many diverse characters. After reading *Dream of the Red Chamber* in its entirety, I now understand why this great work has endured in China up until the present day.

The story begins with the myth of *Nvwa Mending the Sky*, in which a stone created by the goddess was left unused, abandoned under the Qinggeng Peak (a homonym for "love stalk"), until one day when a Buddhist monk and a Taoist priest happened upon it. After listening to the stone's story, they decided to bring it with them to experience the mortal world. Thus, the stone forgot its original identity and was born as a young master named Jia Baoyu, who would go on to experience the prosperity, tragic decline, and emotional entanglements of a wealthy, aristocratic family. From this story, each reader can enlighten their own understanding of the world through the ups and downs of Baoyu's fate and his own understanding of "life." For me, the most influential part of this book is its depiction of Taoism, Confucianism, and Buddhism.

随心所欲。在道家思想中，大自然是一个放松的地方，让人们可以离开社会休息一下。与正统的府邸不同，我认为大观园代表了道家思想的审美和青年人向往的自由的生活方式。比如说，在园中宝玉尽情地享受生活，常常和他的姐妹、朋友玩耍，每天他都花时间写诗，跟丫鬟们厮混，因此忽略了他的学业。虽然在园里长大给了宝玉自在快乐，但是即使长大了，他也没有养成自律的习惯，最终不得不强迫自己面对社会的规矩。

These philosophies can be seen throughout the novel as organized into specific stories, representing the "synthesis of the three religions" from the Ming and Qing dynasties. These stories have helped me not only understand more about Chinese philosophy and values, but they have also opened my eyes to view the meaning of life from three different perspectives.

The story unfolds in a large manor and a place within it called the "Grand View Garden." This garden is where Baoyu, together with his cousins and peers, spends his childhood. In *Dream of the Red Chamber*, the Grand View Garden symbolizes an ideal world where there are no rules, and the youthful Baoyu can do whatever he wishes. In Taoist thought, nature is seen as a place of relaxation where one can seek rejuvenation from greater society. As opposed to the orthodox manor where the rest of the family resides, I believe the Grand View Garden represents the aesthetics of Taoism and the free way of life that is constantly sought by young people. For example, Baoyu enjoys life to the fullest in it, ignoring his studies in favor of playing with his female relatives, and spending every day writing poetry or chasing after love. Although growing up in the Grandview Garden gives Baoyu unrestrained freedom and happiness, as he grows up, he does not develop good habits of self-discipline. Eventually, however, he has no choice but to bring himself to face the rules of society.

In addition to Taoism, *Dream of the Red Chamber* portrays the customs of Confucianism. For example, Baoyu's role as the family's eldest male heir defines his duties. Within the manor, his family members expect him to study hard and take the imperial examinations. Baoyu's success is so crucial to the entire family because they are relying on him to maintain a good relationship with the emperor, which will allow them to continue accumulating their wealth. This applies especially to Jia Zheng, Baoyu's father, who wants Baoyu to listen to his demands, thus ensuring the success of the entire family. Once he grows up, Baoyu's life changes from unrestrained freedom to dutifully fulfilling his responsibilities. Although Baoyu finds this reality difficult to face, he can only passively accept the expectations of his family and greater society. Once Baoyu's beloved childhood sweetheart dies, he hardens his resolve and gradually begins to show filial piety to his parents by marrying the wife they choose for him, starting a family of his own, and passing the imperial examination. However, after finally fulfilling his family's greatest hopes, Baoyu suddenly chooses to give up his wealth, status, and family, once again

除了道家思想，《红楼梦》还有儒家思想的表现。比如说，既然宝玉作为家族的继承人，角色定义了他的职责，家人就期望宝玉努力学习，参加科举。府邸内，宝玉的成功之所以对家族至关重要，是因为他们需要和皇帝保持良好的关系才能积累他们的财富。尤其是宝玉的父亲贾政，他希望宝玉听从他的意愿和安排来确保整个家族的成功。长大后，宝玉的人生从自由、无拘无束变成了履行责任。虽然宝玉很难接受这个现实，但是他也只能被动接受家人和社会的期望。心爱的人死了以后，宝玉变得更加心如止水，开始慢慢地孝顺父母，还和家人给他挑选的妻子结婚，最后参加了科举。然而，在终于完成了家族最大的愿望以后，宝玉突然决定放弃自己的功名、地位和家人，再次改变他追求的生命意义。

最终，经过在道家的自由与儒家的规矩两种相反的思想之间长期的挣扎，宝玉最终选择了皈依佛门。虽然宝玉对自己的身份或者财富都没兴趣，但是他从小到大认为情感依恋是他一生中最重要的方面。可悲的是，当宝玉失去了一生中的挚爱时，他就认为佛家是他唯一的应对方法。经受如此痛苦之后，宝玉慢慢感觉到人生如梦，解除自己痛苦的唯一方法就是放弃自己曾经的执着，所以他离开父母、妻子，最终选择出家做和尚。在结尾的时候，宝玉又幻化成岩石，一生的悲剧被刻在上面，伫立在青埂峰上。

对我而言，《红楼梦》是一部非常有价值的、给人警示的作品。正如我们看到的，宝玉的结局是他自己行为的结果，从小到大他从一个极端走向另一个极端，没有平衡不同处境的方法和思想。我认为宝玉受苦是因为他从来没有学会如何控制自己的欲望。比如，他很小的时候生活无忧无虑，直到家族开始衰败，他不得不去考取功名，可最终他还是无法妥协，一直处在选择和放弃两端之间，面对着极大的幸福和极大的悲伤。这让我意识到人们不但应该学会平衡自己的愿望和职责，而且还要学习融合三种哲学思想，用儒家入世的积极态度和责任心、道

altering the meaning of his life.

In the end, after a long struggle between the two opposing ideas of Taoist freedom and Confucian expectations, Baoyu finally chooses to convert to Buddhism. Although, ever since he was young, Baoyu never had much interest in his own status or wealth, he considered his sentimental attachments to be the most important aspect of his life. Once Baoyu loses the love of his life, he sees Buddhism as the only way of coping. After enduring such pain, Baoyu gradually begins to feel that life is but a dream, and the only way to relieve his pain is to give up his desires. He leaves his parents and wife, choosing at last to become a monk. At the end of the story, Baoyu returns to his original existence as a rock, once again standing alone atop the Qinggeng Peak, with the tragedy of his life engraved on his surface.

For me, *Dream of the Red Chamber* is a valuable, precautionary work. As we can see, Baoyu's ending is the result of his own actions. From childhood to adulthood, he passed from one extreme to the other, without the means with which to balance the different stages of his life. I believe Baoyu experienced so much suffering because he never learned how to moderate his

家无拘无束的出世态度以及佛教超脱的境界来对抗痛苦。

当然，这也许正是《红楼梦》悲剧意义所在。读完宝玉的故事，体会到作者把人性的弱点用最极致的方式表现出来，把人生的梦想撕碎在我们的面前，让我们反复思考。《红楼梦》虽然是一部古典名著，却依然能穿越时空，引领我们每个人学会如何过好自己的一生。

own desires. For example, when he was young he was able to live a carefree life, until the family began to decline, and he had no choice but to take the imperial examination. However, in the end, Baoyu could not maintain his compromises, always stuck between two extreme choices and abandonment, which caused him to face both great happiness and then great sadness. This brought me to the conclusion that we should not only learn to balance our desires and responsibilities, but also learn to integrate these three schools of thought by utilizing Confucianism's positive attitude and responsibility to engage in work, Taoism's carefree spirit to enjoy our own inner worlds, and the transcendent non-attachment of Buddhism to fight against suffering.

However, this may also be the significance of the tragedy in *Dream of the Red Chamber*. After reading Baoyu's story, readers come to realize that the author acutely expresses the weakness of human nature, shredding the dream of life before us, and letting us appreciate and reflect on our own lives again and again. I think this is the very reason *Dream of the Red Chamber* is considered a classical Chinese masterpiece and has been able to travel through time and space to guide each of us to lead better lives.

朱自清的《背影》

作者：陈嘉仪　指导教师：李可宁　密歇根大学

> 这篇文章令我反思，意识到父母多么爱我。

朱自清是一位很有名的作家，他于1898年在中国出生。朱自清家很穷，他于1916年考入北京大学，并与妻子武钟谦结婚。朱自清大学毕业后，为了养家糊口，开始四处教书为生，他去杭州、扬州、上海、宁波等地当老师。朱自清还写了很多文章和诗，其中有一篇文章叫《春》。《春》这篇散文短小精悍，从各个方面表现了春天的美丽、无限的生机和创造力。作品先写对春天的盼望，然后勾画出春天的轮廓，最后具体地描绘出春草、春花、春风、春雨四幅春光图。因此，《春》也被称为朱自清最真挚的散文。现在，为了通过中国国家普通话水平考试，全国的考生都要练习朗诵这篇文章。1929年，朱自清的妻子武钟谦去世了。后来，朱自清去伦敦访学，跟陈竹隐结了婚，又回到中国，在清华大学当教授。1948年，朱自清去世。

今天我解读的是朱自清的《背影》，这是一个很有意义的故事。作者当时是一个20岁的年轻人，祖母刚去世，父亲又刚好失业。父亲只好卖掉家里的东西还债，再借钱给祖母办丧事。祖母的葬礼结束后，作者要回北京上学，父亲要去南京找工作。父亲本来委托一个熟识的茶房送儿子去北京，后来还是不放心，又决定亲自送儿子去车站。作者觉得父亲过分担心，因为他已经20岁了，而且也往来北京好几次了。因为作者的行李太多，他们到了车站以后，得给脚夫付一些

"The View from the Rear" by Zhu Ziqing

Author: Carolyn Chen　Instructor: Kening Li　University of Michigan

> This article made me reflect and realize how much my parents love me.

Zhu Ziqing is a well-known writer who was born in China in 1898. He came from a poor family, but in 1916, he was admitted to Peking University and married his wife Wu Zhongqian. After graduating from university, in order to support his family, Zhu Ziqing started teaching in various places such as Hangzhou, Yangzhou, Shanghai, and Ningbo. At the same time, he also wrote many articles and poems, one of which is called "Spring." "Spring" is a concise and powerful prose that depicts the beauty, boundless vitality, and creativity of spring from various aspects. The work first writes about the expectation of spring, then sketches the outline of spring, and vividly depicts the four spring scenery of spring grass, spring flowers, spring breeze, and spring rain. Therefore, "Spring" is also known as Zhu Ziqing's most sincere prose. Now, in order to pass the Chinese National Mandarin Proficiency Test, students nationwide need to practice reading aloud this article. In 1929, his wife Wu Zhongqian passed away. Zhu Ziqing later went to London for a visit and in 1932, he married Chen Zhuyin before returning to China to teach at Tsinghua University. He passed away in 1948.

Today, I am analyzing Zhu Ziqing's "The View from the Rear," which is a profound story. At the time, the author was a twenty-year-old young man. His grandmother had just passed away and his father had just lost his job. His father had to sell things in their home to pay off debts and borrow money for his grandmother's funeral. After his grandmother's funeral, the author had to return to Beijing for school, and his father had to go to Nanjing to find work. His father had originally entrusted a friend to send his son to Beijing, but then he decided to

小费才能过去。作者觉得父亲讨价还价的时候，说话不够漂亮，不够标准，自己忍不住插嘴。上车后，作者说：“爸爸，你走吧。”可是他父亲还要去给他买橘子。买橘子要穿过铁道，从月台上跳下去，再爬上去。作者看着父亲步履蹒跚地走向铁道，拖着肥胖的身子努力爬上月台的背影，眼泪很快流下来了。作者感受到父亲对自己深深的爱。

这篇文章是我妈妈推荐的。理解故事的意思以后，我觉得这个故事令人很感动，也令人很伤感。作者当时 20 岁，我现在 19 岁，所以我更能理解他的感情。有时候也觉得我父母咄咄逼人，平常提醒我打扫房间，照顾弟弟，天天洗碗。如果他们不让我跟我朋友出去玩儿，我就觉得我一点儿自由都没有。可是，上大学以后，我发现自己对他们的态度有了重大转变。因为我到密歇根大学上学后，没有机会天天见到他们，所以非常想念他们。

这篇文章令我反思，意识到父母多么爱我。当父母真的不容易，尤其是作为移民子女的父母。从中国到美国来生活，压力很大。我知道爸爸妈妈工作很辛苦，为了让我、姐姐、弟弟得到更多的机会和更好的生活条件，他们每天辛勤地工作。最重要的是，他们每天都很用心地照顾我们。比如说，从小到大，每次我做作业的时候，父母都会切好水果，送到我的房间。我以前已经习惯他们给我切水果，而且也觉得切水果没什么。可是现在想起来，他们每天给我切水果都是为

personally send his son to the train station. The author thought his father was overly worried because the author was already twenty years old and had been to Beijing several times. Because the author had too much luggage, they had to pay some tips to the porters at the station. The author felt that his father's bargaining was not eloquent and embarrassing; he couldn't help but interject. After getting on the train, the author said, "Dad, you can go now." But his father still wanted to buy him oranges. Buying oranges required crossing the railroad tracks, jumping off the platform, and climbing back up. The author watched as his father walked toward the railroad tracks with his cumbersome body, struggling to climb up the platform, and tears quickly fell. The author realized how much his father loved him.

My mother recommended this article to me. After understanding the meaning of the story, I found it very touching and poignant. The author was twenty years old at the time, and I am now nineteen, so I can better understand his emotions. Sometimes I also feel that my parents are nagging me, reminding me to clean my room, take care of my younger brother, and wash dishes every day. If they don't let me leave my house and hang out with my friends, it can feel like I have no freedom at all. However, after going to college, I found that my attitude toward them has changed. After going to the University of Michigan, I didn't have the opportunity to see them every day, so I realized how much I missed them.

This article made me reflect and realize how much my parents love me. Being a parent is really not easy, especially being a parent of immigrant children. There's a lot of pressure moving from China to the United States. I know that my father and mother work very hard every day to provide my siblings and me with more opportunities and better living conditions. Most importantly, they care for us with love and compassion every day. For example, from when I was young until now, every time I did my homework, my parents would cut up fruit and bring it to my room. I used to take it for granted, but now I realize that they did it every day to help me focus on my studies. This example may not seem very special, but to me, it shows how much my parents love me and are always thinking about how to take care of me.

My favorite paragraph is when Zhu Ziqing describes his father's actions and appearance. I especially like Zhu Ziqing's writing style. He wrote, "But when he crossed the railway and climbed up to the other platform, it was not easy. He pushed off the upper platform with both

了让我集中精力好好学习。这个例子听起来一点儿也不特别，可是对我来说，这说明父母很爱我，天天在想怎样照顾好我。

我最喜欢的段落是朱自清描写父亲的动作和样子。我特别喜欢朱自清的写作风格。他写道："可是他穿过铁道，要爬上那边月台，就不容易了。他用两手攀着上面，两脚再向上缩；他肥胖的身子向左微倾，显出努力的样子。这时我看见他的背影，我的泪很快地流下来了。"这些句子让我感动和难过，我也特别同情他父亲。读了以后，我意识到，父母会逐渐衰老，身体也不会永远健康，所以我们更应该对他们心存感恩。我特别喜欢这篇文章，因为文章立意很深刻。虽然这篇文章很短，但文笔很优美，读者读过这篇文章后，能够理解文章的意图，能够更加理解和感激自己的父母。

hands and pulled himself up with his feet. His plump body leaned slightly to the left, showing his struggle. At that moment, I saw his back, and tears quickly flowed down my face." These sentences moved me and made me feel sad, and I also sympathized with his father. After reading this, I realized that parents will gradually age, and their health will not always be good, so we should be more grateful to them. I particularly like this article because it has a profound theme. Although it is short, the writing is beautiful, and readers can understand the emotion of the article and appreciate their parents even more after reading it.

华裔文学作品对我的影响

作者：蒋一乐　指导教师：陆原　爱荷华大学

> 要了解美国现代文化中这些至关重要且充满生机的组成部分，阅读华裔文学作品是一个很好的途径。

我一直对华裔文学作品非常感兴趣，所以我想和大家谈一谈美国华裔文学作品对我的影响。通过阅读华裔作家谭恩美的作品，通过阅读当代作家李翊云的小说，我听到了许多华侨华人的故事，了解了许多华人华侨的历史和文化，同时也对复杂的中美文化差异有了更深刻的理解。

几年前，我在高中的课上读了很多回忆录和小说，其中最让我赞叹的作品之一就是谭恩美的《喜福会》。这部小说讲述了二十世纪八十年代旧金山四对华裔母女的故事。故事中的女儿都是在美国长大的，在成长过程中，她们常常与母亲产生矛盾，小说内容也是作者本人经历的折射。谭恩美在一次采访中提到，父母希望她在成为一个美国人的同时，又能继承中式的思维方式，从而造成了家庭关系的紧张。这部小说对二元文化进行了探讨，作者幽默诗意的遣词造句十分引人入胜，为我展示了独特的中式家庭文化，使我对广阔的外部世界产生了强烈的好奇。

后来，我又喜爱上了作家李翊云的小说。那时我得知李翊云曾经在我现在就读的爱荷华大学研习过小说创作和创意写作，于是就对她的作品产生了好奇。

The Influence of Chinese American Authors' Works on Me

Author: Kyler Johnson   Instructor: Yuan Lu   University of Iowa

I am very interested in Chinese American authors' works. In this essay, I am going to write about the influence of Chinese American author's works on me. Through reading classic novels by authors like Amy Tan or more contemporary novels written by writer Yiyun Li, I get to know the stories, history and culture of Chinese people residing abroad and come to understand many of the complex differences between Chinese and American culture.

> Reading Chinese-American literature is a great way of understanding an important and living piece of American modern culture.

Several years ago, as a high school student, I read a variety of memoirs and novels for my classes, yet one of the most remarkable stories I encountered was Amy Tan's *The Joy Luck Club*. The novel follows four different mother-daughter relationships of Chinese Americans in the 1980s in San Francisco. The four daughters, having been brought up in America, often clash with their Chinese mothers.

This bicultural tension is something that Amy Tan herself faced growing up in the United States. In an interview, Tan said her parents wanted her to be American, yet they wanted her to hold on

李翊云出生在中国，而成年后的大部分时间都是在美国度过的。无论是讲述中国故事还是美国故事，描摹战争或是爱情，李翊云笔下的作品都与亲身经历过的文化冲突息息相关，这使得她的读者能以开放的视角，与主流社会中的边缘群体产生共情。

总的来说，作为一个突出的文学类型，美国华裔文学深入探讨了中美文化的差异，让读者对中华文化产生共鸣，同时也记录了与华裔移民相关的重大历史事件。因此，我认为，要了解美国现代文化中这些至关重要且充满生机的组成部分，阅读华裔文学作品是一个很好的途径。

to Chinese ways of thinking, and this caused a lot of tension. Her novel offers an intriguing exploration of bicultural heritage and, for me, it illuminated aspects of Chinese family culture that led me to be more curious about the larger world. Additionally, its humor and poetic nature makes an impactful read that can hook anybody.

Later, I fell in love with Yiyun Li's novels. What first drew me to Yiyun Li is that she studied both fiction and creative non-fiction at the University of Iowa, where I go to school. While having grown up in China, Yiyun Li has lived in the United States for over half her life. Whether set in China or America and whether following stories of war or of love, her stories speak to the culturally bifurcated life Yiyun Li herself has lived and they open up readers' mind to empathize with those on the outskirts of mainstream society.

As a whole, Chinese-American literature functions as a wonderful genre that explores aspects of both Chinese and American culture, evokes a strong echo in readers for Chinese culture and records impactful events related to Chinese immigration to America. As a result, reading Chinese-American literature is a great way of understanding an important and living piece of American modern culture.

我读唐诗《登鹳雀楼》

作者：喜儿　指导教师：温晓虹　休斯敦大学

我虽然是个美国人，但我的身体里流着中国人的血液，因为我母亲是个中国人。我希望能更多地学习中国文化，更多地了解我们家的历史。我最喜欢中国历史上的唐朝。对于唐代人来说，“敬、德、仁”是他们重要的行为标准。我想将唐代道德标准融入我的生活。我特别要说的是唐诗，这是因为好几首唐诗一直在激励我，使我能够克服困难，实现我的愿望。

> 这首诗不但鼓励人们要有韧性，充满勇气，而且要为自己的目标更加努力，只有更加努力才能看到最美丽的风景。

我想谈一谈唐朝诗人王之涣的《登鹳雀楼》。这首诗仅有四句二十个字，但是说的道理很深刻。下面是这首诗和我的解释：

白日依山尽，（美丽的风景和美好的未来，用山来做比喻）

黄河入海流。（也是美丽的风景和成功的未来，用水来做比喻）

欲穷千里目，（如果一个人想拥有更美好的未来，看到最好的风景）

更上一层楼。（那必须越来越努力，到最高峰才能成功）

这首诗不但鼓励人们要有韧性，充满勇气，而且要为自己的目标更加努力，只有更加努力才能看到最美丽的风景。在日常生活中，这首诗常常鼓励我不断地进步，不断地要求自己。最深刻的一次印象是几年前在中国的时候，我和四个朋

Reading the Tang Peom "Climbing the Stork Tower"

Author: Sierra Shepherd Instructor: Xiaohong Wen University of Houston

This poem not only encourages people to be resilient and courageous, but also to work harder for their goals. The most beautiful scenery can only be seen by working harder for what you want.

Although I am American, I have Chinese blood because my mother is Chinese. I wish to learn more about Chinese culture and the history of my family. I like the Tang Dynasty in Chinese history best. For people of the Tang Dynasty, "respect, virtue and benevolence" were their standards of conduct. I want to incorporate the moral standards of the Tang Dynasty into my life. I would like to talk about Tang poems in particular, because the poems of the Tang Dynasty have inspired me to overcome many difficulties and make my wish come true.

More specifically, I would like to talk about "Climbing the Stork Tower" by Wang Zhihuan, a poet of Tang Dynasty. The poem is very short, but it holds deep meanings. This is the poem and my interpretation of it: The bright sun sets past the mountains (beautiful scenery and a bright future, using mountains as a metaphor); The Yellow River flows into the sea (also a beautiful landscape and a successful future, with water as a metaphor).

If you wish to see a thousand miles (if one wants to have a better future and see all the best scenery), you must climb up one more floor (you must work harder and harder to reach a higher level to be more successful).

This poem not only encourages people to be resilient and courageous, but also to work harder for their goals. The most beautiful scenery can only be seen by working harder for what

友约好去登长城。登上长城是我从小的愿望，每次看到长城的图片和视频我都想要登上长城的最高峰。那是一个炎热的夏日，我们已经徒步走了三十多分钟，非常疲倦。最后每个人都想停下来。我也很累，但是天空在我眼前是如此美丽，而长城仍然在等着我登上最高峰。我想看到北京最美丽的景色。正当我犹豫想放弃时，王之涣的诗在我的脑海里出现了。我想看到那美丽的景色（白日依山尽，黄河入海流），但我知道，如果我想到达山顶（欲穷千里目），就必须不断攀登，挑战极限（更上一层楼）。我跟朋友们说了王之涣的这首诗，大家都觉得这首诗很激励人。我一直在心里反复地背诵这四句诗，觉得爬得更快了。就这样，我们克

you want. In my daily life, this poem often encourages me to keep improving and work harder for my goals. An example of this was when I was in China a few years ago. Four friends and I decided to take a journey to climb the Great Wall of China. Climbing up the Great Wall was a dream since my childhood. Every time I saw pictures and videos of the Great Wall, I wished to climb its highest peak. It was a hot summer day, we had been walking for more than thirty minutes, and we were very tired. In the end, everyone wanted to stop. I was tired too, but the sky held so much beauty and I still had not climbed to the highest peak. I wanted to see the most beautiful view of Beijing. Just when I was considering giving up, Wang Zhihuan's poem popped up in my mind. I wanted to see the beautiful scenery (The sun sets past the mountains, the Yellow River flows into the sea), but I know that if I want to reach the top of the mountain and see a beautiful view (If you want to see a thousand miles), I have to keep climbing and challenging myself to reach my goals (I must climb another level). I told my friends about this poem by Wang Zhihuan. Everyone found the poem very inspiring. I kept repeating those four lines in my mind and walked faster. As such, we overcame difficulties and kept moving forward. When we climbed to the top of the Great Wall, I felt so happy! Not only did I see all the beautiful scenery, but I was also very happy that I could encourage my friends to overcome difficulties together and "go to the next level!"

This poem not only helped me get through the challenges I encountered in various activities, but also helped me overcome the difficulties I encountered in my studies. This year has been the hardest year in my studies. I took advanced courses that required countless hours of study, especially my economics class. Economics is not my field of expertise nor is it my favorite subject. But I felt that since I was going to take this course, I had to learn it well. I studied an average of 15 hours a week, especially when I was about to take an exam, I studied 40 hours a week. Even after all that, I failed my first exam. I was very frustrated and felt like a failure. I almost dropped the class. However, whenever faced with difficulties, I would always think of this poem. Wang Zhihuan reminds me not to give up. If I want to have a successful future, I can't give up. Since then, I have been working harder and harder. By the end of the year, my grades in the class improved and I passed the course with a high score.

I love Tang poetry and the standard of life in the Tang Dynasty. Respecting others, being

服困难，不断向前。爬到长城的最高处时，我觉得好幸福！我不但看到了最好的风景，还为自己能鼓励朋友一起克服困难，“更上一层楼”而感到高兴！

这首诗不仅帮助我面对了各种活动中遇到的挑战，而且还让我克服了学习中遇到的困难。今年是我学习中最艰难的一年。我修了高级课程，需要无数小时的学习，特别是有一门经济学的课。经济不是我的喜好和专长，但是我觉得既然我要修这门课就得学好。我平均每周学习 15 个小时，尤其是即将参加考试时，我每周学习 40 个小时。即使这样，我的第一次考试还是没有通过。我感到非常沮丧，觉得自己很失败，差点儿放弃这门课。但是，每当遇到困难时，我就会想到这首诗。王之涣在提醒我不要放弃。如果我想有一个成功的未来，我就不能放弃。从那以后，我越来越努力。到年底，我的成绩提上来了，以高分通过了这门课。

我喜欢唐诗和唐朝的做人标准，尊重他人、有道德、善良、不断地进取、克服困难，对我来说是最重要的。虽然王之涣是一千多年前的中国诗人，但他的诗仍在引导我们今天的生活，不论是在中国、美国，还是在世界其他地方。

moral, kind, and constantly moving forward to overcome difficulties is the most important thing to me. Although Wang Zhihuan was a Chinese poet more than a thousand years ago, his poetry still guides our lives today, be it in China, the United States or the rest of the world.

三位诗人笔下的杨贵妃

作者：王一　指导教师：顾利程　西北大学

> 无论是哪一位诗人的描写，都反映了杨贵妃的一个侧面，都反映了那个时代对杨贵妃的理解。

作为一代传奇人物，杨贵妃的故事被无数文人骚客传颂至今。她有着倾国的容貌、显赫的地位与传奇的经历，无怪乎诸如李白、杜甫和白居易这样唐诗史上的名家也不能免俗，纷纷为她留下墨迹。关于杨贵妃，三人的作品贯穿始终的是一个“美”字，但是他们却采用了不同的艺术手法来描写主人公的美。

在李白的三首《清平调》中，他着重描写了杨贵妃亦真亦幻的仙容花貌。一句“云想衣裳花想容”，便用美丽的事物衬托出杨贵妃的如花似玉，挑起了读者对其样貌的浮想联翩；再一句“春风拂槛露华浓”，更将杨贵妃那绰约的身姿、如玉的肌肤深深印入读者的脑海。而后，李白更用虚幻女神嫦娥和汉朝丽人赵飞燕与杨贵妃对比，衬托出其令他人黯然失色的美。李白笔下的杨贵妃，美得沉鱼落雁，美得如花似玉，美得胜过天仙。

杜甫的《丽人行》却从另一个角度描写了杨贵妃的美。“绣罗衣裳照暮春，蹙金孔雀银麒麟”。如此富贵，这般雕琢，若不是杨贵妃，又有谁配得上呢？头上是“翠微㔩叶垂鬓唇”，身上是“珠压腰衱稳称身”，精致的头饰，贴身的华服，为杨贵妃本就肉感的身姿增添了几许沉甸甸的庄重，给杨贵妃如花似月的面容点

Imperial Consort Yang as Described by Three Poets

Author: Yi Wang Instructor: Licheng Gu Northwestern University

> Regardless of the poets' written descriptions, all their works reflect a specific aspect of Imperial Consort Yang and reveal the societal understanding of her character at that time.

As a generational legend, Imperial Consort Yang's story has been passed on by countless literati and poets to the present day. She has an extremely beautiful physical appearance, a prominent status, and legendary experiences. It is no wonder that famous poets from the Tang Dynasty including Li Bai, Du Fu, and Bai Juyi all couldn't help but write about her in their poetry, leaving permanent literary marks in history. When describing Imperial Consort Yang, the theme of the three poets' works is centered on "beauty," but they've employed different literary techniques to describe the beauty of the protagonist.

In his three-poem collection "Qingpingdiao," Li Bai focused on describing Imperial Consort Yang's beguiling and heavenly appearance. The sentence "I think of her silver clothing at the sight of drifting clouds and her stunning appearance at the sight of flowers" makes effective use of beautiful objects to show Imperial Consort Yang's exceptional flower-like beauty; the next sentence "Caressed by vernal breeze, freshened by morning dew" further ingrains Imperial Consort Yang's graceful figure and jade-like skin into the readers' minds. Later, Li Bai even incorporated the illusory goddess Chang'e and the Han Dynasty's beauty Zhao Feiyan into his works, bringing out Imperial Consort Yang's dazzling beauty that made the appearance of others pale in comparison. The Imperial Consort Yang described by Li Bai is so beautiful that she would make the wild geese alight and fish dive down for shame, so

缀了一抹金灿灿的魅力。杜甫笔下的杨贵妃，美得雍容华贵，美得高高在上，美得华光熠熠。

而在白居易的《长恨歌》中，杨贵妃却展现了另外一种美。美到了什么程度？“回眸一笑百媚生，六宫粉黛无颜色”。泱泱唐宫，里面的姑娘哪一个不是

beautiful that she was like flowers and jades, so beautiful that her beauty exceeded that of a goddess.

In his poem "The Beauty Walks," Du Fu chose to describe Imperial Consort Yang's beauty from another perspective: "Embroidered with peacocks in gold and unicorns in silver, her dress in rich silks shines so bright when spring is old," so rich, so flawless, if it isn't Imperial Consort Yang who is adorned with jewels, who else could be worthy of such splendor? On her head are "Emerald pendant leaves hanging down like silver threads," and on her body are the "perfectly fitted waistbands embroidered with pearls," the exquisite headdress and the close-fitting costumes add a dash of solemnity to Imperial Consort Yang's sensual figure, and adds a touch of golden charm to Imperial Consort Yang's flower and moon-like face. The Imperial Consort Yang described by Du Fu is so gracefully and luxuriously beautiful, so beautiful that she rises above all else, so beautiful that she shines brilliantly.

However, in Bai Juyi's "Eternal Sorrows," Imperial Consort Yang exhibits another type of beauty. How beautiful is she? "Turning her head she smiled so sweet and full of grace, that she outshone in six palaces the fairest face." In the Tang Palace, all the girls were unique and had appearances like peach blossoms. But only Imperial Consort Yang had the appearance of a goddess descended to the earth, making other beauties instantly become ordinary with the turn of her head and a smile. It's no wonder that "In the inner palace dwelt three thousand ladies fair, on her alone was lavished royal love and care." But the beauty of Imperial Consort Yang as written by Bai Juyi was not only limited to the appearance; moreover, it stemmed from the heart. When she took refuge with the emperor, even as a female, she was willing to sacrifice herself to save her husband and the future of the Tang Dynasty; she was truly respectable and valiant, even willing to defend her country "until she was killed before the steed." Afterwards, despite retiring to Mount Fairyland, she still didn't forget her lover's oath, "In the sky, we'd be two lovebirds flying wing to wing; on the earth, we'd be two branches twined together." The depth of her love and the extent of her courage and righteousness, how can it not make people exclaim and gasp? The Imperial Consort Yang described by Bai Juyi is so beautiful that she could captivate the country, so perpetually beautiful that even death wouldn't reduce her value, so impressively beautiful that she could move the sky above and shake the earth below.

人面桃花，应该都不是俗物，可是杨贵妃回眸一笑便令这些丽人变成庸脂俗粉。杨贵妃的确有天女下凡之容，无怪乎“后宫佳丽三千人，三千宠爱在一身”。然而，白居易笔下的杨贵妃的美不止于外表，更来自心灵。与唐明皇避难之时，她一届女流，竟然为了救自己的郎君，为了大唐的将来，宁愿牺牲自己，“宛转蛾眉马前死”，实属可敬。而后虽归隐仙山，但仍不忘情郎的誓言，“在天愿做比翼鸟，在地愿为连理枝”，可谓情至深，义至大，怎能不令人感叹唏嘘？白居易笔下的杨贵妃，美得倾国倾城，美得至死不渝，美得感天动地。

三位诗人对于杨贵妃的美有不同的描写和理解，也是与他们的经历及写作风格息息相关。作为一代浪漫派的代表人物，“诗仙”李白的写作手法飘逸不羁，天马行空，想象力丰富，所以笔下的杨贵妃才如同天女下凡一般。而杜甫作为一代“诗圣”，作品大多体现百姓疾苦，为民抱不平，“朱门酒肉臭，路有冻死骨”，所以笔下的杨贵妃虽然朱唇皓齿，但是奢靡浪费。在杜甫的眼里，美丽的杨贵妃的背后是老百姓的累累白骨。与前二者不同，白居易官位显赫，加之所处年代也相对较晚，杨贵妃早已成为一个传奇人物，故作者才会加入自己的想象，将杨贵妃的美描写得如仙如梦，让人如醉如痴，为之感叹伤神。

无论是哪一位诗人的描写，都反映了杨贵妃的一个侧面，都反映了那个时代对杨贵妃的理解。

The three poets have different descriptions and understandings of Imperial Consort Yang's beauty, which are closely related to their unique experiences and writing styles. As a representative of the romanticism era, "Fairy Poet" Li Bai's writing style is elegant and unrestrained, imaginative and full of creativity, so he writes about Imperial Consort Yang as if she is a goddess descending to earth. On the other hand, as the generational "Poet Sage," Du Fu's works mostly reflect the suffering and poverty of the common people, and he seeks to defend the people's rights. Therefore, although he describes Imperial Consort Yang's red lips and white teeth, she is also depicted as overly extravagant and wasteful: "While the rich wine and dine, the poor die of cold by the roadside." In Du Fu's eyes, Imperial Consort Yang's beauty is built on the sacrifices and bones of the common people. Unlike these two, Bai Juyi was a prominent official and lived in a later generation where Imperial Consort Yang had already become a legendary historical figure, so the author could freely incorporate his own imaginations. Bai Juyi described the beauty of Imperial Consort Yang as surreal and dream-like, making people feel captivated and disoriented.

Regardless of the poets' written descriptions, all their works reflect a specific aspect of Imperial Consort Yang and reveal the societal understanding of her character at that time.

《饮食男女》的精彩人物

作者：刘栗菁　指导教师：徐雅晴　西北大学

> 朱家的大事件都发生在用餐时间，是李安展示家庭动态的一种方式。

李安的《饮食男女》是一部很有趣的电影。给我留下深刻印象是老朱宣布自己和梁锦荣恋爱关系的场景。我很惊讶，因为我一直以为老朱和梁妈妈会结为夫妻，完全没想到竟然是老朱跟梁妈妈的女儿梁锦荣走到了一起。虽然我们看到老朱对梁锦荣的女儿珊珊非常宠爱，但我们没有看到老朱与梁锦荣关系的进展，所以我没想到会有这样的结局。我对这个结局不是很满意，因为惊喜没有得到回应，显得像一个情节的装饰。因为老朱太老了，而锦荣太年轻了，所以观众以为二者之间不会有任何关系。他们唯一的关系是老朱给锦荣的女儿珊珊做午饭。唯独这一点与主题有关。是什么东西把两个年龄如此悬殊的人联系到一起的呢？可能就是老朱做的那些诱人的饭菜。老朱和珊珊的关系，以至于和梁锦荣的关系，都是通过饮食建立的。这就完美地契合了这部电影的主题——饮食男女。

上课时，我们讨论了电影名字的由来，了解到片名来自孔子讲过的话。我以前并不完全理解“饮食男女”对这部电影的意义。听到王教授的解释以后，我终于懂了：朱家的大事件都发生在用餐时间，是李安展示家庭动态的一种方式。每个角色都使身边男女关系有所改变，这也导致了老朱家庭成员的人际关系的变化。无论是像二女儿朱家倩和小女儿朱家宁一样，从家里搬出去，还是像老朱和

Interesting Characters in *Eat Drink Man Woman*

Author: Kai Liu Instructor: Ya-ching Hsu Northwestern University

Ang Lee's *Eat Drink Man Woman* is a very interesting movie. What stood out to me was the scene when Lao Zhu announced his romantic relationship with Liang Jinrong. I was surprised because I had always thought Lao Zhu and Jinrong's mother would be married, but I didn't expect him to get together with the daughter, Liang Jinrong, at all. Although we saw Lao Zhu treating Liang Jinrong's daughter Shanshan very dotingly, we didn't see the progression of Lao Zhu's relationship with Liang Jinrong, so I wasn't expecting such an end. I was not very satisfied with the end because the surprise was not reciprocated and it appeared like a plot decoration. Because Lao Zhu is too old and Jinrong is too young, the audience thought there would be no connection between the two. The only relationship they have is that Lao Zhu makes lunch for Jinrong's daughter Shanshan. This is the only point that is relevant to the theme. What is it that brings two people of such disparate ages together? It could be the tempting meals that Lao Zhu cooks. Lao Zhu's relationship with Shanshan and with Liang Jinrong is established through food and drink. This fits perfectly with the theme of the movie – *Eat Drink Man Woman*.

The major events in the Zhu family all take place during mealtime, a way for Ang Lee to portray the family dynamic.

In class, we discussed the origin of the movie's title and learned that it came from the words of Confucius. I didn't fully understand the purpose of naming "*Eat Drink Man Woman*" to this movie before. After hearing Professor Wang's explanation, I finally got it: the major events in the Zhu family all take place during mealtime, a way for Ang Lee to portray the family dynamic. Each character brings about a change in the relationships between the men and

大女儿朱家珍一样，把家庭关系搞得一地鸡毛家。每个角色都经历了一拨又一拨的家庭变化。有的是爱情和住宿地点的外部变化，有的是胃口上的内部变化。不过最后，每个人都分别找到了属于自己的快乐。

我认为李安的《饮食男女》和他的另一部电影《喜宴》有一个共同点，就是它们都很重视父亲和子女的关系。在此之前，我从来没有看到过这类主题的电影。在我看过的电影里，亚裔美国人的故事大多是讲母亲和子女的关系。在李安的这两部电影里，父亲是一个被充分展现的角色，他们给读者留下了深刻的印象，在子女的生活中起着关键的作用。《饮食男女》和《喜宴》应该只是一个起点，我希望看到更多展示亚裔老年美国人（尤其是亚裔美国父亲）形象的电影。

women around them, which also leads to a change in the interpersonal relationships among Zhu's family members. Whether it's moving out of the family, as in the case of second and youngest daughters Zhu Jiaqian and Zhu Jianing, or making family relationships a mess of the family, as in the case of Lao Zhu and his oldest daughter Zhu Jiazhen, each character has gone through one set of family changes after another. Some are external changes in their romantic relationships and places to stay, and some are internal changes in their appetites. In the end, though, each person finds their own happiness separately.

One thing I think Ang Lee's *Eat Drink Man Woman* and his another movie *The Wedding Banquet* have in common is that they both place a lot of emphasis on the relationship between fathers and their children. Previously, I had never seen a movie with this type of theme. In the movies I had seen, most of the Asian-American stories were about the relationship between mothers and their children. In both of Ang Lee's movies, fathers are well-developed characters who leave a deep impression on the audience and play a key role in the lives of their children. *Eat Drink Man Woman* and *The Wedding Banquet* should only be a starting point, and I would like to see more nuanced portrayals of Asian fatherhood.

《我的少女时代》观后感

作者：赵心宁　指导教师：代德馨　爱荷华大学

> 一颗善良的、乐于助人的心，会带你走向幸福。

小时候，我是在内布拉斯加州长大的。因为内布拉斯加华人很少，所以除了我的家人以外，我没有机会认识很多华人。但是我还是想了解中国文化，所以我就开始找中国电影看。功夫电影、爱情电影、剧情片我都喜欢。我比较喜欢台湾拍的电影，最爱看的是一部叫作《我的少女时代》的电影，又好笑又暖心。

第一次看《我的少女时代》的时候，我正在台湾探望我的家人。当时，我快要上高中了，跟电影的女主角林真心一样，我不太自信，因为我的头发短短的，不太漂亮，跟她一样，蛮尴尬的。而且，我是一个混血儿，所以我感觉自己跟谁都不一样，总觉得自己跟这个世界格格不入。当看到电影里的林真心的时候，我觉得她跟我很像。看到林真心克服了重重困难，还找到了真爱，让我很高兴，因为我希望自己长大后能跟她一样。

我一直到现在都很喜欢这部电影，因为它的主题很有意义。《我的少女时代》的主题有善良、友谊和命运。第一个主题，善良是很重要的。电影的女主角林真心，真的是个有真心的人。在电影里，林真心认识了一个坏男生叫徐太宇。虽然一开始徐太宇欺负她，但是林真心还是每天辅导徐太宇功课。徐太宇是一个帮派大哥，很喜欢打架。因为担心徐太宇的身体，林真心一直都拜托他不要再打架了。

Reflections after Watching the Movie *Our Times*

Author: Serina Kendrick　Instructor: Dexin Dai　University of Iowa

> If you are dedicated to being a good person, have compassion, and love to help others, you will live a happy life.

As a kid, I grew up in Nebraska. Since there aren't many Chinese people in Nebraska, I didn't know many Chinese people other than my family. However, I still wanted to learn about Chinese culture, so I started watching Chinese movies. I liked to watch kung fu movies, romance movies, and dramas. My favorite Chinese movie is one called *Our Times* (《我的少女时代》), which is a funny and heart-warming movie made in Taiwan.

The first time I ever watched *Our Times,* I was in Taiwan visiting my family. At that time, I was about to start high school. Just like the heroine of the movie, Lin Truly, I was not very confident. I felt like I understood Truly's character well because my hair was short, I was not pretty, and I was awkward like her. In addition, I am of mixed blood, so I felt like I was different from everyone else. It made me so happy to see Truly really overcome these obstacles and find love. I wished to be like her when I grew up.

To this day, I've always loved *Our Times* because its themes are meaningful. The movie talks about kindness, friendship, and fate. The first topic of kindness spreads an important message. The heroine of the movie, Lin Truly, is really a sincere person. In the movie, Truly met a gangster boy named Xu Taiyu. Although at first Xu Taiyu bullied her, Lin Truly still helped him with his homework and encouraged him to study hard every day. Xu Taiyu was a gang leader who liked to get into fights. Out of worry about Xu Taiyu's health, Lin Truly always asked him not to fight. As time passed, the two of them became good friends because Truly

因为林真心是很真诚的人，徐太宇感觉他能在林真心身边做他自己。后来，他们两个就成了好朋友。他们的友谊非常美好，他们帮助对方克服了自己青春期的困难，所以最后林真心爱上了徐太宇，徐太宇也爱上了林真心。

可是那个时候，林真心以为徐太宇喜欢另一个女孩儿，所以她还帮着徐太宇跟那个女孩儿约会。因为林真心是非常无私的，在她心里，看到她爱的人高兴就够了，所以她不敢告诉徐太宇自己爱上他了。她只想看到自己的好朋友快乐，即使这让她很难过。

第二个主题，友谊，也很有意思。虽然这是一部爱情片，但是电影里花了更

was a sincere, kind person, making Xu Taiyu feel like he could be himself around her. Their friendship was beautiful and helped the two of them overcome personal problems together, so at the end the two protagonists fell in love with each other.

However, Lin Truly thought Xu Taiyu had a crush on another girl, so she helped Xu Taiyu to date the girl. Lin Truly was very selfless, in her heart, seeing the person she loved happy was enough. So, she did not dare tell Xu Taiyu she had fallen in love with him. She only wanted to see her good friend happy, even if it made her sad. The second theme, friendship, is also interesting. Although *Our Times* is a romance movie, it spends more time talking about friendship. When Lin Truly and Xu Taiyu became friends, they helped the other person overcome obstacles in life. I think this topic is very important because many young girls think that finding love is important, but finding good friends may be not that important. In the movie after Lin Truly got to know Xu Taiyu well, she realized that Xu Taiyu was an angry and violent person because his good friend died when he was a freshman in high school. Lin Truly used patience to help Xu Taiyu control his emotions after realizing what he had been through. Seeing Truly's kindness, Xu Taiyu started to be a good student, stopped fighting, and started to help other students just like Truly.

In addition to Lin Truly helping Xu Taiyu become a better person, Xu Taiyu also helped her. Xu Taiyu was a confident person, very different from Lin Truly. He found that Lin Truly always worried others didn't like her because she was not pretty enough. So he often encouraged Truly and told her how lovely she was. He helped her realize that it was other high school students being superficial if they couldn't find her kind and true.

The last theme is fate. Toward the end of the movie, Lin Truly and Xu Taiyu graduated from high school, and Xu Taiyu moved to the United States to go to college. Truly was not able to keep in touch with him. The two friends never dated, and never even realized they were in love with each other. One day, they met at an Andy Lau's concert. The two of them have been missing the other person all these years. Now, they finally had a chance to fall in love, as if fate brought them together. Because Lin Truly was a kind and sincere person since childhood, she finally found happiness.

Although *Our Times* looks like a simple romance movie from the outside, after watching

多时间讲友谊。林真心和徐太宇成为朋友的时候，他们都帮助对方克服了自己的问题。我觉得这个主题很重要，因为很多年轻的女孩儿觉得找到真爱很重要，对友谊却没有那么看重。在电影里，林真心跟徐太宇相处久了以后，才明白之所以徐太宇是个意气用事、容易生气的人，是因为他上高一的时候，他的好朋友去世了。林真心了解这个事情以后，她耐心地帮助徐太宇，让他更好地控制情绪。徐太宇看到了林真心的善良，在她的影响下，他开始当好学生，不但不打架了，还开始像林真心一样帮助别的学生。

除了林真心帮助徐太宇变成一个更好的人以外，徐太宇也帮助了林真心。徐太宇跟林真心很不一样，他非常自信。他发现林真心总是担心自己不够漂亮，得不到别人的喜欢。所以他总是鼓励林真心，告诉林真心她有多可爱。还开导她，那些看不到她的善良和真诚的人都是肤浅的。

最后一个主题就是命运。电影快结束的时候，林真心和徐太宇高中毕业了。徐太宇要去美国上大学，林真心也没办法一直跟他联络。他们从来没有跟对方告白过，都不知道已经爱上了彼此。有一天，他们终于在刘德华音乐会上重逢了。原来他们两个这些年竟然一直都在思念对方。现在，他们终于有机会相爱，就好像是命运的安排。因为林真心从小到大就是一个善良的、真诚的人，她终于收获了属于她的幸福。

《我的少女时代》看起来只是一部普通的爱情电影，可是看完后，你会接收到很多对少女很重要的讯息。这个电影告诉我们：不用担心任何人对你的印象不好。成长的过程中，大家都想当最聪明、最漂亮的人，可是这些东西不是一生中最重要的。一颗善良的、乐于助人的心，会带你走向幸福。

it, you will understand that it includes some important themes for girls. This movie shows us: Don't worry about what others think of you. When you are young, everyone wants to be the smartest and most popular person, but these things are not the most important things in life. If you are dedicated to being a good person, have compassion, and love to help others, you will live a happy life.

中国电影中的新女性

作者：吴敏　指导教师：解芳　弗吉尼亚军事学院

女性的职能从待在家里转变为走向社会。

女性在社会上的职能是什么？从古至今，女性在社会上的地位正逐渐发生改变。一开始，女性都在家里，扮演妈妈和妻子的角色。二十世纪以后，女性在社会上的职能改变了。她们不再希望做家庭主妇，而是希望走出家庭，去外面工作。在中国，这种改变可以从电影中看出来。比方说，《新女性》（1935），《红色娘子军》（1961）和《杜拉拉升职记》（2010），这些电影用艺术的形式向观众展现了女性在不同时期的社会地位。

《新女性》是1935年蔡楚生导演的一部默片。这部电影体现了二十世纪初期女性在社会上的地位和职能。当时，中国女性仍然禁锢在妻子和母亲的角色里。到了二十世纪三十年代，女性受到启蒙，想要独立生活。虽然这部电影是一部默片，但却显示了女性强有力的声音。她们要挣脱社会的枷锁，找到新的生活。

在这部电影里，女主人公韦明在上海一所学校做音乐老师。同时，她也写作，想要成为一名作家。校长王博士喜欢韦明，想让韦明做他的情妇。但韦明拒绝了王博士。王博士得不到韦明，就把她开除了。这个时候，韦明的姐姐带着韦明的孩子去上海找她。因为韦明的孩子生病了，需要很多钱看病。韦明丢了工作，希望通过写小说赚稿费，可是却受到了出版商的刁难。于是，韦明只好去做妓女。谁知，她的第一个客人竟然是王博士，这让韦明很羞愧，她逃跑了。后来，韦明

The Changing Roles of Women in Chinese Movies

Author: Lauren Wolf Instructor: Laura Xie Virginia Military Institute

> Women's roles have developed from staying at home to going to the society.

What are the roles of women in society? Women's roles have been changing throughout history. At first, women were at home and played the roles of wives and mothers. However, with the turn of the 20th century, they've refused to be identified as housewives and aspired to go out of their families to pursue professional career paths. In China, these changes can be seen in numerous movies, such as *New Woman* (1935), *The Red Detachment of Women* (1961), and *Go Lala Go*! (2010), which artistically manifest women's different social status in society during different periods.

The silent movie *New Woman*, made in 1935, directed by Cai Chusheng, shows women's status and roles in society in the early 20th century. At that time, women were still mostly being confined to the norm of wives and mothers. Into the 1930s, women were enlightened and beginning to search for their own means of living independently. This movie, even though it is silent, shows a powerful message of the struggles of women attempting to escape the expectations of society and search for their own path in China.

In this movie, Wei Ming works as a music teacher for a girls' school, harboring the dream of becoming a writer. Dr. Wang, the school principal, likes Wei Ming and wants her to become his concubine. Wei Ming ignores his advances. Dr. Wang, angered by Wei Ming's rejection, retaliates against Wei Ming and fires her. At the same time, Wei Ming's older sister who takes care of Wei Ming's daughter comes to Shanghai to see her as they are in need of money because of her daughter's disease. Now that Wei Ming has lost her income as a teacher, and she hopes to receive payment from the novel she has written. But the publisher refuses to pay

的孩子死了，韦明也选择了自杀。她的朋友发现她自杀，把她送到了医院。韦明在临死前觉醒了，她说：“我想生活，我想报仇。”

在《新女性》这部电影里，韦明试图过独立的生活，可是她没能成功。因为在当时的社会，人们对女性的期待就是漂亮的“花瓶”，待在家里。“新女性”指的就是韦明。她不想依靠男性，想要在社会上独立生存。但女性为此要经历很多困难和挑战。男性常常压制女性，利用女性。电影里的男性都想得到韦明，得不到就想破坏她。韦明被逼到了绝路，所以才在临死前喊着要报仇，要跟伤害她的人做斗争。

any compensation. Under such harsh circumstances, Wei Ming decides to prostitute herself. Unexpectedly, her first client is Dr. Wang. Wei Ming feels so embarrassed that she runs away. She helplessly watches her daughter die, then commits suicide afterwards. Her friend finds her and takes her to hospital. Before she dies, Wei Ming is awakened and cries out, "I want to live. I want to revenge."

In the movie *New Woman*, Wei Ming tries to live independently, but fails in her attempts. Because at that time, women were expected to stay at home and serve as pretty "vases." "New Woman" refers to Wei Ming, who struggles to live independently without the help of men. She faces many difficulties and challenges because of her struggles. Men often suppress women and make use of them. The men in the movie all want to have Wei Ming, and destroy her as they fail to have her. Wei Ming is driven to desperation, so she cries at her last breath to revenge and fights against those who hurt her.

The movie *The Red Detachment of Women*, made in 1961, directed by Xie Jin, shows the change of women's roles under the leadership of the Communist Party of China. In this movie, Wu Qionghua is a maidservant of the landlord Nan Batian and suffers from his torture in his underground prison. She is rescued by the Party Representative, Hong Changqing, and gets free. Guided by Hong Changqing, she joins the Women's Detachment of Red Army. Her political consciousness improves very fast. She has made mistakes, but corrected them soon. Later, Wu Qionghua sneaks into Nan Batian's fort and plans to capture Nan Batian alive. However, the crafty Nan Batian escapes and reports the situation to the Kuomintang. The Red Army is besieged by the Kuomintang. In a battle to cover the retreat, Hong Changqing is killed. After that, Wu Qionghua becomes the successive Party Representative. She organizes an operation to destroy Nan Batian's forces and has Nan Batian executed.

This movie represents how the oppressed and enslaved women are able to grow into revolutionaries and earn respect in the male-dominated military. The female characters in this movie are all "new" women as they participate in political affairs and can be good leaders. *The Red Detachment of Women* differs from *New Woman* in numerous ways. First, the heroine in *The Red Detachment of Women* escapes from miserable life. In the past, she was oppressed by men. But in the new society, she gets free. Next, the men in *The Red Detachment of Women* do not

《红色娘子军》是1961年谢晋导演的一部电影。这部电影展示了共产党领导下的女性社会地位的改变。在电影里，女主人公吴琼花是地主南霸天家的丫头。她被关在地牢里，受尽折磨。后来吴琼花被一个叫洪常青的党代表救了，获得了自由。洪常青鼓励吴琼花加入红色娘子军。吴琼花加入娘子军以后，思想觉悟提高得很快。她犯过错误，但是很快改正了。后来，吴琼花跟洪常青混进南霸天家，打算活捉南霸天，可是南霸天逃跑了，并且把红色娘子军的情况报告给国民党。国民党派部队包围娘子军，在撤退的时候，洪常青为了掩护娘子军，英勇牺牲了。洪常青死后，吴琼花成了党代表。她重新组织力量，捣毁了南霸天的巢穴，处死了罪大恶极的南霸天。

在这部电影里，我们看到受压迫受奴役的女性逐渐成长为革命者的经历。在男性占据优势的军队里，女性也得到了尊重。电影里的女性都是"新女性"，因为她们参加战斗，也参与政治，并能成长成为优秀的领导者。《红色娘子军》和《新女性》有很多不同的地方。首先，《红色娘子军》里的女主人公逃离了悲惨的生活。在过去，她受到男性的压迫，在新社会里，她得到了自由。其次，《红色娘子军》里的男性不在乎女性的样貌，他们鼓励女性跟随共产党，争取自己的权利。当然，这也说明，男性给予女性这种争取权利的力量。男性是女性的老师，指导她们成长。与《新生活》中的情形比较，女性在新社会中的地位取得了一定的进步。

《杜拉拉升职记》是2010年徐静蕾导演的一部电影。这部电影表现了女性在当今社会的生活现状。这部电影的女主人公杜拉拉是一个二十多岁的女性。她在一家国际大公司工作，有很多想法，能力很强，很快引起了上司的注意，并且在爱情和工作之间取得平衡。杜拉拉也是一位"新女性"。她在社会上独立地生活、工作。跟《新女性》不一样，杜拉拉对她的生活有更多的掌控。跟《红色娘子军》

mind women's appearance. They encourage women to follow the Communist Party and fight for their own rights. This manifests that men give women the power of fighting for their rights. They play the roles of mentoring women's growth. Compared to the situation in *New Woman*, women's status in the new society has been improved to some extent.

The modern movie *Go Lala Go!*, shown in 2010 and directed by Xu Jinglei, aims to show a much more modern point of view on how women function in current Chinese society. In this movie, Du Lala is a woman in her late twenties who works in a prestigious international firm. Hard-working, dedicated, and overflowing with ideas and energy, she quickly catches the eyes of her superior and finds the balance between her love life and her career. Du Lala is a "new woman" as well. She lives and works independently in society. Unlike the characters in *New Woman*, Du Lala has more control of her life. And unlike the characters in *The Red Detachment of Women*, Du Lala does not need the encouragement and assistance of men. However, this movie still demonstrates how men do not want women to be as capable as them and hinder women's

也不一样，杜拉拉不需要男性的鼓励和帮助。但是，男性阻碍女性在社会上前进，却依然存在。在电影里，男性不想看到女性跟男性一样能干。所以在工作上，女性要付出更多的努力。

这三部电影都显示了女性在社会地位和职能上的变化。女性的职能从待在家里转变为走向社会。在当代中国，人们可以看到女性正在成长。今天，大部分中国女性都有自己的工作。她们成为导演、学者、总经理等等；很多女性以党代表、人大代表的身份参与政治，参与国家事务管理。研究女性在社会上地位和职能的变迁，可以帮助我们理解过去、当下以及未来的中国女性。

progress in society. Therefore, women need to make more efforts in their career.

All of these three movies show the changes of women's status and function in society. Women's roles have developed from staying at home to going to the society. Today, Chinese women are seen to be growing. Most of them have their own jobs. They take the roles of directors, scholars, executive managers, etc. Many women participate in the management of political and national affairs. The research on the ever-changing roles of women in society will help with a better understanding of the past, present and future of Chinese women.

休闲冥想

作者：李宇晨　朱乐怡　张栋圭　指导教师：齐润清　科罗洛达大学

不让自己的生活被别人影响，过既简单又幸福的生活。

现代许多年轻人每天忙着上班，没有多少自己的时间，很难放松下来。有的时候，我们被各种小事所困扰，很难做到享受生活。如果你想给你自己休息放松的时间，可以试一试冥想。躺在草地上，慢慢地闭上眼睛。天气很暖和，阳光很好，空气很新鲜。不知不觉，进入梦乡。现在，想象你不是在草地上，而是在一个中国重庆有名的茶馆儿里。

在空气中，你可以闻到茶叶的香味。你看，有很多人在茶馆儿里一边喝茶，一边聊天儿。你可以听到人们聊天儿的声音，茶杯的叮当声和打麻将的声音。哇，你闻到了吗？你可以闻到豆腐花儿还有辣馄饨的香味，它们闻起来很好吃。

吃完小吃后，你可以请采耳师帮你掏耳朵。先掏耳朵，再做头、颈、肩部的按摩，能让你感觉飘飘欲仙，不知不觉进入梦乡。之后你会觉得很放松。现在你的耳朵也干净了，所以你听得更清楚了。你听到有人在前面说话。在茶馆儿的前面有一个老人在讲评书。这听起来是个有意思的故事，他的声音很舒缓。你累不累？如果累了，你可以坐在竹椅上，竹椅坐着很舒服，可以半躺着睡一觉。闭上眼睛一分钟……

现在你从冥想之旅中回来了。你明白了，你可以通过冥想让自己放松一下，这很容易，也很舒服。每天在我们的生活中会有很多事情让我们感觉有压力。

Leisure Meditation

Author: Nelsen Brandon Joyce Chu Jang Donggyu Instructor: Runqing Qi
University of Colorado Boulder

Don't let your life be easily affected by others – just live a simple and happy life.

Today, many young people are busy with work every day and have very little time for themselves, so it's difficult to relax. Sometimes, we're troubled by all kinds of trivial things, so it's difficult to truly enjoy life. If you want to give yourself some time to rest and relax, you can try meditation. Lie down on the grass and slowly close your eyes. The weather is warm, the sun is shining brightly, and the air is fresh. Before you know it, you fall into dreamland. Now, imagine that you're not on the grass, but in a famous teahouse in Chongqing, China.

生活已经很难了，不要让每件不开心的小事影响你。相反，每天留给自己几分钟时间休息。休息的时候，不要去想已经发生过的事情或者还没到来的事情，只关注现在就好。这样，你可以让你自己真正放松下来，休息以后你会感觉舒服一点儿。

周末的时候，你可能不太累，可以做很多别的事情。与其躺在床上看视频，不如花时间跟你的朋友在一起。比如，你们可以一起聊天儿、烧烤、钓鱼、玩儿游戏等等。如果你真的学会了如何让生活简单一点儿，你就会感觉非常舒服，非常享受。

生活就是由小事组成的，慢慢来，观察你的周围。做让你自己快乐的事。不让自己的生活被别人影响，过既简单又幸福的生活。

In the air, you can smell the aroma of tea leaves. You can see a lot of people drinking tea while chatting in the teahouse. You can hear people talking, clinking teacups, and playing mahjong. Wow, can you smell it? It's the delicious smell of condensed bean curd jelly and spicy wonton.

After eating the snacks, you can ask an ear picker to help you clean your ears. After ear picking, they massage your head, neck, and shoulders, making you feel light like a fairy as you unconsciously fall into a deep slumber. Afterwards, you will feel very relaxed – since your ears are also clean, and you'll be able to hear things more clearly. You hear someone talking up front. In front of the teahouse, an old man is telling a story. It sounds like an interesting story, and his voice is soothing to the ear. Are you tired? If you're tired, you can sit on the bamboo chair, which is very comfortable and allows you to sleep. Close your eyes for a minute...

Now, you're back from your meditation journey. You realize that you can make yourself feel relaxed by meditating, an easy and comfortable process. Every day, there are many things in our lives that make us stressed out. Life is already hard, so you shouldn't let every unpleasant little thing affect you. Instead, you should take a few minutes out of each day to rest. When you take a break, don't think about what's already happened or what's yet to come; just focus on the present. This way, you can allow yourself to truly relax, and you'll feel more comfortable after being well-rested.

On weekends, you might not feel too tired, so you can do a lot of other things. Rather than lying in bed to watch videos, spend some time with your friends instead. For example, you can chat, barbecue, fish, play games, the list goes on. If you've really learned how to make life a little simpler, you'll feel that life is very comfortable and enjoyable.

Life is made of various small components, so take your time and observe your surroundings. Do what makes you happy. Don't let your life be easily affected by others – just live a simple and happy life.

时事评论

Current Affairs Commentary

导 读

本板块的十三篇文章都属于时事评论。一篇好的时事评论应该有一个引人注目的题目。开篇第一段就要破题，介绍本文的主要内容，譬如发生了一件什么事情，一个人怎么了，周围的人有什么反应等等。在第一段里，作者可以开诚布公地表达自己对这一事件的看法。第二段就可以分析这个事件的来龙去脉，以及对社会的影响，对环境的影响。譬如说为什么发生了这样的事情，在多大范围内产生了作用，对将来会有什么影响。最后一段可以提出解决问题的建议，譬如如何管控分歧，如何消除误会，如何避免战争等等。

读者可以先看一看这十三篇文章的题目是否醒目:《北京冬奥会》《我看ChatGPT》《网络啊，网络》《城市的另一面》《科幻、人工智能和中国梦》《浅谈中国的绿色信贷政策》《中国的城镇化与北漂现象》《甲烷监测卫星及其影响》《风能在中国》《以和为贵》《中国不是美国的敌人》《哈佛大学中国论坛有感》《中美互惠互利，健康竞争》。看到以上这些题目以后，读者就可以大略知道每篇文章会讨论什么问题了。

给文章命题以后，再来看看一篇文章是怎么破题的。《北京冬奥会》的第一段就写道：“2022 年北京更是受到全世界的关注，这不仅因为北京是历史上第一个既举办夏季奥运会又举办冬季奥运会的城市，是‘双奥之城’，也是因为面对疫情这样特殊的挑战，北京兑现承诺，做了充分的准备，为全世界奉献了一场精彩的体育盛事——2022 年冬奥会！”《我看 ChatGPT》的第一段写道：“ChatGPT很厉害，几乎什么问题都能回答。你可以让它帮你写一篇关于历史的文章，设计一个计算机程序评论……”《网络啊，网络》第一段就写道：“这篇文章将以网络

Introduction

The thirteen essays in this section are all related to commentaries on current affairs. A commentary on current affairs should have a catchy title. The opening paragraph should introduce the main content of the essay, such as describing an event that has taken place, the situation of a person, or the reactions of people around them. In the first paragraph, the author can frankly express his/her own views on the event. The second paragraph analyzes the background and context of the event, as well as its social and environmental impact. For example, why the event occurred, what scale of impact it had, and what implications it might have for the future. The final paragraph makes suggestions for solving the problem, such as how to manage disagreements, eliminate misunderstandings, avoid conflicts and wars, etc.

Readers can first take a look at whether the titles of these thirteen essays are eye-catching: "The Beijing Winter Olympics," "My Views on ChatGPT," "The Internet, ah, the Internet!" "The Other Side of the City," "Sci-Fi, AI and the Chinese Dream," "China's Green Credit Policy," "China's Urbanization and the Beijing Floaters," "Methane Satellites and Their Impact," "Wind Power in China," "Harmony Is Most Valuable," "China Is Not the Enemy of the United States," "My Thoughts on Harvard College China Forum," and "Mutually-beneficial 'Healthy Competition' between the U.S. and China." After reading these titles, readers can have a rough idea of what each essay will discuss.

After assigning titles to the essays, let's examine how an essay begins. The first paragraph of "The Beijing Winter Olympics" states that in the face of the challenges posed by the pandemic, "In 2022, Beijing has attracted worldwide attention; not only is it the first city in history to host both the Summer and Winter Olympics, becoming the 'double Olympic city,' but it also, despite the special challenge of the pandemic, fulfilled its commitments, made full preparations, and dedicated a wonderful sports event to the world – the 2022 Winter Olympic Games!" In the first paragraph of "My Views on ChatGPT," the author writes, "ChatGPT is very powerful and is able to respond to nearly any query. You can use it to help you write

为例，分析科技发展对社会的影响。”

破题之后，接着就是对这个问题从不同的角度进行不同层次的讨论，特别是要讨论出现问题的缘由。在《中国的城镇化与北漂现象》一文中，作者指出：“国际投资和经济发展使许多城市迅速繁华起来，从而吸引了大量人口涌向城市。”在分析地球温室效应的缘由的时候，《甲烷监测卫星及其影响》的作者明确指出，“动物在生长过程中都会产生甲烷。科学家们发现，大气中甲烷浓度上升会加剧地球表面温室效应。”

发现了问题的缘由和影响范围以后，作者就应该提出解决问题的方法。《浅谈中国的绿色信贷政策》一文的作者写道：“要想知道一个政策好不好，我们首先要明确这项政策的目标，其次需要追踪持续研究，随时调整政策，最后我们要密切关注这个政策产生的实际效果。”在讨论如何改善中美关系的时候，《以和为贵》的作者强调：“我们应该放下不同的政治观点，坐下来认真讨论这些问题。”《中美互惠互利，健康竞争》的作者建议道：“中国和美国应及时设计一个有远见的应对气候变化的方案，设计一个‘健康竞争’方案，竞争建设发展中国家的绿色经济。”《哈佛大学中国论坛有感》的作者强调说：“中美关系的改善需要两国年轻一代的合作，需要媒体的合作，需要政治家的远见卓识，想要打败对手的零和思维只会毁掉两国。”

读完这篇导读以后，读者可以从批判的角度来欣赏本板块内十三篇时事评论的题目、首段的破题介绍、中间的解释分析以及结尾的总结建议。

a history essay, design a computer program..." The first paragraph of "The Internet, ah, the Internet" begins with, "Using the internet as an example, this article will analyze the impact of technological development on society."

After setting up the topic, the next step is to discuss it from different perspectives and levels, particularly focusing on the reasons behind the issues. In the essay "China's Urbanization and the Beijing Floaters," the author points out, "Foreign investment and economic development have allowed many cities to prosper rapidly, attracting swaths of people to urban areas." When analyzing the causes of the global greenhouse effect, the author of "Methane Satellites and Their Impact" explicitly states, "Plants and animals produce methane when they grow. Scientists have found that rising concentrations of methane in the atmosphere can exacerbate the greenhouse gas effect on the Earth's surface."

Once the causes and scope of influence of the issue have been identified, the author should propose solutions to the problem. In the essay "China's Green Credit Policy," the author writes, "To determine whether or not a policy is good, first you need to clearly understand the goal of the policy. Secondly, you must continuously follow up with research. Following this, you need to pay close attention to the practical effects of the policy." When discussing how to improve Sino-U.S. relations, the author of "Harmony Is Most Valuable" emphasizes, "We should put aside our prejudices and different political opinions, and sit down to discuss these issues seriously." The author of "Mutually-beneficial 'Healthy Competition' between the U.S. and China" suggests, "China and the United States should soon develop a far-sighted plan to deal with climate change and design scheme of 'healthy competition' to help developing countries build green economies." In the essay "My Thoughts on Harvard College China Forum," the author emphasizes, "The improvement of Sino-U.S. relations requires the cooperation of the younger generation of the two countries, the cooperation of the media, and the foresight of statesmen. The zero-sum mentality of wanting to defeat the opponent will only destroy the two countries."

After reading this section, readers can appreciate the titles, introductory paragraphs, analytical discussions, and concluding recommendations of the thirteen commentaries on current affairs in this section from a critical perspective.

北京冬奥会

作者：银杰瑞　指导教师：纪晶晶　西北大学

体育是无国界的！

北京——中国的首都——是中国的文化和政治中心。这座城市是传统与现代建筑的完美结合，所以是每个人一生中都必须去参观的！2022年北京更是受到全世界的关注，这不仅因为北京是历史上第一个既举办夏季奥运会又举办冬季奥运会的城市，是“双奥之城”，也是因为面对疫情这样特殊的挑战，北京兑现承诺，做了充分的准备，为全世界奉献了一场精彩的体育盛事——2022年冬奥会！

今年冬奥会开始后，我一直在看。在所有的赛事里，我最关注滑雪，在所有的滑雪运动员里，我又最关注谷爱凌。

谷爱凌是中国运动员，可是是在美国出生长大的。她现在住在加州，是斯坦福大学的学生。我喜欢她主要有三个原因。首先，她是一个特别棒的运动员。她从小就非常努力地练习滑雪，她的付出最终有了回报。在2022年的奥运会上，她赢了两场比赛，获得了两个项目的金牌，一个项目的银牌。

我喜欢谷爱凌的另外一个原因是我也很喜欢滑雪。很小的时候，我在瑞士住了一年。在瑞士我没上学，只练习滑雪！在那里我了解了

The Beijing Winter Olympics

Author: Jared Silver Instructor: Jingjing Ji Northwestern University

Sports know no borders!

Beijing – the capital of China – is the cultural and political center of the nation. The city is a perfect combination of traditional and modern architecture, making it a must visit for all at some point in their life! In 2022, Beijing has attracted worldwide attention; not only is it the first city in history to host both the Summer and Winter Olympics, becoming the "double Olympic city," but it also, despite the special challenge of the pandemic, fulfilled its commitments, made full preparations, and dedicated a wonderful sports event to the world – the 2022 Winter Olympic Games!

I've been watching the Winter Olympics since its commencement this year. Out of all the competitions, I pay the most attention to skiing, and among all the skiers, to Eileen Gu.

Eileen Gu is a Chinese athlete, but she was born and raised in the United States. She now lives in California and is an undergraduate at Stanford University. I like her for three main reasons. First, she's an amazing athlete! She has practiced skiing zealously since she was a child, and her hard work finally paid off. At the Olympics in 2022, she won gold medals in two events and silver medal in one.

Another reason I like Eileen Gu is that I also love to skiing. When I was young, I lived in Switzerland for a year. While there, I never went to school, just skied! It was there that I learned about many different types of skiing, my favorite being freestyle skiing. Eileen Gu is a fantastic freestyle skier. I hope that one day I can win the Olympics like her.

Besides this, Eileen Gu's success has inspired millions of young Chinese girls to start skiing. I think this is her greatest achievement: her positive impact on the Chinese community (in China and abroad). Gu has a dual cultural background of China and the United States.

许多不同类型的滑雪。我最喜欢的是自由式滑雪。谷爱凌是非常出色的自由式滑雪运动员。我希望有一天我可以跟她一样拿奥运会冠军。

除此之外，谷爱凌的成功鼓励了数百万年轻的中国女孩儿开始滑雪。我觉得这是谷爱凌最大的成就：她对华人社会（中国以及海外）的积极影响。谷爱凌具有中美双重文化背景，她在美国出生长大，但她的家人来自中国。谷爱凌作为中西方文化的桥梁，她这次参加冬奥会，美国和中国都有很多支持者。她的参赛经历也是体育精神的最佳展示，体育是无国界的！

Born and raised in the States, but with family ties from China. Acting as a bridge between the Chinese and Western cultures, when Gu participated in the Winter Olympics, she had many supporters from both the United States and China. Her competition experience is the best demonstration of sportsmanship and the idea that sports know no borders!

我看 ChatGPT

作者：蒋大为　指导教师：顾利程　西北大学

ChatGPT 是一个聊天儿机器人，是一个可以回答用户提问或者跟用户聊天儿的计算机程序。ChatGPT 很厉害，几乎什么问题都能回答。你可以让它帮你写一篇关于历史的文章，设计一个计算机程序评论，总结一篇文章，你甚至都可以让它帮你写一首歌或者一首诗。ChatGPT 是 OpenAI 公司设计的，于 2022 年 11 月上线。OpenAI 是美国的一家人工智能公司，由很多很有名的商人和计算机科学家于 2015 年投资创建。比如，埃隆・马斯克（Elon Musk）和彼得・泰尔（Peter Thiel）就是这家公司创始人中的两位佼佼者。这个公司也设计了其他软件，像 Dall-E——一个根据书面文字生成图像的人工智能系统。

ChatGPT 是一个聊天儿机器人，是一个可以回答用户提问或者跟用户聊天儿的计算机程序。

ChatGPT 比其他的搜索软件更有用，因为普通的搜索软件只能给用户一些链接或者网站，用户得自己查这些资料，而且有时候搜索软件给的资料有可能跟用户问的问题没有关系。可是，ChatGPT 会帮你总结网上的全部资料，然后写一个相当全面的总结报告。用户甚至可以告诉 ChatGPT 他们想要什么样的报告。这样，用户就可以节约很多的时间和精力去做更有创造性的工作。

我也用过 ChatGPT，觉得很好用。比如说，如果我有问题，但是在网上找不到答案时，我就会问 ChatGPT。如果 ChatGPT 给的答案不正确，用户可以告诉 ChatGPT 哪里错了，然后 ChatGPT 会立即改进它的回答。更加令人惊讶的是，如果十几个人同时要 ChatGPT 给他们写一篇文章，而且输入同样的指令，ChatGPT

My Views on ChatGPT

Author: David Jiang Instructor: Licheng Gu Northwestern University

ChatGPT is a chatbot, a program that is capable of conversing with and answering the questions of a user. ChatGPT is very powerful and is able to respond to nearly any query. You can use it to help you write a history essay, design a computer program, summarize an article, or even compose a song or poem. ChatGPT was designed by a company called OpenAI, and was made available to the public in November, 2022. OpenAI is an Artificial Intelligence company based in the United States, and was founded in 2015 by many renowned businessmen and computer scientists. For example, Elon Musk and Peter Thiel were some of the brilliant minds behind Open AI. This company was also responsible for designing other programs, such as Dall-E, an AI program that generates images based on written text.

ChatGPT is a chatbot, a program that is capable of conversing with and answering the questions of a user.

ChatGPT is more useful than other search engines because ordinary search engines can only provide users with links or relevant websites. Users have to browse the websites for answers themselves, and sometimes the links recommended by ordinary search engines have nothing to do with the query at all. In contrast, ChatGPT scans all available information on the internet, and then writes a summary report of the findings for the user. The user can even specify how they want their report to be written, saving lots of time and energy for more creative endeavors.

I have used ChatGPT in the past, and found it very convenient. For example, if I have a question that I cannot find the answer to online, I'll just use ChatGPT. If ChatGPT's answer is wrong, the user can even tell ChatGPT what the error is, and ChatGPT will immediately correct its future responses. Even more surprising, if several users ask ChatGPT to write them

竟然可以给这十几个人十几份内容不完全相同的文章。

2022 年年底，如果你要用 ChatGPT 的话，你得等好几个小时，因为它的服务器带宽不够大，而用的人又太多。后来，OpenAI 增加了 ChatGPT 的服务器带宽，用户访问速度就快多了。

再过几年，因为 ChatGPT 的发展和广泛使用，可能会让很多人失去工作。ChatGPT 几乎可以用在每一个行业。比如说，秘书的工作也能用 ChatGPT 来做，因为 ChatGPT 已经在设计会管理时间的电脑程序。很快甚至连计算机工程师都会受到影响，因为 ChatGPT 现在已经可以写计算机代码了。

ChatGPT 是人工智能的一个新发明。虽然它还很新，但已经是一个很厉害的工具了，而且会越来越厉害。目前谁都不知道人工智能会发展成什么样子，人类

an essay at the same time about an identical prompt, the essays that ChatGPT generates for them will all be different from one another.

If you wanted to use ChatGPT at the end of 2022, you had to wait several hours because there were too many users, and the servers did not have enough bandwidth to process all the requests at once. Afterwards, OpenAI increased ChatGPT's server bandwidth, so users can better access the program.

In a few years, due to ChatGPT's development and widespread use, many people may lose their jobs. ChatGPT is applicable to nearly every single industry. For instance, secretarial work can be replaced with ChatGPT, which is already capable of designing programs for time management. Soon, even computer engineers will be affected since ChatGPT already has the ability to write code.

ChatGPT is a novel development in Artificial Intelligence. Even though it is very new, it is already a very powerful tool that will be more awesome in the future. At this point, no one knows how AI will develop in the coming years, or if humans will be able to control it. I hope that AI engineers will consider these questions and give us a reassuring answer.

Currently, we don't have any regulation regarding AI. Hopefully, the government can quickly craft the appropriate legislation. A pressing issue right now is students often use ChatGPT to cheat. Because ChatGPT can help students write essays, students can get good

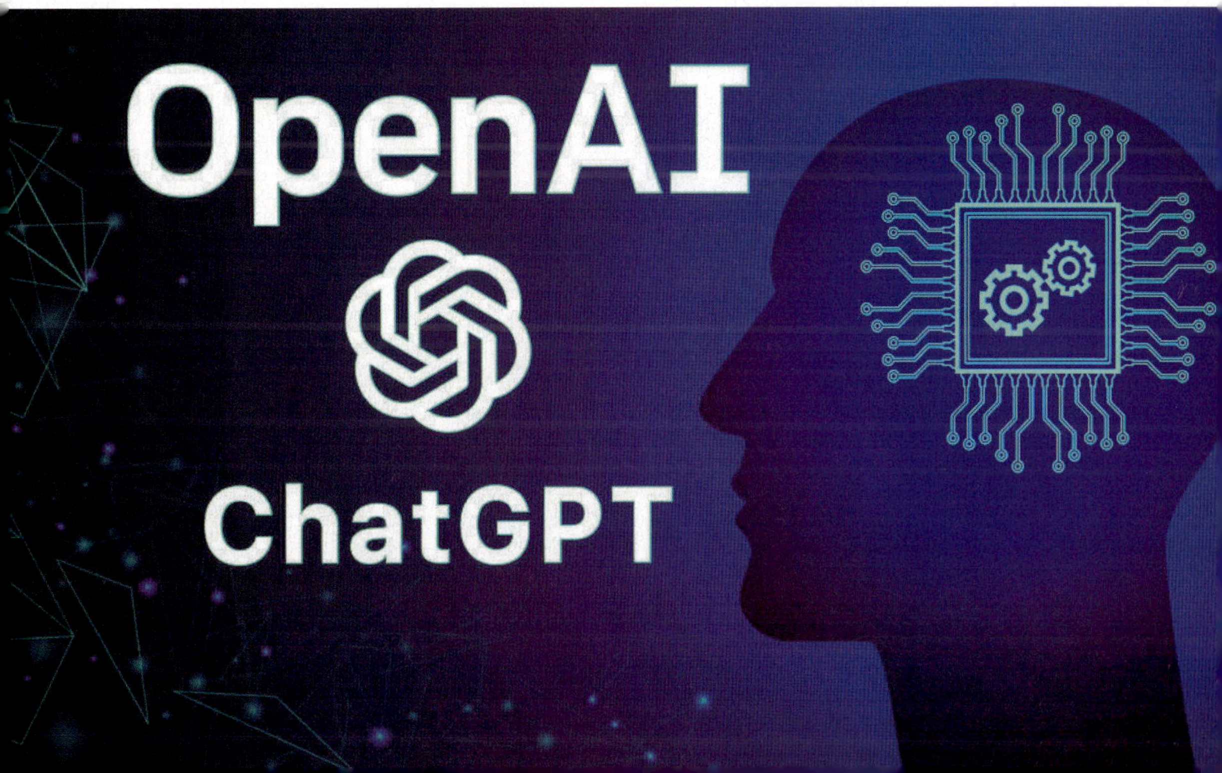

会不会控制不了它。希望人工智能公司的科学家们会考虑这个问题，给我们一个让人放心的答案。

现在我们也没有关于人工智能方面的规则，希望政府很快能制定这方面的法律。一个很大的问题是学生现在常常用 ChatGPT 来作弊。因为 ChatGPT 可以帮助学生撰写论文，学生不需要努力就能拿到好成绩。有一些人想试一试 ChatGPT 写的文章有多好，能不能骗过学校，所以他们就让 ChatGPT 冒充一个学生，在著名的沃顿商学院选修了一门课。结果 ChatGPT 撰写的作业竟然成功地通过了这门课，甚至得了 B。因此，学校得好好关注学生用 ChatGPT 作弊的问题。

总而言之，ChatGPT 又有用又厉害，可是它越厉害就越危险。今后 ChatGPT 肯定会造成更多的问题，社会得考虑如何解决这些问题，确保以后 ChatGPT 是一个有利于人类的工具，而不是一个扰乱社会秩序的祸害。

grades without any effort. Some people wanted to test just how well ChatGPT can write and if they can fool the education system, so they enrolled ChatGPT in a class at the renowned Wharton Business School. The materials submitted by ChatGPT ended up passing the class with a B. Therefore, schools should take measures to prevent students from using ChatGPT to cheat.

In conclusion, ChatGPT is both useful and powerful, but due to its capabilities, it has the potential to be very dangerous as well. ChatGPT will definitely cause more problems in the future, and we must carefully consider how to solve these problems to ensure that ChatGPT is a boon to mankind rather than a force of destruction.

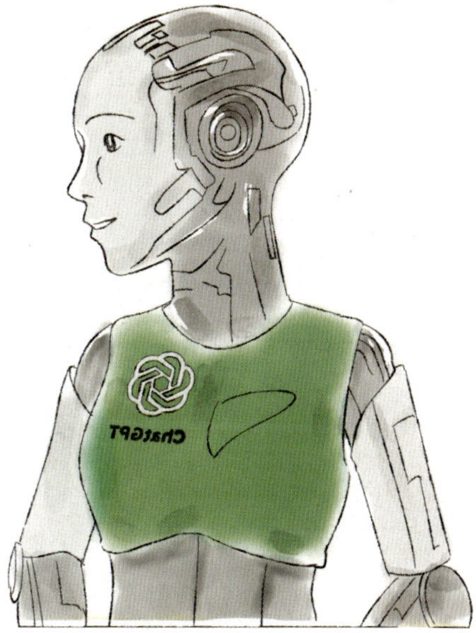

网络啊，网络

作者：普雷顿　指导教师：张锦虹　西北大学

我们的社会每分每秒不断地在变化。随着科技的发展突飞猛进，这个世界到处充满了新事物。有些人因为害怕改变，而对新事物不为所动，甚至不以为然。有些人则对新事物持开放的态度，时时刻刻吸收新知。我认为现代人应该广泛地接受新事物，凡是不愿意接受新事物的人总有一天会被社会淘汰。这篇文章将以网络为例，分析科技发展对社会的影响。

科技发展一方面为人类带来前所未有的进步，但另一方面也伴随着难以避免的“副作用”。

网络是20世纪的新发明，前期只有少数人才能享有这样“高大上”的产物。随着科技的飞速发展，大约千禧年（2000年）后为人类普遍使用，其中最大的改变是我们每个人的生活从此都离不开网络。比方说，我每天用电子邮箱收发邮件，用社交媒体与人沟通，在学习平台上传作业等。这些看来虽是再平常不过的小事，却是上个世纪的人怎么也想不到的进步。此外，当今越来越多的年轻人选择网上交友，然而这样的做法引起了两代人激烈的争论，有些老年人不但反对网上交友这种“开放”的观念，而且一碰到新科技就拒绝学习。因此，当年轻人与上一代交流时，老年人无法了解年轻人的想法，造成了两代人观念上的鸿沟。

科技发展一方面为人类带来前所未有的进步，但另一方面也伴随着难以避免的“副作用”。以社交媒体为例，据统计，社交媒体上瘾对年轻人的心理健康有强烈的负面影响。社交媒体是人人手机里必备的应用程序，最流行的社交平台包括脸书、推特、微信及抖音。微信在中国特别流行，而抖音使用者的平均年龄在逐年下降。这些社交媒体会使人长时间沉浸在一个虚拟的世界里。我认

The Internet, ah, the Internet!

Author: Preston Johnson   Instructor: Chin-hung Chang   Northwestern University

Our society is changing at every moment. With technology's rapid development, the world is full of new developments. Some people fear change and are therefore unmoved or even entirely opposed to anything new. Others have open-minded attitudes toward new things and are always willing to absorb new knowledge. I think that everyone today should accept new things; society will leave everyone who is unwilling to accept new things behind at some point. Using the internet as an example, this article will analyze the impact of technological development on society.

> On one hand, technological development has brought society unprecedented progress; but on the other hand, it also has side-effects that are hard to avoid.

The internet was invented in the 20th century; in its early years, only a small minority of people could enjoy this grand product. As technology quickly developed and it became typical for people to use the internet after 2000, the biggest change to our daily lives is that we cannot leave the internet. For instance, every day I send and receive emails, use social media to communicate with people, and use an online portal to upload homework assignments. Although these changes seem trivial, these improvements were unimaginable in the previous century. Moreover, more and more young people are choosing online dating; this method has led to a debate between two generations, as some older people not only oppose "open-minded" ideas like online dating, but also refuse to learn to use any new technology upon its arrival. Thus, as young people and the previous generation communicate, older people will not be able to understand younger people's idea, resulting in a gap of ideas between the two generations.

On one hand, technological development has brought society unprecedented progress;

为这个虚拟的世界充满了许多肤浅的假象，使用者通常上传他们认为最好玩儿、最酷的事物，呈现最完美的外表。看得太多会使得人的自信心低落。更加糟糕的是，这样的自信低落会促使人们在这个超出现实的世界里进行无谓的竞争，造成青少年的心理问题，进而伤害他们自己的身体。除此之外，社交媒体上瘾也会影响人们的时间管理。年轻人过于专注社交媒体，极少花时间在家人和朋友身上，更别说像做功课这样的正事了。尽管这些影响是负面的，但是我认为社交媒体上瘾不是科技的问题，而是人们自我管理的问题。如果你是一个负责任的人，给自己一定的约束，使用社交媒体能有效地保持与家人朋友的联系，拉近人与人之间的心理距离。

除了时间管理以外，网络也在一定的程度上改变了整个社会的运作方式。比如网上购物的流行就是其中之一。在中国，人们通常用淘宝购物。在美国，亚马逊则是最受欢迎的网店。网上购物提供了一个方便的渠道，也让全人类开始重视物流运送的重要性。

网络啊网络，成也是你，败也是你，叫我说你什么好！

but on the other hand, it also has side-effects that are hard to avoid. For example, according to statistical studies, social media addiction has a strong negative effect on young people's mental health. Social media apps are must-haves on everyone's phones. The most popular platforms include Facebook, Twitter, WeChat, and TikTok. WeChat is especially popular in China and the average age of TikTok users has declined year after year. These social media apps immerse users into a virtual world for a long time. I think this virtual world is full of superficial illusions; users typically upload what they believe are the most fun and cool events and present their most beautiful appearances. Looking at this too much can make one's self-confidence decrease. Even worse, this type of self-confidence decrease will prompt people in this illusory world to engage in unnecessary competition, resulting in young people's mental health problems, and then their physically harming themselves. Besides mental health problems, social media addiction also affects how people manage their time. When young people excessively focus on social media, they spend less time with their family and friends, and even worse, less time doing things like homework. Even though these impacts are negative, I believe that social media addiction is not a technology problem, but rather, a self-management problem. If you are responsible and give yourself well-defined constraints, using social media can be a great way to keep in touch with family and friends while bringing people closer together psychologically.

Apart from time management, the internet has also – to a certain extent – changed the way our entire society operates. The popularization of online shopping is a way in which our society's operations have changed. In China, people typically use Taobao to shop online. In the United States, Amazon is the most popular online shopping platform. Online shopping has not only supplied a convenient way to shop, but also has made people pay attention to the importance of logistics and transportation.

The internet, ah, the internet! Either success or failure is due to you! What can be said about you?

城市的另一面

作者：葛安妮　指导教师：蔡罗一　杜克大学

我是杜克大学的学生。第一个学期是在中国的杜克—昆山大学上的。在中国留学的生活节奏和新鲜的生活体验让我感到很兴奋。作为一名国际学生，我很幸运地看到这种快节奏生活积极的一面，这包括中国高速发展的经济、便捷的公共交通和大量的工作机会。我很少注意到那些维护街道清洁的清洁工人的生活，为我送餐的外卖骑手的生活，以及餐馆服务员的生活，尽管这些人每天都出现在我的生活里，为我提供各种各样的服务。直到有一天，在网上读到了一篇关于北漂外卖骑手的文章，我才有机会了解他们生活。

这些外地打工人为了追逐梦想来到城市。他们渴望赚到足够的钱寄回家，或者组建自己的家庭。

这些外地打工人为了追逐梦想来到城市。他们渴望赚到足够的钱寄回家，或者组建自己的家庭。但实际上，每一个梦想的实现都不容易。比如，在大城市里，你最常看到的打工人就是外卖骑手。尽管送外卖的收入还不错，但是工作时间长、工作强度大，有时还会被客户误解。在城市辛苦工作多年后，他们发现自己既无法返回家乡，也无法融入大城市的生活。这些外地打工人大多来自比较贫困的农村地区，如果回到家乡，他们担心别人把他们视为失败者。跟城市相比，农村地区的教育水平、资源状况、就业机会、生活质量都相对较差。而如果留在城市，他们觉得自己无法完全融入，因为他们的工作生活面临各种各样的困难。由于受到户口制度的限制，这些外地打工人往往无法享受跟城市居民一样的资源，比如送孩子去公立学校上学。

The Other Side of the City

Author: Erin Greig   Instructor: Luoyi Cai   Duke University

I am a student at Duke University. In my first semester, I studied at Duke Kunshan University. I was excited about the pace of life and the new, fresh experience of studying abroad in China. As an international student, I was lucky to see the positive side of this fast-paced lifestyle, including China's rapid economic development, convenient public transportation, and a vast number of job opportunities. I seldom thought deeply about the lives of those sweeping the streets, delivery drivers who brought me meals, and the restaurant workers even though they were present in my life every day providing all types of services. That was until one day when I read an online article about delivery drivers in Beijing, and I had the opportunity to learn about their lives.

These migrant workers come to the city in pursuit of their dreams, eager to send money to their families or start a new family of their own.

These migrant workers come to the city in pursuit of their dreams, eager to send money to their families or start a new family of their own. But in reality, achieving these dreams is not easy. For example, in larger cities, the migrant workers most commonly seen are delivery drivers. Although the income for a delivery driver is not bad, the working hours are long, the work is incredibly intense, and they are often mistreated by customers. After many tough years of living in the city, they find that they can neither return home nor fully integrate into life in the big city. Most of these migrant workers come from poorer rural areas and worry that if they return to their hometowns, they will be seen as failures. Compared to cities, the education level, available resources, job opportunities, and overall quality of life in rural areas are relatively poor. If they stay in the city, they feel that they cannot fully integrate because of the various

农村人口面临的最严峻的问题之一就是就业问题。在城市里，很多大公司每天都在创造新的就业机会。而农村更多地依赖于体力劳动。近年来，农民正在被机器取代。由于农村生活水平提高得较慢，工作机会逐渐减少，以致农村的很多年轻人更愿意离开家乡去大城市找工作。像文章里的外卖骑手一样，他们工作辛苦，大多从事体力劳动，在医疗和子女的教育方面遇到了不少问题。

为了解决城乡差别和贫富差距的问题，中国政府一方面采取了一系列有力措施，帮助农村地区发展。中国的精准扶贫计划是世界瞩目、卓有成效的。例如，为在农村学校就读的学生提供免费午餐。另外，中国政府启动了新农村发展计划，试图增加农村收入，改善道路等基础设施，提高农民的生活水平。这可能有助于创造就业机会。为了改善农村地区的教育状况，中国政府增加了教育支出，为当地的教师和校长提供专业培训，同时选派大学毕业生去农村任教。

difficulties of their working lives. Due to the restrictions of the *hukou* system, migrant workers are unable to enjoy the same resources as urban residents, such as sending their children to public schools.

One of the most serious problems facing the rural population involves employment. In cities, many large companies create new job opportunities every day, and rural areas rely more on manual labor. In recent years, rural workers have been replaced by machines. Because of the slow improvement in rural living standards, job opportunities are gradually decreasing, so many young people in rural areas are more willing to leave their hometowns to find jobs in big cities. Like the delivery drivers in the article, these people work hard, engage mostly in manual labor, and have encountered many problems with medical care and education of their children.

In order to solve the problems of urban-rural disparity and the gap between the rich and poor, the Chinese government has adopted a series of powerful measures to help the development of rural areas. The targeted poverty alleviation programs in China are world-renowned and highly effective. For example, one of those programs has provided free lunches to students attending rural schools. In addition, the Chinese government has launched the new rural development plan, attempting to increase rural income, improve infrastructure such as roads, and improve farmers' standard of living, which could help create job opportunities. To improve education in rural areas, the Chinese government has increased educational spending, provided professional training for local teachers and principals, and selected new university graduates to teach in rural areas.

On the other side, for the thousands of migrant workers who choose to move to work in cities, the Chinese government has also adopted many specific measures to reduce their burden and improve their living conditions. In recent years, the Chinese government has introduced a series of policies that have simplified the process for children of migrant workers to attend urban public schools, provided suitable medical insurance for migrant workers and their children, and made them feel safer and more comfortable working in cities. One of the most common difficulties faced by migrant workers is being owed wages. Therefore, the government has set up a helpline for migrant workers; migrant workers who do not receive their wages on time can call the hotline for help. The Ministry of Human Resources and Social

另一方面，针对成千上万选择在城市打工的农民工，中国政府也采取了很多具体措施减轻他们的负担，改善他们的生活条件。近年来，中国政府出台了一系列政策，大大简化了农民工子女就读城市公立学校的流程，为农民工及其子女提供合适的医疗保险，使他们在城市里工作得更安心、更放心。在城市里的外地打工人最常面临的困难之一就是被拖欠工资。因此，政府为外地打工人开设了求助热线，没有按时收到工资的外地打工人可以拨打热线求助，而人力资源和社会保障部会将拖欠员工工资的公司列入黑名单。除了帮助解决外地打工人的经济问题以外，政府还针对外地打工者和失业者开展职业培训计划，帮助他们提高职业技能。如果外地打工人选择返乡，当地政府还会帮助他们在当地找工作或创业。这些计划有助于减轻外地打工人对城市缺乏归属感和担心回乡失败的焦虑。

尽管如此，城乡差距问题仍然有待解决，在城市里的外地打工人也仍然面临着各种各样的困难。要解决这些困难，除了政府以外，生活在城市里的每一个人都应该做出力所能及的努力。对我来说，行动的第一步是读一读、听一听这些外地打工人的故事。这样我们才能产生共情，而共情能推动我们一起来改善我们的社会！

Security blacklists the companies that owe wages to their employees. In addition to helping solve the economic problems of migrant workers, the government also conducts vocational training programs for migrant workers and the unemployed to help them develop their skills. If migrant workers choose to return to their hometowns, the local government will also help them find jobs or start businesses locally. These programs help alleviate the anxiety of migrant workers over their lack of belonging in the city and their fear of returning home as a failure.

Nevertheless, the gap between urban and rural areas remains to be resolved and migrant workers in cities still face all kinds of difficulties. To solve these challenges, in addition to the government, everyone living in the city should put in the effort. For me, the first step is to read and listen to the stories of these migrant workers. Only in this way can we develop empathy, and empathy can push us to improve our society together!

科幻、人工智能和中国梦

作者：孙立欣　指导教师：俞巧娜　维克森林大学

> 具有激发创新和未来独特思维能力的科幻类型小说，正在被用来帮助中国实现这一梦想。

在2061年，太阳即将燃尽，地球上的人必须团结起来拯救地球、拯救人类。这是由刘慈欣创作的中国科幻小说以及2019年据此改编的电影《流浪地球》的情节。电影中的一个关键场景描绘了先进的AI计算机莫斯（Moss）与我们的反叛力量代表人类英雄宇航员刘培强之间斗智斗勇。场景揭示了基于逻辑和功利主义的莫斯是与我们英雄的目标相悖的。简而言之，莫斯通过数学计算，得出的结论是：若要拯救全人类，便无法拯救地球。为了保证地球不被摧毁，莫斯会抹除全人类的痕迹。相反的，我们人类的主角刘培强却看到了完全不同的东西，他看到了拯救地球和人类的机会——他看到了希望。

随着剧情的发展，不同立场的团体都试图扼杀对方，直到最后，人类的反抗终于占了上风。我们的英雄做了所有英雄所做的事，他决定牺牲自己，拯救世界。除了电影中先进的科幻画面外，电影本身也是一场卓越的中国科技大型展示，体现了中国技术在未来的发展潜力。

这种强大的科幻作品能激发创造灵感。对于那些希望得到未来指引的人们来说，它的启发功能和教育功能甚至大于文学性。美国的科技公司，如微软、谷歌和苹果，经常委托科幻作家来创造“设计小说”。这些科幻小说的智囊团以未来派的叙事为主题，旨在开发出适销对路的产品。今年，美国国家航空航天局（NASA）负责人证实，他们正在与演员汤姆·克鲁斯（Tom Cruise）合作，创作

Sci-Fi, AI and the Chinese Dream

Author: Alex Casale Instructor: Qiaona Yu Wake Forest University

> The science fiction genre, with its ability to inspire innovation and deliver a unique vision of the future, is helping China pursue their technological dreams.

In 2061, the sun is dying, and the people on the Earth must band together to save the planet... or at the very least save the human race. This is the plot of the popular Chinese Sci-Fi book and its 2019 movie adaptation entitled *The Wandering Earth* by Liu Cixin. A pivotal scene in the movie depicts a battle-of-wits between the advanced AI computer called Moss and our rebel human hero, astronaut Liu Peiqiang. The scene reveals that Moss, based on logic and utilitarianism, is at odds with our hero's goals. In a nutshell, Moss runs the numbers and concludes that in order for humanity to survive, the earth cannot be saved. In order for the Earth to be saved, Moss will obliterate the traces of all humanity. On the contrary, our human protagonist Liu Peiqiang sees something quite different... he sees a chance to save the earth and humanity – he sees hope.

As the scene progresses, each entity attempts to stifle the other, until human resistance prevails at last. Our hero does what heroes do – he decides to sacrifice himself and save the world. Besides depicting the superior sci-fi scenes, the film is also an outstanding display of China's technology, revealing the potential for China's technological future. This powerful sci-fi work can inspire creativity. It is even more enlightening and educational than literary for those who wish to guide the world. American tech companies, such as Microsoft, Google, and Apple often commission sci-fi writers to do something called "design fiction." Here, science fiction think-tanks run through futuristic narratives with the goal of leading to marketable products and services. For example, the head of the National Aeronautics and Space Administration

一部太空题材的科幻电影。尽管不是设计小说，美国国家航空航天局希望借此激发新一代有志于此的工程师和科学家向太空发起探索。

美国并不是唯一一个利用科幻力量和影响力的国家，作为世界第二大经济体的中国，对于科幻力量的使用也已经引起了人们的关注。例如，中国著名智能手机公司小米的老板雷军，已经将刘慈欣的《三体》列为员工必读书。这也许是因为小米的工作专注于创新。此外，2015 年在刘慈欣获得雨果奖的几天后，中国国家副主席李源潮会见了以刘慈欣为代表的科幻作家代表团。在这次访问中，李副主席呼吁中国科幻小说作家“激发年轻人实现中国梦的信念”。

这种新兴技术的顶峰是人工智能。当一个叫作阿尔法围棋（AlphaGo）的人工智能游戏系统击败了世界围棋冠军柯洁时，利用科幻力量发展科技的想法在 2017 年得到了强化。那年晚些时候，中国公布了“下一代人工智能发展规划”，该文件阐明了到 2030 年中国将成为世界主要人工智能创新中心的战略，为中国公民提供了新的视野。谷歌中国前负责人李开复宣称：“人工智能将改变一切。不了解即将到来的人工智能革命，将有被抛在后面的风险。”

(NASA) recently confirmed that they are working with actor Tom Cruise to create a science fiction film in space. While not designing fiction, NASA hopes this film will inspire a new generation of engineers and scientists throughout the U.S. to explore space.

America isn't the only country utilizing the power and influence of sci-fi. As the world's second largest economy, China has been noticed for using the power of sci-fi. For example, Lei Jun, the CEO of Xiaomi, has made Liu Cixin's *Three Body Trilogy* a required reading for the employees of Xiaomi, a famous smartphone company in China. This may be because Xiaomi's work focuses on innovation. In addition, in 2015, a few days after Liu Cixin received the Hugo Award – the Vice President of the People's Republic of China, Li Yuanchao, met with Liu and

简而言之，具有激发创新和未来独特思维能力的科幻类型小说，正在被用来帮助中国实现这一梦想。现在，中国正在经历科幻小说的复兴。中国科幻小说不仅在中国很流行，在全球各地也越来越流行。最终，就像《流浪地球》的人类主角一样，科幻小说会用一种极为人性的东西提供拯救人类的希望。

a delegation of science fiction writers. During this visit, Vice President Li called on Chinese science fiction writers to "fuel the faith of the youth in realizing the fulfillment of the Chinese Dream."

The pinnacle of this emerging technology is artificial intelligence (AI). This idea likely gained strength in 2017, when an AI gaming system called AlphaGo defeated the world champion, Chinese go player Ke Jie. Later that year, China unveiled its "Next Generation Artificial Intelligence Development Plan," a document laying out the country's strategy to become the AI global leader by 2030. This plan gave Chinese citizens a new vision of the future. In fact, Kai-Fu Lee, former head of Google China, declared: "AI is going to change everything. To not understand the coming AI revolution is to risk getting left behind."

Overall, the science fiction genre, with its ability to inspire innovation and deliver a unique vision of the future, is helping China pursue their technological dreams. China is now in the midst of a science fiction renaissance. China's sci-fi is popular not only in China, but also all over the world. Ultimately, just like our protagonist from *The Wandering Earth*, science fiction provides us with the hope to rescue humanity in a very human way.

浅谈中国的绿色信贷政策

作者：欧勤爱　指导教师：周赫璇　乔治华盛顿大学

按照绿色信贷政策的规定，银行在贷款的时候，需要考察这个公司的项目是否符合环境保护的标准。

近年来，美国政府跟中国政府都越来越重视对环境的保护。中美两国都发现，全球日益恶化的气候危机将严重影响各国的经济发展。为了解决气候危机，一些负责任的国家相继出台了一系列的环保政策。通过这些政策，他们希望减少碳排放和空气污染。中国的绿色信贷政策就是其中重要的一项。在我看来，跟其他国家的绿色金融政策相比，中国的绿色信贷政策显然更加有效。

要想知道一个政策好不好，我们首先需要明确这项政策的目标，其次需要追踪持续研究，随时调整政策，最后我们需要密切关注这个政策产生的实际效果。本文将从四个方面来讲述中国的绿色信贷政策：一是中国的绿色信贷政策到底是什么，二是中国绿色信贷政策的优点，三是中国绿色信贷政策的不足，四是美国应该不应该采取一样的政策。

通过研究我发现，绿色信贷构成了绿色金融体系的重要组成部分。为了控制高耗能、高污染产业的规模扩大，中国环保总局、人民银行、银监会这三个部门于 2007 年 7 月 12 日联合提出了一项全新的绿色信贷政策《关于落实环境保护政策法规防范信贷风险的意见》。绿色信贷对经济的可持续发展产生了巨大效益，而且也大大促进了环境保护。因为绿色信贷可以减少企业对环境的破坏，所以中国政府认真研究，最后制定了一系列综合政策。中国政府的政策对中国

China's Green Credit Policy

Author: Olivia Pfeiffer Instructor: Hexuan Zhou George Washington University

> According to the rules of the green credit policy, when a bank gives a loan to a company, it needs to investigate whether or not that company's goals comply with environmental protection.

In recent years, both the American government and Chinese government have increasingly placed importance on environmental protection. Both China and the U.S. discovered that the worsening worldwide climate crisis will have a serious effect on the economic development of various countries. In order to solve the climate crisis, some countries have taken the responsibility to take steps to introduce environmental protection policies. Through these policies, these countries hope to reduce carbon emissions and air pollution. China's green credit policy is one of their most important initiatives. In my opinion, compared to other countries' green finance policies, China's green credit policy is evidently more effective.

To determine whether or not a policy is good, first you need to clearly understand the goal of the policy. Secondly, you must continuously follow up with research. Following this, you need to pay close attention to the practical effects of the policy. This article will introduce China's green credit policy from four aspects: the first is what exactly China's green credit policy is; the second is China's green credit policy's strengths; the third is China's green credit policy's weaknesses; the fourth is whether or not the U.S. should adopt a similar policy.

Through my research, I found that the green credit policy has become an important part of the green financial system. In order to control high energy consumption and the scale and expansion of high polluting industries, on July 12th, 2007 the Chinese Environmental Protection Administration, People's Bank of China, and China Banking Regulatory

企业有举足轻重的影响。按照绿色信贷政策的规定，银行在贷款的时候，需要考察这个公司的项目是否符合环境保护的标准。如果发现这个项目符合环境保护的标准，政府就批准银行发放贷款；如果发现这个项目不符合环境保护的标准，政府就不批准银行发放贷款。从这个角度来看，中国政府在环境保护方面所采取措施的力度是相当大的，而绿色信贷就是其中重要的组成部分。中国的这个可持续发展模式给别的国家树立了一个好榜样。

因为绿色信贷和社会风险管理有很密切的关系，所以绿色信贷政策越强，社会风险管理就越好。中国有句话，“摸着石头过河”，意思是你应该有一种务实的态度。我觉得“摸着石头过河”形象地体现了中国政府的态度。在我看来，虽然这个政策还不完善，但是通过很多措施可以看出这是一个很好的政策。中国政府的绿色信贷政策的重点包括：一，把风险管理系统变得更强大；二，用准实验研究来监测碳排放，每两年对这些公司进行信用评估；三，提倡并且执行净零能耗；四，

Commission – these three departments – all jointly proposed a new green credit policy. This green credit policy is helpful to the sustainable development of economy, but also to environmental protection. Because green credit policy can reduce companies' damage to the environment, the Chinese government researched diligently and finally executed a series of comprehensive regulations. The Chinese government's policies have a crucial impact on Chinese companies. According to the rules of the green credit policy, when a bank gives a loan to a company, it needs to investigate whether or not that company's goals comply with environmental protection. If the bank discovers the company's goals comply with environmental protection standards, then the government will approve the bank to issue a loan. If the bank discovers the company's goals do not comply with environmental protection standards, then the government will not approve the bank to issue a loan. From this point of view, the steps that the Chinese government takes in strengthening environmental protection are quite large, and green credit policy is an important part of this. China's sustainable development model sets a very good example for other countries.

Because green credit policy and social risk management are closely related, then the stronger the green credit policy is, the better social risk management is. There is a Chinese saying that goes, "crossing the river by feeling for stones." It means that you should always have a pragmatic attitude. I believe that this saying, "crossing the river by feeling for stones," vividly reflects the attitude of the Chinese government. In my opinion, although this policy is not

中国的每家银行都要制定绿色信贷与绿色借贷规定。

一般来说，中国科学家用两种统计方法评估中国的绿色信贷政策对环境的影响。通过这两种统计方法，科学家可以评估空气污染的严重性，同时对全球变暖的研究也很重要。这两种统计方法是倾向得分匹配法和双重差分法（PSM-DID）。通过研究，我们可以发现，中国的绿色信贷政策已经产生了积极的影响。绿色信贷政策要求中国公司报告商业运营信息，这就是一个企业社会责任的体现。在很多科学家看来，企业社会责任和财务业绩是联系在一起的，公司的企业社会责任感越强，财务业绩就会越好。与此同时，绿色信贷政策也创造了绿色供应链。所谓的绿色供应链，就是用环保的方式保障供应链。比如农场采用环保的方式种植棉花，纺织厂用环保的方式纺纱织布，服装厂用环保的方式制造、销售产品。随着绿色供应链的发展，经济也必将持续发展。中国国家主席习近平非常关注中国

perfect, through the many steps that have been taken, it can be seen as a very good policy. The most important parts of the Chinese governments green credit policy include: making social risk management stronger, using quasi-experimental studies to monitor carbon emissions by conducting a credit evaluation every two years, advocating and implementing net zero energy consumption, and finally every bank in China must execute green credit and green lending regulations.

Generally speaking, Chinese scientists utilize two statistical methods to assess the environmental impact of China's green credit policy. Through these two statistical methods, scientists can measure the severity of air pollution. At the same time, it is very helpful for research on global warming. The two statistical methods are the propensity score matching method and the difference-in-difference method (PSM-DID). Through research we can discover that China's green credit policy has already had a positive impact. Green credit policy requires Chinese companies to report information on business operations, and this is one characteristic of corporate social responsibility. In the opinion of many scientists, corporate social responsibility and financial performance are linked to one another. The stronger a company's corporate social responsibility is, the higher its financial performance will be. At the same time, green credit policies have also created green supply chains. These so-called green supply chains use environmentally friendly methods to protect supply chains. For example, farms use environmentally friendly methods to grow cotton, textile mills use environmentally friendly methods in spinning fabrics, and apparel factories use environmentally friendly methods to manufacture and sell products. With the development of green supply chains, the economy will also continue to develop. Chinese President Xi Jinping is very concerned about the sustainable development of China's economy, and every year he participates in the G20 summit which leaves a good impression on people. Aside from this, the climate crisis has also attracted the attention of many young Chinese people, who increasingly feel very seriously about the sustainable development of the economy. Therefore, I recognize that the Chinese youth urgently hope that the government will adopt practical and feasible policies in order to solve the climate crisis. All of these points demonstrate that the Chinese government and the Chinese people are very concerned about environmental protection.

Recently, many people believe that the Chinese government can further improve this

经济的可持续发展，他每年都会参加 G20 峰会。这给人们留下了很好的印象。另外，气候危机也引起了很多中国年轻人的注意，他们越来越重视经济的可持续性发展。所以我认为，中国的年轻人迫切希望政府采取切实可行的政策，以缓解气候危机。这些都说明中国政府和中国人民都非常关心环境保护。

最近，很多人认为中国政府还可以进一步完善这个制度。一方面，绿色信贷政策会产生一种溢出效应。也就是说，有些不负责任的企业会跑到比较偏远的地区去建厂开矿，污染那里的环境。一般来说，不可持续的工商活动比较简单，而且费用又低，所以一些公司和银行可能不会遵守这些可持续发展的规定。现在这个溢出效应对中国西北地区已经造成了比较大的威胁。因为大部分西北地区还没有实施这样的政策，如果一家公司和银行不想遵守绿色信贷的规定，他们会决定搬到这些还没有实施这些政策的地区去发展。在我看来，中国政府应该严格控制这样的公司和银行，这样，这些公司就无法通过别的方式来制造空气污染。另一方面是中国的银行和政府都需要更顺畅的沟通。中国的各家银行也需要跟公众建立更多联系。有些科学家建议中国的所有银行都应该更严格地遵守绿色信贷政策。如果能够做到这一点，绿色信贷政策的效果会更显著。中国政府和年轻人非常重视保护环境，因此，中国的绿色信贷政策必将日益完善。

最后，我认为美国也应该出台类似的绿色信贷政策。因为中国的绿色信贷政策证明这是一个可持续发展的良好模式，给各国树立了一个好榜样。可惜的是，在环境保护方面，美国政府和美国的银行做得还远远不够。在美国，虽然我们也有几项可持续发展模式的政策，但是我认为很多大公司和银行都没有遵守这些政策的规定，所以这是很大的问题。因此，我真切希望美国政府能够跟中国政府更多地交流这个话题。我相信美国政府将来一定会出台一个适合美国国情的可持续发展的模式，与世界上许多国家一起，保护好我们的家园——地球。

system. On the one hand, green credit policies can have spillover effects. In other words, some irresponsible companies will move to remote areas to build factories and mines, and pollute the environment there. Generally speaking, engaging in unsustainable business activities is significantly simpler and the fees are much lower, therefore some companies and banks may not comply with sustainable development regulations. Currently this spillover effect has posed a relatively large threat to the northwestern region of China. Because a majority of the northwest territories have not implemented such policies, if a company or bank does not want to follow the green credit policy regulations, they will decide to move to these areas where this policy is not practiced. In my opinion, the Chinese government should more strictly control these companies and banks. In this way, these companies are unable to create air pollution through other methods. On the other hand, both the Chinese banks and the government need to communicate more smoothly with one another. Chinese banks also need to establish more communication with the public. Some scientists suggest that all the banks in China should more strictly follow this green credit policy. If this can be done, the effect of the green credit policy will be more significant. The Chinese government and youth both greatly prioritize environmental protection. Therefore, China's green credit policy is bound to increasingly improve.

Finally, I feel that the U.S. should also implement a similar green credit policy. Because the Chinese green credit policy has proven to be a good model for sustainable development, and also set a good example for various countries to follow. It is a pity that in regards to environmental protection, the American government and American banks have not done enough. Although, in the U.S., we also have several sustainable development models and policies, I feel that many large American companies and banks do not follow these policies regulations, so this is still a very big problem. Therefore, I greatly hope the American government together with the Chinese government can communicate more in regards to this topic. I believe that in the future, the American government can certainly carry out a suitable sustainable development model, and the many countries of the world can unite to protect our home – the Earth.

中国的城镇化与北漂现象

作者：康睿　指导教师：张恒煜　耶鲁大学

> 所谓“北漂”，就是在北京工作的外地人。他们的生活不稳定，所以就像漂在水上的树叶一样。

改革开放以来，中国的经济发生了日新月异的变化。一些小渔村变成了大城市，大城市变成了国际大都市。改革开放和城镇化有着密切的关系。从经济上来说，城镇化提高了中国人民的生活水平。但是，城镇化的转型过程也造成了一些社会问题，而其中最严重的问题就是城乡人口迁徙。

国际投资和经济发展使许多城市迅速繁华起来，从而吸引了大量人口涌向城市。虽然大城市里五彩缤纷的生活十分诱人，但是城市居民却需要承受着较大的工作和生活压力。由于大学毕业生基本上都选择留在大城市里工作和生活，加上许多乡镇人口也都涌进城里寻找就业机会，因此城市的交通和住房压力越来越大，人们的工作压力也越来越大。有的城市居民的工作压力非常之大，以至于抽不出时间在工作之余跟朋友见面。而涌入大城市的乡镇人口，生活更是不易。因为这些人没有北京、上海、广州、深圳这些大城市的户口，所以他们的子女就不能在大城市的学校就近入学。这些孩子就需要返回家乡上学。这样父母就无法陪伴孩子，也无法满足孩子的需求。

由于快速的城镇化，许多当地的传统文化也在快速消失。中国各地区自古以

China's Urbanization and the Beijing Floaters

Author: Jacques Cornec   Instructor: Hengyu Zhang   Yale University

The so-called "Beijing floaters" are non-locals working in Beijing. Their lives are unstable and as such, they are like leaves drifting on the surface of the water.

Since China's reform and opening-up policy, the country's economy has undergone rapid changes. Small fishing villages have become large cities and large cities have become international megacities. Reform and opening-up and China's urbanization are inextricably linked. Economically, urbanization has improved the living standards of Chinese people. However, the urbanization process has also given rise to a host of social problems, the most serious of which is urban-rural migration.

Foreign investment and economic development have allowed many cities to prosper rapidly, attracting swaths of people to urban areas. Although the colorful life of big cities can be attractive, urban residents also have to bear a lot of pressure at work and in their daily life. Since college graduates basically all choose to stay in big cities to work and live there, and many rural people flock to the cities to find employment as well, pressures on housing and transportation are increasing, as is pressure in the workplace. Some city dwellers are under so much stress that they cannot find time to meet friends outside of work. The influx of people from the countryside makes life even harder. Since these people do not have the *hukou* of big cities such as Beijing, Shanghai, Guangzhou, and Shenzhen, their children cannot attend school in the city. These children then need to return to their hometown to attend school there. It prevents parents from being with their children and meet their needs.

来就各有特色。文化、饮食、习俗和方言都不同。深圳是城镇化最明显的例子。40 年以前，深圳居民都说粤语，可是现在，深圳人主要说普通话。另外，具有当地传统文化色彩的建筑也在渐渐消失。现在，中国“一线城市”的当地文化流失很多，都变成了现代化国际大都市。

当然，城镇化有它积极的一面。市民的日常生活水平提高了，经济发展了，等等。但是，城镇化的好处不是平等的：有的人的生活水平提高了，而有的人的生活水平却提高得不多。在我看来，未来怎么控制城镇化值得中国政府关注，因为城镇化的速度和力度是可以控制的。

以北京为例，城镇化带来的一个问题就是“北漂族”的出现。所谓“北漂”，就是在北京工作的外地人。他们的生活不稳定，所以就像漂在水上的树叶一样。

为了搞懂“北漂”的情况，我们先需要了解中国的城乡差距。改革开放以后，中国的经济发展得很快，因为跨国公司想在大城市里投资，所以公司的资源都集

Rapid urbanization is also leading to the disappearance of traditional local culture. Since ancient times, each region of China has had its own local characteristics. Culture, food, customs, and dialect are all different. Shenzhen is the most obvious example of this. Forty years ago, all Shenzhen residents spoke Cantonese, but now, Shenzhen people mainly speak Mandarin. Furthermore, traditional buildings are gradually disappearing too. Now, China's "first-tier cities" have lost a lot of their local culture and instead become modern, international metropolitan cities.

Of course, urbanization also has its positives. The living standard of citizens has improved, the economy has grown, and so on. However, the benefits of urbanization are not equally distributed: Some people's living standards have improved, while others' lives have not improved much. In my opinion, the issue of how to control urbanization in the future deserves the attention of the Chinese government, because the speed and intensity of urbanization can be controlled.

In Beijing for example, one of the problems brought about by urbanization is the emergence of "Beijing floaters." The so-called "Beijing floaters" are non-locals working in Beijing. Their lives are unstable and as such, they are like leaves drifting on the surface of the water.

In order to understand the situation of "Beijing floaters," we first need to understand the rural-urban divide in China. After the reform and opening-up, China's economy has developed rapidly, and many international corporations wanted to invest in large cities, leading to a concentration of resources in urban areas. As a result, big cities grew rapidly, while smaller cities were having a hard time attracting college graduates to come and work there. There is no point denying that large cities have a rich and colorful life and many more job opportunities. Most big international companies have branches in first-tier cities like Beijing, Shanghai, Shenzhen, and Guangzhou, so these first-tier cities have more and better job opportunities. However, life in big cities can also be hard: cost of living is high, and rent is expensive, whereas rent is not a problem in small cities. However, young people would rather work in large cities than in small ones. Non-locals working in Beijing cannot buy a house or send their children to public schools if they do not have a Beijing *hukou*, so they are called "Beijing floaters."

中在大城市。这样一来，大城市发展得很快，相反，小城市就很难吸引大学毕业生去工作。不可否认，大城市里有丰富多彩的生活，而且也有更多的工作机会。大多数国际大公司都在像北京、上海、深圳、广州这些一线城市里设立分支机构，所以在这些一线城市，人们可以获得更多、更好的工作机会。可是，大城市的生活也很辛苦：生活费用很高，房租很贵，在小城市里房租则不是什么问题。可是，年轻人宁可去大城市工作，也不去小城市。在北京工作的外地人，如果没有北京户口，那就买不了房子，孩子也上不了公立学校，所以称之为“北漂”。

在我看来，“北漂”的问题与政府的政策不能说完全没有关系。现在，中国政府已经意识到城镇化所带来的问题，也正在想办法解决“北漂”这样的问题。他们正在考虑做两件事情：改革户口制度和促进中小城市的发展。首先是帮助“北漂”的孩子在北京当地上学。其次是帮助中小城市发展，在政策上引导资金流向中小城市，发展当地经济。政府还在鼓励外资流向农业，帮助当地农民建立大规模机械化农业。最后，为了吸引更多大学毕业生去中小城市工作，政府也在给中小城市投资，建设和发展文化、娱乐活动。我相信中国政府一定会解决“北漂”的问题，提高大多数中国人的生活水平。

In my opinion, the problem of "Beijing floaters" cannot be regarded as completely unrelated to government policies. The Chinese government is now aware of the problems caused by urbanization and is trying to resolve the issue of "Beijing floaters." They are considering two things: Reforming the *hukou* system and promoting the development of small and medium-sized cities. The first step is to help children of "Beijing floaters" go to school in Beijing. The second step is to help the economic development of small and medium-sized cities by directing capital flows to them. The government is also encouraging the flow of foreign capital to agriculture to help local farmers establish large-scale mechanized agricultural operations. Finally, in order to attract more university graduates to work in small and medium-sized cities, the government is also investing in those cities to build and develop cultural and recreational activities. I believe the government will solve the problem of "Beijing floaters" and improve the living standard of most Chinese people.

甲烷监测卫星及其影响

作者：陈美恩　指导教师：张恒煜　耶鲁大学

希望全世界各国携起手来，保护我们地球的环境。因为，我们只有一个地球。

2019 年，美国和中国政府宣布，清华大学与美国环境保护基金会（Environmental Defense Fund，简称 EDF）建立新的合作伙伴关系，携手研究环境保护问题。随着两国经济的发展，气候变化所带来的问题变得越来越突出。两国希望可以通过这种新型伙伴关系加强合作，共同减少碳排放。专家普遍认为，绿色金融是解决环境污染问题最有效的方法。所谓“绿色金融”是指金融业如何促进环境保护和经济社会的可持续发展。绿色金融包括政府制定有效的保护环境政策、严格限定企业对自然资源的消耗、个人对自己的碳足迹负责等等。实现可持续发展面临许多困难，特别是在如何收集准确的数据方面。为了减少数据收集中的不确定风险，双方一致认为，有必要开发更准确的数据收集工具，特别是甲烷排放监测工具。

动植物在生长过程中都会产生甲烷。科学家们发现，大气中甲烷浓度上升会加剧地球表面温室效应。然而，甲烷排放的监测是一个非常困难的事情。很长时间以来，人们还没有开发出监测甲烷排放的有效工具。值得庆幸的是，最近几年，越来越多的环保机构开始用卫星来收集大规模甲烷排放的数据。美国环境保护基金会新近制造了一颗卫星，叫作 MethaneSAT，中文翻译为甲烷监测卫星。制造这颗卫星的目的不仅是为了监测某一地区的甲烷排放，也是为了监测全球的甲烷排放。然后将甲烷监测卫星收集的数据公开，以更好地帮助各国制定有效的环境保护政策。甲烷监测卫星使用一种对流层监测仪（TROPOMI）来感知大规模的甲

Methane Satellites and Their Impact

Author: Anna Tran Instructor: Hengyu Zhang Yale University

> We hope that all countries in the world will join hands to protect the environment of our planet. Because we have only one Earth.

In 2019, the United States government and Chinese government announced a new partnership between Tsinghua University and the U.S. Environmental Defense Fund to cooperate on environmental protection issues. Climate change issues have become increasingly prominent with the economic development of these two countries. Both China and the United States hope to strengthen cooperation between the two nations through this partnership to jointly reduce carbon emissions. Generally, experts believe that "green finance" is the most effective way to solve the environmental pollution problem. This so-called "green finance" refers to how the financial industry can promote environmental protection and sustainable economic development. Green finance includes governmental support in formulating effective environmental protection policies, limiting the consumption of natural resources by businesses, and individuals being responsible for their own carbon footprints. There are many challenges to achieving sustainable development, especially when it comes to collecting accurate data. To reduce the risk of uncertainty in data collection, both parties agreed that it is necessary to develop more accurate data collection tools, especially for the detection of methane emissions.

Plants and animals produce methane when they grow. Scientists have found that rising concentrations of methane in the atmosphere can exacerbate the greenhouse gas effect on the Earth's surface. However, monitoring methane emissions proves to be a challenge. Effective tools for monitoring

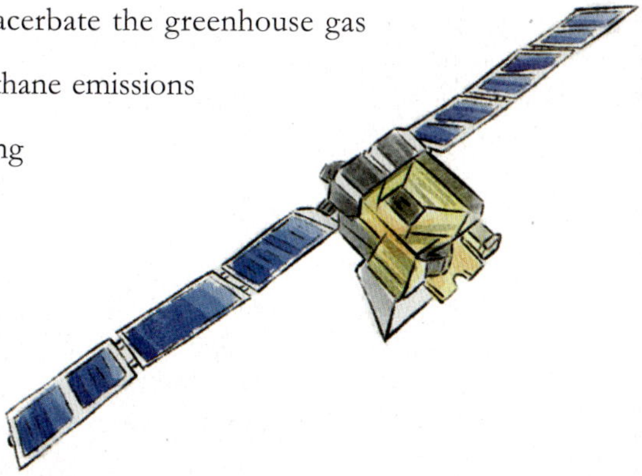

烷排放。该工具已被证明是行之有效的。这颗卫星和有效的传感器将会对环境保护产生深远的影响。

人们对甲烷监测卫星的反应各不相同。首先，2021 年 1 月美国环境保护基金会宣布他们将与私人公司 SpaceX 合作发射甲烷监测卫星。人们都知道，SpaceX 是由埃隆·马斯克（Elon Musk）建立的。虽然人们相信合作发射甲烷监测卫星一定会成功，但是许多人认为如此重要的项目不应该由一家私人公司来完成。其次，发射甲烷监测卫星的本意是好的，但是监测全球的甲烷排放量是一个很复杂的工程。虽然美国与中国以及欧洲一些国家建立了伙伴关系，但是世界上还有其他尚未加入伙伴关系的国家，他们会认为甲烷监测卫星侵犯了他们国家的信息安

methane emissions have not been developed for a long time. The good news is, in recent years, more and more environmental agencies have begun to use satellites to collect data on large-scale methane emissions. The U.S. Environmental Defense Fund recently created a satellite called MethaneSAT, which translates to "methane satellite" in Chinese. The purpose of this satellite is not only to monitor methane emissions in a certain region, but also to monitor methane emissions globally. The data collected by the satellite will then be made public to better help countries formulate effective environmental protection policies. MethaneSAT uses a Tropospheric Monitor Instrument (TROPOMI) to sense large-scale methane emissions. This tool has proven to be effective. This satellite and effective sensor will have a profound impact on environmental protection.

People's responses to MethaneSAT have been varied. Firstly, the U.S. Environmental Defense Fund announced that they would launch MethaneSAT in partnership with the private company, SpaceX. Everyone knows that SpaceX was founded by Elon Musk. While people believe that the MethaneSAT project will be successful, many believe that a private company should not be overseeing such an important project. Next, while the original intentions of launching MethaneSAT are good, the act of monitoring global methane emissions is complicated. Although the United States has partnered with China and some European countries, there are other countries in the world that have not yet joined the partnership, and they might believe that methane monitoring encroaches on their country's information security and privacy, resulting in destabilized international relations. In the future, no one knows what the impact of the MethaneSAT launch will have, but for now, the launch of MethaneSAT represents a huge potential for strengthening the Sino-U.S. cooperation on environmental protection. Methane-monitoring satellites will have a huge impact – not only on the field of green finance, but also on all aspects of global environmental protection.

Since the formation of the partnership between the U.S. Environmental Defense Fund and Tsinghua University, there has been a growing number of climate projects and exchanges between China and the United States. Major companies such as McDonald's, Walmart, and Amcor all employed EDF researchers to conduct projects on how their companies can further sustainable improvements, such as energy management strategies or supply chain analysis. More

全，这样会使国际关系不稳定。未来，没人知道甲烷监测卫星的发射会带来什么影响，但现在，发射甲烷监测卫星代表了中美在环境保护方面加强重要伙伴关系的巨大潜力。甲烷监测卫星不仅在绿色金融领域，而且在全球环境保护的各个方面都会产生巨大影响。

自从美国环境保护基金会与清华大学建立伙伴关系以来，中美之间的气候项目和交流活动越来越多。麦当劳、沃尔玛和安姆科等大公司都允许美国环境保护基金会的研究员来研究他们公司如何进一步做出可持续的改进，比如提出能源管理战略或供应链分析。到目前为止，全球一百多个国家签署了协议，同意到21世纪末将甲烷排放量减少30%。解决气候变化问题的道路还很长，但这些行动让我们看到了希望，美国和中国可以共同为甲烷监测卫星项目树立榜样。希望全世界各国携起手来，保护我们地球的环境。因为，我们只有一个地球。

than 100 countries around the world have signed agreements to reduce methane emissions by 30% by 2030. There is still a long way to go to address climate change, but these actions give us hope that, together, the United States and China can set an example for environmental protection partnerships. We hope that all countries in the world will join hands to protect the environment of our planet. Because we have only one Earth.

风能在中国

作者：何丽晶　苏月梅　指导教师：翟梦莹　夏威夷大学

各国政府都应该制定奖励绿色能源的政策，支持和扶植绿色工业，保护环境。

在过去的几十年中，中国的经济经历了高速的发展，而高速发展的经济需要大量能源。由于中国一直以来主要依靠燃煤来提供能源，所以中国面临着严重的环境污染问题。自 1978 年以来，中国积极采取措施，将可再生能源纳入经济计划当中，以帮助解决环境污染问题。从那时候起，中国就成为了世界风能领域的引领者。

刮风是地球上的一个自然现象，不需要多少人力、物力，我们就可以享用大自然给人类的馈赠。今天有些地方，风车还在吱吱呀呀地转着，为人们推碾子磨磨、汲水浇灌。科技发展到今天，人们已经发明用风力涡轮机来发电，制造清洁能源。简而言之，风力涡轮机发电与我们日常使用的电风扇工作原理相同，作用相反。涡轮机并不是使用电力来制造风，而是利用空气中的风力来发电，一个是电能转化为风能，一个是风能转化为电能。取之不尽用之不竭的风力吹动风扇的叶片，叶片连接到发电机上。当风力吹动叶片旋转时，发电机中的转子也跟着旋转，从而产生电力。发电机产生的电能可以储存在电池中或输送到电力公司。电力公司通过能源网络分配电力，供客户使用。虽然风能高效而且环保，但它的缺点是不太可靠。因为天气是不可预测的，没有风的时候，无法实现风能转化为电能。

中国对可再生风能的投资始于 20 世纪 50 年代，当时他们开始研究使用小

Wind Power in China

Author: Jessielyn Ho　Olivia Sou　Instructor: Mengying Zhai
University of Hawai'i

> All governments must formulate policies to reward green energy, support and foster green industries, and protect the environment.

China's economy has experienced rapid growth over the past few decades, which needed much energy. China has long since relied upon burning coal to provide for its energy needs, so it is facing severe environmental pollution problems. Since 1978, China has taken active measures, bringing renewable energy into its economic planning to solve the problem of environment pollution. Since then, China has become a world leader in wind energy.

Wind blowing is a natural phenomenon on the Earth. We can enjoy the gift of nature without spending much manpower or material resources. Even today, windmills are still used to turn rollers for milling and to draw water for irrigation. As science developed, wind turbines were invented to generate electricity and produce clean energy. Simply put, wind turbines work on the same principle as electric fans, but they produce opposite effects. Instead of using electricity to make wind, turbines use wind to make electricity. The blades on wind turbines are connected to a generator, and when wind spins the blades, the rotor in the generator spins simultaneously, which generates electricity. The electric energy is then either stored in batteries or transported to electricity companies and distributed to customers through energy grids. Although wind energy is highly efficient and environmentally friendly, one disadvantage is that the energy production is not reliable. Since weather can be unpredictable, it is impossible to convert wind energy into electricity if there is no wind. China's investment in wind-powered renewable energy started in the 1950s when they started research on small-scale wind turbines.

型风力涡轮机发电。然而，当时经济、政治和技术的限制阻碍了他们的进展。1978年以后，中国政府推出了新的风能政策，风力发电研究才得以继续发展。在20世纪90年代，中国引进了更先进的、能源容量更高的风力发电机。截至2019年，中国的风电场已经超过4000座，大大增加了风力的发电量。

中国成为世界风能领域的领导者背后的原因，可能是在20世纪70年代的能源危机中，石油禁运导致石油价格上涨。中国及时意识到了过度依赖进口石油的危险性，所以转向其他途径，开始开发可再生能源，比如风能。

哈佛大学与清华大学合作研究发现，如果中国选择依靠风能而不再依靠化石能源，中国的潜在风能强大到可以产生足够的电力，其产生的积极影响足以抵消未来很多甚至全部温室气体带来的负面影响。中国的北部和西部地区拥有巨大的风能潜力，比如新疆、甘肃、西藏和内蒙古。中国这些地区人口稀少，经济和工业不太发达，对能源的需求很低。因此，当地产生的电能需要用高压输电线输送到电力消耗较大的地区，如江浙沪地区。根据国际专家分析，如果中国对可再生能源进行足够的投资，那么仅风能就可以满足大量的能源需求。

中国已迅速成为风能领域的全球领导者，装机容量排名世界第一。但中国

However, the economic, political, and technological restrictions at that time halted their progress. It was not until 1978 that the Chinese government rolled out new policies that finally allowed wind energy to continue to develop. In the 1990s, China imported more advanced wind turbines with higher energy capacities. As of 2019, there are over 4,000 wind farms in China, creating an enormous impact on wind powered electricity output.

China is the world leader in wind energy. This may be due to the energy crisis of the 1970s that led to the inflation of oil prices. China realized the danger of excessive dependence on imported oil, so it turned to other ways to secure its energy consumption, such as wind energy.

One cooperative research effort between Harvard University and Tsinghua University found that if China chooses to rely on wind energy instead of fossil energy, the electricity generated from China's potential wind energy would offset the negative repercussions from present and future greenhouse gasses. The northern and western regions of China, such as Xinjiang, Gansu, Xizang, and Inner Mongolia, have huge wind energy potentials. These regions in China are sparsely populated, economically, and industrially underdeveloped, and have low demand for energy. This means that the excess power generated in these regions may be transmitted to areas with large power consumption by high-voltage transmission lines – areas such as Jiangsu, Zhejiang, and Shanghai. According to the analysis of international experts, if China continues to invest in renewable energy, wind energy alone can generate enough energy to meet the demands.

China has rapidly become a global leader in the field of wind energy, with its installed capacity ranking first in the world. However, China also faces huge challenges in its development of wind-powered technology. Currently, the biggest challenge is that the region with the largest potential for wind energy production is far away from major cities. Transferring energy generated in western China to the east requires a tremendous amount of resources, thus requiring careful planning. Due to its rapid development in recent years, China's international influence is growing. Whether China chooses to use fossil fuels or completely rely on renewable energy will undoubtedly affect other countries in the world.

World powers hold the capability of changing the Earth's future; therefore, they also have

在风能开发上也面临着巨大的挑战，其中最大的挑战就是风能潜力最大的地区离能源消耗的主要城市很远。将中国西部产生的能量传送到东部，需要大量的人力、物力，所以需要认真地规划。中国由于近些年的迅速发展，国际影响力越来越大，中国是选择使用化石燃料还是完全依赖可再生能源，这无疑将影响世界上其他国家。

世界大国掌握着地球未来的走向，所以也有责任尽最大努力保护环境。各国政府都应该制定奖励使用绿色能源的政策，支持和扶植绿色工业，保护环境。除了发展风能以外，还可以发展其他的再生能源，比如太阳能、水能、地热能、生物能等等。保护环境是每个人的责任。我们应该弥补以前的过失，否则我们的家园可能会不复存在。

the responsibility to do their best to protect the environment. Indeed, all governments must formulate policies to reward green energy, support and foster green industries, and protect the environment. In addition to the development of wind energy, other renewable energy sources can also be developed, such as solar energy, hydropower, geothermal energy, and bio-energy. It is everyone's responsibility to protect the environment. We should make up for our past mistakes, or else our home may cease to exist.

以和为贵

作者：路劲挺　指导教师：陈红　洛尤拉大学

只有和平与合作，我们人类才能更加强大，才能共同面对今天的困难和挑战。

我们的世界缺少了什么？

我一直在想这个问题。在新冠病毒大流行的时候，我在想这个问题；在中美贸易战不断升级的时候，我在想这个问题；在针对亚裔的暴力事件越来越多的时候，我在想这个问题；在地球的环境逐渐恶化的时候，我在想这个问题；在世界各地战争频繁发生的时候，我还在思考这个问题。我们今天的世界到底怎么了？我认为我们的世界缺少一个“以和为贵”的心态。

中国和美国是两个很了不起的国家。美国有世界上最先进的科学技术，来自世界各地的优秀人才，一流的大学教育，追求自由平等的人民。中国有着五千年的悠久历史文化，改革开放后飞速发展的经济，勤奋努力、热爱生活的人民。目前，我们在很多方面遇到了前所未有的困难和挑战。如何尽快控制疫情，让经济恢复正常？如何降低关税壁垒，促进国际贸易？如何建立国际合作，降低二氧化碳排放，保护好地球环境，让青山绿水常在？如何消灭种族歧视，真正实现平等自由？如何在世界范围内停止战争，通过谈判解决国际纠纷？如果不解决好这些问题，人们就不会长期享受和平幸福的生活。

我认为，我们应该放下偏见，放下不同的政治观点，坐下来认真讨论这些问题。无论我们在哪个国家，是什么种族和肤色，属于什么党派，我们都是人类，都应该以诚相待。为了控制疫情，我们不能只责备某一个种族、某一个国家。为了全世界人民的安全健康，各国必须在研制疫苗和特效药等方面通力合作，互相

Harmony Is Most Valuable

Author: Timothy Rooney Instructor: Hong Chen Loyola University

> Only through peace and cooperation, can we human beings become stronger and face the difficulties and challenges together.

What's missing in our world?

This is a question I've thought about a lot. During the COVID-19 pandemic, I've thought about this question; during the ongoing trade war between China and the United States, I've thought about this question; as incidents of violence against Asian people increase, I've thought about this question; as the Earth's environment continues to deteriorate, I've thought about this question; as conflicts and wars continue to occur around the world, I continue to think about this question. What has happened to our world today? I believe that what our world is missing is the attitude of "Harmony is most valuable."

China and the United States are two amazing countries. The United States has the world's most advanced science and technology, talented people from around the world, first-class university education, and people who seek freedom and equality. China has a long history and profound culture of 5,000 years, a rapidly developing economy following reform and opening-up, and people who work hard and love life. Currently, we are facing unprecedented difficulties and challenges in many areas: How can we quickly control the pandemic and restore our economies to normal? How can we reduce tariffs and promote international trade? How can we establish international cooperation, reduce carbon dioxide emissions, and protect the environment to keep the mountains green and the water clear? How can we eliminate racial discrimination and achieve true equality and freedom? How can we stop wars worldwide and resolve international disputes through negotiation? If these problems are not solved, people will not be able to enjoy peaceful and happy lives for long.

帮助。只有全球的人们都得到了疫苗及特效药，疫情才能最终被控制住。为了结束贸易战，国家之间必须坐下来谈判，找到合作共赢的道路，因为贸易战没有赢家，给贸易战买单的是各国的老百姓。为了结束种族歧视，我们要宣传博爱，平等待人，相互尊重，同时还要通过立法，严惩种族歧视的罪行。为了保护我们的地球，每一个人都要从自己做起，从现在做起。过俭朴的生活，远离奢华，保护野生动物，回收废弃物，使用绿色能源。我们只有一个地球，要给我们的后人保留一个适合居住的环境。国家之间如果发生矛盾，要坐下来谈判，不能靠武力解决问题。今天已经是核武器的时代，这个时代的战争没有你赢我输，只有人类的共同毁灭。我们应该放下武器，不要传播仇恨，而是团结起来合力解决我们面临的共同挑战！

以和为贵，这是一种大智慧。只有和平与合作，我们人类才能更加强大，才能共同面对今天的困难和挑战。让我们一起加油努力！

I believe that we should put aside our prejudices and different political opinions, and sit down to discuss these issues seriously. Despite our nationalities, races, skin colors, and affiliated political parties, we are all human beings and we should treat each other with respect. In order to keep the pandemic under control, we should not blame any single race or any single country. For the sake of safety and health of all the people in the world, all countries should cooperate and support each other in developing vaccines and specific medicines. Only when all the people in the world get vaccinated and have access to specific medicines, can the pandemic be really under control. In order to stop the trade wars, all countries should sit down and negotiate to find a common ground. There is no winner in trade wars. It is the people of those countries who suffer in the trade wars. In order to stop racial discrimination, we should promote universal love, equality, and mutual respect. At the same time, laws should be passed to punish the crimes of racial discrimination. In order to protect our Earth, each of us should start from ourselves, start from present, live simple lives and say good-bye to luxuries. We should protect wild animals, recycle and use renewable energy. We have only one Earth, we should leave behind with our children the Earth that they can live on. If two countries have any conflicts, they should sit down and negotiate. They should not resort to military powers. We have already entered an era of nuclear weapons. There is no winner or loser in nuclear wars; there is only total destruction of us all. We should all put down our arms, stop spreading hatred, and put our efforts together to face our common challenges!

Harmony between all people and all nations is a great wisdom. Only through peace and cooperation, can we human beings become stronger and face the difficulties and challenges together. Let's combine our efforts!

中国不是美国的敌人

作者：杜可若　指导教师：潘 越　堪萨斯大学

> 这个地球够大，太平洋够宽，容得下中国和美国同时高速发展。

从科学技术方面把中国和美国做系统比较，会让我们更好地了解当代的中国。从发展的角度来看，中国利用40多年的时间，从一个经济不太发达的国家发展成为世界最强经济体之一，这个过程说明中国跟美国有很多相似之处。虽然今天的中国实际上与今天的美国没有太大的差别，但是一般美国民众仍然认为美国和中国的差别很大，甚至不少美国民众认为中国是美国的敌对国家。这完全是西方媒体夸大了中美之间的不同和利益冲突。

《中国新闻网》采访了美国著名智库布鲁金斯学会的主任李成博士，并于2022年2月22日发表了一篇文章，分析了有关美国人对中国和中国人的看法。数据统计表明，美国年轻人对中国的看法大大不同于他们的前辈。文章说，美国90后、00后对中国好感度比他们的前辈高出很多。原因有很多，其中就包括“美国青年的冷战思维不像前几代人那么强，前几代美国人是在冷战时期的20世纪80年代中期长大的”。还有，“美国青年受保守的极端宗教的影响比较小”，以及跟中国年轻人打交道时获得的经验。然而大多数美国人是旧式白人，他们往往是保守的，也有歧视他人的倾向。这些人往往觉得中国的高速发展对美国是一种威胁，中国是美国的敌人。美国媒体则更是推波助澜，延续刻板印象，把中国塑造

China Is Not the Enemy of the United States

Author: Keira Dobbs Instructor: Yue Pan University of Kansas

> The Earth is big enough and the Pacific Ocean is wide enough to simultaneously accommodate the development of China and the U.S.

Using a systematic comparison of science and technology between China and the United States, we can gain a better understanding of contemporary China. Looking at China's development, the nation has rapidly evolved from a economically developing country to a country with one of the strongest economies in the world in over 40 years. China and the United States have many similarities in this regard. Although China and the United States actually do not possess a great many differences today, the American public generally believe the two countries are quite different to the point where some Americans feel that China is a hostile nation. Western media is largely to blame for exaggerating the differences and conflicts of interest between China and the United States.

China News interviewed Dr. Li Cheng, Director of the well-known American think tank Brookings Institute, and published an article on how Americans view China and Chinese people on February 22, 2022. The statistics in the article reveal that the young people in the United States view China differently from past generations. The article states Americans born in the 1990s and the 2000s have a much higher opinion on China. There are many reasons for this, including the fact that "American youth do not possess as strong of a Cold War mentality as previous generations that grew up during the Cold War in the mid-1980s." In addition, "American youth are relatively less influenced by conservative extremist religions" and have

成美国的敌人，所以美国的一般民众对中国有误解，不太友善。

中国是一个发展中国家。虽然以前经济不太发达，但是目前中国的经济发展得很快。中国的社会主义市场经济体系，与世界接轨，使中国的经济发生了日新月异的变化。从中华人民共和国成立到21世纪初，发达国家对中国没有信心。他们怀疑中国会像许多其他发展中国家一样，会停滞不前，会留在原地。让西方国家意想不到的是，中国避免了“拉美陷阱”现象，GDP赶超了很多发达国家。1978年改革开放以后，高速的经济发展让中国受到了世界的瞩目，并且影响了全世界。各种中国制造和中国创造丰富了世界各国人民的日常生活，包括（但不限于）技术、环境、政治、主流媒体、流行服饰、电视剧等等。

再具体一点儿，有两个例子很好地体现出中国在科技方面的发展速度：付款方式和私家汽车。别的国家的付款方式

experience dealing with Chinese youth. However, a significant portion of Americans are traditional white people who tend to hold conservative and discriminatory views. These types of people often think China's rapid development threatens the United States, and they make China out to be an enemy of the United States. American media adds more fuel to the fire by perpetuating the stereotypes and portraying China as a national enemy in the news, resulting in the general American public believing common misunderstandings and treating Chinese people unkindly.

China is a developing country. Although the economy was not very developed before, China's current economy has been developing quite quickly. China's socialist market economy system, integrating with the world market, has brought about the ever-changing Chinese economy. From the founding of the People's Republic of China to the start of the 21st century, developed countries had no confidence in China. They suspected that China would stagnate and be unable to progress like many other developing countries. To the surprise of Western countries, China avoided what's known as the "Latin American bottleneck" phenomenon and its GDP surpassed many developed countries. After the policy of reform and opening-up in 1978, China's rapid economic development has not only attracted the world's attention but also begun to influence the world. All sorts of inventions that are manufactured or created in China enrich the daily lives of people around the world, including but not limited to technology, environment, politics, mainstream media, fashion trends, TV shows, etc.

To be more specific, two good topics exemplifying the speed of China's development in technology are payment methods and private cars. Other countries' payment methods have developed slowly in comparison, like in the case of the United States. The U.S. first used cash (and still does use cash) for purchases. The 20th century brought about the use of checks and credit cards by the public in the U.S. Using a cellphone to make payments is only now starting to spread in densely populated areas of the U.S., but it's not as common elsewhere. Paying with your cell phone in China, however, has become the dominant mode of payment in the country. People can pay with their cell phones anytime and anywhere. From this perspective, China is more modern than the United States. We can look at the development of private cars as well. Although China's public transportation system is very developed, Chinese people have been

发展缓慢，比如美国。美国先用（现在依然用）现金付款，然后 20 世纪开始用支票和信用卡。现在美国人口密集的地区开始用手机付款，可是不太普遍。相反，在中国用手机付款已经成为最主要的付款方式。人们随时随地都可以用手机付款。从这个角度看，中国和美国相比，中国更现代一些。再看看私家汽车的发展。虽然中国的公共交通已经非常发达，但是中国人受到西方的影响，拥有私家车也成为一种生活方式。在中国的城市里，越来越多的家庭拥有了私家车。现在中国每年新车数量的增长速度远远高于美国新车数量的增长速度。

总结起来，中国走了一条具有中国特色的道路，这是一条独一无二的道路。因此很多传统保守的美国人看不惯。他们在保守的媒体和一些别有用心的政客的误导下，认为中国的发展影响了美国的发展，把中国的崛起看成是对美国的威胁，所以他们把中国看成是美国的敌人。实际上中国的高速发展并没有危害到美国的利益。这个地球够大，太平洋够宽，容得下中国和美国同时高速发展。虽然中国和美国在文化上有很大差别，但是这两个国家面临着差不多同样的问题，所以未来都应该努力解决自己国内的问题。在国际上，双方更应该努力合作，达到双赢的目的。中国不是美国的敌人，最多只是一个竞争对手。

influenced by the West, and owning a private car has also become a way of life. In Chinese cities, more and more families have private cars. The number of new cars in China is now growing at a significantly faster rate than the number of new cars in the U.S.

Overall, China has taken a path of development with unique Chinese characteristics. Therefore, many traditionally conservative Americans cannot tolerate it. They are misled by conservative media and politicians with ulterior motives to believe that China's development affects the development of the United States. They interpret China's rapid rise to the global stage as a threat to the United States and make China out to be a national enemy. In reality, China's quick development has not harmed the interests of the United States. The Earth is big enough and the Pacific Ocean is wide enough to simultaneously accommodate the development of China and the U.S. Although China and the U.S. have very different cultures, both countries face similar issues, so, in the future, both countries should focus on trying to solve these domestic problems. On a global scale, the two nations should work together for their mutual benefit. China is not an enemy of the United States, at most a competitor.

哈佛大学中国论坛有感

作者：铁白玲　指导教师：金德华　康涅狄格学院

> 我认为中美关系的改善需要两国年轻一代的合作，需要媒体的合作，需要政治家的远见卓识，想要打败对手的零和思维只会毁掉两国。

2022年4月15日至16日，我参加了在波士顿举办的哈佛中国论坛，聆听了专家、学者、政府官员、经济学家讨论如何解决日益恶化的中美关系。此次论坛有三个方面给我留下了深刻的印象。

首先，尽管论坛是关于中美关系的，但是参加论坛的美国学生却寥寥无几，这让我开始质疑关心中美问题的美国学生到哪里去了。他们对这类话题不感兴趣吗？我们有可能把美国学生的冷漠态度归咎于美国教育体系。在美国的中学和大学的历史与政治科学课上，除了讨论美国历史和政治以外，很少涉及其他国家的内容。有人可能会说："那当然啊，在美国就应该学习美国呀。"我个人不完全同意这种说法。美国不是在真空中存在的，一个国家的历史和制度往往是由与其他国家的关系来定义的。再者，美国是一个移民国家，每个人都有独特的视角，接纳不同的视角可以帮助学生开阔视野，增强全球观念。虽然大学教育更加多样化，但仍不完美。在大多数大学中，国际教师短缺，如果教授某个地区相关课程的教授真的来自该地区，那就更好了。这并不是说教授除了与自己的祖国相关的内容不能教其他东西，而是说如果学生从国际教师内部的视角和美国教师的外部视角同时观察世界，他们会对美国以外的世界产生兴趣。可

My Thoughts on Harvard College China Forum

Author: Sbidag Demerjian　Instructor: Tek-wah King　Connecticut College

> I think the improvement of Sino-U.S. relations requires the cooperation of the younger generation of the two countries, the cooperation of the media, and the foresight of statesmen. The zero-sum mentality of wanting to defeat the opponent will only destroy the two countries.

On April 15-16, 2022, I attended Harvard College China Forum in Boston, where I listened to experts, academics, government officials, and economists discuss how to resolve the deteriorating Sino-U.S. relationship. Three aspects of this forum left a deep impression on me.

First, even though the forum was about Sino-U.S. relations, there were very few American students participating in the forum, which made me question where the American students, who are concerned about Sino-U.S. issues, are. Are they not interested in such topics? Maybe the American education system is to be blamed for the indifference of American students. In the history and political science classes in U.S. high schools and colleges, there is little content from other countries other than America. Some people may say, "Of course, in the United States, you should learn about the United States." I personally don't fully agree with this statement. The United States does not exist in a vacuum, and the nation's history and institutions are often defined by its relationships with other nations. Furthermore, the United States is a country of immigrants, where everyone has a unique perspective, and embracing different perspectives can help students broaden their horizons and enhance their global perspectives.

惜的是，美国的教育系统没有能够做到这一点。

其次，中美合作不仅对世界经济福祉至关重要，对全球总体安全也极为紧迫。中国和美国都是全球经济的重要参与者，两国经济相互依存，互相进出口货物，如果这种关系终止，世界将面临悲剧性后果，因为经济安全是实现全球和平与安全的先决条件。所以美国学生应该密切关注中美关系的发展。

最后，媒体应该拿出勇气来避免坠入修昔底德陷阱（Thucydides Trap），以改善陷于危机中的中美关系。修昔底德陷阱是由美国政治学家格雷厄姆·T·艾利森（Graham T. Allison）提出的概念，用于说明一个新兴大国必然会挑战守成大国

While a college education is more diverse, it's still not perfect. In most universities, there is a shortage of international teachers. It would be better if the professors teaching a region-related course were actually from that region. This is not to say that professors cannot teach anything other than content relevant to their home countries, but that students will become interested in the world outside of the United States if they observe the world from both the perspectives of international teachers and the external perspectives of American teachers. Unfortunately, the American education system has not achieved this yet.

Second, Sino-U.S. cooperation is not only critical to the well-being of the world economy, but also extremely urgent to overall global security. Both China and the United States are important players in the global economy. The two economies are interdependent, importing and exporting goods from each other. If this relationship is terminated, the world will face tragic consequences, because economic security is a prerequisite for global peace and security. So American students should pay close attention to the development of Sino-U.S. relations.

Finally, the media should show the courage to avoid falling into Thucydides Trap to improve the dilemma of Sino-U.S. relations. Thucydides Trap is a concept proposed by American political scientist Graham T. Allison to illustrate that a rising power will inevitably challenge the hegemony of an established power, while the established power will inevitably take measures to contain and suppress the emerging power, and conflicts or even wars will inevitably occur between the two sides. Some politicians today have fallen deeply into this Thucydides Trap. The media have the responsibility and obligation to break the Thucydides Trap and pull politicians out of it. China and the United States should treat each other as friends and equal partners. They should be complementary teammates, not mortal enemies. Every country in the world has a chance to succeed. The Pacific Ocean is so big that it can accommodate more trade cargo ships; the earth is so big that it can accommodate the development of all countries. It is a pity that the media often use false news and propaganda to further deteriorate the relationship between the two countries in order to win more people's attention. Therefore, it is urgent to stop the spread of fake news. The media should report the facts, suppress the evil, and combat the spread of fake news, so as to eliminate the misunderstanding and hatred between the two countries.

的霸主地位，而守成大国也必然会采取措施遏制和打压新兴大国，双方不可避免会发生冲突甚至战争。当今一些政治家已经深深地掉进了这个修昔底德陷阱。媒体有责任、有义务打破修昔底德陷阱，把政客们从这个陷阱中拉出来。中美应该把对方当作朋友和平等的伙伴，中国和美国应该是互补的队友，而不是你死我活的敌人。世界上每个国家都有成功的机会。太平洋之大，容得下更多的贸易货船；地球之大，容得下所有国家的发展。可惜的是，媒体经常通过不实的新闻和宣传，使对立的两国关系进一步恶化，以博取更多人的眼球。因此制止假新闻的传播十分迫切。媒体应该报道事实，以正压邪，打击假新闻的传播，这样才能消弭两国之间的误解和仇恨。

我认为中美关系的改善需要两国年轻一代的合作，需要媒体的合作，需要政治家的远见卓识，想要打败对手的零和思维只会毁掉两国。希望未来有更多的美国青年能对这个话题感兴趣，并花时间思考可行的方案，好让中美关系早日脱离困境，回到正确的轨道上来。如果那样，那就是中美两国人民的福音、世界人民的福音。

I think the improvement of Sino-U.S. relations requires the cooperation of the younger generation of the two countries, the cooperation of the media, and the foresight of statesmen. The zero-sum mentality of wanting to defeat the opponent will only destroy the two countries. Hopefully in the future, more American young people will be interested in this topic and take the time to think about feasible solutions, so that Sino-U.S. relations can get out of the predicament as soon as possible and return to the right track. This will be great news for the people of China and the United States, and great news for the people of the world.

中美互惠互利，健康竞争

作者：克里斯·卡特　指导教师：丰华　哈佛大学

> 中国和美国应及时设计一个有远见的应对气候变化的方案，设计一个“健康竞争”方案，竞争建设发展中国家的绿色经济。

在一篇发表于2018年《金融时报》的文章里，亨利·基辛格说道：“历史上会偶尔出现这样的人物——他们的到来会标志着一个时代的结束并迫使社会放弃旧时代的观念。特朗普就是这样的人物之一。”2017年1月，特朗普就职，成为美国第45任总统，中美关系进入了一个新时代。特朗普对中国所持的强硬态度严重影响了中美关系。在美国2017年国家安全战略和2018年国防战略中，美国政府开始将中美关系定义为“大国竞争”。

特朗普是如何改变美国的外交政策的呢？首先，美国近30年的外交冲突都是与小国家发生的，所以美国使用了一种“平叛”战略。然而，根据美国2018年国防战略，美国的国防部开始实行打压其他大国的战略，也就是所谓的“大国竞争”战略。此外，在经济方面，为了遏制中国前所未有的经济发展，美国对中国商品加征了很高的关税，引发了贸易战。还有特朗普政府的孤立主义政策，让美国与包括中国在内的很多国家的合作日趋减少，给中美关系以及世界秩序带来了巨大的负面影响。美国退出的条约、协定和机构不在少数，包括应对全球气候变化的

Mutually-beneficial "Healthy Competition" between the U.S. and China

Author: Kris Carter Instructor: Hua Feng Harvard University

> China and the United States should soon develop a far-sighted plan to deal with climate change and design scheme of "healthy competition" to help developing countries build green economies.

In a 2018 *Financial Times* article, Henry Kissinger said, "I think Trump may be one of those figures in history who appears from time to time to mark the end of an era and to force it to give up its old pretenses." Indeed, when former President Donald Trump took office as the 45th president of the United States in January 2017, Sino-U.S. relations entered a new era. Trump's hardline stance toward China left a lasting mark on Sino-U.S. relations. The 2017 U.S. National Security Strategy and 2018 National Defense Strategy used a new term to define this era: great power competition.

In what ways did Trump change the U.S. foreign policy? The 2018 National Defense Strategy that introduced the rhetoric of great power competition marked a shift from the America's foreign policy focusing on smaller countries over the last 30 years. Besides this, on the economic front, the United States imposed high tariffs on Chinese goods to counter China's unprecedented economic development, triggering a trade war. Following the isolationist policy of the Trump administration, there has been less cooperation between the United States and other countries including China, bringing great negative influence on Sino-U.S. relations and world order. The United States withdrew from many treaties, agreements, and institutions,

《巴黎协定》、伊朗核问题协议、《全面与进步跨太平洋伙伴关系协定》、《北美自由贸易协定》、联合国教科文组织和联合国人权理事会等。

相反，中国政府意识到了多边主义的重要性，尤其是和众多发展中国家的多边关系。中国近年来大规模增加了对外投资，“一带一路”倡议就是最好的例子。从 2010 年到 2019 年十年间，除了 2016 年以外，中国每年都向世界银行采购了大量的项目设施和设备。同时，中国也是全球基础设施基金垂直型基金的最大贡献者。通过这样的经济支持，中国已在发展中国家站稳脚跟，并提高了国际影响力。自 2000 年起，中国在 19 个巴基斯坦能源项目上投资了 206 亿美元（同时期，世界银行只投资了 44 亿美元）。目前来看，中国的战略是行之有效的。2022 年 4 月，中国和所罗门群岛签署了一项战略性的安全协议。

在忽视了发展中国家几年后，美国逐渐意识到争取这些国家的战略重要性。

健康竞争 绿色经济

including *The Paris Agreement*, the Iranian nuclear deal, *Comprehensive and Progressive Agreement for Trans-Pacific Partnership*, *the North American Free Trade Agreement*, UNESCO, and the United Nations Human Rights Council.

In contrast, the Chinese government has realized the strategic importance of multilateralism, especially developing relations with developing countries. China has sharply increased its foreign investments in recent years, notably with the Belt and Road Initiative. Except in 2016, from 2010 to 2019, China purchased the most facilities and equipment contracts from the World Bank annually. China is also typically the largest contributor to global infrastructure funds. Through such economic support, China has gained a firm foothold in developing countries and increased its international influence. For example, since 2000, China has invested $20.6 billion in 19 Pakistani energy projects (the World Bank only invested $4.4 billion over the same period of time). So far, China's strategy has produced its desired outcome, including a strategic security agreement between China and the Solomon Islands in April 2022.

The United States has also gradually realized the strategic importance of winning over developing countries. The United States is concerned that China's growing influence in the South Pacific islands will hinder its "free and open Indo-Pacific" policy. In response to the agreement between the Solomon Islands and China, the United States immediately sent a high-level delegation to the Solomon Islands. It goes without saying that developing countries, especially those in the South Pacific region, have become entangled in the competition between China and the United States.

Although China and the United States have different positions, pre-Trump administrations recognized areas for cooperation, such as mitigating global warming. In the Obama era, China and the United States cooperated far more, including on joint initiatives to reduce carbon emissions, the greatest achievement on that front being *The Paris Agreement*. In 2014, 2015, and 2016, China and U.S. leaders also issued three consecutive joint statements on climate change and set goals for reducing carbon emissions. Researchers from the two countries also worked together to establish the Sino-U.S. Climate Change Working Group and the Sino-U.S. Clean Energy Joint Research Center.

美国担心中国在南太平洋岛屿越来越大的影响力会阻碍自己的“自由开放的印太地区”战略。作为对所罗门群岛和中国的协议的回应，美国马上派出了一个高级代表团访问所罗门群岛。不言而喻，发展中国家，尤其是南太平洋地区，已变成中美竞争的一部分。

虽然中美两国立场不同，但是特朗普之前的政府还是认识到双方存在一些利益共同点，比如减缓全球变暖。在奥巴马时代，中美合作还比较多，包括减少碳排放。在这方面，最大的成就是应对全球气候变化的《巴黎协定》。2014 年、2015 年、2016 年，中美元首连续发表了三个应对气候变化的联合声明。两国还共同设计了关于降低全球碳排放的目标。两国研究人员也通力合作，建立了美中气候变化工作组和美中清洁能源联合研究中心。

不过，特朗普任职期间，这些合作明显倒退。因为特朗普政府的外交政策立足于孤立主义，美国退出了许多协定，包括《巴黎协定》。同时，美国共和党不重视全球变暖问题，政府环保部门的人员和经费都非常短缺。

目前，虽然拜登总统要扭转特朗普的外交政策，但是在短期内，中美关系难以回到以前合作时期的水平。因为近年美国在环保方面不进反退，中国政府对美国环保政策非常失望。虽然美国和中国都加入了 2021 年的《格拉斯哥气候公约》，但是该公约还没发挥实质作用。美国最高法院限制联邦政府出台环保政策的权力以后，中国强调美国不能只“喊口号”。依目前的情况，中国和美国合作的可能性不太大，得寻找其他办法减少全球碳排放。

如今的全球变暖危机是史无前例的，全球变暖的危害也是显而易见的，特别是在发展中国家，因为这些国家往往社会不太稳定、设施不过硬、经济不景气。在全球面临严重粮食危机的 2.58 亿人中，多数都受到气候冲击和极端天气影响。全球变暖也使得更多人被各种各样的病毒传染。红十字会估算超过 500 万人同时

During Trump's tenure, however, those cooperations went backward. Because of the Trump administration's isolationist foreign policy, the United States has withdrawn from many agreements, including *The Paris Agreement.* At the same time, U.S. Republican Party downplays the issue of global warming, so the environmental protection agencies are short of personnel and funds.

Although President Biden now wants to reverse Trump's foreign policy, in the short term, it is difficult for Sino-U.S. relations to return to pre-Trump levels of cooperation. As the United States has deprioritized environmental protection, China has grown frustrated with U.S. climate policy. Although both the United States and China joined the recent 2021 *Glasgow Climate Pact*, the pact has yet to have a substantial impact. After the U.S. Supreme Court limited the power of the federal government to issue environmental protection policies, China emphasized that the U.S. should not just "shout slogans." Under the current circumstances, the possibility of cooperation between China and the United States is not very high – a different solution must be found to reduce global carbon emissions.

Today's global warming crisis is unprecedented, and the harms of global warming are abundantly evident, especially in developing countries, as these countries have relatively unstable domestic political situations, poor infrastructure, and struggling economies. Of the 258 million people facing severe food insecurity globally, the majority are affected by climate shocks and extreme weather. Studies have found that the social effects of global warming also make more people vulnerable to infection from various viruses, and the Red Cross estimates that more than 5 million people are affected by both the corona virus and global warming. The World Bank estimates that by 2030, 100 million more people will be living below the poverty line due to the effects of climate change. Additionally, extreme weather resulting from climate change costs $520 billion in damages and repair costs and impoverishes 26 million people annually. According to a Stanford study, the gap between developing and developed countries has been widened by 25 percent since 1960.

Historically, Chinese culture has nurtured the idea of combating global warming. From Guan Zhong, a Qi State reformer in the Spring and Autumn Period, to modern scholars and artists, Chinese intellectuals are relatively aware of the causation between economic

受到新冠病毒和全球变暖的影响。世界银行估计，到 2030 年，由于气候变化的影响，处于贫困线以下的人会新增 1 亿。此外，每年极端天气导致 5200 亿美元的损失，并使 2600 万人陷入贫困。据斯坦福研究报告，自 1960 年以来，发展中国家和发达国家之间的差距扩大了 25%。

历史上，中国文化培育出了对抗全球变暖的思想。从春秋时期齐国的改革者管仲，到现代的学者，中国的知识分子都意识到了经济发展和破坏环境的关系。管仲曾经说，在草原别养太多牛，要不草原无法恢复；农作物的种植不要太密集，要不土壤肥力不够。近年来，中国的环保意识在逐步提高。现在，中国决定将“生态文明”放在第一位，甚至连中小学的课堂里也增加了环保课程。

美国在环保方面不如中国积极。因为美国有虚假新闻泛滥的问题，大众对全球变暖持两种截然不同的态度。有些人非常重视环保，有些人不相信全球变暖是真的。再有，石油公司在政治上拥有巨大的影响力。最近美国最高法院的判决是美国社会和环保关系复杂的最好例证。2022 年 6 月 30 日，美国最高法院以 6 比 3 的投票，否决了美国环保局有关限制排放二氧化碳的规定。最高法院指出，只有在国会授权的情况下，环保局才可以限制美国油气公司的开采以及油气排放的标准。

减少全球变暖的核心不仅仅是个科学问题，还是个社会问题。美国如何出台一个政治上可接受的、有效的环保政策？解决方案就在眼前：和中国竞争，看谁能够为拯救全球环境做出更大的贡献，而不是追求霸权的“大国竞争”。近 6 年美国的孤立主义思想已给全球造成了困扰和挑战。希望美国和中国共同担当起“大国责任”，展开一场“健康的竞争”。

这里建议的“健康竞争”包括帮助发展中国家发展绿色经济，推动多边开发银行、基础设施的建设以及绿色技术的发展。希望两国政府出台政策鼓励私人在

development and environmental damage. Guan Zhong once said, "Don't raise too many cattle in the grassland, or the grassland will not recover; don't plant too dense crops, or the soil is not fertile enough." In recent years, the awareness of environmental protection has once again been increasing in China. China has decided to put "ecological civilization" first, and environmental studies courses have even made their way into middle and elementary school curricula.

The U.S. has not pursued environmental protection as actively as China. Because there is a flood of fake news in the U.S., the public has two completely different attitudes toward climate change: some people take it very seriously, and some people do not even believe that it is real. Oil companies have great influence in politics. The recent Supreme Court's decision demonstrated this complex relationship between American society and environment protection. On June 30, 2022, the Supreme Court voted six to three to limit the U.S. Environmental Protection Agency's (EPA) ability to regulate carbon dioxide emissions. The Supreme Court ruled that the EPA needs the authorization of Congress to limit the production of U.S. oil and gas companies and set standards for oil and gas emissions.

Addressing global warming is not only a scientific issue, but also a social issue. How can

发展中国家投资绿色经济，比如税收优惠。这样，中国和美国的私人投资者会去竞争发展中国家丰富的投资机会。中美的“健康竞争”是有先例的。2014 年，美国承诺捐款 30 亿美元给联合国的绿色气候基金。一年以后，中国为了对抗全球变暖，保证给发展中国家捐款 31 亿美元。

总而言之，中国和美国应及时设计一个有远见的应对气候变化的方案，设计一个“健康竞争”方案，竞争建设发展中国家的绿色经济。这样的规划不仅会得到人民的支持，也会逐步地解决全球气候变化问题，一举两得。这样的政策不会给世界秩序带来混乱，反而会给许多贫困国家带来繁荣。这是两国应该承担的“大国责任”。

the United States devise a politically acceptable and effective environmental protection policy? The solution is right in front of us: compete to make a greater contribution to saving the global environment, rather than continue the "great power competition" for hegemony. In the past six years, the isolationist thinking of the U.S. has brought confusion and challenge to the whole world. It is hoped that both the U.S. and China will jointly shoulder the "responsibility of great powers" by initiating a "healthy competition."

The "healthy competition" suggested here includes aiding developing countries in building green economies, promoting the establishment of multilateral development banks and green technology and infrastructure contracts in developing countries. The governments of the two countries would introduce policies to encourage private investment in the green economies in developing countries, such as tax incentives. Chinese and American private investors would compete for the abundant investment opportunities in developing countries. There is precedent for "healthy competition" between China and the United States. In 2014, the United States pledged \$3 billion to the United Nations' Green Climate Fund, and a year later China responded by pledging to donate \$3.1 billion to developing countries to combat global warming.

All in all, China and the United States should soon develop a far-sighted plan to deal with climate change and design scheme of "healthy competition" to help developing countries build green economies. Such a plan will both have public support and gradually alleviate the problem of global climate change. Instead of bringing chaos to world order, such a policy would lend a helping hand to developing countries, fulfilling the "responsibility of great powers" that the United States and China ought to carry.

致谢

在多方的鼓励和支持下，这本《东西交汇：美国大学生优秀作文100篇》终于问世了。这是对美国中文教学成果的展现和总结，值得庆贺！

在此，我首先要感谢西北大学给我提供的支持。校长夏彼洛教授亲自给这本文集写了致读者的信。他在信中热情洋溢地祝贺同学们发表了自己的文章，在学习中文、了解中国文化的道路上迈出了坚实的一步。西北大学主管国际合作的副校长格林斯潘博士，还有她的助手瑞帕女士、派帕女士及杰瑞德女士都给予了我巨大的帮助。她们帮我挑选插图画手、挑选封面设计，她们是我征集来的稿件的第一批读者。由于我是电脑技术的劣等生，每当我有技术问题时，总是找派帕女士帮忙。她能够在第一时间帮助我解决一切技术问题，如远程录像、照片的像素等问题。

我所在的西北大学亚洲语言与文化系也给予了我巨大的支持，特别是原系主任布鲁克教授、现任系主任麦考利教授及系办公室秘书戴文女士。在本书的编写过程中，她们给我配备了两名学生助手：马筠淇同学帮我做中译英的工作，

Acknowledgements

With the encouragement and support from various parties, *East Meets West: 100 Essays from University Students in the U.S.A.* has finally been published. This is a showcase and summary of the achievements of Chinese language teaching in the United States, and it is truly worth celebrating!

First, I would like to thank Northwestern University for all the support. The president, Professor Schapiro, personally wrote a "Letter to Readers" for this collection. In the letter, he warmly congratulated the students for getting their essays published, and they have taken a solid step on the road of learning Chinese and understanding Chinese culture. Dr. Dévora Grynspan, Northwestern University's Vice President for International Relations, and her assistants, Ms. Kim Rapp, Ms. Janka Pieper, and Ms. Jennifer Gerrard, all provided me with a lot of help as well. They helped me choose illustrators, select cover designs, and they were the first readers of the collection. Since I am not that tech-savvy, whenever I had technical problems, I would always turn to Ms. Pieper for help. She was able to help me solve all technical problems right away, such as remote video recording, photo pixels, and other issues.

Northwestern University's Department of Asian Languages and Cultures, where I work, also gave me immense support, especially Professor Laura Brueck, the former chair of the department, Professor Melissa Macauley, the current department chair, and Ms. Jean Deven,

优质高效地翻译了大量材料；马凡同学帮我拍摄这本书的宣传片，并且为此采访了多位西北大学和周边学校的学生作者。

我也要感谢给这本书推荐稿件的全美众多大学的中文教学同行们。他们作为指导教师，在每篇文章里都有署名。我也要感谢所有给这本文集供稿的同学们。因为篇幅有限，不能接受全部投稿，但是我深为同学们优异的写作水平感到骄傲。有一些同学还给他们的文章提供了自己的照片，起到了锦上添花的作用。在此我们统一感谢了。

如果说这本书的编辑工作一半是在美国完成的，那么另一半是在中国完成的。所以我要感谢北京语言大学及其出版社为这本书做出的贡献。首先要感谢校长刘利教授的大力支持。他在百忙当中亲自动笔，为本书写下热情洋溢的序言。刘教授在序言中引经据典，详细阐明了学习中文、了解中国文化的重要性。我要感谢北语出版社各位领导的鼎力支持。他们运筹帷幄，与语合中心教材处密切合作，组织强大的编辑团队，确保本书高质量、高速度按时出版发行。他们是北京语言大学出版社董事长、我的老朋友郝运先生，社长赵中平先生，总编辑郭风岚女士，副社长陈万超先生，国际中文部主任付彦白先生，审读质检中心主任郑炜先生，图书责任印制周燚先生，出版社北美分社袁世奇先生、李泊华先生及康健先生。

这本文集的作者都是美国不同大学的在读或者毕业的大学生，有在美国出生长大的华裔，更多的是非华裔，所以他们写出来的中文作品难免有不少瑕疵。学生作文中经常会有一些句子，看起来合乎语法，可是感觉就是有些不自然，作为主编的我有时也不知道怎么改好。出版社中文编审老师们对此一一做出了修改和编辑，使每一篇文章最终都变成了一篇完美的作文，完全可以供美国学中文的学生模仿、学习。所以我要感谢中文编审老师们的辛勤劳动。我从

the Business Manager. During the writing process of this book, they assigned me two student assistants: Angela Ma helped me with the Chinese-to-English translation, translating many essays with high quality and high efficiency; Rosa Fan Ma helped me film a promotional video for the book, interviewing student authors from Northwestern University and surrounding schools.

I would also like to thank the Chinese teaching colleagues in many universities across the United States who recommended essays for this book. Their names are listed next to the author's byline on each essay as the instructor. I would also like to thank all the students who submitted their essays to this book. Although we cannot accept all the submissions due to the limit of space, we are still deeply impressed by the excellence in their essays. I would also like to thank the student authors who included photos in their essays. These photos have definitely made their essays more interesting in this book.

If we say that half of the editing work for this book was completed in the United States, the other half was completed in China. So, I would like to give a special thank you to Beijing Language and Culture University and its Press for their contributions to this book. First and foremost, I would like to thank Professor Liu Li, the university president, for his strong support. Despite his busy schedule, he wrote a passionate preface for this book. In the preface, Professor Liu quoted classic texts and elaborated on the importance of learning Chinese and understanding Chinese culture. I would also like to thank the leaders of the Press for their support. They made meticulous arrangements and closely collaborated with the Textbook Division of the Center for Language Education and Cooperation, organizing a strong editorial team to ensure the high-quality and timely publication of this book. They include Mr. Hao Yun, Chairman of Beijing Language and Culture University Press and my old friend; Mr. Zhao Zhongping, the President; Ms. Guo Fenglan, the Editor-in-Chief; Mr. Chen Wanchao, the Vice President; Mr. Fu Yanbai, Director of the International Chinese Department; Mr. Zheng Wei, Director of the Review and Quality Inspection Center; Mr. Zhou Yi, in charge of book printing; and Mr. Yuan Shiqi, Mr. Li Bohua, and Mr. Kang Jian from the North American branch of the Press.

The authors of the collection of essays are current or graduated college students from

心底佩服他们扎实的中文功底和敬业精神。他们是中文复审上官雪娜女士、中文终审王俊毅先生。

这是一本中英对照的文集，当然也要有美方提供的英文文本。原以为出版社只会修改编辑美方提供的中文文本，而对英文文本全盘接受，没有想到我和美国大学生编写的英文稿件几乎每一篇都或多或少得到了出版社英文编辑老师的润色和拔高。仔细读来，发现英文编辑老师们的编辑确实起到了精益求精的效果。所以我要感谢英文编辑张轶鋆女士、英文复审侯晓娟女士。为两位英文编辑老师的功底和自信点赞！

这是一本图文并茂的文集，缺不了精美的插图锦上添花。所以我当然也要感谢北京青侣文化创意有限公司的插画师黄莉女士及装帧设计师邱彬先生。他们绘制的每一幅插图、设计的封面和版式都给文集起到了画龙点睛的作用。

我最后，也是最隆重感谢的是这本书的责任编辑唐琪佳老师。顾名思义，责任编辑就是全面负责的意思。唐老师绝对是一位负责任的编辑。因为这本书需要在2023年9月之前完成，所以我们不能等待全部100篇文章征集齐再编辑。为了提高工作效率，我们决定流水作业。只要征集到10篇文章，就走一个审读流程，即对这一组文章做中文的初审、复审、终审。都通过以后，再在定稿的基础上译成英文。然后英文还要经过初审、复审、终审的过程。与此同时，每一篇文章还需要配上插图。要经过脚本、线稿、彩稿三道手续，有的插图几易其稿，修改数次。唐老师在中国北京，我这个主编在美国芝加哥，两地有着14个小时的时差。这无疑使整个合作的过程变得更加复杂。唐老师统筹全局，精心安排与中英文复审、终审的流水工作，安排与插画师、设计师的合作。唐老师与我这个主编保持着密切的沟通，随时随地通过邮箱和微信联系。从画手的挑选，到封面和版式的修改，唐老师都给我提供三个以上的选项，供

various universities across the United States. Among them are Chinese Americans who were born and raised in the United States, and the majority are non-Chinese students. Therefore, it is natural that their Chinese writings have some flaws. In student essays, there are often sentences that seem grammatically correct but feel somewhat unnatural, and as the chief editor, I sometimes struggle with figuring out how to improve them. The Chinese editors at the Press have made modifications and edits to each piece, turning them into perfect compositions that can be used as examples for American students learning Chinese. Therefore, I would like to express my gratitude to the diligent work of the Chinese editors. I sincerely admire their proficient Chinese language skills and professionalism. They are Ms. Shangguan Xuena, the Chinese copy editor, and Mr. Wang Junyi, the final Chinese editor.

Since this is a bilingual collection of essays, there should naturally be English essays provided by the American side as well. I initially thought that the Press would only modify and edit the Chinese texts provided by the American side, while accepting the English essays as they were. However, to my surprise, almost every piece of English writing composed by myself and the American university students received some degree of refinement and enhancement from the English editors in the Press. Upon careful reading, I realized that the edits made by the English editors truly achieved an excellent result. Therefore, I would like to express my gratitude to Ms. Zhang Yijun, the English editor, and Ms. Hou Xiaojuan, the English copy editor. I commend the expertise and confidence of these two English editors at the Press!

This is a collection of essays that is complemented by beautiful illustrations, which add an extra touch of elegance. Therefore, I must express my gratitude to Ms. Huang Li from Beijing Qinglu Cultural Creativity Co., Ltd. for her illustrations, as well as Mr. Qiu Bin from the same company for his book cover and layout design. Each illustration they created and every aspect of the book's design, including the cover and layout, have added the perfect finishing touch to the collection.

Lastly, and most importantly, I want to express my utmost gratitude to the managing editor of this book, Ms. Tang Qijia. As the name implies, a managing editor is responsible for overseeing all aspects of a publication. Ms. Tang is truly a responsible and dedicated editor. Since this book needed to be completed before September 2023, we couldn't wait until we had

我参考。对我不懂的事情她总是耐心给我解释，直到我明白为止。我的每一封邮件唐老师都会及时回复。到目前为止，为了编辑这本书我们已经往复了几百封邮件。我们前后编辑了130多篇学生的文章，而工作过程文件则多达上千个，不同的中文版本和英文译稿，每篇文章的插图过程稿，中英文初审、复审、终审。等都定稿了以后，有的学生作者又提出不同的修改意见。这些工作都需要谨慎处理。工作量之大不可想象。稍有不慎就会张冠李戴，出现混乱。因此，我要特别感谢唐老师的耐心、细致、专业、井井有条的工作，而这方面恰恰是我的弱项。没有唐老师投入大量的时间和精力，这本书不可能如此高质量、高速度地出版。感谢唐琪佳老师！

collected all 100 essays to begin editing. To improve efficiency, we decided to work in parallel. As soon as we received a batch of 10 essays, we would go through the process of preliminary review, copyediting, and final editing in Chinese. Once they were approved, we would translate them into English based on the finalized Chinese versions. The English translations also went through a process of preliminary review, copyediting, and final editing. Meanwhile, each essay needed to be accompanied by illustrations, which involved scriptwriting, sketching, and final artwork, with some illustrations undergoing multiple revisions. Ms. Tang is based in Beijing, China, while I, as the chief editor, am in Chicago, U.S.A., with a 14-hour time difference between the two locations. Undoubtedly, this made the entire collaboration process more complex. Ms. Tang managed the overall situation meticulously, carefully coordinating the workflow with Chinese and English review and editing, as well as the collaboration with the illustrators. She maintained close communication with me, the chief editor, through email and WeChat, regardless of time and location. From selecting the illustrators to modifying the book cover and layout, Ms. Tang always provided me with three or more options for reference. She patiently explained things to me that I didn't understand until I grasped the concepts and promptly responded to every email I sent. So far, we have exchanged hundreds of emails in the process of editing this book. We have edited over 130 essays by students, and the number of documents involved in the workflow has reached thousands, including different versions of Chinese essays and English translations, drafts of illustrations for each essay, and the Chinese and English stages of preliminary review, copyediting, and final editing. Even after finalizing everything, some student authors had additional modification requests, which needed to be handled with caution. The workload is unimaginable, and any slight negligence could lead to confusion and mistakes. Therefore, I want to express my special gratitude to Ms. Tang for her patience, meticulousness, professionalism, and well-organized work, which happens to be my weakness. Without her dedicating a significant amount of time and effort, it would have been impossible to publish this book with such high quality and speed. Thank you, Ms. Tang Qijia!

Published by Phoenix Tree Publishing Inc.

West Meets East: 100 Essays from University Students in the U.S.A.
By Licheng Gu
ISBN: 9781625753397
Library of Congress Control Number: 2023914895
First Edition
First Printing: June 2023
Printed in China

Editor: Tang Qijia   Zhang Yijun
Phoenix Tree Publishing Inc.
5660 N. Jersey Ave · Chicago, IL 60659
Phone: 773.250.0707 · Fax: 773.250.0808
Email: marketing@phoenixtree.com

For information about special discounts for bulk purchases,
please contact the publisher at the address above.

Find out more about Phoenix Tree Publishing at
www.phoenixtree.com